Exploring Java

Exploring Java

Patrick Niemeyer and Joshua Peck

O'Reilly & Associates, Inc.

Bonn · Cambridge · Paris · Sebastopol · Tokyo

Exploring Java
by Patrick Niemeyer and Joshua Peck

Copyright © 1996 O'Reilly & Associates, Inc. All rights reserved.
Printed in the United States of America.

Published by O'Reilly & Associates, Inc., 101 Morris Street, Sebastopol, CA 95472.

Editors: Mike Loukides and Paula Ferguson

Production Editor: Mary Anne Weeks Mayo

Printing History:

        May 1996:   First Edition

This book is printed on acid-free paper with 85% recycled content, 15% post-consumer waste. O'Reilly & Associates is committed to using paper with the highest recycled content available consistent with high quality.

ISBN: 1-56592-184-4

This book is dedicated to those who fight for our freedom of speech and its realization in a free and independent Internet.

Table of Contents

Preface

This book is about the Java language and programming environment. If you've been at all active on the Internet in the past year, you've heard a lot about Java. It's one of the most exciting developments in the history of the Internet, rivaling the creation of the World Wide Web. Java became the darling of the Internet programming community as soon as the alpha version was released. Immediately, thousands of people were writing Java applets to add to their Web pages. Interest in Java only grew with time, and support for Java in Netscape Navigator guaranteed it would be a permanent part of the Net scene.

What, then, is Java? Java is a language for network programming that was developed by Sun Microsystems. It's already in widespread use for creating animated Web pages. However, this is only the start. The Java language and environment are rich enough to support entirely new kinds of applications, like dynamically extensible browsers. There has been talk about new kinds of computer platforms (Java terminals or Java pads) that download all their software over the network. In the coming years, we'll see what Java is capable of doing; fancy Web pages are fun and interesting, but they certainly aren't the end of the story. If Java is successful (and that isn't a foregone conclusion), it could change the way we think about computing in fundamental ways.

This book sets out to give you a head start on a lot of Java fundamentals. *Exploring Java* attempts to live up to its name by mapping out the Java language, its class libraries, programming techniques, and idioms. We'll dig deep into interesting areas, and at least scratch the surface of the rest. Other titles in the O'Reilly & Associates Java series will pick up where we leave off and provide more comprehensive information on specific areas and applications of Java.

Whenever possible, we'll provide meaningful, realistic examples and avoid simply cataloging features. The examples are simple but hint at what can be done. We won't be developing the next great "killer Internet app" in these pages, but we hope to give you a starting point for many hours of experimentation and tinkering that will lead you to learn more on your own.

Audience

This book is for computer professionals, students, technical people, and Finnish hackers. It's for everyone who has a need for hands-on experience with the Java language with an eye towards building real applications. This book could also be considered a crash course in object-oriented programming; as you learn about Java, you'll also learn a powerful and practical approach to object-oriented software development.

Superficially, Java looks like C or C++, so you'll be in the best position to use this book if you've some experience with one of these languages. If you do not, you might want to reference books like O'Reilly's *Practical C Programming* for a more thorough treatment of basic C syntax. However, don't make too much of the syntactic similarities between Java and C or C++. In many respects, Java acts like more dynamic languages such as Smalltalk and Lisp. Knowledge of another object-oriented programming language should certainly help, although you may have to change some ideas and unlearn a few habits. Java is considerably simpler than languages like C++ and Smalltalk.

Much of the interest in Java has centered around World Wide Web applets. Although we encourage you to take a broader view, you would have every right to be disappointed if we ignored the Web. Much of the book does discuss Java as a language for World Wide Web applications, so you should be familiar with the basic ideas behind Web browsers, servers, and Web documents.

Using This Book

This book divides roughly into three sections:

- Chapters 1 and 2 provide a basic introduction to Java concepts and a tutorial to give you a jump start on Java programming.

- Chapters 3 through 6 discuss tools for working with Java (the compiler, the interpreter, HTML support, etc.) and the language itself. Chapter 6 covers the language's thread facilities, which should be of particular interest to advanced programmers.

- Chapters 7 through 11 discuss the class libraries. Chapter 7 covers basic utilities; Chapter 8 covers I/O facilities; Chapter 9 covers networking; and Chapters 10 and 11 cover the Abstract Windowing Toolkit (AWT), which provides graphics and GUI support.

If you're like us, you don't read books from front to back. If you are really like us, you usually don't read the preface at all. However, on the off chance that you will see this in time, here are a few suggestions.

If you are an experienced programmer who has to learn Java in the next five minutes, you are probably looking for the examples. You might want to start by glancing at the tutorial in Chapter 2. If that doesn't float your boat, you should at least look at the information in Chapter 3, which tells you how to use the compiler and interpreter, and gives you the basics of a standalone Java application. This should get you started.

Chapter 9 is essential if you are interested in writing advanced networked applications. This is probably the most interesting and important part of Java. Unfortunately, we are still waiting for Sun to release a production version of HotJava, or for someone else to release a browser that implements all of Java's networking features.* Until then, you can still write interesting standalone applications that use the Net. Maybe you'll even write the browser we're waiting for.

Chapter 11 discusses Java's graphics features. You will need to read this if you are interested in animation and other live displays.

Getting Wired

There are many online sources for information about Java. Sun Microsystem's official Web site for Java topics is *http://www.javasoft.com/*; look here for the latest news, updates, and Java releases. *www.javasoft.com* is where you'll find the Java Developers Kit (JDK), which includes the compiler, the interpreter, and other tools. Another good source of Java information, including free applets, utility classes, and applications, is the Gamelan site, run by EarthWeb; its URL is *http://www.gamelan.com.*

You should also visit O'Reilly & Associates' Java site at *http://www.ora.com/info/java.* There you'll find information about other books in O'Reilly's Java series, and a pointer to the home page for *Exploring Java, http://www.ora.com/catalog/expjava/*, where you'll find the source code and examples for this book.

---

* Just before this book went to press, Sun released a "pre-beta 1" version of HotJava. That's definitely good news, though the pre-beta version doesn't support downloadable content and protocol handlers. These are promised for the "real" beta release.

The *comp.lang.java* newsgroup can be a good source of information, announcements, and a place to ask intelligent questions.

Conventions Used in This Book

The font conventions used in this book are quite simple.

Italic is used for:

- UNIX pathnames, filenames, and program names

- Internet addresses, such as domain names and URLs

- New terms where they are defined

Boldface is used for:

- Names of GUI buttons and menus

`Typewriter Font` is used for:

- Anything that might appear in a Java program, including method names, variable names, and class names

- Command lines and options that should be typed verbatim on the screen

- Tags that might appear in an HTML document

In the main body of text, we always use a pair of empty parentheses after a method name to distinguish methods from variables and other creatures.

In the Java source listings, we follow the coding conventions most frequently used in the Java community. Class names begin with capital letters; variable and method names begin with lowercase. All the letters in the names of constants are capitalized. We don't use underscores to separate words in a long name; following common practice, we capitalize individual words (after the first) and run the words together. For example: `thisIsAVariable`, `thisIsAMethod()`, `ThisIsAClass`, and `THISISACONSTANT`.

Acknowledgments

Many people contributed to putting this book together under a schedule that became increasingly rushed as time passed. Thanks to their efforts, we gave birth to something we can all be proud of.

Foremost we would like to thank Tim O'Reilly for giving us the opportunity to write this book. Special thanks to Mike Loukides, the series editor, whose endless patience and experience got us through the difficult parts and to Paula Ferguson, whose organizational and editing abilities got the material into its final form. It's due largely to Mike and Paula's tireless efforts that this book has gotten to you as quickly as it has. We could not have asked for a more skillful or responsive team of people with whom to work.

Particular thanks are due to our technical reviewers: Andrew Cohen, Eric Raymond, and Lisa Farley. All of them gave thorough reviews that were invaluable in assembling the final draft. Eric contributed many bits of text that eventually found their way into the book.

Speaking of borrowings, the original version of the glossary came from David Flanagan's book, *Java in a Nutshell*. We also borrowed the class hierarchy diagrams from David's book. These diagrams were based on similar diagrams by Charles L. Perkins. His original diagrams are available at *http://rendezvous.com/java/*.

Thanks also to Marc Wallace and Steven Burkett for reading the book in progress. As for the crowd in St. Louis: a special thanks to LeeAnn Langdon of the Library Ltd. and Kerri Bonasch. Deepest thanks to Victoria Doerr for her patience and love. Finally, thanks for the support of the "lunch" crowd: Karl "Gooch" Stefvater, Bryan "Butter" O'Connor, Brian "Brian" Gottlieb, and the rest of the clan at Washington University.

Many people in O'Reilly's production and design groups contributed their blood, sweat, and tears to the project. Mary Anne Weeks Mayo was production editor and copy editor, and had the stress-filled job of working under a very tight deadline with chapters arriving asynchronously (which means at random and later than expected). Seth Maislin wrote the index, and Stephen Spainhour adapted David Flanagan's glossary for this book. Chris Reilley converted rough diagrams into professional technical illustrations. Erik Ray, Ellen Siever, and Lenny Muellner converted HTML files into SGML and made sure we could convert electrons into paper without mishap. Lenny also implemented a new design for this book, which was created by Nancy Priest. Hanna Dyer created the back cover; Edie Freedman designed the front cover.

1

Yet Another Language?

The greatest challenges and most exciting opportunities for software developers today lie in harnessing the power of networks. Applications created today, whatever their intended scope or audience, will almost certainly be run on machines linked by a global network of computing resources. The increasing importance of networks is placing new demands on existing tools, and fueling the demand for a rapidly growing list of completely new kinds of applications.

We want software that works—consistently, anywhere, on any platform—and that plays well with other applications. We want dynamic applications that take advantage of a connected world, capable of accessing disparate and distributed information sources. We want truly distributed software that can be extended and upgraded seamlessly. We want intelligent applications—like autonomous agents that can roam the Net for us, ferreting out information and serving as electronic emissaries. We know, at least to some extent, what we want. So why don't we have it?

The problem has been that the tools for building these applications have fallen short. The requirements of speed and portability have been, for the most part, mutually exclusive, and security has largely been ignored or misunderstood. There are truly portable languages, but they are mostly bulky, interpreted, and slow. These languages are popular as much for their high level functionality as for their portability. And there are fast languages, but they usually provide speed by binding themselves to particular platforms, so they can meet the portability issue only half way. There are even a few recent safe languages, but they are primarily offshoots of the portable languages and suffer from the same problems.

Enter Java

The Java programming language, developed at Sun Microsystems under the guidance of Net luminaries James Gosling and Bill Joy, is designed to be a machine-independent programming language that is both safe enough to traverse networks and powerful enough to replace native executable code. Java addresses the issues raised here and may help us start building the kinds of applications we want.

Right now, most of the enthusiasm for Java stems from its capabilities for building embedded applications for the World Wide Web; these applications are called *applets*. This book will teach you how to build applets. But there is more to Java than applets, and I'll also try to show you the "more." The book will also show you how to use the tools of Java to accomplish real programming tasks, such as building networked applications and creating functional user interfaces. By the end of the book, you will be able to use these tools to build powerful Java applets and standalone applications.

Coffee Beans

The seeds of Java were planted in 1990 by Sun Microsystems patriarch and chief researcher, Bill Joy. Since Sun's inception in the early '80s, it has steadily pushed one idea: "The network is the computer." At the time though, Sun was competing in a relatively small workstation market, while Microsoft was beginning its domination of the more mainstream, Intel-based PC world. When Sun missed the boat on the PC revolution, Joy retreated to Aspen, Colorado to work on advanced research. He was committed to accomplishing complex tasks with simple software, and founded the aptly named Sun Aspen Smallworks.

Of the original members of the small team of programmers assembled in Aspen, James Gosling is the one who will be remembered as the father of Java. Gosling first made a name for himself in the early '80's as the author of Gosling Emacs, the first version of the popular Emacs editor that was written in C and ran under UNIX. Gosling Emacs became popular, but was soon eclipsed by a free version, GNU Emacs, written by Emacs's original designer. By that time, Gosling had moved on to design Sun's NeWS window system, which briefly contended with the X Window System for control of the UNIX graphic user interface (GUI) desktop in 1987. While some people would argue that NeWS was superior to X, NeWS lost out because Sun kept it proprietary and didn't publish source code, while the primary developers of X formed the X Consortium and took the opposite approach.

Designing NeWS taught Gosling the power of integrating an expressive language with a network-aware windowing GUI. It also taught Sun that the Internet programming community will refuse to accept proprietary standards, no matter how good they may be. The seeds of Java's remarkably permissive licensing scheme were sown by NeWS's failure. Gosling brought what he had learned to Bill Joy's nascent Aspen project, and in 1992, work on the project led to the founding of the Sun subsidiary, FirstPerson, Inc. Its mission was to lead Sun into the world of consumer electronics.

The FirstPerson team worked on developing software for information appliances, such as cellular phones and personal digital assistants (PDA). The goal was to enable the transfer of information and real-time applications over cheap infrared and packet-based networks. Memory and bandwidth limitations dictated small and efficient code. The nature of the applications also demanded they be safe and robust. Gosling and his teammates began programming in C++, but they soon found themselves confounded by a language that was too complex, unwieldy, and insecure for the task. They decided to start from scratch, and Gosling began working on something he dubbed "C++ minus minus."

With the floundering of the Apple Newton, it became apparent that the PDA's ship had not yet come in, so Sun shifted FirstPerson's efforts to interactive TV (ITV). The programming language of choice for ITV set-top boxes was the near ancestor of Java, a language called Oak. Even with its elegance and ability to provide safe interactivity, Oak could not salvage the lost cause of ITV. Customers didn't want it, and Sun soon abandoned the concept.

At that time, Joy and Gosling got together to decide on a new strategy for their language. It was 1993, and the explosion of interest in the Internet, and the World Wide Web in particular, presented a new opportunity. Oak was small, robust, architecture independent, and object oriented. As it happens, these are also the requirements for a universal, network-savvy programming language. Sun quickly changed focus, and with a little retooling, Oak became Java.

Future Buzz?

I don't think it's overdoing it to say that Java has caught on like wildfire. Even before its first official release, while Java was still a nonproduct, nearly every major industry player jumped on the Java bandwagon. A major coup for Sun came as Microsoft decided to license Java for its Internet-related products.

As we begin looking at the Java architecture, you'll see that much of what is exciting about Java comes from the self-contained, virtual machine environment in which Java applications run. Java has been carefully designed so that this supporting architecture can be implemented either in software, for existing computer platforms, or in customized hardware, for new kinds of devices. Sun and other industry giants have announced their intentions to produce cheap, fast Java chips, the first of which should be available by the time you read this. Hardware implementations of Java could power inexpensive network terminals, PDAs, and other information appliances, to take advantage of transportable Java applications.

Many people see Java as part of a trend toward cheap, Net-based, "operating system-less" appliances that will extend the Net into more and more consumer-related areas. Only time will tell what people will do with Java, but it's probably worth at least a passing thought that the applet you write today might well be running on someone's wristwatch tomorrow.

A Virtual Machine

Java is both a compiled and an interpreted language. Java source code is turned into simple binary instructions, much like ordinary microprocessor machine code. However, whereas C or C++ source is refined to native instructions for a particular model of processor, Java source is compiled into a universal format—instructions for a virtual machine.

Compiled Java byte-code, also called J-code, is executed by a Java run-time interpreter. The run-time system performs all the normal activities of a real processor, but it does so in a safe, virtual environment. It executes the stack-based instruction set and manages a storage heap. It creates and manipulates primitive data types, and loads and invokes newly referenced blocks of code. Most importantly, it does all this in accordance with a strictly defined open specification that can be implemented by anyone who wants to produce a Java-compliant virtual machine. Together, the virtual machine and language definition provide a complete specification. There are no features of Java left undefined or implementation dependent. For example, Java specifies the sizes of all its primitive data types, rather than leave it up to each implementation.

The Java interpreter is relatively lightweight and small; it can be implemented in whatever form is desirable for a particular platform. On most systems, the interpreter is written in a fast, natively compiled language like C or C++. The interpreter can be run as a separate application, or it can be embedded in another piece of software, such as a Web browser.

All of this means that Java code is implicitly portable. The same Java application can run on any platform that provides a Java run-time environment, as shown in Figure 1–1. You don't have to produce alternate versions of your application for different platforms, and you never have to distribute source code to end users.

The fundamental unit of Java code is the *class*. As in other object-oriented languages, classes are application components that hold executable code and data. Compiled Java classes are distributed in a universal binary format that contains

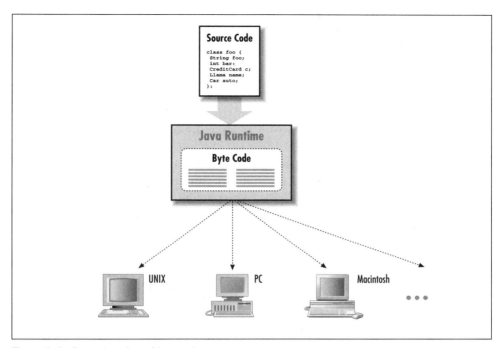

Figure 1–1: Java virtual machine environment

Java byte-code and other class information. Classes can be maintained discretely and stored in files or archives on a local system or on a network server. Classes are located and loaded dynamically at run-time, as they are needed by an application.

In addition to the platform-specific run-time system, Java has approximately 22 fundamental classes that contain architecture-dependent methods. These *native methods* serve as Java's gateway to the real world. These methods are implemented in a native language on the host platform. They provide access to resources such as the network, the windowing system, and the host filesystem. The rest of Java is written entirely in Java, and is therefore portable. This includes fundamental Java utilities like the Java compiler, which is also a Java application and is therefore immediately available on all Java platforms.

In general, interpreters are slow, but because the Java interpreter runs compiled byte-code, Java is a fast interpreted language. Java has also been designed so that software implementations of the run-time system can optimize their performance by compiling byte-code to native machine code on the fly. This is called "just in time" compilation. Sun claims that with just in time compilation, Java code can execute nearly as fast as native compiled code and maintain its transportability and security. The one performance hit that natively compiled Java code will always suffer is array bounds checking. But on the other hand, some of the basic design features of Java place more information in the hands of the compiler, which allows for certain kinds of optimizations not possible in C or C++.

Java Compared

Java is a new language, but it draws on many years of programming experience with other languages in its choice of features. So a lot can be said in comparing and contrasting Java with other languages. There are at least three pillars necessary to support a universal language for network programming today: portability, speed, and security. Figure 1–2 shows how Java compares to other languages.

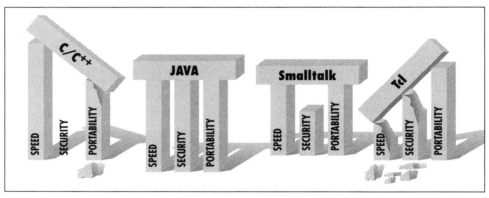

Figure 1–2: Programming languages compared

You may have heard that Java is a lot like C or C++, but that's really not true, except at a superficial level. When you first look at Java code, you'll see that the basic syntax looks a lot like C or C++. But that's where the similarities end. Java is by no means a direct descendant of C or a next generation C++. If you compare language features, you'll see that Java actually has more in common with languages like Smalltalk and Lisp. In fact, Java's implementation is about as far from native C as you can imagine.

The surface-level similarities to C and C++ are worth noting, however. Java borrows heavily from C and C++ syntax, so you'll see lots of familiar language constructs, including an abundance of curly braces and semicolons. Java also subscribes to the C philosophy that a good language should be compact; in other words, it should be sufficiently small and regular so that a programmer can hold all the language's capabilities in his or her head at once. As C is extensible with libraries, packages of Java classes can be added to the core language components.

C has been successful because it provides a reasonably featureful programming environment, with high performance and an acceptable degree of portability. Java also tries to balance functionality, speed, and portability, but it does so in a very different way. While C trades functionality to get portability, Java trades speed for portability. Java also addresses security issues, while C doesn't.

Java is an interpreted language, so it won't be as fast as a compiled language like C. But Java is fast enough, especially for interactive, network-based applications, where the application is often idle, waiting for the user to do something or waiting for data from the network. For situations where speed is critical, a Java implementation can optimize performance by compiling byte-code to native machine code on the fly.

Scripting languages, like Tcl, Perl, and Wksh, are becoming quite popular, and for good reason. There's no reason a scripting language could not be suitable for safe, networked applications (e.g., Safe Tcl), but most scripting languages are not designed for serious, large-scale programming. The attraction to scripting languages is that they are dynamic; they are powerful tools for rapid prototyping. Some scripting languages, like awk and Perl, also provide powerful tools for text-processing tasks more general-purpose languages find unwieldy. Scripting languages are also highly portable.

One problem with scripting languages, however, is that they are rather casual about program structure and data typing. Most scripting languages (with a hesitant exception for Perl 5.0) are not object oriented. They also have vastly simplified type systems and generally don't provide for sophisticated scoping of variables and functions. These characteristics make them unsuitable for building large, modular applications. Speed is another problem with scripting languages; the high-level, fully interpreted nature of these languages often makes them quite slow.

Java offers some of the essential advantages of a scripting language, along with the added benefits of a lower-level language.[*] Incremental development with object-oriented components, combined with Java's simplicity, make it possible to develop applications rapidly and change them easily, with a short concept to implementation time. Java also comes with a large base of core classes for common tasks such as building GUIs and doing network communications. But along with these features, Java has the scalability and software-engineering advantages of more static languages. It provides a safe structure on which to build higher-level networked tools and languages.

---

[*] Don't confuse Java with JavaScript. JavaScript is an object-based scripting language being developed by Netscape and is designed to create dynamic, interactive Web applications. JavaScript is a very different language from Java in most respects. For more information on JavaScript, check out Netscape's Web site (*http://home.netscape.com*).

As I've already said, Java is similar in design to languages like Smalltalk and Lisp. However, these languages are used mostly as research vehicles, rather than for developing large-scale systems. One reason is that they never developed a standard portable binding to operating-system services analogous to the C standard library or the Java core classes. Smalltalk is compiled to an interpreted byte-code format, and it can be dynamically compiled to native code on the fly, just like Java. But Java improves on the design by using a byte-code verifier to ensure the correctness of Java code. This verifier gives Java a performance advantage over Smalltalk because Java code requires fewer run-time checks. Java's byte-code verifier also helps with security issues, something that Smalltalk doesn't address. Smalltalk is a mature language though, and Java's designers took lessons from many of its features.

Throughout the rest of this chapter, we'll take a bird's eye view of the Java language. I'll explain what's new and what's not so new about Java; how it differs from other languages, and why.

Safety of Design

You have no doubt heard a lot about the fact that Java is designed to be a safe language. But what do we mean by safe? Safe from what or whom? The security features that attract the most attention for Java are those features that make possible new types of dynamically portable software. Java provides several layers of protection from dangerously flawed code, as well as more mischievous things like viruses and trojan horses. In the next section, we'll take a look at how the Java virtual machine architecture assesses the safety of code before it's run, and how the Java class loader builds a wall around untrusted classes. These features provide the foundation for high-level security policies that allow or disallow various kinds of activities on an application-by-application basis.

In this section though, we'll look at some general features of the Java programming language. What is perhaps more important, although often overlooked in the security din, is the safety that Java provides by addressing common design and programming problems. Java is intended to be as safe as possible from the simple mistakes we make ourselves, as well as those we inherit from contractors and third-party software vendors. The goal with Java has been to keep the language simple, provide tools that have demonstrated their usefulness, and let users build more complicated facilities on top of the language when needed.

Syntactic Sweet 'n Low

Java is parsimonious in its features; simplicity rules. Compared to C, Java uses few automatic type coercions, and the ones that remain are simple and well-defined. Unlike C++, Java doesn't allow programmer-defined operator overloading. The string concatenation operator + is the only system-defined, overloaded operator in Java. All methods in Java are like C++ virtual methods, so overridden methods are dynamically selected at run-time.

Java doesn't have a preprocessor, so it doesn't have macros, `#define` statements, or conditional source compilation. These constructs exist in other languages primarily to support platform dependencies, so they are not needed in Java. Another common use for conditional compilation is for debugging purposes. Debugging code can be included directly in your Java source code by making it conditional on a constant (i.e., `static` and `final`) variable. The Java compiler is smart enough to remove this code when it determines that it won't be called.

Java provides a well-defined package structure for organizing class files. The package system allows the compiler to handle most of the functionality of *make*. The compiler also works with compiled Java classes because all type information is preserved; there is no need for header files. All of this means that Java code requires little context to read. Indeed, you may sometimes find it faster to look at the Java source code than to refer to class documentation.

Java replaces some features that have been troublesome in other languages. For example, Java supports only a single inheritance class hierarchy, but allows multiple inheritance of interfaces. An interface, like an abstract class in C++, specifies the behavior of an object without defining its implementation, a powerful mechanism borrowed from Objective C. It allows a class to implement the behavior of the interface, without needing to be a subclass of the interface. Interfaces in Java eliminate the need for multiple inheritance of classes, without causing the problems associated with multiple inheritance.

As you'll see in Chapter 4, Java is a simple, yet elegant, programming language.

Type Safety and Method Binding

One attribute of a language is the kind of type checking it uses. When we categorize a language as static or dynamic we are referring to the amount of information about variable types that is known at compile time versus what is determined while the application is running.

In a strictly statically typed language like C or C++, data types are etched in stone when the source code is compiled. The compiler benefits from having enough information to enforce usage rules, so that it can catch many kinds of errors before the code is executed. The code doesn't require run-time type checking, which is advantageous because it can be compiled to be small and fast. But statically typed languages are inflexible. They don't support high-level constructs like lists and collections as naturally as languages with dynamic type checking, and they make it impossible for an application to safely import new data types while it's running.

In contrast, a dynamic language like Smalltalk or Lisp has a run-time system that manages the types of objects and performs necessary type checking while an application is executing. These kinds of languages allow for more complex behavior, and are in many respects more powerful. However, they are also generally slower, less safe, and harder to debug.

The differences in languages have been likened to the differences between kinds of automobiles.[*] Statically typed languages like C++ are analogous to a sports car—reasonably safe and fast—but useful only if you're driving on a nicely paved road. Highly dynamic languages like Smalltalk are more like an offroad vehicle: they afford you more freedom, but can be somewhat unwieldy. It can be fun (and sometimes faster) to go roaring through the back woods, but you might also get stuck in a ditch or mauled by bears.

Another attribute of a language deals with when it binds method calls to their definitions. In an early-binding language like C or C++, the definitions of methods are normally bound at compile-time, unless the programmer specifies otherwise. Smalltalk, on the other hand, is a late-binding language because it locates the definitions of methods dynamically at run-time. Early-binding is important for performance reasons; an application can run without the overhead incurred by searching method tables at run-time. But late-binding is more flexible. It's also necessary in an object-oriented language, where a subclass can override methods in its superclass, and only the run-time system can determine which method to run.

Java provides some of the benefits of both C++ and Smalltalk; it's a statically typed, late-binding language. Every object in Java has a well-defined type that is known at compile time. This means the Java compiler can do the same kind of static type checking and usage analysis as C++. As a result, you can't assign an object to the wrong type of reference or call nonexistent methods within it. The Java compiler goes even further and prevents you from messing up and trying to use uninitialized variables.

---

* The credit for the car analogy goes to Marshall P. Cline, author of the C++ FAQ.

However, Java is fully run-time typed as well. The Java run-time system keeps track of all objects and makes it possible to determine their types and relationships during execution. This means you can inspect an object at run-time to determine what it is. Unlike C or C++, casts from one type of object to another are checked by the run-time system, and it's even possible to use completely new kinds of dynamically loaded objects with a level of type safety.

Since Java is a late-binding language, all methods are like virtual methods in C++. This makes it possible for a subclass to override methods in its superclass. But Java also allows you to gain the performance benefits of early-binding by declaring (with the `final` modifier) that certain methods can't be overridden by subclassing, removing the need for run-time lookup.

Incremental Development

Java carries all data-type and method-signature information with it from its source code to its compiled byte-code form. This means that Java classes can be developed incrementally. Your own Java classes can also be used safely with classes from other sources your compiler has never seen. In other words, you can write new code that references binary class files, without losing the type safety you gain from having the source code. The Java run-time system can load new classes while an application is running, thus providing the capabilities of a dynamic linker.

A common irritation with C++ is the "fragile base class" problem. In C++, the implementation of a base class can be effectively frozen by the fact that it has many derived classes; changing the base class may require recompilation of the derived classes. This is an especially difficult problem for developers of class libraries. Java avoids this problem by dynamically locating fields within classes. As long as a class maintains a valid form of its original structure, it can evolve without breaking other classes that are derived from it or that make use of it.

Dynamic Memory Management

Some of the most important differences between Java and C or C++ involve how Java manages memory. Java eliminates ad hoc pointers and adds garbage collection and true arrays to the language. These features eliminate many otherwise insurmountable problems with safety, portability, and optimization.

Garbage collection alone should save countless programmers from the single largest source of programming errors in C or C++: explicit memory allocation and deallocation. In addition to maintaining objects in memory, the Java run-time system keeps track of all references to those objects. When an object is no longer in use, Java automatically removes it from memory. You can simply throw away references to objects you no longer use and have confidence that the system will clean them up at an appropriate time. Sun's current implementation of Java uses a conservative, mark and sweep garbage collector that runs intermittently in the background, which means that most garbage collecting takes place between mouse clicks and keyboard hits. Once you get used to garbage collection, you won't go back. Being able to write air-tight C code that juggles memory without dropping any on the floor is an important skill, but once you become addicted to Java you can "realloc" some of those brain cells to new tasks.

You may hear people say that Java doesn't have pointers. Strictly speaking, this statement is true, but it's also misleading. What Java provides are *references*—a safe kind of pointer—and Java is rife with them. A reference is a strongly typed handle for an object. All objects in Java, with the exception of primitive numeric types, are accessed through references. If necessary, you can use references to build all the normal kinds of data structures you're accustomed to building with pointers, like linked lists, trees and so forth. The only difference is that with references you have to do so in a type-safe way.

Another important difference between a reference and a pointer is that you can't do pointer arithmetic with references. A reference is an atomic thing; you can't manipulate the value of a reference except by assigning it to an object. References are passed by value, and you can't reference an object through more than a single level of indirection. The protection of references is one of the most fundamental aspects of Java security. It means that Java code has to play by the rules; it can't peek into places it shouldn't.

Unlike C or C++ pointers, Java references can point only to class types. There are no pointers to methods. People often complain about this missing feature, but you will find that most tasks that call for pointers to methods, such as callbacks, can be accomplished using interfaces instead. It's another case of a choice for simplicity in the initial design of Java.

Finally, arrays in Java are true, first-class objects. They can be dynamically allocated and assigned like other objects. Arrays know their own size and type, and although you can't directly define array classes or subclass them, they do have a well-defined inheritance relationship based on the relationship of their base types. Having true arrays in the language alleviates much of the need for pointer arithmetic like that in C or C++.

Error Handling

Java's roots are in networked devices and embedded systems. For these applications, it's important to have robust and intelligent error management. Java has a powerful exception-handling mechanism, somewhat like that in newer implementations of C++. Exceptions provide a more natural and elegant way to handle errors. Exceptions allow you to separate error-handling code from normal code, which makes for cleaner, more readable applications.

When an exception occurs, it causes the flow of program execution to be transferred to a predesignated catcher block of code. The exception carries with it an object that contains information about the situation that caused the exception. The Java compiler requires that a method either declare the exceptions it can generate or catch and deal with them itself. This promotes error information to the same level of importance as argument and return typing. As a Java programmer, you know precisely what exceptional conditions you must deal with, and you have help from the compiler in writing correct software that doesn't leave them unhandled.

Multithreading

Applications today require a high degree of parallelism. Even a very single-minded application can have a complex user interface. As machines get faster, users become more sensitive to waiting for unrelated tasks that seize control of their time. Threads provide efficient multiprocessing and distribution of tasks. Java makes threads easy to use because support for them is built into the language.

Concurrency is nice, but there's more to programming with threads than just performing multiple tasks simultaneously. In many cases, threads need to be synchronized, which can be tricky without explicit language support. Java supports synchronization based on the monitor and condition model developed by C.A.R. Hoare—a sort of lock and key system for accessing resources. A keyword, `synchronized`, designates methods for safe, serialized access within an object. Only one synchronized method within the object may run at a given time. There are also simple, primitive methods for explicit waiting and signaling between threads interested in the same object.

Learning to program with threads is an important part of learning to program in Java. See Chapter 6 for a complete discussion of this topic.

Scalability

At the lowest level, Java programs consist of classes. Classes are intended to be small, modular components. They can be separated physically on different systems, retrieved dynamically, and even cached in various distribution schemes. Over classes, Java provides packages, a layer of structure that groups classes into functional units. Packages provide a naming convention for organizing classes and a second level of organizational control over the visibility of variables and methods in Java applications.

Within a package, a class is either publicly visible or protected from outside access. Packages form another type of scope that is closer to the application level. This lends itself to building reusable components that work together in a system. Packages also help in designing a scalable application that can grow without becoming a bird's nest of tightly coupled code dependency.

Safety of Implementation

It's one thing to create a language that prevents you from shooting yourself in the foot; it's quite another to create one that prevents others from shooting you in the foot.

Encapsulation is a technique for hiding data and behavior within a class; it's an important part of object-oriented design. It helps you write clean, modular software. In most languages however, the visibility of data items is simply part of the relationship between the programmer and the compiler. It's a matter of semantics, not an assertion about the actual security of the data in the context of the running program's environment.

When Bjarne Stroustrup chose the keyword `private` to designate hidden members of classes in C++, he was probably thinking about shielding you from the messy details of a class developer's code, not the issues of shielding that developer's classes and objects from the onslaught of someone else's viruses and trojan horses. Arbitrary casting and pointer arithmetic in C or C++ make it trivial to violate access permissions on classes without breaking the rules of the language. Consider the following code:

```
// C++

class Finances {
    private:
        char creditCardNumber[16];
        ...
    };

main() {
    Finances finances;

    // Forge a pointer to peek inside the class
    char *cardno = (char *)finances;
    printf("Card Number = %s\n", cardno);
}
```

In this little C++ drama, we have written some code that violates the encapsulation of the `Finances` class and pulls out some secret information. If this example seems unrealistic, consider how important it is to protect the foundation (system) classes of the run-time environment from similar kinds of attacks. If untrusted code can corrupt the components that provide access to real resources, such as the filesystem, the network, or the windowing system, it certainly has a chance at stealing your credit-card numbers.

In Visual BASIC, it's also possible to compromise the system by peeking, poking, and, under DOS, installing interrupt handlers. Even some recent languages that have some commonalities with Java lack important security features. For example, the Apple Newton uses an object-oriented language called NewtonScript that is compiled into an interpreted byte-code format. However, NewtonScript has no concept of public and private members, so a Newton application has free reign to access any information it finds. General Magic's Telescript language is another example of a device-independent language that does not fully address security concerns.

If a Java application is to dynamically download code from an untrusted source on the Internet and run it alongside applications that might contain confidential information, protection has to extend very deep. The Java security model wraps three layers of protection around imported classes, as shown in Figure 1–3.

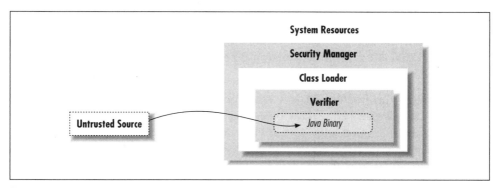

Figure 1–3: The Java security model

At the outside, application-level security decisions are made by a security manager. A security manager controls access to system resources like the filesystem, network ports, and the windowing environment. A security manager relies on the ability of a class loader to protect basic system classes. A class loader handles loading classes from the network. At the inner level, all system security ultimately rests on the Java verifier, which guarantees the integrity of incoming classes.

The Java byte-code verifier is an integral part of the Java run-time system. Class loaders and security managers, however, are implemented by applications that load applets, such as applet viewers and Web browsers. All these pieces need to be functioning properly to ensure security in the Java environment.[*]

The Verifier

Java's first line of defense is the byte-code *verifier*. The verifier reads byte-code before they are run and makes sure they are well-behaved and obey the basic rules of the Java language. A trusted Java compiler won't produce code that does otherwise. However, it's possible for a mischievous person to deliberately assemble bad code. It's the verifier's job to detect this.

Once code has been verified, it's considered safe from certain inadvertent or malicious errors. For example, verified code can't forge pointers or violate access permissions on objects. It can't perform illegal casts or use objects in ways other than they are intended. It can't even cause certain types of internal errors, such as overflowing or underflowing the operand stack. These fundamental guarantees underlie all of Java's security.

You might be wondering, isn't this kind of safety implicit in lots of interpreted languages? Well, while it's true that you shouldn't be able to corrupt the interpreter with bogus BASIC code, remember that the protection in most interpreted languages happens at a higher level. Those languages are likely to have heavyweight interpreters that do a great deal of run-time work, so they are necessarily slower and more cumbersome.

By comparison, Java byte-code is a relatively light, low-level instruction set. The ability to statically verify the Java byte-code before execution lets the Java interpreter run at full speed with full safety, without expensive run-time checks. Of course, you are always going to pay the price of running an interpreter, but that's not a serious problem with the speed of modern CPUs. Java byte-code can also be compiled on the fly to native machine code, which has even less run-time overhead.

The verifier is a type of theorem prover. It steps through the Java byte-code and applies simple, inductive rules to determine certain aspects of how the byte-code will behave. This kind of analysis is possible because compiled Java byte-code has a lot more type information stored within it than other languages of this kind. The byte-code also has to obey a few extra rules that simplify its behavior. First, most

---

* You may have seen reports about various security flaws in Java. While these weaknesses are real, it's important to realize that they have been found in the implementations of various components, namely Sun's byte-code verifier and Netscape's class loader and security manager, not in the basic security model itself. One of the reasons Sun has released the source code for Java is to encourage people to search for weaknesses, so they can be removed.

byte-code instructions operate only on individual data types. For example, with stack operations, there are separate instructions for object references and for each of the numeric types in Java. Similarly, there is a different instruction for moving each type of value into and out of a local variable.

Second, the type of object resulting from any operation is always known in advance. There are no byte-code operations that consume values and produce more than one possible type of value as output. As a result, it's always possible to look at the next instruction and its operands, and know the type of value that will result.

Because an operation always produces a known type, by looking at the starting state, it's possible to determine the types of all items on the stack and in local variables at any point in the future. The collection of all this type information at any given time is called the *type state* of the stack; this is what Java tries to analyze before it runs an application. Java doesn't know anything about the actual values of stack and variable items at this time, just what kind of items they are. However, this is enough information to enforce the security rules and to insure that objects are not manipulated illegally.

To make it feasible to analyze the type state of the stack, Java places an additional restriction on how Java byte-code instructions are executed: all paths to the same point in the code have to arrive with exactly the same type state.[*] This restriction makes it possible for the verifier to trace each branch of the code just once and still know the type state at all points. Thus, the verifier can insure that instruction types and stack value types always correspond, without actually following the execution of the code.

Class Loader

Java adds a second layer of security with a *class loader*. A class loader is responsible for bringing Java binary classes that contain byte-code into the interpreter. Every application that loads classes from the network must use a class loader to handle this task.

After a class has been loaded and passed through the verifier, it remains associated with its class loader. As a result, classes are effectively partitioned into separate namespaces based on their origin. When a class references another class, the request is served by its original class loader. This means that classes retrieved from a specific source can be restricted to interact only with other classes retrieved from

---

* The implications of this rule are mainly of interest to compiler writers. The rule means that Java byte-code can't perform certain types of iterative actions within a single frame of execution. A common example would be looping and pushing values onto the stack. This is not allowed because the path of execution would return to the top of the loop with a potentially different type state on each pass, and there is no way that a static analysis of the code can determine whether it obeys the security rules.

that same location. For example, a Java-enabled Web browser can use a class loader to build a separate space for all the classes loaded from a given uniform resource locator (URL).

The search for classes always begins with the built-in Java system classes. These classes are loaded from the locations specified by the Java interpreter's class path (see Chapter 3). Classes in the class path are loaded by the system only once and can't be replaced. This means that it's impossible for an applet to replace fundamental system classes with its own versions that change their functionality.

Security Manager

Finally, a security manager is responsible for making application-level security decisions. A security manager is an object that can be installed by an application to restrict access to system resources. The security manager is consulted every time the application tries to access items like the filesystem, network ports, external processes, and the windowing environment, so the security manager can allow or deny the request.

A security manager is most useful for applications that run untrusted code as part of their normal operation. Since a Java-enabled Web browser can run applets that may be retrieved from untrusted sources on the Net, such a browser needs to install a security manager as one of its first actions. This security manager then restricts the kinds of access allowed after that point. This lets the application impose an effective level of trust before running an arbitrary piece of code. And once a security manager is installed, it can't be replaced.

A security manager can be as simple or complex as a particular application warrants. Sometimes it's sufficient simply to deny access to all resources or to general categories of services such as the filesystem or network. But it's also possible to make sophisticated decisions based on high-level information. For example, a Java-enabled Web browser could implement a security manager that lets users specify how much an applet is to be trusted or that allows or denies access to specific resources on a case-by-case basis.

The integrity of a security manager is based on the protection afforded by the lower levels of the Java security model. Without the guarantees provided by the verifier and the class loader, high-level assertions about the safety of system resources are meaningless. The safety provided by the Java byte-code verifier means that the interpreter can't be corrupted or subverted, and that Java code has to use components as they are intended. This, in turn, means that a class loader can guarantee that an application is using the core Java system classes and that these classes are the only means of accessing basic system resources. With these restrictions in place, it's possible to centralize control over those resources with a security manager.

Application and User Level Security

There's a fine line between having enough power to do something useful and having all the power to do anything you want. Java provides the foundation for a secure environment in which untrusted code can be quarantined, managed, and safely executed. However, unless you are content with keeping that code in a little black box and running it just for its own benefit, you will have to grant it access to at least some system resources so that it can be useful. Every kind of access carries with it certain risks and benefits. The advantages of granting an untrusted applet access to your windowing system, for example, are that it can display information and let you interact in a useful way. The associated risks are that the applet may instead display something worthless, annoying, or offensive. Since most people can accept that level of risk, graphical applets and the World Wide Web in general are possible.

At one extreme, the simple act of running an application gives it a resource, computation time, that it may put to good use or burn frivolously. It's difficult to prevent an untrusted application from wasting your time, or even attempting a "denial of service" attack. At the other extreme, a powerful, trusted application may justifiably deserve access to all sorts of system resources (e.g., the filesystem, process creation, network interfaces); a malicious application could wreak havoc with these resources. The message here is that important and sometimes complex security issues have to be addressed.

In some situations, it may be acceptable to simply ask the user to "OK" requests. Sun's HotJava Web browser can pop up a dialog box and ask the user's permission for an applet to access an otherwise restricted file. However, we can put only so much burden on our users. An experienced person will quickly grow tired of answering questions; an inexperienced user may not even be able to answer the questions. Is it okay for me to grant an applet access to something if I don't understand what that is?

Making decisions about what is dangerous and what is not can be difficult. Even ostensibly harmless access, like displaying a window can become a threat when paired with the ability for an untrusted application to communicate off of your host. The Java `SecurityManager` provides an option to flag windows created by an untrusted application with a special, recognizable border to prevent it from impersonating another application and perhaps tricking you into revealing your password or your secret recipe collection. There is also a grey area, in which an application can do devious things that aren't quite destructive. An applet that can mail a bug report can also mail-bomb your boss. The Java language provides the tools to implement whatever security policies you want. However, what these policies will be ultimately depends on who you are, what you are doing, and where you are doing it.

To fully exploit the power of Java, we need to have some basis on which to make reasonable decisions about the level of trust an application should have. Web browsers such as HotJava start by defining a few rules and some coarse levels of security that restrict where applets may come from and what system resources they may access. These rules are sufficient to keep the waving Duke applet from clutching your password file, but they aren't sufficient for applications you'd like to trust with sensitive information. What if you want to implement a secure applet to carry a credit-card number to the mall, or more likely the credit-card company? How are people to trust that the applet they are using is really secure? If it's named the "Bank of Boofa" applet, how do they know it's legit?

You might think of trusting only certain hosts for these kinds of applications. However, as Java class files begin to fill the Net, the situation will become more complicated. Hosts can be impersonated. If your communications pass through an untrusted network, you can't be sure you're talking to the intended entity. Furthermore, class files may need to be cached or retrieved through complicated distribution mechanisms. For these kinds of applications, what we really need is a mechanism for verifying the authorship and authenticity of an item and making sure that it has not been tampered with by the time that you received it. Fortunately, this is a problem solved a while ago by your friendly neighborhood cryptographers.

Signing Classes

Digital signatures provide a means of authenticating documents. Like their inky analogs, they associate a name with an item in a way that is supposed to be difficult to forge. Unlike pen on paper, though, electronic digital signatures are actually difficult to forge when used properly. By their nature, digital signatures also provide the benefit that, if authenticated, a document is known not to have been altered in transit. In other words, you can't clip out a digital signature and attach it to a new document.

The details of cryptography are a bit beyond the scope of this book but the basics are important and interesting.[*] Digital signatures are one side of the coin of public-key cryptography. Public-key algorithms rely on the fundamental mathematical difficulty of factoring arbitrarily large numbers. In a public-key system, there are two pieces of information: a public key (as you might have guessed) and a private one. These keys have a special asymmetric relationship such that a message

---

[*] See Bruce Schneier's encyclopedic *Applied Cryptography* (John Wiley & Sons).

encrypted with one key can be decrypted only by knowing the other. This means that by giving you my public key, you can send me messages that only I can read. No one else, including you, has enough information to decrypt the encoded message, so it's safe to send it over untrusted networks. Now, by reversing this process, I can encrypt something with my private key so that anyone can use my public key to read the message. The important thing in this case is that the task of creating such a message without the private key is just as difficult as decoding the message in the first scenario. Since no one else knows my private key, only the real me could have sent the message. This is the basis for digital signatures.

We can imagine this process being used to authenticate Java class files and other types of objects sent over the network. The author of a class signs the code with a digital signature, and we authenticate it when we retrieve it. Now we know that we have the authentic class, or do we? There is one problem that a digital signature alone doesn't solve, namely, at some point we still have to assume we have the author's authentic public key. This is where a key-certification agency comes into play.

A key-certification agency validates a key by issuing a certificate that lists a name and an official public key. The certificate is signed with the agency's own digital signature. The agency presumably has a well-known public key to verify the certificate. Of course, this doesn't solve the problem entirely, but it reduces the number of people you have to trust and the amount of information you have to transport reliably. Presumably the agency is a reputable organization, its private keys are well guarded, and it certifies keys only after some kind of real-world validation such as person-to-person contact.

As you can see, there is a lot to the issue of authentication and the solutions continue to evolve. Some of the APIs for working with signed classes should be available with a future release of Sun's HotJava browser and with an upcoming release of Netscape Navigator. The important thing is, as always, to know who you are dealing with and what kind of software and security you have in place before sending any kind of confidential information over the Net. Don't become paranoid, just keep yourself informed so that you can weigh the risks and the benefits.

Java and the World Wide Web

Alice was beginning to get very tired of sitting by her sister on the bank, and of having nothing to do: once or twice she had peeped into the book her sister was reading, but it had no pictures or conversations in it, "and what is the use of a book," thought Alice, "without pictures or conversations?"

—*Alice in Wonderland*

The application-level safety features of Java make it possible to develop new kinds of applications not necessarily feasible before now. A Web browser that implements the Java run-time system can incorporate Java applets as executable content inside of documents. This means that Web pages can contain not only static hypertext information but also full-fledged interactive applications. The added potential for use of the WWW is enormous. A user can retrieve and use software simply by navigating with a Web browser. Formerly static information can be paired with portable software for interpreting and using the information. Instead of just providing some data for a spreadsheet, for example, a Web document might contain a fully functional spreadsheet application embedded within it that allows users to view and manipulate the information.

Applets

The term *applet* is used to mean a small, subordinate, or embeddable application. By embeddable, I mean it's designed to be run and used within the context of a larger system. In that sense, most programs are embedded within a computer's operating system. An operating system manages its native applications in a variety of ways: it starts, stops, suspends, and synchronizes applications; it provides them with certain standard resources; and it protects them from one another by partitioning their environments.

In this book, I'll be describing Java applets, which are Java applications meant to be embedded in and controlled by a larger application, such as a Java-enabled Web browser or an applet viewer. To include an applet as executable content in a Web document, you use a special HTML tag. The `<applet>` tag points to an applet and provides configuration information about the applet.

As far as the Web browser model is concerned, an applet is just another type of object to display. Browsers make a distinction between items presented inline and items anchored via hypertext links and made available by external means, such as a viewer or helper application. If you download an MPEG video clip, for instance, and your browser doesn't natively understand MPEG, it will look for a helper application (an MPEG player) to pass the information to. Java-enabled Web browsers generally execute applets inline, in the context of a particular document, as shown in Figure 1–4. However, less capable browsers could initially provide some support for Java applets through an external viewer.

A Java applet is a compiled Java program, composed of classes just like any Java program. While a simple applet may consist of only a single class, most large applets should be broken into many classes. Each class is stored in a separate class file. The class files for an applet are retrieved from the network as they are needed. A large applet doesn't need to retrieve all its parts or all its data before beginning to interact with the user. Well-designed applets can take advantage of

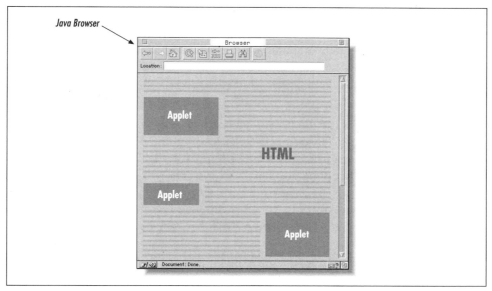

Figure 1–4: Applets in a Web document

multithreading to wait for certain resources in the background, while performing other activities.

An applet has a four-part life cycle. When an applet is initially loaded by a Web browser, it's asked to initialize itself. The applet is then informed each time it's displayed and each time it's no longer visible to the user. Finally, the applet is told when it's no longer needed, so that it can clean up after itself. During its lifetime, an applet may start and suspend itself, do work, communicate with other applications, and interact with the Web browser.

Applets are autonomous programs, but they are confined within the walls of a Web browser or applet viewer, and have to play by its rules. I'll be discussing the details of what applets can and can't do as we explore features of the Java language. However, under the most conservative security policies, an applet can interact only with the user and communicate over the network with the host from which it originated. Other types of activities, like accessing files or interacting directly with outside applications, are typically prevented by the security manager that is part of the Web browser or applet viewer. But aside from these restrictions, there is no fundamental difference between a Java applet and a standalone Java application.

New Kinds of Applications

Sun's HotJava Web browser is written entirely in Java. Because it's a Java application, HotJava is immediately available on any platform with the Java run-time system. This goes a long way towards the goal of a Web browser serving as a universal access point for resources on the Net. And where one Web browser leads the way, more will surely follow.

In addition to displaying Java applets as executable content in Web pages, the Hot-Java application dynamically extends itself by loading Java code from the Net. Hot-Java uses *protocol handlers* and *content handlers* to provide this functionality.[*] Protocol handlers and content handlers are classes in the Java API that let an application implement new types of URLs and interpret the objects retrieved from them. A Web browser that supports this functionality can load handlers from a remote location and effectively upgrade itself on the fly to use new protocols and access new kinds of information.

Like applets, content handlers and protocol handlers can be served by a Web site, along with the information they interpret. As an example, consider the new Portable Network Graphics (PNG) format, a freely distributable alternative to GIF. By supplying a PNG content handler along with PNG images on our server, we give users the ability to use the new image format, just as they would a built-in format. We don't have to create a new standard and force every Web browser to support the new format. Instead, the first time a user loads a document referencing a PNG image from our site, the Web browser will realize it doesn't understand the object and will ask the server if it has a content handler for it. Since we've provided a content handler, the browser can load it and then use it to interpret and display the image dynamically.

In a similar manner, protocol handlers allow a Web browser to start speaking a new protocol with the server. This is especially useful for things like security protocols. If we invent a revolutionary new cryptographic protocol late one night, all we have to do is implement it in the form of a protocol handler and place it on our server. We can then start using URLs that point through our new protocol at objects on our server, and people can immediately begin using it.

These scenarios describe just a few things that safe, transportable code will allow. We will undoubtedly see many other new breeds of application we can't even begin to anticipate.

---

[*] Downloadable content and protocol handlers are not supported in the "pre-beta 1" release of Hot-Java 1.0, but will be supported in a future release.

Java as a General Application Language

The Java applet API is a framework that allows Java-enabled Web browsers to manage and display embedded Java applications within WWW documents. However, Java is more than just a tool for building transportable multimedia applications. Java is a powerful, general-purpose programming language that just happens to be safe and architecture independent. Standalone Java applications are not subject to the restrictions placed on applets; they can do all activities that software written in a language like C does.

Any software that implements the Java run-time system can run Java applications. Applications written in Java can be large or small, standalone or component-like, as in other languages. Java applets are different from other Java applications only in that they expect to be managed by a larger application. In this book, we will build examples of both applets and standalone Java applications. With the exception of the few things applets can't do, such as access files, all of the tools we examine in this book apply to both applets and standalone Java applications.

Availability

By the time you read this book, you should have several choices for Java development environments and run-time systems. As this book goes to press, Sun's Java Development Kit (JDK) is available for Solaris, Windows NT, and Windows 95. The JDK provides an interpreter and a compiler for building general-purpose Java applications. There's also a beta version of the JDK for the Macintosh, but it supports writing Java applets only, not standalone applications. Visit Sun's Java Web site, *http://www.javasoft.com/* for more information about the JDK. There are also a number of JDK ports for various platforms; see the Java FAQ from the *comp.lang.java* newsgroup for current information.

Sun and other vendors are also developing integrated, graphical development environments for Java. Sun's Java WorkShop is a Web-based Java development environment written entirely in Java that is available for Solaris, Windows NT, and Windows 95. Symantec Cafe (*http://www.symantec.com/*) is another commercial Java development tool for Windows NT and Windows 95 systems. Microsoft, Borland, IBM, and ParcPlace have also announced plans for Java implementations; check their respective Web sites for more information.

There are efforts under way to produce a free clone of Java, redistributable in source form. The Java Open Language Toolkit (JOLT) Project is working to assemble a high-quality Java implementation that will pass Sun's validation tests and earn a Java stamp. The JOLT Project Web page is accessible from *http://www.redhat.com/*.

The Netscape Navigator Web browser comes with its own implementation of the Java run-time system that runs Java applets. Netscape also provides a `-java` switch that lets you execute Java applications (including the Java compiler) and applets and run nongraphical applications. Netscape's Web site is located at *http://home.netscape.com/*. Check there for information on the latest version of Netscape Navigator.

2

A First Applet

Before we turn our attention to the details of the language, let's take a crash course and jump right into some Java code. In this chapter, we'll build a contrived but friendly little applet that illustrates a number of techniques we use throughout the book. I'll take this opportunity to introduce general features of the Java language and of Java applets. However, many details won't be fleshed out here, but in subsequent chapters.

This chapter also serves as a brief introduction to the object oriented and multi-threaded features of Java. If these concepts are new to you, you can take comfort in the knowledge that encountering them for the first time in Java should be a straightforward and pleasant experience. If you have worked with another object-oriented or multithreaded programming environment, clear your mind; you will especially appreciate Java's simplicity and elegance.

I can't stress enough the importance of experimentation as you learn new concepts. If you follow along with the online examples, be sure to take some time and compile them locally. Play with them; change their behavior, break them, fix them, and, as Java developer Arthur van Hoff would say: "Have fun!"

Hello Web!

In the tradition of all good introductory programming texts, we begin with Java's equivalent of the archetypal "Hello World" application. In the spirit of our new world, we'll call it "Hello Web!"

I'll take four passes at this example, adding features and introducing new concepts along the way. Here's a minimalist version:

```
public class HelloWeb extends java.applet.Applet {

    public void paint( java.awt.Graphics gc ) {
        gc.drawString("Hello Web!", 125, 95 );
    }
}
```

Place this text in a file called *HelloWeb.java.* Now compile this source:

```
% javac HelloWeb.java
```

This produces the Java byte-code binary class file *HelloWeb.class.*

We need an HTML document that contains the appropriate <applet> tag to display our example. Place the following text in a file called *HelloWeb.html* in the same directory as the binary class file:

```
<html>
<head>
</head>
<body>
    <applet code=HelloWeb width=300 height=200></applet>
</body>
</html>
```

Finally, you can point your Java-enabled Web browser at this document with a URL such as:

```
http://yourServer/wherever/HelloWeb.html
```

or

```
file:/wherever/HelloWeb.html
```

You should see the proclamation shown in Figure 2–1. Now congratulate yourself: you have written your first applet! Take a moment to bask in the glow of your monitor.

HelloWeb may be a small program, but there is actually quite a bit going on behind the scenes. Those five lines represent the tip of an iceberg. What lies under the surface are layers of functionality provided by the Java language and its foundation class libraries. In this chapter, I'll cover a lot of ground quickly in an effort to show you the big picture. I'll try to offer enough detail for a complete understanding of what is happening in each example without exhaustive explanations until the appropriate chapters. This holds for both elements of the Java language and the object-oriented concepts that apply to them. Later chapters will provide more detailed cataloging of Java's syntax, components, and object-oriented features.

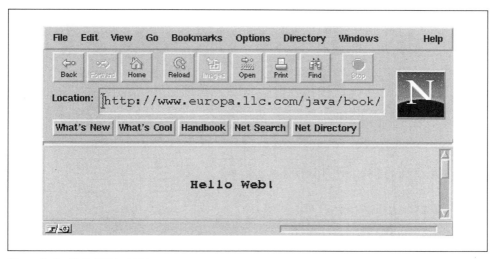

Figure 2–1: Hello Web! applet

Classes

The previous example defines a *class* named `HelloWeb`. Classes are the fundamental building blocks of most object-oriented languages. A class in Java is akin to the C++ concept of a class. Specifically, it's a group of data items (à la a C struct), with associated functions that perform operations on this data. The data items in a class are called *fields* or *variables*; the functions are called *methods*. A class might represent something concrete, like a button on a screen or the information in a spreadsheet, or it could be something more abstract, such as a sorting algorithm or possibly the sense of ennui in your MUD character. A hypothetical spreadsheet class might, for example, have variables that represent the values of its individual cells and methods that perform operations on those cells, such as "clear a row" or "compute values."

Our `HelloWeb` class is the container for our Java applet. It holds two general types of variables and methods: those we need for our specific applet's tasks and some special predesignated ones we provide to interact with the outside world. The Java run-time environment, in this case a Java-enabled Web browser, periodically calls methods in `HelloWeb` to pass us information and prod us to perform actions, as depicted in Figure 2–2. Our simple `HelloWeb` class defines a single method called `paint()`. The `paint()` method is called by Java when it's time for our application to draw itself on the screen.

You will see that the `HelloWeb` class derives some of its structure from another class called `Applet`. This is why we refer to `HelloWeb` as an applet.

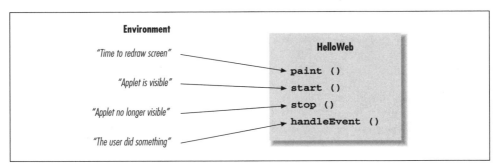

Figure 2–2: Method invocation in the Java environment

Class Instances and Objects

A class represents a particular thing; it contains methods and variables that assist in that representation. Many individual working copies of a given class can exist while an application is active. These individual incarnations are called *instances* of the class. Two instances of a given class may contain different states, but they always have the same methods.

As an example, consider a `Button` class. There is only one `Button` class, but many actual working instances of buttons can be in an application. Furthermore, two `Button` instances might contain different data, perhaps giving each a different appearance or specifying a different message for each to send when pushed. In this sense, a class can be considered a mold for making the object it represents: something like a cookie cutter stamping out working instances of itself in the memory of the computer. As you'll see later, there's a bit more to it than that—a class can in fact share information among its instances—but this explanation suffices for now.

The term *object* is very general and in some other contexts is used almost interchangeably with class. Objects are the abstract entities all object-oriented languages refer to in one form or another. I will use object as a generic term for an instance of a class. I might, therefore, refer to an instance of the `Button` class as a `Button`, a `Button` object, or, indiscriminately, as an object.

A Java-enabled Web browser creates an instance of our `HelloWeb` class when we first use our applet. If we had included the `HelloWeb` applet tag in our HTML document twice (causing it to appear twice on the screen), the browser would create and manage two separate HelloWeb objects (two separate instances of the `HelloWeb` class).

Variables

In Java, every class defines a new *type*. A variable can be of this type and then hold instances of that class. A variable could, for example, be of type `Button` and hold an instance of the `Button` class, or of type `SpreadSheetCell` and hold a `SpreadSheetCell` object, just as it could be any of the more familiar types such as `integer` or `float`. In this way, by having variables containing complex objects, a class may use other classes as tools within itself. Using classes in this way is called *composition*. Our examples in this chapter are somewhat unrealistic in that we are building only a single class of our own. However, we will be using many classes as tools within our applet.

You have seen only one variable so far in our simple `HelloWeb` example. It's found in the declaration of our lonely `paint()` method:

```
public void paint( java.awt.Graphics gc ) {...}
```

Just like functions in C (and many other languages), a method in Java declares a list of variables that hold its arguments, and it specifies the types of those arguments. Our `paint()` method takes one argument named (somewhat tersely) `gc`, which is of type `Graphics`. When the `paint()` method is invoked, a `Graphics` object is assigned to `gc`, which we use in the body of the method. I'll say more about `paint()` and the `Graphics` class in a moment.

But first, a few words about variables. I have loosely referred to variables as holding objects. In reality, variables that have complex types (class types) don't so much contain objects as point to them. Class-type variables are *references* to objects. A reference is a pointer to, or another name for, an object.

Simply declaring a variable doesn't imply that any storage is allocated for that variable or that an instance of its type even exists anywhere. When a reference-type variable is first declared, if it's not assigned to an instance of a class, it doesn't point to anything. It's assigned the default value of `null`, meaning "no value." If you try to use a variable with a `null` value as if it were pointing to a real object, a run-time error (NullPointerException) occurs.

This discussion begs the question as to where to get an instance of a class to assign to a variable in the first place. The answer, as you will see later, is through the use of the `new` operator. In our first two passes at this example, we are dealing only with objects handed to us prefabricated from somewhere outside of our class. We examine object creation later in the chapter.

Inheritance

Java classes are arranged in a parent-child hierarchy, in which the parent and child are known as the *superclass* and *subclass*, respectively. In Java, every class has exactly one superclass (a single parent), but possibly many subclasses. Of course, a class' superclass probably has its own superclass.

The declaration of our class in the previous example uses the keyword `extends` to specify that `HelloWeb` is a subclass of the `Applet` class:

```
public class HelloWeb extends java.applet.Applet {...}
```

A subclass may be allowed to inherit some or all of the variables and methods of its superclass. Through *inheritance*, the subclass can use those members as if it has declared them itself. A subclass can add variables and methods of its own, and it can also override the meaning of inherited variables and methods. When we use a subclass, overridden variables and methods are hidden (replaced) by the subclass' own versions of them. In this way, inheritance provides a powerful mechanism whereby a subclass can refine or extend its superclass.

For example, the hypothetical spreadsheet class might be subclassed to produce a new scientific spreadsheet class with extra mathematical functions and special built-in constants. In this case, the source code for the scientific spreadsheet might declare methods for the added mathematical functions and variables for the special constants, but the new class automatically has all the variables and methods that constitute the normal functionality of a spreadsheet; they are inherited from the parent spreadsheet class. This means the scientific spreadsheet maintains its identity as a spreadsheet, and we can use it anywhere the simpler spreadsheet is used.

Our `HelloWeb` class is a subclass of the `Applet` class and inherits many variables and methods not explicitly declared in our source code. These members function in the same way as the ones we add or override.

Applet

The `Applet` class provides the framework for building applets. It contains methods that support the basic functionality for a Java application that is displayed and controlled by a Java-enabled Web browser or other Java-enabled software.

We override methods in the `Applet` class in a subclass to implement the behavior of our particular applet. This may sound restrictive, as if we are limited to some predefined set of routines, but that is not the case at all. Keep in mind that the methods we are talking about are means of getting information from the outside world. A realistic application might involve hundreds or even thousands of classes, with legions of methods and variables and multiple threads of execution. The vast majority of these are related to the particulars of our job. The inherited methods of the `Applet` class, and of other special components, serve as a framework on which to hang code that handles certain types of events and performs special tasks.

The `paint()` method is an important method of the `Applet` class; we override it to implement the way in which our particular applet displays itself on the screen. We don't override any of the other inherited members of `Applet` because they provide basic functionality and reasonable defaults for this (trivial) example. As `HelloWeb` grows, we'll delve deeper into the inherited members and override additional methods. Inherited members will allow us to get information from the user and give us more control over what our applet does. We will also add some arbitrary, application-specific methods and variables for the needs of `HelloWeb`.

If you want to verify for yourself what functionality the `Applet` class is providing our example, you can try out the world's least interesting applet: the `Applet` base class itself. Just use the class name `java.applet.Applet` in your HTML code, instead of `HelloWeb`:

```
<applet code=java.applet.Applet width=300 height=200></applet>
```

You should get a blank area of screen. I told you it's not very interesting.

Relationships and Finger Pointing

We can correctly refer to `HelloWeb` as an `Applet` because subclassing can be thought of as creating an "is a" relationship, in which the subclass is a kind of its superclass. `HelloWeb` is therefore a kind of `Applet`. When we refer to a kind of object, we mean any instance of that object's class or any of its subclasses. Later, we will look more closely at the Java class hierarchy and see that `Applet` is itself a subclass of the `Panel` class, which is further derived from a class called `Container`, and so on, as shown in Figure 2–3.

In this sense, an `Applet` is a kind of `Panel`, which is, itself, a kind of `Container` and each of these can ultimately be considered to be a kind of `Component`. You'll see later that it's from these classes that `Applet` inherits its basic graphical user interface functionality and the ability to have other graphical components embedded within it.

`Component` is a subclass of `Object`, so all of these classes are a kind of `Object`. As you'll see later, the `Object` class is at the top of the Java class hierarchy; `Object` doesn't have a superclass. Every other class in the Java API inherits behavior from `Object`, which defines a few basic methods, as you'll see in Chapter 5.

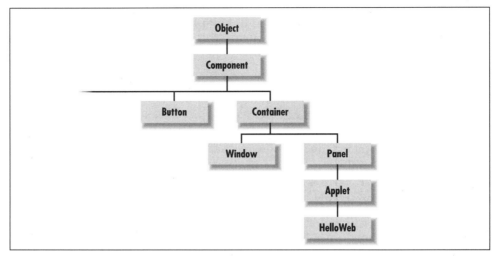

Figure 2–3: Part of the Java class hierarchy

The terminology here can become a bit muddled. I'll continue to use the word "object" (lowercase o) in a generic way to refer to an instance of any class; I'll use Object to refer specifically to that class.

Packages

In our previous example, the Applet class is referenced by its fully qualified name java.applet.Applet:

```
public class HelloWeb extends java.applet.Applet {...}
```

The prefix on the class name identifies it as belonging to the java.applet package. Packages provide a means for organizing Java classes. A *package* is a group of Java classes that are related by purpose or by application. Classes in the same package have special access privileges with respect to one another and may be designed to work together. Package names are hierarchical and are used somewhat like Internet domain and host names, to distinguish groups of classes by organization and application. Classes may be dynamically loaded over networks from arbitrary locations; within this context, packages provide a crude namespace of Java classes.[*]

---

[*] There are many efforts under way to find a general solution to the problem of locating resources in a globally distributed computing environment. The Uniform Resource Identifier Working Group of the IETF has proposed Uniform Resource Names (URNs). A URN would be a more abstract and persistent identifier that would be resolved to a URL through the use of a name service. We can imagine a day when there will exist a global namespace of trillions of persistent objects forming the infrastructure for all computing resources. Java provides an important evolutionary step in this direction.

`java.applet` identifies a particular package that contains classes related to applets. `java.applet.Applet` identifies a specific class, the `Applet` class, within that package. The `java.` hierarchy is special. Any package that begins with `java.` is part of the core Java API and is available on any platform that supports Java. Figure 2–4 illustrates the core Java packages, showing a representative class or two from each package.

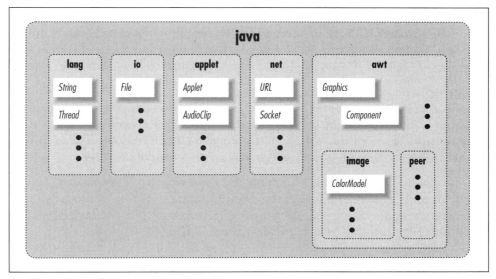

Figure 2–4: The core Java packages

Some notable core packages include: `java.lang`, which contains fundamental classes needed by the Java language itself; `java.awt`, which contains classes of the Java Abstract Windowing Toolkit; and `java.net`, which contains the networking classes.

A few classes contain methods that are not written in Java, but are instead part of the native Java implementation on a particular platform. Approximately 22 such classes are in the `java` package hierarchy; these are the only classes that have to be ported to a new platform. They form the basis for all interaction with the operating system. All other classes are built on or around these and are completely platform independent.

The paint() Method

The source for our `HelloWeb` class defines just one method, `paint()`, which overrides the `paint()` method from the `Applet` class:

```
public void paint( java.awt.Graphics gc ) {
    gc.drawString("Hello Web!", 125, 95 );
}
```

The `paint()` method is called by Java when it's time for our applet to draw itself on the screen. It takes a single argument, a `Graphics` object, and doesn't return any type of value (`void`) to its caller.

Modifiers are keywords placed before classes, variables, and methods to alter their accessibility, behavior, or semantics. `paint()` is declared as `public`, which means it can be invoked (called) by methods in classes other than `HelloWeb`. In this case, it's the Java windowing environment that is calling our `paint()` method. A method or variable declared as `private` is inaccessible from outside of its class.

The `Graphics` object, an instance of the `Graphics` class, represents a particular graphical drawing area and is also called a graphics context. It contains methods the applet calls to draw in this area, and variables that represent characteristics such as clipping or drawing modes. The particular `Graphics` object we are passed in the `paint()` method corresponds to our applet's area of the screen.

The `Graphics` class provides methods for rendering primitive shapes, images, and text. In `HelloWeb`, we invoke the `drawString()` method of our `Graphics` object to scrawl our message at the specified coordinates. (For a description of the methods available in the `Graphics` class, see Chapter 11.)

As in C++, a method or variable of an object is accessed in a hierarchical way by appending its name with a "." (dot) to the object that holds it. We invoked the `drawString()` method of the `Graphics` object (referenced by our `gc` variable) in this way:

```
gc.drawString( "Hello Web!", 125, 95 );
```

You may need to get used to the idea of our application is drawn by a method that is called by an outside agent at arbitrary times. How can we do anything useful with this? How do we control what gets done and when? These answers will be forthcoming. For now, just think about how you would structure applications that draw themselves on command.

Hello Web! II: The Sequel

Let's make our applet a little more interactive, shall we? The following improvement, `HelloWeb2`, allows us to drag the message around with the mouse. `HelloWeb2` is also customizable. It takes the text of its message from a parameter of the `<applet>` tag of the HTML document.

HelloWeb2 is a new applet—another subclass of the Applet class. In that sense, it's a sibling of HelloWeb. Having just seen inheritance at work, you might wonder why we aren't creating a subclass of HelloWeb and exploiting inheritance to build upon our previous example and extend its functionality. Well, in this case, that would not necessarily be an advantage, and for clarity we simply start over.[*] Here is HelloWeb2:

```java
import java.applet.Applet;
import java.awt.*;

public class HelloWeb2 extends Applet {
    int messageX = 125, messageY = 95;
    String theMessage;

    public void init() {
        theMessage = getParameter("message");
    }

    public void paint( Graphics gc ) {
        gc.drawString( theMessage, messageX, messageY );
    }

    public boolean mouseDrag(Event evt, int x, int y ) {
        messageX = x;
        messageY = y;
        repaint();
        return true;
    }
}
```

Place the text of this example in a file called *HelloWeb2.java* and compile it as before. You should get a new class file, *HelloWeb2.class*, as a result. We need to create a new <applet> tag for HelloWeb2. You can either create another HTML document (copy *HelloWeb.html* and modify it) or simply add a second <applet> tag to the existing *HelloWeb.html* file. The <applet> tag for HelloWeb2 has to use a parameter; it should look like:

```html
<applet code=HelloWeb2 width=300 height=200>
<param name="message" value="Hello Web!" >
</applet>
```

Feel free to substitute your own salacious comment for the value of message.

Run this applet in your Java-enabled Web browser, and enjoy many hours of fun, dragging the text around with your mouse.

---

* You are left to consider whether such a subclassing would even make sense. Should HelloWeb2 really be a kind of HelloWeb? Are we looking for refinement or just code reuse?

Import

So, what have we added? First you may notice that a couple of lines are now hovering above our class:

```
import java.applet.Applet;
import java.awt.*;

public class HelloWeb2 extends Applet {
...
```

The `import` statement lists external classes to use in this file and tells the compiler where to look for them. In our first `HellowWeb` example, we designated the `Applet` class as the superclass of `HelloWeb`. `Applet` was not defined by us and the compiler therefore had to look elsewhere for it. In that case, we referred to `Applet` by its fully qualified name, `java.applet.Applet`, which told the compiler that `Applet` belongs to the `java.applet` package so it knew where to find it.

The `import` statement is really just a convenience; by importing `java.applet.Applet` in our newer example, we tell the compiler up front we are using this class and, thereafter in this file, we can simply refer to it as `Applet`. The second import statement makes use of the wildcard "*" to tell the compiler to import all of the classes in the `java.awt` package. But don't worry, the compiled code doesn't contain any excess baggage. Java doesn't do things like that. In fact, compiled Java classes don't contain other classes at all; they simply note their relationships. Our current example uses only the `java.awt.Graphics` class. However, we are anticipating using several more classes from this package in the upcoming examples.

The `import` statement may seem a bit like the C or C++ preprocessor `#include` statement, which injects header files into programs at the appropriate places. This is not true; there are no header files in Java. Unlike compiled C or C++ libraries, Java binary class files contain all necessary type information about the classes, methods, and variables they contain, obviating the need for prototyping.

Instance Variables

We have added some variables to our example:

```
public class HelloWeb2 extends Applet {
    int messageX = 125, messageY = 95;
    String theMessage;
...
```

messageX and messageY are integers that hold the current coordinates of our movable message. They are initialized to default values, which should place a message of our length somewhere near the center of the applet. Java integers are always 32-bit signed numbers. There is no fretting about what architecture your code is running on; numeric types in Java are precisely defined. The variable theMessage is of type String and can hold instances of the String class.

You should note that these three variables are declared inside the braces of the class definition, but not inside any particular method in that class. These variables are called *instance variables* because they belong to the entire class, and copies of them appear in each separate instance of the class. Instance variables are always visible (usable) in any of the methods inside their class. Depending on their modifiers, they may also be accessible from outside the class.

Unless otherwise initialized, instance variables are set to a default value of 0 (zero), false, or null. Numeric types are set to zero, boolean variables are set to false, and class type variables always have their value set to null, which means "no value." Attempting to use an object with a null value results in a run-time error.

Instance variables differ from method arguments and other variables that are declared inside of a single method. The latter are called *local variables*. They are effectively private variables that can be seen only by code inside the method. Java doesn't initialize local variables, so you must assign values yourself. If you try to use a local variable that has not yet been assigned a value, your code will generate a compile-time error. Local variables live only as long as the method is executing and then disappear (which is fine since nothing outside of the method can see them anyway). Each time the method is invoked, its local variables are recreated and must be assigned values.

Methods

We have made some changes to our previously stodgy paint() method. All of the arguments in the call to drawString() are now variables.

Two new methods have appeared in our class. Like paint(), these are methods of the base Applet class we override to add our own functionality. init() is an important method of the Applet class. It's called once, when our applet is created, to give us an opportunity to do any work needed to set up shop. init() is a good place to allocate resources and perform other activities that need happen only once in the lifetime of the applet. A Java-enabled Web browser calls init() when it prepares to place the Applet on a page.

Our overridden `init()` method does one thing; it sets the text of the `theMes-sage` instance variable:

```
public void init() {
    theMessage = getParameter("message");
}
```

When an applet is instantiated, the parameters given in the `<applet>` tag of the HTML document are stored in a table and made available through the `getPa-rameter()` method. Given the name of a parameter, this method returns the value as a `String` object. If the name is not found, it returns a `null` value.

So what, you may ask, is the type of the argument to the `getParameter()` method? It, too, is a `String`. With a little magic from the Java compiler, quoted strings in Java source code are turned into `String` objects. A bit of funny-business is going on here, but it's simply for convenience. (See Chapter 7 for a complete discussion of the `String` class.)

`getParameter()` is a public method we inherited from the `Applet` class. We can use it from any of our methods. Note that the `getParameter()` method is invoked directly by name; there is no object name prepended to it with a dot. If a method exists in our class, or is inherited from a superclass, we can call it directly by name.

In addition, we can use a special read-only variable, called `this`, to explicitly refer to our object. A method can use `this` to refer to the instance of the object that holds it. The following two statements are therefore equivalent:

```
theMessage = getParameter("message");
```

or

```
theMessage = this.getParameter("message");
```

I'll always use the shorter form. We will need the `this` variable later when we have to pass a reference to our object to a method in another class. We often do this so that methods in another class can give us a call back later or can watch our public variables.

Events

The last bit of `HelloWeb2` is the `mouseDrag()` method we added to get informa-tion from the mouse. Each time the user performs an action, such as hitting a key on the keyboard, moving the mouse, or perhaps banging his or her head against a touch-sensitive screen, Java generates an *event*. An event represents an action that has occurred; it contains information about the action, such as its time and location. Events can usually be associated with a particular graphical user interface (GUI) component in an application. A keystroke, for instance, could correspond to a character being typed into a particular text entry field. Pressing a mouse button could cause a certain graphical button on the screen to activate. Even just moving the mouse within a certain area of the screen could be intended to trigger effects such as highlighting or changing the cursor to a special mouse cursor.

Every area of real estate on the screen belongs to a particular GUI component. These components are designed to respond to different types of events within their boundaries. As with all things in Java, GUI components are objects. When an event occurs, Java determines to which component the action belongs and delivers the event to the appropriate object. Information about an event is wrapped up in an instance of the `java.awt.Event` class. The event is delivered by invoking a method in the receiving object; the `Event` object is passed as an argument to that method.

Events are discussed in detail in Chapter 10. For now, all you need to know is that in this example our applet serves as the single component to which events are delivered. The `mouseDrag()` method is one of a suite of routines we can override to handle specific types of events when they are delivered to it.

```
public boolean mouseDrag(Event evt, int x, int y ) {
    messageX = x;
    messageY = y;
    repaint();
    return true;
}
```

As the mouse is dragged, Java calls the `mouseDrag()` method repeatedly to update us on the position of the mouse. Each invocation of `mouseDrag()` corresponds to a discrete position of the mouse.

The first argument to `mouseDrag()` is the `Event` object that contains information about this event. We assign the `Event` to the `evt` variable. It contains, among other things, data specifying the type of event (mouse movement), the component in which it happened (our applet), and and the x,y coordinates of the event (the current mouse position). The last two arguments to `mouseDrag()` are integers which, redundantly, contain the x,y coordinates of the mouse position.

This may be a bit confusing. If the `Event` object has all the information, why do we have a specific method for this type of event, and why are we passed the x,y coordinates in separate variables? The answer is that `mouseDrag()` is a programming convenience. A lower-level method looks at the `Event` first and, based on its type, dispatches it to one of several more specific methods. In this case, we don't have to bother with the `Event` argument to `mouseDrag()`, and we can simply use the x,y coordinates to do our work. There could, however, be situations in which we would need to differentiate between events before acting on them. This issue should become clearer when we discuss how events are delivered when there are multiple user-interface components in our application.

Our implementation of the `mouseDrag()` method does three things. First, the `messageX` and `messageY` instance variables of our class are set to the current position of the mouse. Now, having changed the coordinates for the message, we would like `HelloWeb2` to redraw itself. At first glance, it might seem logical for us to call the `paint()` method. However, you might notice that we can't invoke `paint()` directly because we don't have a `Graphics` context to pass to it. What to do?

The repaint() Method

We can use the `repaint()` method of the `Applet` class to request our applet be redrawn. `repaint()` causes the Java windowing system to schedule a call to our `paint()` method at the next possible time; Java supplies the necessary `Graphics` object, as shown in Figure 2–5.

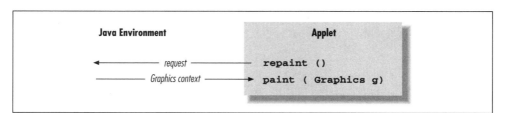

Figure 2–5: Invoking the repaint() method

This mode of operation isn't just an inconvenience brought about by not having the right graphics context handy at the moment. The foremost advantage to this mode of operation is that the repainting is handled by someone else, while we are free to go about our business. The Java system has a separate, dedicated thread of execution that handles all `repaint()` requests. It can schedule and consolidate `repaint()` requests as necessary, which helps to prevent the windowing system from being overwhelmed during painting-intensive situations like scrolling. Another advantage is that all of the painting functionality can be kept in our `paint()` method; we aren't tempted to spread it throughout the application.

Finally, our `mouseDrag()` method returns a value to the method that called it. `mouseDrag()` returns a `boolean` value that indicates whether we have actually

handled the event. Here we return `true`, indicating that we did indeed respond to
the event and that no further processing is necessary. What would happen if we
said that we had not? Well, in this example, not much. However, as you will see in
the next section, certain types of components can act as containers for other components, creating a hierarchy. In this case, events that are not handled by the component where it occurred are passed upward to the container component that
holds it. This gives us the option of having general event-handling routines that
manage a number of components.

Hello Web! III: The Button Strikes!

Well, now that we have those concepts under control, we can move on to some fun
stuff. `HelloWeb3` brings us a new graphical interface component: the `Button`.
We add a `Button` component to our applet that changes the color of our text
each time the button is pressed. Our new example is shown below.

```
import java.applet.*;
import java.awt.*;

public class HelloWeb3 extends Applet {
    int messageX = 125, messageY = 95;
    String theMessage;
    Button theButton;
    Color[] someColors = {
        Color.black, Color.red, Color.green,
        Color.blue, Color.magenta };
    int colorIndex;

    public void init() {
        theMessage = getParameter("message");
        theButton = new Button("Change Color");
        add(theButton);
    }

    public void paint( Graphics gc ) {
        gc.setColor( currentColor() );
        gc.drawString( theMessage, messageX, messageY );
    }

    public boolean action ( Event e, Object arg ) {
        if ( e.target == theButton ) {
            changeColor();
            return true;
        }

        return false;
    }

    public boolean mouseDrag(Event evt, int x, int y ) {
        messageX = x;
```

```
        messageY = y;
        repaint();
        return true;
    }

    synchronized private Color currentColor() {
        return someColors[ colorIndex ];
    }

    synchronized private void changeColor() {
        if ( ++colorIndex == someColors.length )
            colorIndex = 0;
        theButton.setForeground( currentColor() );
        repaint();
    }
}
```

Create `HelloWeb3` just as the other applets and put an `<applet>` tag referencing it in an HTML document. An `<applet>` tag just like the one for `HelloWeb2` will do nicely. Run the example, and you should see the display shown in Figure 2–6. Drag the text. Each time you press the button the color should change. Call your friends! They should be duly impressed.

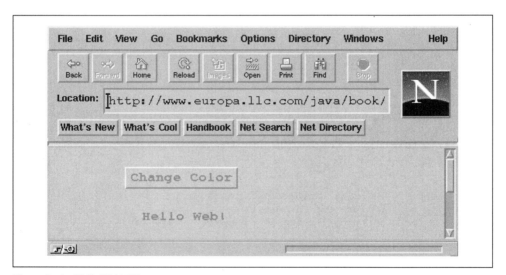

Figure 2–6: Hello Web! III

The New Operator

So what have we added this time? Well, for starters we have a new variable:

```
Button theButton;
```

The `theButton` variable is of type `Button` and is going to hold an instance of the `java.awt.Button` class. The `Button` class, as you might expect, represents a graphical button, which should look like other buttons in your windowing system.

Two additional lines in `init()` actually create the button and cause it to be displayed in our applet:

```
theButton = new Button("Change Color");
add(theButton);
```

The first line brings us to something new. The `new` keyword is used to create an instance of a class. Recall that the variable we have declared is just an empty reference and doesn't yet point to a real object—in this case, an instance of the `Button` class. This is a fundamental and important concept. We have dealt with objects previously in our examples. We have assigned them to variables, and we have called methods in them. So far, however, these objects have always been handed to us ready to go, and we have not had to explicitly create them ourselves. In the case of our `paint()` method, we were given a `Graphics` object with which to draw. The system created this instance of the `Graphics` class for our area of the screen and passed it to us in the parameter variable `gc`. Our `theMessage` variable is of type `String`, and we used it to hold a `String` that was returned by the `getParameter()` method. In each case, some other method instantiated (created a new instance of) the class for us.

The closest we came to actually instantiating an object was when we passed the name of the HTML `<applet>` parameter as an argument to the `getParameter()` method. In that case, we created a `String` object and passed it as the argument, but we did it in a rather sneaky fashion. As I mentioned previously, `String` objects have special status in the Java language. Because strings are used so frequently, the Java compiler creates an instance of the `String` class for us whenever it comes across quoted text in our source code. `String` objects are, in all other respects, normal objects. (See Chapter 7.)

The `new` operator provides the general mechanism for instantiating objects. It's the feature of the Java language that creates a new instance of a specified class. It arranges for Java to allocate storage for the object and then calls the constructor method of the objects' class to initialize it.

Constructors

A *constructor* is a special method that is called to set up a new instance of a class. When a new object is created, Java allocates storage for it, sets variables to their default values, and then calls the constructor method for the class to do whatever application-level setup is required.

A constructor method looks like a method with the same name as its class. For example, the constructor for the `Button` class is called `Button()`. Constructors don't have a return type; by definition they return an object of that class. But like other methods, constructors can take arguments. Their sole mission in life is to configure and initialize newly born class instances, possibly using whatever information is passed to them in parameters.

It's important to understand the difference between a constructor and a method like our `init()` method. Constructors are special methods of a class that help set up and initialize an instance of a class when it's first created. The `init()` method of the `Applet` class serves a very similar purpose; however, it's quite different. Constructors are a feature of the Java language. Every class, including `Applet`, has constructors. `init()`, however, is just a method of the `Applet` class like any other. It's an application-level phenomenon that happens to perform initialization.

An object is created by using the `new` operator with the constructor for the class and any necessary arguments. The resulting object instance is returned as a value. In our example, we create a new instance of `Button` and assign it to our `theButton` variable:

```
theButton = new Button("Change Color");
```

This `Button` constructor takes a `String` as an argument and, as it turns out, uses it to set the label of the button on the screen. A class could also, of course, provide methods that allow us to configure an object manually after it's created or to change its configuration at a later time. Many classes do both; the constructor simply takes its arguments and passes them to the appropriate methods. The `Button` class, for example, has a public method, `setLabel()`, that allows us to set a `Button`'s label at any time. Constructors with parameters are therefore a convenience that allows a sort of short hand to set up a new object.

Method Overloading

I said this `Button` constructor because there could be more than one. A class can have multiple constructors, each taking different parameters and possibly using them to do different kinds of setup. When there are multiple constructors for a class, Java chooses the correct one based on the types of arguments that are passed to it. We call the Button constructor and pass it a String argument, so Java locates the constructor method of the Button class that takes a single String argument and uses it to set up the object. This is called *method overloading*. All methods in Java, not just constructors, can be overloaded; this is one aspect of the object-oriented programming principle of polymorphism.

A constructor method that takes no arguments is called the *default constructor*. As you'll see in Chapter 7, default constructors play a special role in the initialization of inherited class members.

Garbage Collection

I've told you how to create a new object with the new operator, but I haven't said anything about how to get rid of an object when you are done with it. If you are a C programmer, you're probably wondering why not. The reason is that you don't have to do anything to get rid of objects when you are done with them.

The Java run-time system uses a *garbage collection* mechanism to deal with objects no longer in use. The garbage collector sweeps up objects not referenced by any variables and removes them from memory. Garbage collection is one of the most important features of Java. It frees you from the error-prone task of having to worry about details of memory allocation and deallocation.

Components

I have used the terms *component* and *container* somewhat loosely to describe graphical elements of Java applications. However, you may recall from Figure 2–3 that these terms are the names of actual classes in the java.awt package.

Component is a base class from which all of Java's GUI components are derived. It contains variables that represent the location, shape, general appearance, and status of the object, as well as methods for basic painting and event handling. The familiar paint() and mouseDrag() methods we have been using in our example are actually inherited from the Component class. Applet is, of course, a kind of Component and inherits all of its public members, just as other (perhaps simpler) types of GUI components do.

The Button class is also derived from Component and therefore shares this functionality. This means that the developer of the Button class had methods like paint() and mouseDrag() available with which to implement the behavior of the Button object, just as we did when creating our applet.[*] What's exciting is that we are perfectly free to further subclass components like Button and override their behavior to create our own special types of user-interface components.

Both Button and Applet are, in this respect, equivalent types of things. However, the Applet class is further derived from a class called Container, which gives it the added ability to hold other components and manage them.

Containers

A Button object is a simple GUI component. It makes sense only in the context of some larger application. The Container class is an extended type of Component that maintains a list of child components and helps to group them. The Container causes its children to be displayed and arranges them on the screen according to a particular scheme. A Container may also receive events related to its child components. As I mentioned earlier, if a component doesn't respond to a particular type of event by overriding the appropriate event-handling method and handling the event, the event is passed to the parent Container of the component. This is the default behavior for the standard Java AWT components, which gives us a great deal of flexibility in managing interface components. We could, for example, create a smart button by subclassing the Button class and overriding certain methods to deal with the action of being pressed. Alternatively, we could simply have the Button's container note which Button is pressed and handle the event appropriately. In the interest of keeping our examples contained in a single class, I am using the gestalt view and letting our Button's container, HelloWeb3, deal with its events.

Remember that a Container is a Component too and, as such, can be placed alongside other Component objects in other Containers, in a hierarchical fashion, as shown in Figure 2–7. Our HelloWeb3 applet is a kind of Container and can therefore hold and manage other Java AWT components and containers like buttons, sliders, text fields, and panels.

In Figure 2–7, the italicized items are components, and the bold items are containers. The keypad is implemented as a container object that manages a number of keys. The keypad itself is contained in the GizmoTool container object.

---

* At the time of this writing, there are some limitations with respect to which events can be caught and handled by certain types of components. Not all types of components can currently intercept all types of events. The problem arises from the complications of using native windowing system GUI components in Java implementations. It's the Java development team's goal to correct this situation.

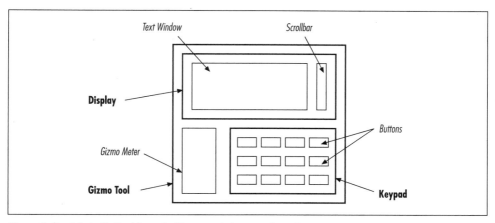

Figure 2–7: A hypothetical layout of Java containers and components

Layout

After creating the `Button` object, we'd like to stick it in our applet. To do so, we invoke the `add()` method of `Applet`, passing the `Button` object as a parameter:

```
add(theButton);
```

`add()` is a method inherited by our `Applet` from the `Container` class. It appends our `Button` to the list of components `HelloWeb3` manages. Thereafter, `HelloWeb3` is responsible for the `Button`: the applet causes the button to be displayed, it determines where in our part of the screen the button should be placed, and it receives events when the button is pushed.

Java uses an object called a `LayoutManager` to determine the precise location in `HelloWeb3`'s screen area the `Button` is displayed. A `LayoutManager` object embodies a particular scheme for arranging components on the screen and adjusting their sizes. You'll learn more about layout managers in Chapter 10. There are several standard layout managers to choose from, and we can, of course, create new ones. In our case, we have not specified a layout manager, so we get the default one, which means our button appears centered at the top of the applet.

Subclassing and Subtypes

If you look up the `add()` method of the `Container` class, you'll see that it takes a `Component` object as an argument. But in our example we've given it a `Button` object. What's going on?

Well, if you check the inheritance diagram in Figure 2–3 again, you'll see that Button is a subclass of the Component class. Because a subclass is a kind of its superclass and has, at minimum, the same public methods and variables, we can use an instance of a subclass anywhere we use an instance of its superclass. This is a very important concept, and it's a second aspect of the object-oriented principle of polymorphism. Button is a kind of Component, and any method that expects a Component as an argument will accept a Button.

As you'll see later, it's not possible to create an instance of the Component class. This class is an abstract class that exists solely to be subclassed into usable forms. (See Chapter 5.)

action()

We have added another method to our class:

```
public boolean action ( Event e, Object arg ) {
    if ( e.target == theButton ) {
        changeColor();
        return true;
    }

    return false;
}
```

The action() method is another in the suite of event-handing routines like mouseDrag(). As the name *action* might suggest however, it's slightly more general in purpose. Components like buttons, toggle switches, and sliders all cause an event to be sent whenever they are used. These types of events are categorized as action events and are delivered to the action() method of the object in which they occurred. In our example, all of the action events from the **Change Color** button are passed to its container, HelloWeb3 and handled by our action() method.

In this case, there's only one Button object, and it's the only component that can cause action events in HelloWeb3. However, in a more realistic situation, our applet could contain many such components, and our event-handling methods would then have to make a determination as to which component was responsible for the event before acting on it. We would therefore be remiss not to take a little care and add the appropriate check in our action() method. (Just in case someone slips another Button into HelloWeb3 when we're not looking.)

An event contains a field called target that references the component that generated the event. Here we use the "==" operator in an expression to check if our Button (the one referenced by theButton) is indeed that same object that generated the event. If the `Event` we are passed does have `Button` as its target, we then call our new method `changeColor()` and return `true`, indicating that we handled this event. If the event was instigated by some other object, we do nothing and return `false`.

It's worth noting at this point that, in Java, the "`==`" operator is a test for identity and not equality. Here we are testing to see if `e.target` and `theButton` are the same object, not just equivalent but possibly different objects. The distinction is important. When two references are identical, they point to the same object. When we say two references are equivalent, that generally means they point to two different objects that have the same data. We would, for example, consider two `String` objects to be equivalent if they have exactly the same characters in the same sequence. They would be, by that measure, equivalent. They are, however, not the same object. In Chapter 5, we'll look at the `equals()` method, which can be used to compare two instances of a class for equivalence.

You may be wondering why we don't have to change `mouseDrag()` now that we have a `Button` in our applet. The rationale is that the coordinates of the event are all that matter for this method. We are not particularly concerned if the event happens to fall within an area of the screen occupied by another component. This means that you can drag the text right through the `Button` and even lose it behind the `Button` if you aren't careful: try it and see!

Color Commentary

To support `HelloWeb3`'s colorful side we have added a couple of new variables and two helpful methods. We create and initialize an array of `Color` objects representing the colors through which we cycle when the button is pressed. We also declare an integer variable that serves as an index to this array, specifying the current color:

```
Color[] someColors = {
    Color.black, Color.red, Color.green, Color.blue, Color.magenta };
int colorIndex;
```

A number of things are going on here. First let's look at the `Color` objects we are putting into the array. Instances of the `java.awt.Color` class represent colors and are used by all classes in the `java.awt` package that deal with color graphics. Notice that we are referencing variables such as `Color.black` and `Color.red`. These look like normal references to an object's instance variables; however `Color` is not an object, it's a class. What is the meaning of this?

Static Members

If you recall our discussion of classes and instances, I hinted then that a class can contain methods and variables that are shared among all instances of the class. These shared members are called *static variables* and *static methods*. The most common use of static variables in a class is to hold predefined constants or unchanging objects all of the instances can use.

There are two advantages to this approach. The more obvious advantage is that static members take up space only in the class; the members are not replicated in each instance. The second advantage is that static members can be accessed even if no instances of the class exist. A hypothetical `Component` class might have a static variable called `maximumWidth`. Some other class that has to deal with this component, such as a layout manager, might want to know the maximum width of such a component, even if there aren't any around at the moment. Since `maximumWidth` is a static variable, the layout manager can get this information.

An instance of the `Color` class represents a color. For convenience, the `Color` class contains some static, predefined color objects with friendly names like `green`, `red` and (my favorite) `magenta`. `Color.green` is thus a predefined `Color` object that is set to a green color. In this case, these static members of `Color` are not changeable, so they are effectively constants and can be optimized as such by the compiler. Constant static members make up for the lack of a `#define` construct in Java. However, static variables don't, in general, have to be constant. I'll say more about static class members in Chapter 5. The alternative to using these predefined colors is to create a color manually by specifying its red, green, blue (RGB) components using a `Color` class constructor.

Arrays

Next, we turn our attention to the array. We have declared a variable called `some-Colors`, which is an array of `Color` objects. Arrays are syntactically supported by the Java language; however, they are true, first-class objects. This means that an array is, itself, a type of object that knows how to hold an indexed list of some other type of object. An array is indexed by integers; when you index an array, the resulting value is the object in the corresponding slot in the array. Our code uses the `colorIndex` variable to index `someColors`. It's also possible to have an array of simple primitive types, rather than objects.

When we declare an array, we can initialize it by using the familiar C-like curly brace construct. Specifying a comma-separated list of elements inside of curly braces is a convenience that instructs the compiler to create an instance of the array with those elements and assign it to our variable. Alternatively, we could have just declared our someColors variable and, later, allocated an array object for it and assigned individual elements to that array's slots. See Chapter 4 for a complete discussion of arrays.

Our Color Methods

So, we now have an array of Color objects and a variable with which to index them. What do we do with them? Well, we have declared two private methods that do the actual work for us. The private modifier on these methods specifies that they can be called only by other methods in the same instance of the class. They are not visible outside of the object. We declare members to be private to hide the detailed inner workings of a class from the outside world. This is called *encapsulation* and is another tenet of object-oriented design, as well as good programming practice. Private methods are also often created as helper functions for use solely within the class implementation.

The first method, currentColor(), is simply a convenience routine that returns the Color object representing the current text color. It returns the Color object in the someColors array at the index specified by our colorIndex variable:

```
synchronized private Color currentColor() {
    return someColors[ colorIndex ];
}
```

We could just as readily have used the expression someColors[colorIndex] everywhere we use currentColor(); however, creating methods to wrap common tasks is another way of shielding ourselves from the details of our class. In an alternative implementation, we might have shuffled off details of all color-related code into a separate class. We could have created a class that takes an array of colors in its constructor and then provided two methods: one to ask for the current color and one to cycle to the next color (just some food for thought).

The second method, changeColor(), is responsible for incrementing the colorIndex variable to point to the next Color in the array. changeColor() is called from our action() method whenever the button is pressed.

```
synchronized private void changeColor() {
    if ( ++colorIndex == someColors.length )
        colorIndex = 0;
    theButton.setForeground( currentColor() );
    repaint();
}
```

We increment `colorIndex` and compare it to the length of the `someColors` array. All array objects have a variable called `length` that specifies the number of elements in the array. If we have reached the end of the array, we reset our index to zero and start over. After changing the currently selected color, we do two things. First, we call a method in our `Button` object to set the color of its label to the current color, just for consistency. Then we call `repaint()` to cause the applet to be redrawn with the new color for the draggable message.

So, what is the `synchronized` keyword that appears in front of our `current-Color()` and `changeColor()` methods? Synchronization has to do with threads, which we'll examine in the next section. For now, all you need know is that the `synchronized` keyword indicates these two methods can never be running at the same time. They must always run one after the other.

The reason is that in `changeColor()` we increment `colorIndex` before testing its value. That means that for some brief period of time while Java is running through our code, `colorIndex` can have a value that is past the end of our array. If our `currentColor()` method happened to run at that same moment, we would see a run-time "array out of bounds" error. There are, of course, ways in which we could fudge around the problem in this case, but this simple example is representative of more general synchronization issues we need to address. In the next section, you'll see that Java makes dealing with these problems easy through language-level synchronization support.

Finally, our `paint()` method has been modified to set the current color in its graphics context before doing any drawing:

```
public void paint( Graphics gc ) {
    gc.setColor( currentColor() );
    gc.drawString( theMessage, messageX, messageY );
}
```

Subsequent drawing calls on this `Graphics` object, like the one we make to `drawString()`, render in that color. We must set the color from our `paint()` method because we are handed a new `Graphics` object on each invocation—a blank slate if you will. We are responsible for remembering everything about how we draw our applet's face.

In contrast, you might recall that our `Button` object has its own `paint()` method and is therefore responsible for remembering its own appearance, including its current color. That is why we can safely set that property for the `Button` once, right in the `changeColor()` method.

Hello Web! IV: Netscape's Revenge

We have explored quite a few features of Java with our first three revisions of the `HelloWeb` applet. But until now, our applet has been rather passive; it has waited patiently for events to come its way and responded to the whims of the user. Now our applet is going to take some initiative—`HelloWeb4` will blink! The code for our latest version is shown below.

```java
import java.applet.*;
import java.awt.*;

public class HelloWeb4 extends Applet implements Runnable {
    int messageX = 125, messageY = 95;
    String theMessage;
    Button theButton;
    Color[] someColors = {
        Color.black, Color.red, Color.green,
        Color.blue, Color.magenta };
    int colorIndex = 0;
    Thread blinkThread;
    boolean blinkState;

    public void init() {
        theMessage = getParameter("message");

        theButton = new Button("Change Color");
        add(theButton);
    }

    public void paint( Graphics gc ) {
        gc.setColor( blinkState ? Color.white : currentColor() );
        gc.drawString( theMessage, messageX, messageY );
    }

    public boolean action ( Event e, Object arg ) {
        if ( e.target == theButton ) {
            changeColor();
            return true;
        }
        return false;
    }

    public boolean mouseDrag(Event evt, int x, int y ) {
        messageX = x;
        messageY = y;
        repaint();
        return true;
    }

    synchronized private Color currentColor() {
        return someColors[ colorIndex ];
    }
```

```
synchronized private void changeColor() {
    if ( ++colorIndex == someColors.length )
        colorIndex = 0;
    theButton.setForeground( currentColor() );
    repaint();
}

public void run() {
    while ( true ) {
        blinkState = !blinkState;
        repaint();

        try {
            Thread.sleep(500);
        }
        catch (InterruptedException e ) {
        }
    }
}

public void start() {
    if ( blinkThread == null ) {
        blinkThread = new Thread(this);
        blinkThread.start();
    }
}

public void stop() {
    if ( blinkThread != null ) {
        blinkThread.stop();
        blinkThread = null;
    }
}
}
```

If you create HelloWeb4 as you have the other applets and then run it in a Java-enabled Web browser, you'll see that the text does in fact blink. My apologies if you don't like blinking text—I'm not overly fond of it either—but it does make for a simple, instructive example.

Threads

All the changes we've made in HelloWeb4 have to do with setting up a separate thread of execution to make the text of our applet blink. Java is a *multithreaded* language, which means there can be many threads running at the same time. A *thread* is a separate flow of control within a program. Conceptually, threads are similar to processes, except that unlike processes, multiple threads share the same address space, which means that they can share variables and methods (but they have their own local variables). Threads are also quite lightweight in comparison to processes, so it's conceivable for a single application to be running hundreds of threads concurrently.

Multithreading provides a way for an application to handle many different tasks at the same time. It's easy to imagine multiple things going on at the same time in an application like a Web browser. The user could be listening to an audio clip while scrolling an image, and in the background the browser is downloading an image. Multithreading is especially useful in GUI-based applications, as it can improve the interactive performance of these applications.

Unfortunately for us, programming with multiple threads can be quite a headache. The difficulty lies in making sure routines are implemented so they can be run by multiple concurrent threads. If a routine changes the value of a state variable, for example, then only one thread can be executing the routine at a time. Later in this section, we'll examine briefly the issue of coordinating multiple thread's access to shared data. In other languages, synchronization of threads can be an extremely complex and error-prone endeavor. You'll see that Java gives you a few simple tools that help you deal with many of these problems. Java threads can be started, stopped, suspended, and prioritized. Threads are preemptive, so a higher priority thread can interrupt a lower priority thread when vying for processor time. See Chapter 6 for a complete discussion of threads.

The Java run-time system creates and manages a number of threads. I've already mentioned the AWT thread, which manages `repaint()` requests and event processing for GUI components that belong to the `java.awt` package. A Java-enabled Web browser typically has at least one separate thread of execution it uses to manage the applets it displays. Until now, our example has done most of its work from methods of the `Applet` class, which means that is has been borrowing time from these threads. Methods like `mouseDrag()` and `action()` are invoked by the AWT thread and run on its time. Similarly, our `init()` method is called by a thread in the Web browser. This means we are somewhat limited in the amount of processing we do within these methods. If we were, for instance, to go into an endless loop in our `init()` method, our applet would never appear, as it would never finish initializing. If we want an applet to perform any extensive processing, such as animation, a lengthy calculation, or communication, we should create separate threads for these tasks.

The Thread Class

As you might have guessed, threads are created and controlled as `Thread` objects. We have added a new instance variable, `blinkThread`, to our example to hold the `Thread` that handles our blinking activity:

```
Thread blinkThread;
```

An instance of the `Thread` class corresponds to a single thread. It contains methods to start, control, and stop the thread's execution. Our basic plan is to create a `Thread` object to handle our blinking code. We call the `Thread`'s `start()` method to begin execution. Once the thread starts, it continues to run until we call the `Thread`'s `stop()` method to terminate it.

But Java doesn't allow pointers to methods, so how do we tell the thread which method to run? Well, the `Thread` object is rather picky; it always expects to execute a method called `run()` to perform the action of the thread. The `run()` method can, however, with a little persuasion, be located in any class we desire.

We specify the location of the `run()` method in one of two ways. First, the `Thread` class itself has a method called `run()`. One way to execute some Java code in a separate thread is to subclass `Thread` and override its `run()` method to do our bidding. In this case, we simply create an instance of this subclass and call its `start()` method.

But it's not always desirable or possible to create a subclass of `Thread` to contain our `run()` method. In this case, we need to tell the `Thread` which object contains the `run()` method it should execute. The `Thread` class has a constructor that takes an object reference as its argument. If we create a `Thread` object using this constructor and call its `start()` method, the `Thread` executes the `run()` method of the target object, rather than its own. In order to accomplish this, Java needs to have a guarantee that the object we are passing it does indeed contain a compatible `run()` method.

Interfaces

Java uses a construct called an *interface* to provide this guarantee. An interface is a specification of the behavior of an object. An interface is very much like a class, except that an interface may not implement any methods itself. The role of an interface is simply to list a set of methods that might be implemented by a class. A class that contains all of these methods is then said to *implement* that interface.

As with classes, every interface defines a corresponding type. Any object whose class implements the interface can be said to be of that type. This may sound trivial, but it's actually a powerful feature. It means we can write a method that acts on any object that implements a certain interface. We don't have to limit ourselves to just a single class of objects or even to a single part of the inheritance hierarchy. We can specify an interface as the type of the argument, so that any object that implements the interface is acceptable. Interfaces may be subinterfaced, much as classes may be subclassed.

In other languages such as C++, accomplishing this type of behavior requires allowing classes to inherit from multiple superclasses. Conceptually, multiple inheritance makes a lot of sense, but in practice it can be quite messy. As you will see in Chapter 5, interfaces in Java eliminate most of the need for multiple inheritance of classes, without many of the associated problems.

The Runnable Interface

The second technique I described for creating a `Thread` object involved passing a target object to the `Thread` constructor. This target object must implement an interface called `Runnable`. The `Runnable` interface specifies that the object contains a `run()` method that takes no arguments and returns no value.

Sticking with our technique for implementing our applet in a single class, we have opted to add the `run()` method for `blinkThread` to our `HelloWeb4` class. This means that `HelloWeb4` needs to implement the `Runnable` interface. We indicate that the class implements the interface in our class declaration:

```
public class HelloWeb4 extends Applet implements Runnable {...}
```

At compile time, the Java compiler checks to make sure we abide by this statement. We have carried through by adding an appropriate `run()` method to our applet. Our `run()` method has the task of changing the color of our text a couple of times a second. It's a very short routine, but I'm going to delay looking at it until we tie up some loose ends in dealing with the `Thread` itself.

start() and stop()

Now that we know how to create a `Thread` to execute our applet's `run()` method, we need to figure out where to actually do it. The `start()` and `stop()` methods of the `Applet` class are similar to `init()`. The `start()` method is called when an applet is first displayed. If the user then leaves the Web document or scrolls the applet off the screen, the `stop()` method is invoked. If the user subsequently returns, the `start()` method is called again, and so on. Unlike `init()`, `start()` and `stop()` can be called repeatedly during the lifetime of an applet.

The `start()` and `stop()` methods of the `Applet` class have absolutely nothing to do with the `Thread` object, except that they are a good place for an applet to start and stop a thread. An applet is responsible for managing the threads that it creates. It would be considered rude for an applet to continue such tasks as animation, making noise, or performing extensive calculations long after it's no longer visible on the screen. It's common practice, therefore, to start a thread when an applet becomes visible and stop it when the applet is no longer visible.

Here's the `start()` method from `HelloWeb4`:

```
public void start() {
    if ( blinkThread == null ) {
        blinkThread = new Thread(this);
        blinkThread.start();
    }
}
```

The method first checks to see if there is an object assigned to `blinkThread`; recall that an uninitialized instance variable has a default value of `null`. If not, the method creates a new instance of `Thread`, passing the target object that contains the `run()` method to the constructor. Since `HelloWeb4` contains our `run()` method, we pass the special variable `this` to the constructor to let the thread know where to find the `run()` method it should run. `this` always refers to our object. Finally, after creating the new `Thread`, we call its `start()` method to begin execution.

Our `stop()` method takes the complimentary position:

```
public void stop() {
    if ( blinkThread != null ) {
        blinkThread.stop();
        blinkThread = null;
    }
}
```

This method checks to see if `blinkThread` is empty. If not, it calls the thread's `stop()` method to terminate its execution. By setting the value of `blinkThread` back to `null`, we have eliminated all references to the thread object we created in the `start()` method, so the garbage collector can dispose of the object.

run()

Our `run()` method does its job by setting the value of the variable `blinkState`. We have added `blinkState`, a `boolean` value, to represent whether we are currently blinking on or off:

```
boolean blinkState;
```

The `setColor()` line of our `paint()` method has been modified slightly to handle blinking. The call to `setColor()` now draws the text in white when `blinkState` is true:

```
gc.setColor( blinkState ? Color.white : currentColor() );
```

Here we are being somewhat terse and using the C-like ternary operator to return one of two alternate color values based on the value of `blinkState`.

Finally, we come to the `run()` method itself:

```
public void run() {
    while ( true ) {
        blinkState = !blinkState;
        repaint();

        try {
            Thread.sleep(500);
        }
        catch (InterruptedException e ) {
        }
    }
}
```

At its outermost level, `run()` uses an infinite `while` loop. This means the method will run continuously until the thread is terminated by a call to the controlling `Thread` object's `stop()` method.

The body of the loop does three things on each pass:

- Flips the value of `blinkState` to its opposite value using the `not` operator, `!`.

- Calls `repaint()` so that our `paint()` method can have an opportunity to redraw the text in accordance with `blinkState`.

- Uses a `try/catch` statement to trap for an error in our call to the `sleep()` method of the `Thread` class. `sleep()` is a static method of the `Thread` class. The method can be invoked from anywhere and has the effect of putting the current thread to sleep for the specified number of milliseconds. The effect here is to give us approximately two blinks per second.

Exceptions

The `try/catch` statement in Java is used to handle special conditions called *exceptions*. An exception is a message that is sent, normally in response to an error, during the execution of a statement or a method. When an exceptional condition arises, an object is created that contains information about the particular problem or condition. Exceptions act somewhat like events. Java stops execution at the place where the exception occurred, and the exception object is said to be *thrown* by that section of code. Like events, an exception must be delivered somewhere and handled. The section of code that receives the exception object is said to *catch* the exception. An exception causes the execution of the instigating section of code to abruptly stop and transfers control to the code that receives the exception object.

The `try/catch` construct allows you to catch exceptions for a section of code. If an exception is caused by a statement inside of a `try` clause, Java attempts to deliver the exception to the appropriate `catch` clause. A `catch` clause looks like a method declaration with one argument and no return type. If Java finds a catch clause with an argument type that matches the type of the exception, that catch clause is invoked. A try clause can have multiple catch clauses with different argument types; Java chooses the appropriate one in a way that is analogous to the selection of overloaded methods.

If there is no try/catch clause surrounding the code, or a matching catch clause is not found, the exception is thrown up the call stack to the calling method. If the exception is not caught there, it's thrown up another level, and so on until the exception is handled. This provides a very flexible error-handling mechanism, so that exceptions in deeply nested calls can bubble up to the surface of the call stack for handling. As a programmer, you need to know what exceptions a particular statement can generate, so methods in Java are required to declare the exceptions they can throw. If a method doesn't handle an exception itself, it must specify that it can throw that exception, so that the calling method knows that it may have to handle it. See Chapter 4 for a complete discussion of exceptions and the try/catch clause.

So, why do we need a try/catch clause around our sleep() call? What kind of exception can Thread's sleep() method throw and why do we care about it, when we don't seem to check for exceptions anywhere else? Under some circumstances, Thread's sleep() method can throw an InterruptedException, indicating that it was interrupted by another thread. Since the run() method specified in the Runnable interface doesn't declare it can throw an InterruptedException, we must catch it ourselves, or the compiler will complain. The try/catch statement in our example has an empty catch clause, which means that it handles the exception by ignoring it. In this case, our thread's functionality is so simple it doesn't matter if it's interrupted. All of the other methods we have used either handle their own exceptions or throw only general-purpose exceptions that are assumed to be possible everywhere and don't need to be explicitly declared.

A Word About Synchronization

At any given time, there can be a number of threads running in the Java interpreter. Unless we explicitly coordinate them, these threads will be executing methods without any regard for what the other threads are doing. Problems can arise when these methods share the same data. If one method is changing the value of some variables at the same time that another method is reading these variables, it's possible that the reading thread might catch things in the middle and get some variables with old values and some with new. Depending on the application, this situation could cause a critical error.

In our `HelloWeb` examples, both our `paint()` and `mouseDrag()` methods access the `messageX` and `messageY` variables. Without knowing the implementation of our particular Java environment, we have to assume that these methods could conceivably be called by different threads and run concurrently. `paint()` could be called while `mouseDrag()` is in the midst of updating `messageX` and `messageY`. At that point, the data is in an inconsistent state and if `paint()` gets lucky, it could get the new x value with the old y value. Fortunately, in this case, we probably would not even notice if this were to happen in our application. We did, however, see another case, in our `changeColor()` and `currentColor()` methods, where there is the potential for a more serious "out of bounds" error to occur.

The `synchronized` modifier tells Java to acquire a *lock* for the class that contains the method before executing that method. Only one method can have the lock on a class at any given time, which means that only one synchronized method in that class can be running at a time. This allows a method to alter data and leave it in a consistent state before a concurrently running method is allowed to access it. When the method is done, it releases the lock on the class.

Unlike synchronization in other languages, the `synchronized` keyword in Java provides locking at the language level. This means there is no way that you can forget to unlock a class. Even if the method throws an exception or the thread is terminated, Java will release the lock. This feature makes programming with threads in Java much easier than in other languages. See Chapter 6 for more details on coordinating threads and shared data.

Whew! Now it's time to say goodbye to `HelloWeb`. I hope that you have developed a feel for the major features of the Java language, and that this will help you as you go on to explore the details of programming with Java.

3

Tools of the Trade

As I described at the end of Chapter 1, by now you should have a number of options for Java development environments. The examples in this book were developed using the Solaris version of the Java Development Kit (JDK), so I'm going to describe those tools here. When I refer to the compiler or interpreter, I'll be referring to the command-line versions of these tools, so the book is decidedly biased toward those of you who are working in a UNIX or DOS-like environment with a shell and filesystem. However, the basic features I'll be describing for Sun's Java interpreter and compiler should be applicable to other Java environments as well.

In this chapter, I'll describe the tools you'll need to compile and run Java applications. I'll also cover the HTML `<applet>` tag and other information you'll need to know to incorporate Java applets in your Web pages.

The Java Interpreter

A Java interpreter is software that implements the Java virtual machine and runs Java applications. It can be a separate piece of software like the one that comes with the JDK, or part of a larger application like the Netscape Navigator Web browser. It's likely that the interpreter itself is written in a native, compiled language for your particular platform. Other tools, like Java compilers and development environments, can (and one could argue, should) be written in Java.

The Java interpreter performs all of the activities of the Java run-time system. It loads Java class files and interprets the compiled byte-code. It verifies compiled classes that are loaded from untrusted sources by applying the rules discussed in

Chapter 1. In an implementation that supports dynamic, or "just in time," compilation, the interpreter also serves as a specialized compiler that turns Java byte-code into native machine instructions.

Throughout the rest of this book, we'll be building both standalone Java programs and applets. Both are kinds of Java applications run by a Java interpreter. The difference is that a standalone Java application has all of its parts; it's a complete program that runs independently. An applet, as I described in Chapter 1, is more like an embeddable program module; it relies on an applet viewer for support. Although Java applets are, of course, compiled Java code, the Java interpreter can't directly run them because they are used as part of a larger application. An applet-viewer application could be a Web browser like Sun's HotJava or Netscape Navigator, or a separate applet viewer application like the one that comes with Sun's Java Development Kit. All of Sun's tools, including HotJava, are written entirely in Java. Both HotJava and the applet viewer are standalone Java applications run directly by the Java interpreter; these programs implement the additional structure needed to run Java applets.

Sun's Java interpreter is called *java*. To start a standalone application with it, you specify an initial class to be loaded. You can also specify options to the interpreter, as well as any command-line arguments that are needed for the application:

```
% java [interpreter options] class name [program arguments]
```

The class should be specified as a fully qualified class name including the class package, if any. Note, however, that you don't include the *.class* file extension. Here are a few examples:

```
% java animals.birds.BigBird
% java test
```

java searches for the class in the current *class path*, which is a list of locations where packages of classes are stored. I'll discuss the class path in detail in the next section, but for now you should know that you can set the class path with the `-classpath` option.

There are a few other interpreter options you may find useful. The `-cs` or `-checksource` option tells *java* to check the modification times on the specified class file and its corresponding source file. If the class file is out of date, it's automatically recompiled from the source. The `-verify`, `-noverify`, and `-verifyremote`options control the byte-code verification process. By default, *java* runs the byte-code verifier only on classes loaded from an untrusted source; this is the `-verifyremote` option. If you specify `-verify`, the byte-code verifier is run on all classes; `-noverify` means that the verifier is never run.

Once the class is loaded, *java* follows a very C-like convention and looks to see if the class contains a method called `main()`. If it finds an appropriate `main()` method, the interpreter starts the application by executing that method. From there, the application can start additional threads, reference other classes, and create its user interface or other structures, as shown in Figure 3–1.

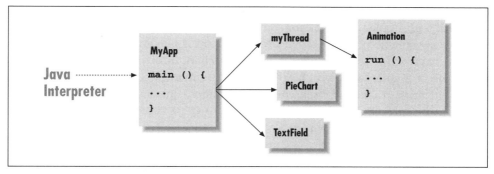

Figure 3–1: The Java interpreter starting a Java application

In order to run, `main()` must have the right *method signature*. A method signature is a collection of information about the method, as in a C prototype or a forward function declaration in other languages. It includes the method's name, type, and visibility, as well as its arguments and return type. In this case, `main()` must be a `public`, `static` method that takes an array of `String` objects as its argument and does not return any value (`void`):

```
public static void main ( String [] myArgs )
```

Because `main()` is a `public` method, it can be accessed directly from any other class using the name of the class that contains it. We'll discuss the implications of visibility modifiers such as `public` in Chapter 5.

The `main()` method's single argument, the array of `String` objects, holds the command-line arguments passed to *java*. As in C, the name that we give the parameter doesn't matter, only the type is important. Unlike C, the content of `myArgs` is a true array. There's no need for an argument count parameter, because `myArgs` knows how many arguments it contains and can happily provide that information:

```
int argc = myArgs.length;
```

Java also differs from C in another respect here: `myArgs[0]` is the first command-line argument, not the name of the application. If you're accustomed to parsing C command-line arguments, you'll need to be careful not to trip over this difference.

The Java virtual machine continues to run until the `main()` method of its initial class file has returned, and until any threads that it started are complete. Special threads designated as "daemon" threads are silently killed when the rest of the application has completed.

The Class Path

The concept of a path should be familiar to anyone who has worked on a DOS or UNIX platform. It's a piece of environment information that provides an application with a list of places to look for some resource. The most common example is a path for executable programs. In a UNIX shell, the PATH environment variable is a colon-separated list of directories that are searched, in order, when the user types the name of a command. The Java CLASSPATH environment variable, similarly, is a list of locations that can be searched for packages containing Java class files. Both the Java interpreter and the Java compiler use CLASSPATH when searching for files on the local host platform.

Classes loaded from the local host via the class path have special features. For example, the Java interpreter loads classes in the class path just once; after a core class has been loaded, it can't be modified or replaced. The interpreter can also be told to trust classes in the class path and to load them without passing them through the byte-code verification process. This is important because certain kinds of optimizations on Java virtual machine instructions produce valid byte-code that, nonetheless, can't pass the verification process. Byte-code that is precompiled on the native host is an extreme example.

The class path is a list of locations where Java class packages are found. A location can be a path such as a directory name or the name of a class archive file. Java supports archives of class files in the uncompressed ZIP format.[*] It automatically looks inside ZIP archives and retrieves classes, which then allows large groups of classes to be distributed in a single archive file. The precise means and format for setting the class path varies from system to system. On a UNIX system, you set the CLASS-PATH environment variable with a colon-separated list of directories and class archive files:

```
CLASSPATH=/usr/lib/java/classes.zip:/home/vicky/Java/classes:\
    /home/vicky/.netscape/moz2_0.zip:.
```

On a Windows system, the CLASSPATH environment variable is set with a semicolon-separated list of directories and class archive files:

---

[*] The ZIP format is an open standard for file archiving and compression. There are ZIP utilities available for most platforms; you'll need to get one if you want to store Java classes in ZIP archives. Use *ftp://ftp.uu.net/pub/archiving/zip/* to access an archive of freely available ZIP utilities.

```
CLASSPATH=C:\tools\java\classes.zip;D:\users\vicky\Java\classes;.
```

The class path can also be set with the -classpath option to the Java interpreter *java* and the Java compiler *javac*.

The above UNIX example specifies a class path with four locations: a ZIP archive in */usr/lib/java*, a directory in the user's home, another ZIP file in the user's Netscape collection, and the current directory, which is always specified with a dot (.). The last component of the class path, the current directory, is useful when tinkering with classes, but as a general rule, it's bad practice to put the current directory in any kind of path.

The Java interpreter searches each of these four locations, in order, to find classes. *java* expects to find class files in a directory hierarchy or in a directory within a ZIP archive that maps to the fully qualified name of the class. The components of a class-package name become the components of a pathname. Given the above class path, the first time we reference a class with the fully qualified name of ani-mals.birds.BigBird, for example, *java* begins the search with the *classes.zip* archive in */usr/lib/java*. It looks for a class archived under the path *ani-mals/birds/BigBird*. If *java* does not find the class there, it looks for the class in */home/vicky/Java/classes/animals/birds/BigBird*. If it's not found there, *java* moves on to the archive file specified next in the class path, and so on.

If you don't specify the CLASSPATH environment variable or the -classpath option, *java* uses the following default class path:

```
.:$JAVA/classes:$JAVA/lib/classes.zip        UNIX systems
.;$JAVA\classes;$JAVA\lib\classes.zip        Windows systems
```

In this path, $JAVA is the main Java directory on your system. Notice that the current directory (.) is the first location in the default class path; this means the files in your current directory are always available. If you change the class path and don't include the current directory, these files will no longer be accessible.

The Java Compiler

In this section, I'm going to say a few words about *javac*, the Java compiler that is supplied as part of Sun's JDK. (If you are happily working in another development environment, you may want to skip ahead to the next section.) The *javac* compiler is written entirely in Java, so it's available for any platform that supports the Java run-time system. The ability to support its own development environments is an important stage in a language's development. Java makes this bootstrapping automatic by supplying a ready-to-run compiler at the same cost as porting the interpreter.

javac turns Java source code into a compiled class that contains Java virtual machine byte-code. By convention, source files are named with a *.java* extension; the resulting class files have a *.class* extension. *javac* considers a file to be a single compilation unit. As you'll see in Chapter 5, classes in a given compilation unit share certain features like `package` and `import` statements.

javac allows you one `public` class per file and insists the file have the same name as the class. If the filename and class name don't match, *javac* issues a compilation error. A single file can contain multiple classes, as long as only one of the classes is `public`. You should avoid packing lots of classes into a single file. The compiler lets you include extra non-`public` classes in a *.java* file, so that you can implement a class that is tightly coupled to another class without a lot of hassle. But you should have more than one class in a file if the `public` class in the file is the only one that ever uses additional classes.

Now for an example. The source code for the following class should be placed in a file called *BigBird.java*:

```
package animals.birds

public class BigBird extends Bird {
    ...
}
```

We can then compile it with:

```
% javac BigBird.java
```

Unlike the Java interpreter, which takes a class name as its argument, *javac* requires an actual filename to process. The above command produces the class file *BigBird.class* and stores it in the same directory as the source file. While it's useful to have the class file in the same directory as the source when you are working on a simple example, for most real applications you'll need to store the class file in an appropriate place in the class path.

You can use the −d option to *javac* to specify an alternate directory for storing the class files it generates. The specified directory is used as the root of the class hierarchy, so *.class* files are placed in this directory or in a subdirectory below it, depending on the package name of the class. For example, we can use the following command to put our *BigBird.class* file in an appropriate location:

```
% javac -d /home/vicky/Java/classes BigBird.java
```

When you use the −d option, *javac* automatically creates any directories needed to store the class file in the appropriate place. In the above command, the *BigBird.class* file is stored in */home/vicky/Java/classes/animals/birds*.

You can specify multiple *.java* files in a single *javac* command; the compiler simply creates a class file for each source file. But you don't need to list source files for other classes your class references, as long as the other classes have already been compiled. During compilation, Java resolves other class references using the class path. If our class references other classes in `animals.birds` or other packages, the appropriate paths should be listed in the class path at compile time, so that *javac* can find the appropriate class files. You either make sure that the `CLASS-PATH` environment variable is set or use the `-classpath` option to *javac*.

The Java compiler is more intelligent than your average compiler and replaces some of the functionality of a *make* utility. For example, *javac* compares the modification times of the source and class files for all referenced classes and recompiles them as necessary. A compiled Java class remembers the source file from which it was compiled, so as long as the source file is in the same directory as the class file, *javac* can recompile the source if necessary. If, in the above example, class `Big-Bird` references another class, `animals.furry.Grover`, *javac* looks for the source *Grover.java* in an `animals.furry` package and recompiles it if necessary to bring the *Grover.class* class file up to date.

It's important to note that *javac* can do its job even if only the compiled versions of referenced classes are available. Java class files contain all the data type and method signature information source files do, so compiling against binary class files is as type safe (and exception safe) as compiling with Java source code.

The Netscape Alternative

If the JDK is not available for your platform, but you have access to a Java-enabled version of Netscape Navigator, you can take advantage of a special Netscape switch to compile and run Java applications. The `-java` switch provides direct access to Netscape's implementation of the Java run-time system and supports the same command-line options as Sun's *java* interpreter. Here's the general syntax for using the `-java` switch:

```
% netscape -java [interpreter options] class name [program arguments]
```

Before you can use Netscape's `-java` switch, you have to download the JDK; you need the *classes.zip* file that is part of the JDK distribution. After you have unpacked the distribution, set the `CLASSPATH` environment variable to point to both Netscape's class archive and the *classes.zip* file from the JDK:

```
CLASSPATH=/usr/lib/java/classes.zip:/home/vicky/.netscape/moz2_0.zip:.
```

Now you can compile a *.java* file using Netscape's `-java` switch as follows:

```
% netscape -java sun.tools.javac.Main source file
```

In this case, you are actually using the `-java` switch to run the Java compiler, *javac*, and supplying the source file as an argument to the compiler. Recall that *javac* is itself a Java program, which is why you can run it using the `-java` switch. The above command produces a class file and stores it in the same directory as the source file.

After you have compiled a Java application with Netscape, you can use Netscape to run it. You can use the `-java` switch to run nongraphical Java applications. In other words, you can run any application that doesn't use AWT. You can't use the `-java` switch to run applications that use AWT because Netscape has its own toolkit that employs Netscape native components. However, you can use the `-java` switch to compile applets (and applications) that use AWT. As always, you can display these applets using Netscape as a Web browser.

The Applet Tag

Applets are embedded in HTML documents with the `<applet>` tag. The `<applet>` tag resembles the HTML `<img>` image tag.[*] It contains attributes that identify the applet to be displayed and, optionally, give the Web browser hints about how it should be displayed. The standard image tag sizing and alignment attributes, such as `height` and `width`, can be used inside the applet tag. Unlike images, however, applets have both an opening `<applet>` and a closing `</applet>` tag. Sandwiched between these can be any number of `<param>` tags that contain application-specific parameters to be passed to the applet itself:

```
<applet attribute [ attribute ] ...  >
[<param parameter >]
[<param parameter >]
...
<\applet>
```

Attributes

Attributes are name/value pairs that are interpreted by a Web browser or applet viewer. (Many HTML tags besides `<applet>`have attributes.) Attributes of the `<applet>` tag specify general features that apply to all applets, such as size and alignment. The definition of the `<applet>` tag lists a fixed set of recognized

---

[*] If you are not familiar with HTML or other markup languages, you may want to refer to *HTML: The Definitive Guide*, from O'Reilly & Associates, for a complete reference on HTML and structured Web documents.

attributes; specifying an incorrect or nonexistent attribute should be considered an HTML error.

Three attributes, code, width, and height, are always required in the <applet> tag. code specifies the name of the applet to be loaded; width and height determine its initial size. Other attributes are optional.

The following is an HTML fragment for a hypothetical, simple clock applet that takes no parameters and requires no special HTML layout:

```
<applet code=AnalogClock width=100 height=100></applet>
```

The HTML file that contains this <applet> tag needs to be stored in the same directory as the AnalogClock.class class file. The applet tag is not sensitive to spacing, so the above is therefore equivalent to:

```
<applet
    code=AnalogClock
    width=100
    height=100>
<\applet>
```

You can use whatever form seems appropriate.

Parameters

Parameters are analogous to command-line arguments; they provide a way to pass information to an applet. Each <param> tag contains a name and a value that are passed as strings to the applet:

```
<param name = parameter_name value = parameter_value>
```

Parameters provide a means of embedding application-specific data and configuration information within an HTML document.[*] Our AnalogClock applet, for example, might accept a parameter that selects between local and universal time:

```
<applet code=AnalogClock width=100 height=100>
    <param name=zone value=GMT>
<\applet>
```

Presumably, this AnalogClock applet is designed to look for a parameter named zone with a possible value of GMT.

---

[*] If you are wondering why the applet's parameters are specified in yet another type of tag, here's the reason. In the original alpha release of Java, applet parameters were included inside of a single <app> tag along with formatting attributes. However, this format was not SGML-compliant, so the <param> tag was added.

Parameter names and values can be quoted to contain spaces and other special characters. We could therefore be more verbose and use a parameter value like the following:

```
<param name=zone value="Greenwich Mean Time">
```

The parameters a given applet expects are determined by the developer of that applet. There is no fixed set of parameter names or values; it's up to the applet to interpret the parameter name/value pairs that are passed to it. Any number of parameters can be specified, and the applet may choose to use or ignore them as it sees fit. The applet might also consider parameters to be either optional or required and act accordingly.

Hablo Applet?

Web browsers ignore tags they don't understand; if the Web browser doesn't interpret the <applet> or <param> tags, they should disappear and any HTML between the <applet>and </applet> tags should appear normally.

By convention, Java-enabled Web browsers do the opposite and ignore any extra HTML between the <applet> and </applet> tags. This means we can place some alternate HTML inside the <applet> tag, which is then displayed only by Web browsers that can't run the applet.

For our AnalogClock example, we could display a small text explanation and an image of the clock applet as a teaser:

```
<applet code=AnalogClock width=100 height=100>
    <param name=zone value=GMT>
    <strong>If you see this you don't have a Java-enabled Web
    browser. Here's a picture of what you are missing.</strong>
    <img src="clockface.gif">
<\applet>
```

The Complete Applet Tag

We can now spell out the full-blown <applet> tag:[*]

```
<applet
    code = class name
    width = pixels wide
    height = pixels high
    [ codebase = location URL ]
    [ name = instance name ]
```

---

[*] The HTML working group of the IETF is investigating standardization of embedded objects in HTML. A draft document can be found at *ftp://ds.internic.net/internet-drafts/draft-ietf-html-cda-00.txt.* They would prefer a slightly less application-centric name such as <embed>. However, their discussion, for the most part, parallels the <applet> tag.

```
        [ alt = alternate text ]
        [ align = alignment style ]
        [ vspace = vertical pad pixels ]
        [ hspace = horizontal pad pixels ]
    >
    [ <param name = parameter name value = parameter value> ]
    [ <param name = parameter name value = parameter value> ]
    . . .
    [ HTML for non Java aware browsers ]
    <\applet>
```

The width, height, align, vspace, and hspace attributes have the same
meanings as those of the <img> tag and determine the preferred size, alignment,
and padding respectively.

The alt attribute specifies alternate text that is displayed by browsers that understand the <applet> tag and its attributes, but can't actually run applets. This
attribute can also describe the applet, since in this case any alternate HTML
between <applet> and <\applet> is ignored.

The name attribute specifies an instance name for the executing applet. This is a
name specified as a unique label for each copy of an applet on a particular HTML
page. For example, if we include our clock twice on the same page (using two
applet tags), we could give each instance a unique name to differentiate them:

```
<applet code=AnalogClock name="bigClock" width=300 height=300><\applet>
<applet code=AnalogClock name="smallClock" width=50 height=50><\applet>
```

Applets use instance names to recognize and communicate with other applets on
the same page. We could, for instance, create a "clock setter" applet that knows
how to set the time on a AnalogClock applet and pass it the instance name of a
particular target clock on this page as a parameter. This might look something
like:

```
<applet code=ClockSetter>
    <param name=clockToSet value="bigClock">
<\applet>
```

Loading Class Files

The code attribute of the <applet> tag should specify the name of an applet.
This is either a simple class name, or a package path and class name. For now, let's
look at simple class names; I'll discuss packages in a moment. By default, the Java
run-time system looks for the class file in the same location as the HTML document
that contains it. This location is known as the base URL for the document.

Consider an HTML document, *clock.html*, that contains our clock applet example:

```
<applet code=AnalogClock width=100 height=100><\applet>
```

Let's say we retrieve the document at the following URL:

```
http://www.time.ch/documents/clock.html
```

Java tries to retrieve the applet class file from the same base location:

```
http://www.time.ch/documents/AnalogClock.class
```

The `codebase` attribute of the `<applet>` tag can be used to specify an alternative base URL for the class file search. Let's say our HTML document now specifies `codebase`, as in the following example:

```
<applet
    codebase=http://www.joes.ch/stuff/
    code=AnalogClock
    width=100
    height=100>
<\applet>
```

Java now looks for the applet class file at:

```
http://www.joes.ch/stuff/AnalogClock.class
```

Packages

Packages are groups of Java classes; see Chapter 5 for more information. A package name is a little like an Internet hostname, in that they both use a hierarchical, dot-separated naming convention. A Java class file can be identified by its full name by prefixing the class name with the package name. We might therefore have a package called `time` for time-related Java classes, and perhaps a subordinate package called `time.clock` to hold classes related to one or more clock applications.

In addition to providing a naming scheme, packages can be used to locate classes stored at a particular location. Before a class file is retrieved from a server, its package-name component is translated by the client into a relative path name under the base URL of the document. The components of a class package name are simply turned into the components of a path name, just like with classes on your local system.

Let's suppose that our `AnalogClock` has been placed into the `time.clock` package and now has the fully qualified name of `time.clock.AnalogClock`. Our simple `<applet>` tag would now look like:

```
<applet code=time.clock.AnalogClock width=100 height=100><\applet>
```

Let's say the *clock.html* document is once again retrieved from:

```
http://www.time.ch/documents/clock.html
```

Java now looks for the class file in the following location:

```
http://www.time.ch/documents/time/clock/AnalogClock.class
```

The same is true when specifying an alternative `codebase`:

```
<applet
    codebase=http://www.joes.ch/stuff/
    code=time.clock.AnalogClock
    width=100
    height=100>
<\applet>
```

Java now tries to find the class in the corresponding path under the new base URL:

```
http://www.joes.ch/stuff/time/clock/AnalogClock.class
```

One possible package-naming convention proposes that Internet host and domain names be incorporated as part of package names to form a unique identifier for classes produced by a given organization. If a company with the domain name `foobar.com` produced our `AnalogClock` class, they might distribute it in a package called `com.foobar.time.clock`. The fully qualified name of the `AnalogClock` class would then be `com.foo.time.clock.AnalogClock`. This would presumably be a unique name stored on an arbitrary server. A future version of the Java class loader might use this to automatically search for classes on remote hosts.

Perhaps soon we'll run Sun's latest and greatest Web browser directly from its source with:

```
% java com.sun.java.hotjava.HotJava
```

Viewing Applets

Sun's JDK comes with an applet-viewer program aptly called *appletviewer*. To use *appletviewer*, specify the URL of the document on the command line. For example, to view our `AnalogClock` at the URL shown above, use the following command:

```
% appletviewer http://www.time.ch/documents/clock.html
```

The *appletviewer* retrieves all applets in the specified document and displays each one in a separate window. *appletviewer* is not a Web browser; it doesn't attempt to display HTML. It's primarily a convenience for testing and debugging applets. If the document doesn't contain `<applet>` tags, *appletviewer* does nothing.

4

The Java Language

In this chapter, I introduce the framework of the Java language and some of its fundamental tools. I'm not going to try to provide a full language reference here. Instead, I'll lay out the basic structures of Java with special attention to how it differs from other languages. For example, we'll take a close look at arrays in Java, because they are significantly different from those in some other languages. We won't, on the other hand, spend much time explaining basic language constructs like loops and control structures. We won't talk much about Java's object-oriented features here, as that's covered in Chapter 5.

As always, I'll try to provide meaningful examples to illustrate how to use Java in everyday programming tasks.

Text Encoding

Java is a language for the Internet. Since the people of the Net speak and write in many different human languages, Java must be able to handle a number of languages as well. Java supports internationalization through the Unicode character encoding. Unicode uses a 16-bit character encoding; it's a worldwide standard that supports the character sets of most languages.[*]

Java source code can be written using the Unicode character encoding and stored either in its full form or with ASCII-encoded Unicode character values. This makes Java a friendly language for non-English speaking programmers, as these programmers can use their native alphabet for class, method, and variable names in Java code.

---

[*] For more information about Unicode, use the following URL: *http://www.unicode.org/*.

79

The Java `char` type and `String` objects also support Unicode. But if you're concerned about having to labor with two-byte characters, you can relax. The `String` API makes the character encoding transparent to you. Unicode is also ASCII-friendly; the first 256 characters are identical to the first 256 characters in the ISO8859-1 (Latin-1) encoding and if you stick with these values, there's really no distinction between the two.

Most platforms can't display all currently defined Unicode characters. As a result, Java programs can be written with special Unicode escape sequences. A Unicode character can be represented with the escape sequence:

```
\uxxxx
```

xxxx is a sequence of one to four hexadecimal digits. The escape sequence indicates an ASCII-encoded Unicode character. This is also the form Java uses to output a Unicode character in an environment that doesn't otherwise support them.

Java stores and manipulates characters and strings internally as Unicode values. Java also comes with classes to read and write Unicode-formatted character streams, as you'll see in Chapter 8.

Comments

Java supports both C-style block comments delimited by /* and */ and C++-style line comments indicated by //:

```
/*  This is a
        multiline
            comment.    */

// This is a single line comment
// and so // is this
```

As in C, block comments can't be nested. Single-line comments are delimited by the end of a line; extra // indicators inside a single line have no effect. Line comments are useful for short comments within methods because you can still wrap block comments around large chunks of code during development.

By convention, a block comment beginning with /** indicates a special "doc comment." A doc comment is commentary that is extracted by automated documentation generators, such as Sun's *javadoc* program that comes with the Java Development Kit. A doc comment is terminated by the next */, just as with a regular block comment. Leading spacing up to a * on each line is ignored; lines beginning with @ are interpreted as special tags for the documentation generator:

```
/**
 * I think this class is possibly the most amazing thing you will
 * ever see. Let me tell you about my own personal vision and
 * motivation in creating it.
 * <p>
 * It all began when I was a small child, growing up on the
 * streets of Idaho. Potatoes were the rage, and life was good...
 *
 * @see PotatoPeeler
 * @see PotatoMasher
 * @author John 'Spuds' Smith
 * @version 1.00, 19 Dec 1996
 */
```

javadoc creates HTML class documentation by reading the source code and the embedded comments. The author and version information is presented in the output and the @see tags make hypertext links to the appropriate class documentation.

Doc comments can appear above class, method, and variable definitions, but some tags may not be applicable to all. For example, a variable declaration can contain only a @see tag. Table 4–1 summarizes the tags used in doc comments.

Table 4–1: Doc Comment Tags

Tag	Description	Applies to
@see	Associated class name	Class, method, or variable
@author	Author name	Class
@version	Version string	Class
@param	Parameter name and description	Method
@return	Description of return value	Method
@exception	Exception name and description	Method

Types

The type system of a programming language describes how its data elements (variables and constants) are associated with actual storage. In a statically typed language, such as C or C++, the type of a data element is a simple, unchanging attribute that often corresponds directly to some underlying hardware phenomenon, like a register value or a pointer indirection. In a more dynamic language like Smalltalk or Lisp, variables can be assigned arbitrary elements and can effectively change their type throughout their lifetime. A considerable amount of overhead goes into validating what happens in these languages at run-time. Scripting languages like Tcl and awk achieve ease of use by providing drastically simplified type systems in which only certain data elements can be stored in variables, and values are unified into a common representation such as strings.

As I described in Chapter 1, Java combines the best features of both statically and dynamically typed languages. As in a statically typed language, every variable and programming element in Java has a type that is known at compile-time, so the interpreter doesn't normally have to check the type validity of assignments while the code is executing. Unlike C or C++ though, Java also maintains run-time information about objects and uses this to allow safe run-time polymorphism.

Java data types fall into two categories. *Primitive types* represent simple values that have built-in functionality in the language; they are fixed elements like literal constants and numeric expressions. *Reference types* (or class types) include objects and arrays; they are called reference types because they are passed "by reference" as I'll explain shortly.

Primitive Types

Numbers, characters, and boolean values are fundamental elements in Java. Unlike some other (perhaps more pure) object-oriented languages, they are not objects. For those situations where it's desirable to treat a primitive value as an object, Java provides "wrapper" classes (see Chapter 7). One major advantage of treating primitive values as such is that the Java compiler can optimize their usage.

Another advantage of working with the Java virtual-machine architecture is that primitive types are precisely defined. For example, you never have to worry about the size of an int on a particular platform; it's always a 32-bit, signed, two's-complement number. Table 4–2 summarizes Java's primitive types.

Table 4–2: Java Primitive Data Types

Type	Definition
boolean	true or false
char	16-bit Unicode character
byte	8-bit signed two's complement integer
short	16-bit signed two's complement integer
int	32-bit signed two's complement integer
long	64-bit signed two's complement integer
float	32-bit IEEE 754 floating-point value
double	64-bit IEEE 754 floating-point value

If you think the primitive types look like an idealization of C scalar types on a byte-oriented 32-bit machine, you're absolutely right. That's how they're supposed to look. The 16-bit characters were forced by Unicode, and pointers were deleted for other reasons we'll touch on later, but in general the syntax and semantics of Java primitive types are meant to fit a C programmer's mental habits. If you're like most of this book's readers, you'll probably find this saves you a lot of mental effort in learning the language.

Declaration and initialization

Variables are declared inside of methods or classes in C style. For example:

```
int foo;
double d1, d2;
boolean isFun;
```

Variables can optionally be initialized with an appropriate expression when they are declared:

```
int foo = 42;
double d1 = 3.14, d2 = 2 * 3.14;
boolean isFun = true;
```

Variables that are declared as instance variables in a class are set to default values if they are not initialized. In this case, they act much like static variables in C or C++. Numeric types default to the appropriate flavor of zero, characters are set to the null character "\0," and boolean variables have the value false. Local variables declared in methods, on the other hand, must be explicitly initialized before they can be used.

Integer literals

Integer literals can be specified in octal (base 8), decimal (base 10), or hexadecimal (base 16). A decimal integer is specified by a sequence of digits beginning with one of the characters 1-9:

```
int i = 1230;
```

Octal numbers are distinguished from decimal by a leading zero:

```
int i = 01230;              // i = 664 decimal
```

(An interesting, but meaningless, observation is that this would make the number 0 an octal value in the eyes of the compiler.)

As in C, a hexadecimal number is denoted by the leading characters 0x or 0X (zero "x"), followed by digits and the characters a–f or A–F, which represent the decimal values 10–15 respectively:

```
int i = 0xFFFF;             // i = 65535 decimal
```

Integer literals are of type int unless they are suffixed with an L, denoting that they are to be produced as a long value:

```
long l = 13L;
long l = 13;                // equivalent—13 is converted from type int
```

(The lowercase character l ("el") is also acceptable, but should be avoided because it often looks like the numeral 1).

When a numeric type is used in an assignment or an expression involving a type with a larger range, it can be promoted to the larger type. For example, in the second line of the above example, the number 13 has the default type of int, but it's promoted to type long for assignment to the long variable. Certain other numeric and comparison operations also cause this kind of arithmetic promotion. A numeric value can never be assigned to a type with a smaller range without an explicit (C-style) cast, however:

```
int i = 13;
byte b = i;              // Compile time error—explicit cast needed
byte b = (byte) i;       // Okay
```

Conversions from floating point to integer types always require an explicit cast because of the potential loss of precision.

Floating-point literals

Floating-point values can be specified in decimal or scientific notation. Floating-point literals are of type double unless they are suffixed with an f denoting that they are to be produced as a float value:

```
double d = 8.31;
double e = 3.00e+8;
float f = 8.31F;
float g = 3.00e+8F;
```

Character literals

A literal character value can be specified either as a single-quoted character or as an escaped ASCII or Unicode sequence:

```
char a = 'a';
char newline = '\n';
char octalff = \u00ff;
```

Reference Types

In C, you can make a new, complex data type by creating a structure. In Java (and other object-oriented languages), you instead create a class that defines a new type in the language. For instance, if we create a new class called Foo in Java, we are also implicitly creating a new type called Foo. The type of an item governs how it's used and where it's assigned. An item of type Foo can, in general, be assigned to a variable of type Foo or passed as an argument to a method that accepts a Foo value.

In an object-oriented language like Java, a type is not necessarily just a simple attribute. Reference types are related in the same way as the classes they represent. Classes exist in a hierarchy, where a subclass is a specialized kind of its parent class. The corresponding types have a similar relationship, where the type of the child class is considered a subtype of the parent class. Because child classes always extend their parents and have, at a minimum, the same functionality, an object of the child's type can be used in place of an object of the parent's type. For example, if I create a new class, `Bar`, that extends `Foo`, there is a new type `Bar` that is considered a subtype of `Foo`. Objects of type `Bar` can then be used anywhere an object of type `Foo` could be used; An object of type `Bar` is said to be assignable to a variable of type `Foo`. This is called *subtype polymorphism* and is one of the primary features of an object-oriented language. We'll look more closely at classes and objects in Chapter 5.

Primitive types in Java are used and passed "by value." In other words, when a primitive value is assigned or passed as an argument to a method, it's simply copied. Reference types, on the other hand, are always accessed "by reference." A *reference* is simply a handle or a name for an object. What a variable of a reference type holds is a reference to an object of its type (or of a subtype). A reference is like a pointer in C or C++, except that its type is strictly enforced and the reference value itself is a primitive entity that can't be examined directly. A reference value can't be created or changed other than through assignment to an appropriate object. When references are assigned or passed to methods, they are copied by value. You can think of a reference as a pointer type that is automatically dereferenced whenever it's mentioned.

Let's run through an example. We specify a variable of type `Foo`, called `myFoo`, and assign it an appropriate object:

```
Foo myFoo = new Foo();
Foo newFoo = myFoo;
```

`myFoo` is a reference type variable that holds a reference to the newly constructed `Foo` object. For now, don't worry about the details of creating an object; we'll cover that in Chapter 5. We designate a second `Foo` type variable, `newFoo`, and assign it to the same object. There are now two identical references: `myFoo` and `newFoo`. If we change the `Foo` object itself, we will see the same effect by looking at it with either reference. The comparable code in C++ would be:

```
// C++
Foo& myFoo = *(new Foo());
Foo& newFoo = myFoo;
```

We can pass one of the variables to a method, as in:

```
myMethod( myFoo );
```

The reference itself is passed by value. That is, the argument variable that holds the reference in the method is actually a third copy of the reference. The method can alter the `Foo` object itself through that reference, but it can't change the caller's copy of `myFoo`. For the times we want a method to change a reference for us, we have to pass a reference to the object that contains it, as shown in Chapter 5.

Reference types always point to objects, and objects are always defined by classes. However, there are two special kinds of reference types that specify the type of object they point to in a slightly different way. Arrays in Java have a special place in the type system. They are a special kind of object automatically created to hold a number of some other type of object, known as the base type. Declaring an array-type reference implicitly creates the new class type, as you'll see in the next section.

Interfaces are a bit sneakier. An interface defines a set of methods and a corresponding type. Any object that implements all methods of the interface can be treated as an object of that type. Variables and method arguments can be declared to be of interface types, just like class types, and any object that implements the interface can be assigned to them. This allows Java to cross the lines of the class hierarchy in a type safe way, as you'll see in Chapter 5.

A Word About Strings

Strings in Java are objects; they are therefore a reference type. `String` objects do, however, have some special help from the Java compiler that makes them look more primitive. Literal string values in Java source code are turned into `String` objects by the compiler. They can be used directly, passed as arguments to methods, or assigned to `String` type variables:

```
System.out.println( "Hello World..." );
String s = "I am the walrus...";
String t = "John said: \"I am the walrus...\"";
```

The + symbol in Java is overloaded to provide string concatenation; this is the only overloaded operator in Java:

```
String quote = "Four score and " + "seven years ago,";
String more = quote + " our" + " fathers" +  " brought...";
```

Java builds a single `String` object from the concatenated strings and provides it as the result of the expression. We will discuss the `String` class in Chapter 7.

Statements and Expressions

Although the method declaration syntax of Java is quite different from that of C++, Java statement and expression syntax is very like that of C. Again, the design intention was to make the low-level details of Java easily accessible to C programmers, so that they can concentrate on learning the parts of the language that are really different. Java *statements* appear inside of methods and special class initializers and describe all activities of a Java program. Variable declarations and initializations like those in the previous section are statements, as are the basic language structures like conditionals and loops. *Expressions* are statements that produce a result that can be used as part of another statement. Method calls, object allocations, and of course, mathematical expressions are examples of expressions.

One of the tenets of Java is to keep things simple and consistent. To that end, when there are no other constraints, evaluations and initializations in Java always occur in the order in which they appear in the code—from left to right. We'll see this rule used in the evaluation of assignment expressions, method calls, and array indexes, to name a few cases. In some languages, the order of evaluation is more complicated or even implementation dependent. Java removes this element of danger by precisely and simply defining how the code is evaluated. This doesn't, however, mean you should start writing obscure and convoluted statements. Relying on the order of evaluation of expressions is a bad programming habit, even when it works. It produces code that is hard to read and harder to modify. Real programmers, however, are not made of stone, and you may catch me doing this once or twice when I can't resist the urge to write terse code.

Statements

As in C or C++, statements and expressions in Java appear within a *code block*. A code block is syntactically just a number of statements surrounded by an open curly brace ({) and a close curly brace (}). The statements in a code block can contain variable declarations:

```
{
    int dog = "Max";
    setName( dog );
    ...
}
```

Methods, which look like C functions, are in a sense code blocks that take parameters and can be called by name.

Variable declarations are limited in scope to their enclosing code block. That is, they can't be seen outside of the nearest set of braces:

```
...
{
    int i = 5;
}

i = 6;               // compile time error, no such variable i
```

In this way, code blocks can be used to arbitrarily group other statements and variables. The most common use of code blocks, however, is to define a group of statements for use in a conditional or iterative statement.

Since a code block is itself collectively treated as a statement, we define a conditional like an `if/else` clause as follows:

```
if ( condition )
    statement;
[ else
    statement; ]
```

Thus, `if/else` in Java has the familiar functionality of taking either of the forms:

```
if ( condition )
    statement;
```

or:

```
if ( condition )  {
    [ statement; ]
    [ statement; ]
    [ ... ]
}
```

Here the *condition* is a `boolean` expression. In the second form, the statement is a code block, and all of its enclosed statements are executed if the conditional succeeds. Any variables declared within that block are visible only to the statements within the successful branch of the condition. Like the `if/else` conditional, most of the remaining Java statements are concerned with controlling the flow of execution. They act for the most part like their namesakes in C or C++.

The `do` and `while` iterative statements have the familiar functionality, except that their conditional test is also a `boolean` expression. You can't use an integer expression or a reference type; in other words you must explicitly test your value. In other words, while `i==0` is legitimate, `i` is not, unless `i` is `boolean`. Here are the forms of these two statements:

```
while ( conditional )
    statement;

do
    statement;
while ( conditional );
```

The `for` statement also looks like it does in C:

```
for ( initialization; conditional; incrementor )
    statement;
```

The variable initialization expression can declare a new variable; this variable is limited to the scope of the `for` statement:

```
for (int i = 0; i < 100; i++ ) {
    System.out.println( i )
    int j = i;
    . . .
}
```

Java doesn't support the C comma operator, which groups multiple expressions into a single expression. However, you can use multiple, comma-separated expressions in the initialization and increment sections of the `for` loop. For example:

```
for (int i = 0, j = 10; i < j; i++, j-- ) {
    . . .
}
```

The Java `switch` statement takes an integer type (or an argument that can be promoted to an integer type) and selects among a number of alternative `case` branches[*]:

```
switch ( int expression ) {
    case int expression :
        statement;
    [ case int expression
        statement;
    . . .
    default :
        statement;   ]
}
```

No two of the `case` expressions can evaluate to the same value. As in C, an optional `default` case can be specified to catch unmatched conditions. Normally, the special statement `break` is used to terminate a branch of the `switch`:

```
switch ( retVal ) {
    case myClass.GOOD :
        // something good
        break;
    case myClass.BAD :
        // something bad
        break;
    case default :
```

---

[*] An object-based `switch` statement is highly desired and likely to find its way into the language in a future release.

```
            // neither one
            break;
    }
```

The Java `break` statement and its friend `continue` perform unconditional jumps out of a loop or conditional statement. They differ from the corresponding statements in C by taking an optional label as an argument. Enclosing statements, like code blocks and iterators, can be labeled with identifier statements:

```
one:
    while ( condition ) {
        ...
        two:
            while ( condition ) {
                ...
                // break or continue point
            }
        // after two
    }
// after one
```

In the above example, a `break` or `continue` without argument at the indicated position would have the normal, C-style effect. A `break` would cause processing to resume at the point labeled "after two"; a `continue` would immediately cause the two loop to return to its condition test.

The statement `break two` at the indicated point would have the same effect as an ordinary `break`, but `break one` would break two levels and resume at the point labeled "after one." Similarly, `continue two` would serve as a normal `continue`, but `continue one` would return to the test of the one loop. Multilevel `break` and `continue` statements remove much of the need for the evil `goto` statement in C and C++.

There are a few Java statements we aren't going to discuss right now. The `try`, `catch`, and `finally` statements are used in exception handling, as we'll discuss later in this chapter. The `synchronized` statement in Java is used to coordinate access to statements among multiple threads of execution; see Chapter 6 for a discussion of thread synchronization.

On a final note, I should mention that the Java compiler flags "unreachable" statements as compile-time errors. Of course, when I say unreachable, I mean those statements the compiler determines won't be called by a static look at compile-time.

Expressions

As I said earlier, expressions are statements that produce a result when they are evaluated. The value of an expression can be a numeric type, as in an arithmetic expression; a reference type, as in an object allocation; or the special type void, which results from a call to a method that doesn't return a value. In the last case, the expression is evaluated only for its side effects (i.e., the work it does aside from producing a value). The type of an expression is known at compile-time. The value produced at run-time is either of this type or, in the case of a reference type, a compatible (assignable) type.

Operators

Java supports almost all standard C operators. These operators also have the same precedence in Java as they do in C, as you can see in Table 4–3.

Table 4–3: Java Operators

Precedence	Operator	Operand Type	Description
1	++, —	Arithmetic	Increment and decrement
1	+, –	Arithmetic	Unary plus and minus
1	~	Integral	Bitwise complement
1	!	Boolean	Logical complement
1	(*type*)	Any	Cast
2	*, /, %	Arithmetic	Multiplication, division, remainder
3	+, –	Arithmetic	Addition and subtraction
3	+	String	String concatenation
4	<<	Integral	Left shift
4	>>	Integral	Right shift with sign extension
4	>>>	Integral	Right shift with no extension
5	<, <=, >, >=	Arithmetic	Numeric comparison
5	instanceof	Object	Type comparison
6	==, !=	Primitive	Equality and inequality of value
6	==, !=	Object	Equality and inequality of reference
7	&	Integral	Bitwise AND
7	&	Boolean	Boolean AND
8	^	Integral	Bitwise XOR
8	^	Boolean	Boolean XOR
9	|	Integral	Bitwise OR
9	|	Boolean	Boolean OR
10	&&	Boolean	Conditional AND
11	||	Boolean	Conditional OR
12	?:	NA	Conditional ternary operator
13	=	Any	Assignment

Table 4–3: Java Operators (continued)

Precedence	Operator	Operand Type	Description
13	`*=, /=, %=, +=, -=, <<=, >>=, >>>=, &=, ^=, |=`	Any	Assignment with operation

There are a few operators missing from the standard C collection. For example, Java doesn't support the comma operator for combining expressions, although the `for` statement allows you to use it in the initialization and increment sections. Java doesn't allow direct pointer manipulation, so it does not support the reference (`*`), dereference (`&`), and `sizeof` operators.

Java also adds some new operators. As we've seen, the + operator can be used with `String` values to perform string concatenation. Because all integral types in Java are signed values, the `>>` operator performs a right-shift operation with sign extension. The `>>>` operator treats the operand as an unsigned number and performs a right shift with no extension. The `new` operator is used to create objects; we will discuss it in detail shortly.

Assignment

While variable initialization (i.e., declaration and assignment together) is considered a statement, variable assignment alone is an expression:

```
int i, j;
i = 5;                           // expression
```

Normally, we rely on assignment for its side effects alone, but, as in C, an assignment can be used as a value in another part of an expression:

```
j = ( i = 5 );
```

Again, relying on order of evaluation extensively (in this case, using compound assignments in complex expressions) can make code very obscure and hard to read. Do so at your own peril.

null

The expression `null` can be assigned to any reference type. It has the meaning of "no reference." A `null` reference can't be used to select a method or variable and attempting to do so generates a `NullPointerException` at run-time.

Variable access

Using the dot (.) to access a variable in an object is a type of expression that results in the value of the variable accessed. This can be either a numeric type or a reference type:

```
int i;
String s;
i = myObject.length;
s = myObject.name;
```

A reference type expression can be used in further evaluations, by selecting variables or calling methods within it:

```
int len = myObject.name.length();
int initialLen = myObject.name.substring(5, 10).length();
```

Here we have found the length of our name variable by invoking the length() method of the String object. In the second case, we took an intermediate step and asked for a substring of the name string. The substring method of the String class also returns a String reference, for which we ask the length. (Chapter 7 describes all of these String methods in detail.)

Method invocation

A method invocation is basically a function call, or in other words, an expression that results in a value, the type of which is the return type of the method. Thus far, we have seen methods invoked via their name in simple cases:

```
System.out.println( "Hello World..." );
int myLength = myString.length();
```

When we talk about Java's object-oriented features in Chapter 5, we'll look at some rules that govern the selection of methods.

Like the result of any expression, the result of a method invocation can be used in further evaluations, as we saw above. Whether to allocate intermediate variables and make it absolutely clear what your code is doing or to opt for brevity where it's appropriate is a matter of coding style.

Object creation

Objects in Java are allocated with the new operator:

```
Object o = new Object();
```

The argument to new is a *constructor* that specifies the type of object and any required parameters to create it. The return type of the expression is a reference type for the created object.

We'll look at object creation in detail in Chapter 5. For now, I just want to point out that object creation is a type of expression, and that the resulting object reference can be used in general expressions. In fact, because the binding of new is "tighter" than that of the dot-field selector, you can easily allocate a new object and invoke a method in it for the resulting expression:

```
int hours = new Date().getHours();
```

The Date class is a utility class that represents the current time. Here we create a new instance of Date with the new operator and call its getHours() method to retrieve the current hour as an integer value. The Date object reference lives long enough to service the method call and is then cut loose and garbage collected at some point in the future.

Calling methods in object references in this way is, again, a matter of style. It would certainly be clearer to allocate an intermediate variable of type Date to hold the new object and then call its getHours() method. However, some of us still find the need to be terse in our code.

instanceof

The instanceof operator can be used to determine the type of an object at runtime. instanceof returns a boolean value that indicates whether an object is an instance of a particular class or a subclass of that class:

```
Boolean b;
String str = "foo";
b = ( str instanceof String );      // true
b = ( str instanceof Object );      // also true
b = ( str instanceof Date );        // false—not a Date or subclass
```

instanceof also reports if an object implements a particular interface.

Exceptions

Do, or do not... There is no try.

—Yoda (*The Empire Strikes Back*)

Java's roots are in embedded systems—software that runs inside specialized devices like hand-held computers, cellular phones, and fancy toasters. In those kinds of applications, it's especially important that software errors be handled properly. Most users would agree that it's unacceptable for their phone to simply crash or for their toast (and perhaps their house) to burn because their software failed. Given that we can't eliminate the possibility of software errors, a step in the right direction is to at least try to recognize and deal with the application-level errors that we can anticipate in a methodical and systematic way.

Dealing with errors in a language like C is the responsibility of the programmer. There is no help from the language itself in identifying error types, and there are no tools for dealing with them easily. In C and C++, a routine generally indicates a failure by returning an "unreasonable" value (e.g., the idiomatic -1 or null). As the programmer, you must know what constitutes a bad result, and what it means. It's often awkward to work around the limitations of passing error values in the normal path of data flow.* An even worse problem is that certain types of errors can legitimately occur almost anywhere, and it's prohibitive and unreasonable to explicitly test for them at every point in the software

Java offers an elegant solution to these problems with exception handling. (Java exception handling is similar to, but not quite the same as, exception handling in C++.) An *exception* indicates an unusual condition or an error condition. Program control becomes unconditionally transferred or thrown to a specially designated section of code where it's caught and handled. In this way, error handling is some-what orthogonal to the normal flow of the program. We don't have to have special return values for all our methods; errors are handled by a separate mechanism. Control can be passed long distance from a deeply nested routine and handled in a single location when that is desirable, or an error can be handled immediately at its source. There are still a few methods that return -1 as a special value, but these are limited to situations in which there isn't really any error.†

A Java method is required to specify the exceptions it can throw (i.e., the ones that it doesn't catch itself); this means that the compiler can make sure we handle them. In this way, the information about what errors a method can produce is pro-moted to the same level of importance as its argument and return types. You may still decide to punt and ignore obvious errors, but in Java you must do so explicitly.

Exceptions and Error Classes

Exceptions are represented by objects that are instances of the class java.lang.Exception. Various subclasses of Exception hold specialized information (and possibly behavior) for various kinds of problems. Figure 4–1 shows the subclasses of Exception; these classes are defined in various packages in the Java API, as indicated in the diagram.

The Exception object is created by the code at the point where the error condi-tion arises and is passed, along with the flow of control, to the handling block of

---

* The somewhat obscure setjmp() and longjmp() statements in C can save a point in the execu-tion of code and later return to it unconditionally from a deeply buried location. In a limited sense, this is the functionality of exceptions in Java.

† For example, the getHeight() method of the Image class returns -1 if the height isn't known yet. No error has occurred; the height will be available in the future. In this situation, throwing an excep-tion would be overkill.

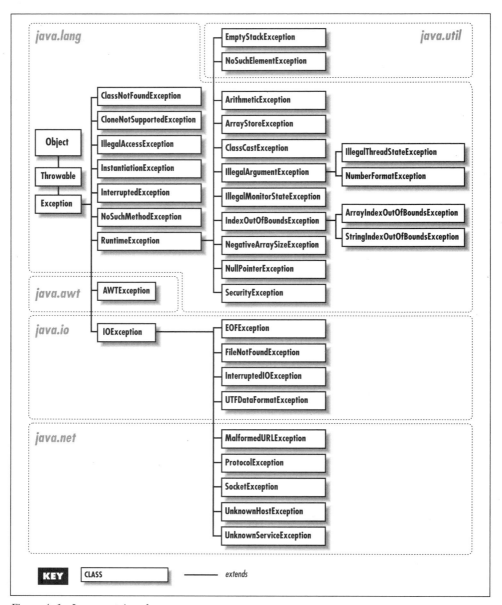

Figure 4–1: Java exception classes

code. This is where the terms "throw" and "catch" come from: the Exception
object is thrown from one point in the code and caught by the other.

The Java API also defines the java.lang.Error class for unrecoverable errors.
The subclasses of Error are shown in Figure 4–2. You needn't to worry about

these errors (i.e., you do not have to catch them); they normally indicate linkage problems or virtual machine errors. An error of this kind usually causes the Java interpreter to display a message and exit.

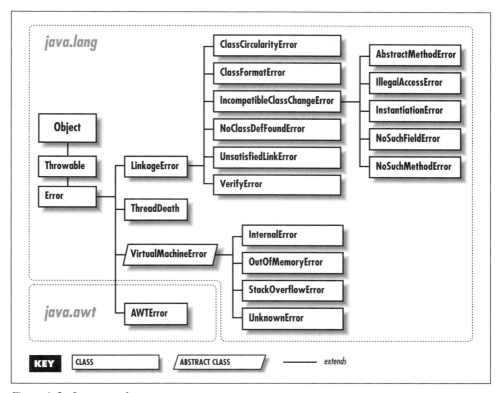

Figure 4–2: Java error classes

Exception Handling

The `try`/`catch` guarding statements wrap a block of code and catch designated types of exceptions that occur within it:

```
try {
    readFromFile("foo");
    ...
}
catch ( Exception e ) {
    // Handle error
    System.out.println( "Exception while reading file: " + e );
    ...
}
```

In the above example, exceptions that occur within the body of the `try` statement are directed to the `catch` clause for possible handling. The `catch` clause acts like a method; it specifies an argument of the type of exception it wants to handle and, if it's invoked, the `Exception` object is passed into its body as an argument. Here we receive the object in the variable e and print it along with a message.

A `try` statement can have multiple `catch` clauses that specify different specific types (subclasses) of `Exception`:

```
try {
    readFromFile("foo");
    ...
}
catch ( FileNotFoundException e ) {
    // Handle file not found
    ...
}
catch ( IOException e ) {
    // Handle read error
    ...
}
catch ( Exception e ) {
    // Handle all other errors
    ...
}
```

The `catch` clauses are evaluated in order, and the first possible (assignable) match is taken. At most one `catch` clause is executed, which means that the exceptions should be listed from most specific to least. In the above example, we'll assume that the hypothetical `readFromFile()` can throw two different kinds of exceptions: one that indicates the file is not found; the other indicates a more general read error. Any subclass of `Exception` is assignable to the parent type `Exception`, so the third `catch` clause acts like the `default` clause in a `switch` statement and handles any remaining possibilities.

It should be obvious, but one beauty of the `try`/`catch` statement is that any statement in the `try` block can assume that all previous statements in the block succeeded. A problem won't arise suddenly because a programmer forgot to check the return value from some method. If an earlier statement fails, execution jumps immediately to the `catch` clause; later statements are never executed.

Bubbling Up

What if we hadn't caught the exception? Where would it have gone? If there is no enclosing `try`/`catch` statement, the exception propagates to the top of the method in which it appears and is, in turn, thrown from that method. In this way, the exception bubbles up until it's caught, or until it pops out of the top of the program, terminating it with a run-time error message.

Let's look at another example. In Figure 4–3, the method getContent() invokes the method openConnection() from within a try/catch statement. open-Connection(), in turn, invokes the method sendRequest(), which calls the method write() to send some data.

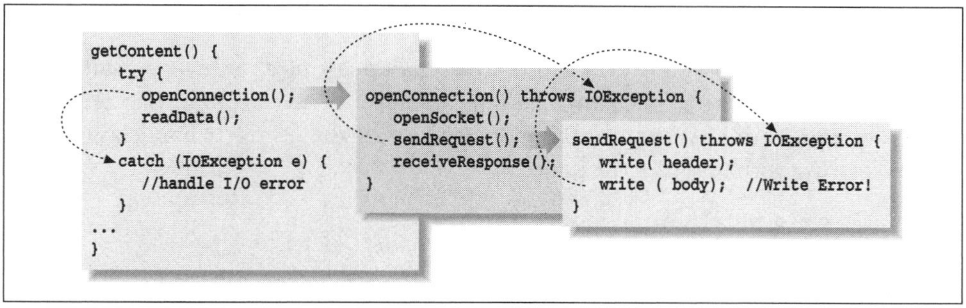

Figure 4–3: Exception propagation

In this figure, the second call to write() throws an IOException. Since sendRequest() doesn't contain a try/catch statement to handle the exception, it's thrown again, from the point that it was called in the method openConnection(). Since openConnection() doesn't catch the exception either, it's thrown once more. Finally it's caught by the try statement in getContent() and handled by its catch clause.

The throws Clause

I mentioned earlier that Java makes us be explicit about our error handling. Any method that throws an exception, either by passively ignoring one that occurs within it or (as we'll see below) generating one itself, must declare it can throw that type of exception in a special throws clause in its method declaration. We haven't yet talked about declaring methods; we'll cover that in detail in Chapter 5. For now all you need know is that methods have to declare the exceptions they can throw.

Again in Figure 4–3, notice that the methods openConnection() and sendRequest() both specify that they can throw an IOException. Multiple exceptions can be specified by separating them with commas:

```
void readFile( String s ) throws IOException, InterruptedException {
    ...
}
```

Throwing Exceptions

We can throw our own exceptions: either instances of Exception or one of its predefined subclasses, or our own specialized subclasses. All we have to do is create an instance of the Exception and throw it with the throw statement:

```
throw new Exception();
```

Execution stops and is transferred to the nearest enclosing try/catch statement. (Note that there is little point in keeping a reference to the Exception object we've created here.) An alternative constructor of the Exception class lets us specify a string with an error message:

```
public void checkRead( String s ) {
    if ( new File(s).isAbsolute() || (s.indexOf("..") != -1) )
        throw new SecurityException(
            x"Access to file : "+ s +" denied.");
}
```

Of course, we can include whatever other information is useful in our own specialized subclasses of Exception. Often though, just having a new type of exception is good enough, because it's sufficient to direct the flow of control for us.

An Exception Among Exceptions

Java is programmer-friendly, it doesn't require that every type of exception be caught everywhere. Instead, exceptions are divided into two categories:

General exceptions
    Exceptions a reasonable application should try to handle gracefully.

Run-time exceptions
    Exceptions from which we would not normally expect our software to try to recover.

The category of general exceptions includes application-level problems like missing files and unavailable hosts. As good programmers (and upstanding citizens), we should design software to recover gracefully from these kinds of conditions. The category of run-time exceptions includes problems such as "out of memory" and "array index out of bounds." While these may indicate application-level programming errors, they can legitimately occur almost anywhere. Fortunately, you don't have to wrap every one of your array-index operations in a try/catch statement.

The Java compiler treats exceptions that are subclasses of the RuntimeException class differently from other exceptions. See Figure 4–1 for the subclasses of

RuntimeException. It's not a compile-time error to ignore the possibility of these exceptions being thrown; additionally, methods don't have to declare they can throw them. In all other respects, run-time exceptions behave the same as other exceptions. We are perfectly free to catch them if we wish; we aren't required to.

Try Creep

The try statement imposes a condition on the statements they guard. It says that if an exception occurs within it, the remaining statements will be abandoned. This has consequences for local variable initialization. If the compiler can't determine whether a local variable assignment we placed inside a try/catch block will happen, it won't let us use the variable:

```
void myMethod() {
    int foo;

    try {
        foo = getResults();
    }
    catch ( Exception e ) {
        ...
    }

    int bar = foo;  // Compile time error—foo may not
                    // have been initialized
```

In the above example, we can't use foo in the indicated place because there's a chance it was never assigned a value. One obvious option is to move the assignment inside the try statement:

```
try {
    foo = getResults();
    int bar = foo;  // Okay because we only get here
                    // if previous assignment succeeds
}
catch ( Exception e ) {
    ...
}
```

Sometimes this works just fine. However, now we have the same problem if we want to use bar later in myMethod(). If we're not careful, we might end up pulling everything into the try statement. The situation changes if we transfer control out of the method in the catch clause:

```
try {
    foo = getResults();
}
catch ( Exception e ) {
    ...
```

```
        return;
    }

    int bar = foo;   // Okay because we only get here
                     // if previous assignment succeeds
```

Your code will dictate its own needs; you should just be aware of the options.

The finally Clause

What if we have some clean up to do before we exit our method from one of the catch clauses? To avoid duplicating the code in each catch branch and to make the cleanup more explicit, Java supplies the finally clause. A finally clause can be added after a try and any associated catch clauses. Any statements in the body of the finally clause are guaranteed to be executed, no matter why control leaves the try body:

```
try {
    // Do something here
}
catch ( FileNotFoundException e ) {
    ...
}
catch ( IOException e ) {
    ...
}
catch ( Exception e ) {
    ...
}
finally {
    // Cleanup here
}
```

In the above example the statements at the cleanup point will be executed eventually, no matter how control leaves the try. If control transfers to one of the catch clauses, the statements in finally are executed after the catch completes. If none of the catch clauses handles the exception, the finally statements are executed before the exception propagates to the next level.

If the statements in the try execute cleanly, or even if we perform a return, break, or continue, the statements in the finally clause are executed. To perform cleanup operations, we can even use try and finally without any catch clauses:

```
try {
    // Do something here
    return;
}
finally {
    System.out.println("Whoo-hoo!");
}
```

Exceptions that occur in a `catch` or `finally` clause are handled normally; the search for an enclosing `try`/`catch` begins outside the offending `try` statement.

Arrays

An array is a special type of object that can hold an ordered collection of elements. The type of the elements of the array is called the *base type* of the array; the number of elements it holds is a fixed attribute called its *length*. (For a collection with a variable length, see the discussion of `Vector` objects in Chapter 7.) Java supports arrays of all numeric and reference types.

The basic syntax of arrays looks much like that of C or C++. We create an array of a specified length and access the elements with the special index operator, `[]`. Unlike other languages, however, arrays in Java are true, first-class objects, which means they are real objects within the Java language. An array is an instance of a special Java array class and has a corresponding type in the type system. This means that to use an array, as with any other object, we first declare a variable of the appropriate type and then use the `new` operator to create an instance of it.

Array objects differ from other objects in Java in three respects:

- Java implicitly creates a special array class for us whenever we declare an array type variable. It's not strictly necessary to know about this process in order to use arrays, but it helps in understanding their structure and their relationship to other objects in Java.

- Java lets us use the special `[]` operator to access array elements, so that arrays look as we expect. We could implement our own classes that act like arrays, but because Java doesn't have user-defined operator overloading, we would have to settle for having methods like `get()` and `put()` instead of using the special `[]` notation.

- Java provides a corresponding special form of the `new` operator that lets us construct an instance of an array and specify its length with the `[]` notation.

Array Types

An array type variable is denoted by a base type followed by empty brackets `[]`. Alternatively, Java accepts a C-style declaration, with the brackets placed after the array name. The following are equivalent:

```
int [] arrayOfInts;
int arrayOfInts [];
```

In each case, `arrayOfInts` is declared as an array of integers. The size of the array is not yet an issue, because we are declaring only the array type variable. We have not yet created an actual instance of the array class, with its associated storage. It's not even possible to specify the length of an array as part of its type.

An array of objects can be created in the same way:

```
String [] someStrings;
Button someButtons [];
```

Array Creation and Initialization

Having declared an array type variable, we can now use the `new` operator to create an instance of the array. After the `new` operator, we specify the base type of the array and its length, with a bracketed integer expression:

```
arrayOfInts = new int [42];
someStrings = new String [ number + 2 ];
```

We can, of course, combine the steps of declaring and allocating the array:

```
double [] someNumbers = new double [20];
Component widgets [] = new Component [12];
```

As in C, array indices start with zero. Thus, the first element of `someNumbers  []` is `0` and the last element is `19`. After creation, the array elements are initialized to the default values for their type. For numeric types, this means the elements are initially zero:

```
int [] grades = new int [30];
grades[0] = 99;
grades[1] = 72;
// grades[2] == 0
```

The elements of an array of objects are references to the objects, not actual instances of the objects. The default value of each element is therefore `null`, until we assign instances of appropriate objects:

```
String names [] = new String [4];
names [0] = new String();
names [1] = "Boofa";
names [2] = someObject.toString();
// names[3] == null
```

This is an important distinction that can cause confusion. In many other languages, the act of creating an array is the same as allocating storage for its elements. In Java, an array of objects actually contains only reference variables and those variables, have the value `null` until they are assigned to real objects.[*] Figure 4–4 illustrates the `names` array of the previous example:

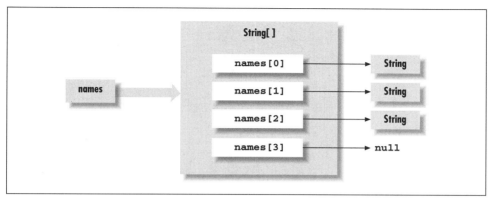

Figure 4–4: The names array

`names` is a variable of type `String[]` (i.e., a string array). The `String[]` object can be thought of as containing four `String` type variables. We have assigned `String` objects to the first three array elements. The fourth has the default value `null`.

Java supports the C-style curly braces `{}` construct for creating an array and initializing its elements when it is declared:

```
int [] primes = { 1, 2, 3, 5, 7, 7+4 };     // primes[2] == 3
```

An array object of the proper type and length is implicitly created and the values of the comma-separated list of expressions are assigned to its elements.

We can use the `{}` syntax with an array of objects. In this case, each of the expressions must evaluate to an object that can be assigned to a variable of the base type of the array, or the value `null`. Here are some examples:

```
String [] verbs = { "run", "jump", someWord.toString() };

Button [] controls = { stopButton, new Button("Forwards"),
    new Button("Backwards") };
```

---

[*] The analog in C or C++ would be an array of pointers to objects. However, pointers in C or C++ are themselves two- or four-byte values. Allocating an array of pointers is, in actuality, allocating the storage for some number of those pointer objects. An array of references is conceptually similar, however, references are not themselves objects. We can't manipulate references or parts of references other than by assignment, and their storage requirements (or lack thereof) are not part of the high-level language specification.

```
// all types are subtypes of Object
Object [] objects = { stopButton, "A word", null };
```

You should create and initialize arrays in whatever manner is appropriate for your application. The following are equivalent:

```
Button [] threeButtons = new Button [3];
Button [] threeButtons = { null, null, null };
```

Using Arrays

The size of an array object is available in the public variable `length`:

```
char [] alphabet = new char [26];
int alphaLen = alphabet.length;              // alphaLen == 26

String [] musketeers = { "one", "two", "three" };
int num = musketeers.length;                 // num == 3
```

`length` is the only accessible field of an array; it is a variable, not a method.

Array access in Java is just like array access in C; you access an element by putting an integer-valued expression between brackets after the name of the array. The following example creates an array of `Button` objects called `keyPad` and then fills the array with `Button` objects:

```
Button [] keyPad = new Button [ 10 ];
for ( int i=0; i < keyPad.length; i++ )
    keyPad[ i ] = new Button( Integer.toString( i ) );
```

Attempting to access an element that is outside the range of the array generates an `ArrayIndexOutOfBoundsException`. This is a type of `RuntimeException`, so you can either catch it and handle it yourself, or ignore it, as we already discussed:

```
String [] states = new String [50];

try {
    states[0] = "California";
    states[1] = "Oregon";
    ...
    states[50] = "McDonald's Land";  // Error—array out of bounds
}
catch ( ArrayIndexOutOfBoundsException err ) {
    System.out.println( "Handled error: " + err.getMessage() );
}
```

It's a common task to copy a range of elements from one array into another. Java supplies the `arraycopy()` method for this purpose; it's a utility method of the `System` class:

```
System.arraycopy( source, sourceStart, destination,
                  destStart, length );
```

The following example doubles the size of the names array from an earlier example:

```
String [] tmpVar = new String [ 2 * names.length ];
System.arraycopy( names, 0, tmpVar, 0, names.length );
names = tmpVar;
```

A new array, twice the size of names, is allocated and assigned to a temporary variable tmpVar. arraycopy() is used to copy the elements of names to the new array. Finally, the new array is assigned to names. If there are no remaining references to the old array object after names has been copied, it will be garbage collected on the next pass.

Multidimensional Arrays

Java supports multidimensional arrays in the form of arrays of array type objects. You create a multidimensional array with C-like syntax, using multiple bracket pairs, one for each dimension. You also use this syntax to access elements at various positions within the array. Here's an example of a multidimensional array that represents a chess board:

```
ChessPiece [][] chessBoard;
chessBoard = new ChessPiece [8][8];
chessBoard[0][0] = new ChessPiece( "Rook" );
chessBoard[1][0] = new ChessPiece( "Pawn" );
...
```

Here chessBoard is declared as a variable of type ChessPiece[][] (i.e., an array of ChessPiece arrays). This declaration implicitly creates the type ChessPiece[] as well. The example illustrates the special form of the new operator used to create a multidimensional array. It creates an array of ChessPiece[] objects and then, in turn, creates each array of ChessPiece objects. We then index chessBoard to specify values for particular ChessPiece elements. (We'll neglect the color of the pieces.)

Of course, you can create arrays of with more than two dimensions. Here's a slightly impractical example:

```
Color [][][] rgbCube = new Color [256][256][256];
rgbCube[0][0][0] = Color.black;
rgbCube[255][255][0] = Color.yellow;
...
```

As in C, we can specify the initial index of a multidimensional array to get an array type object with fewer dimensions. In our example, the variable `chessBoard` is of type `ChessPiece[][]`. The expression `chessBoard[0]` is valid and refers to the first element of `chessBoard`, which is of type `ChessPiece[]`. For example, we can create a row for our chess board:

```
ChessPiece [] startRow =  {
    new ChessPiece("Rook"), new ChessPiece("Knight"),
    new ChessPiece("Bishop"), new ChessPiece("King"),
    new ChessPiece("Queen"), new ChessPiece("Bishop"),
    new ChessPiece("Knight"), new ChessPiece("Rook")
};

chessBoard[0] = startRow;
```

We don't necessarily have to specify the dimension sizes of a multidimensional array with a single new operation. The syntax of the new operator lets us leave the sizes of some dimensions unspecified. The size of at least the first dimension (the most significant dimension of the array) has to be specified, but the sizes of any number of the less significant array dimensions may be left undefined. We can assign appropriate array type values later.

We can create a checkerboard of `boolean` values (which is not quite sufficient for a real game of checkers) using this technique:

```
boolean [][] checkerBoard;
checkerBoard = new boolean [8][];
```

Here, `checkerBoard` is declared and created, but its elements, the eight `boolean[]` objects of the next level, are left empty. Thus, for example, `checkerBoard[0]` is `null` until we explicitly create an array and assign it, as follows:

```
checkerBoard[0] = new boolean [8];
checkerBoard[1] = new boolean [8];
...
checkerBoard[7] = new boolean [8];
```

The code of the previous two examples is equivalent to:

```
boolean [][] checkerBoard = new boolean [8][8];
```

One reason we might want to leave dimensions of an array unspecified is so that we can store arrays given to us by another method.

Note that since the length of the array is not part of its type, the arrays in the checkerboard do not necessarily have to be of the same length. Here's a defective (but perfectly legal) checkerboard:

```
checkerBoard[2] = new boolean [3];
checkerBoard[3] = new boolean [10];
```

Since Java implements multidimensional arrays as arrays of arrays, multidimensional arrays do not have to be rectangular. For example, here's how you could create and initialize a triangular array:

```
int [][][] triangle = new int [5][];
for (int i = 0; i < triangle.length; i++) {
    triangle[i] = new int [i + 1];
    for (int j = 0; j < i + 1; j++)
        triangle[i][j] = i + j;
}
```

Inside Arrays

I said earlier that arrays are instances of special array classes in the Java language. If arrays have classes, where do they fit into the class hierarchy and how are they related? These are good questions; however, we need to talk more about the object-oriented aspects of Java before I can answer them. For now, take it on faith that arrays fit into the class hierarchy; details are in Chapter 5.

5

Objects in Java

In this chapter, we'll get to the heart of Java and explore the object-oriented aspects of the language. Object-oriented design is the art of decomposing an application into some number of objects—self-contained application components that work together. The goal is to break the problem down into a number of smaller problems that are simpler and easier to understand. Ideally, the components can be implemented directly as objects in the Java language. And if things are truly ideal, the components correspond to well-known objects that already exist, so they don't have to be created at all.

An object-oriented design methodology is a system or a set of rules created by someone to help you identify objects in your application domain and pick the real ones from the noise. In other words, such a methodology helps you factor your application into a good set of reusable objects. The problem is that though it wants to be a science, good object-oriented design is still pretty much an art form. While you can learn from the various off-the-shelf design methodologies, none of them will help you in all situations. The truth is that experience pays.

I won't try to push you into a particular methodology here; there are shelves full of books to do that.[*] Instead, I'll provide a few hints to get you started. Here are some

---

[*] Once you have some experience with basic object-oriented concepts, you might want to take a look at *Design Patterns: Elements of Reusable Object Oriented Software* by Gamma/Helm/Johnson/Vlissides (Addison-Wesley). This book catalogs useful object-oriented designs that have been refined over the years by experience. Many appear in the design of the Java API.

general design guidelines, which should be taken with a liberal amount of salt and common sense:

- Think of an object in terms of its interface, not its implementation. It's perfectly fine for an object's internals to be unfathomably complex, as long as its "public face" is easy to understand.

- Hide and abstract as much of your implementation as possible. Avoid public variables in your objects, with the possible exception of constants. Define methods to set and return even simple values. Later, when you need to, you'll be able to modify the implementation of your objects without breaking other classes that rely on them.

- Specialize objects only when you have to. When you use an object in its existing form, as a piece of a new object, you are composing objects. When you change or refine the behavior of an object, you are using inheritance. You should try to reuse objects by composition rather than inheritance whenever possible because when you compose objects you are taking full advantage of existing tools. Inheritance involves breaking down the barrier of an object and should be done only when there's a real advantage. Ask yourself if you really need to inherit the whole public interface of an object, or if you can just delegate certain jobs to the object and use it by composition.

- Minimize relationships between objects and group-related objects in packages. To enhance your code's reusability, write it as if there *is* a tomorrow. Find what one object needs to know about another to get its job done and try to minimize the coupling between them.

Classes

Classes are the building blocks of a Java application. A *class* contains methods and variables; it serves as a blueprint for making class *instances*, which are run-time objects that implement the class structure. You declare a class with the `class` keyword. Methods and variables of the class appear inside the braces of the class declaration:

```
class Pendulum {
    float mass;
    float length = 1.0;
    int cycles;

    float position ( float time ) {
        ...
    }
    ...
}
```

The above class, Pendulum, contains three variables: mass, length, and cycles. It also defines a method called position() that takes a float value as an argument and returns a float value. Variables and method declarations can appear in any order, but variable initializers can't use forward references to uninitialized variables.

Now that we've defined the Pendulum class, we can create an actual Pendulum object as follows:

```
Pendulum p;
p = new Pendulum();
```

Recall that our declaration of the variable p does not create a Pendulum object; it simply creates a variable that refers to an object of type Pendulum. We still have to create the object dynamically, using the new keyword. Now that we've created a Pendulum object, we can access its variables and methods, as we've already seen many times:

```
p.mass = 5.0;
float pos = p.position( 1.0 );
```

Variables defined in a class are called *instance variables*. Every object has its own set of instance variables; the values of these variables in one object can differ from the values in another object, as shown in Figure 5–1. If you don't initialize an instance variable when you declare it, it's given a default value appropriate for its type.

In Figure 5–1, we have a hypothetical TextBook application that uses two instances of Pendulum through the reference type variables bigPendulum and smallPendulum. Each of these Pendulum objects has its own copy of mass, length, and cycles.

As with variables, methods defined in a class are *instance methods*. An instance method is associated with an instance of the class, but each instance doesn't have its own copy of the method. Instead, there's just one copy of the method, but it operates on the values of the instance variables of a particular object. As you'll see later when we talk about subclassing, there's more to learn about method selection.

Accessing Members

Inside of a class, we can access instance variables and call instance methods of the class directly by name. Here's an example that expands upon our Pendulum:

```
class Pendulum {
    ...
    void resetEverything() {
        cycles = 0;
        mass = 1.0;
```

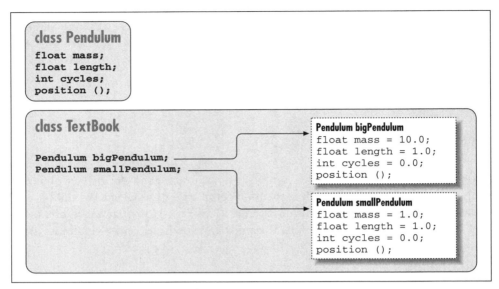

Figure 5–1: Instances of the Pendulum class

```
        ...
        float startingPosition = position( 0.0 );
    }
    ...
}
```

Other classes generally access members of an object through a reference, using the C-style dot notation:

```
class TextBook {
    ...
    void showPendulum() {
        Pendulum bob = new Pendulum();
        ...
        int i = bob.cycles;
        bob.resetEverything();
        bob.mass = 1.01;
        ...
    }
    ...
}
```

Here we have created a second class, TextBook, that uses a Pendulum object. It creates an instance in showPendulum() and then invokes methods and accesses variables of the object through the reference bob.

Several factors affect whether class members can be accessed from outside the class. You can use the visibility modifiers, `public`, `private`, and `protected` to restrict access; classes can also be placed into packages that affect their scope. The `private` modifier, for example, designates a variable or method for use only by other members inside the class itself. In the previous example, we could change the declaration of our variable `cycles` to `private`:

```
class Pendulum {
    ...
    private int cycles;
    ...
```

Now we can't access `cycles` from `TextBook`:

```
class TextBook {
    ...
    void showPendulum() {
        ...
        int i = bob.cycles;            // Compile time error
```

If we need to access cycles, we would probably add a `getCycles()` method to the `Pendulum` class. We'll look at access modifiers and how they affect the scope of variables and methods in detail later.

Static Members

Instance variables and methods are associated with and accessed through a particular object. In contrast, members that are declared with the `static` modifier live in the class and are shared by all instances of the class. Variables declared with the `static` modifier are called *static variables* or *class variables*; similarly, these kinds of methods are called *static methods* or *class methods*.

We can add a class variable to our `Pendulum` example:

```
class Pendulum {
    ...
    static float gravAccel = 9.80;
    ...
```

We have declared the new `float` variable `gravAccel` as `static`. That means if we change its value in any instance of a `Pendulum`, the value changes for all `Pendulum` objects, as shown in Figure 5–2.

Static members can be accessed like instance members. Inside our `Pendulum` class, we can refer to `gravAccel` by name, like an instance variable:

```
class Pendulum {
    ...
    float getWeight () {
        return mass * gravAccel;
```

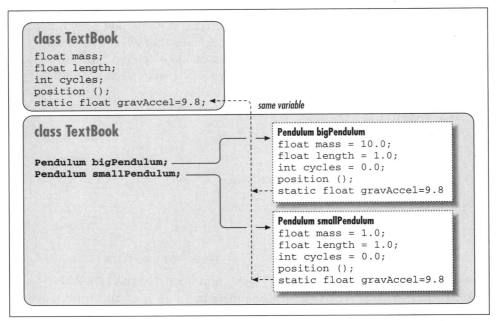

Figure 5–2: A static variable

```
          }
      . . .
   }
```

However, since static members exist in the class itself, independent of any instance, we can also access them directly through the class. We don't need a `Pendulum` object to set the variable `gravAccel`; instead we can use the class name as a reference:

```
Pendulum.gravAccel = 8.76;
```

This changes the value of `gravAccel` for any current or future instances. Why, you may be wondering, would we want to change the value of `gravAccel`? Well, perhaps we want to explore how pendulums would work on different planets. Static variables are also useful if you need to keep a tally of all instances of a class.

We can use static variables to define constant values. In this case, we use the `static` modifier along with the `final` modifier. So, if we cared only about pendulums under the influence of the Earth's gravitational pull, we could change `Pendulum` as follows:

```
class Pendulum {
    ...
    static final float GRAV_ACCEL = 9.80;
    ...
```

We have followed a common convention and named our constant with capital letters; C programmers should recognize the capitalization convention, which resembles C #define statements. Now the value of GRAV_ACCEL is a constant; it can be accessed by any instance of Pendulum (or anywhere, for that matter), but its value can't change.

Constants can also be flag-like identifiers accessed from anywhere. These are especially useful for values needed in the construction of an instance itself. In our example, we might declare a number of static values to represent various kinds of Pendulum objects:

```
class Pendulum {
    ...
    static final int SIMPLE = 0, ONE_SPRING = 1, TWO_SPRING = 2;
    ...
```

We might then use these flags in a method that sets the type of a Pendulum or, more likely, in a special constructor, as we'll discuss shortly:

```
Pendulum pendy = new Pendulum();
pendy.setType( Pendulum.ONE_SPRING );
```

Remember, inside the Pendulum class, we can use static members directly by name as well:

```
class Pendulum {
    ...
    void resetEverything() {
        setType ( SIMPLE );
        ...
    }
    ...
}
```

Methods

Methods appear inside class bodies. They contain local variable declarations and other Java statements that are executed by a calling thread when the method is invoked. Method declarations in Java look like ANSI C-style function declarations with two restrictions:

* A method in Java always specifies a return type (there's no default). The returned value can be a primitive numeric type, a reference type, or the type void, which indicates no returned value.

- A method always has a fixed number of arguments. The combination of method overloading and true arrays removes most of the need for a variable number of arguments. These techniques are type-safe and easier to use than C's variable argument list mechanism.

Here's a simple example:

```
class Bird {
    int xPos, yPos;

    double fly ( int x, int y ) {
        double distance = Math.sqrt( x*x + y*y );
        flap( distance );
        xPos = x;
        yPos = y;
        return distance;
    }
    ...
}
```

In this example, the class `Bird` defines a method, `fly()`, that takes as arguments two integers: `x` and `y`. It returns a `double` type value as a result.

Local Variables

The `fly()` method declares a local variable called `distance` that it uses to compute the distance flown. A local variable is temporary and exists only within the scope of its method. Local variables are allocated and initialized when a method is invoked; they are destroyed when the method returns. They can't be referenced outside the method itself. If the method is executing concurrently in different threads, each thread has its own copies of the method's local variables. A method's arguments also serve as local variables within the scope of the method.

An object created within a method and assigned to a local variable may or may not persist after the method has returned. As with all objects in Java, it depends on whether any references to the object remain. If an object is created, assigned to a local variable, and never used anywhere else, that object will no longer be referenced when the local variable is destroyed, so garbage collection will remove the object. If, however, we assign the object to an instance variable, pass it as an argument to another method, or pass it back as a return value, it may be saved by another variable holding its reference. We'll discuss object creation and garbage collection in more detail shortly.

Shadowing

If a local variable and an instance variable have the same name, the local variable *shadows* or hides the name of the instance variable within the scope of the method. In the following example, the local variables xPos and yPos hide the instance variables of the same name:

```
class Bird {
    int xPos, yPos;
    int xNest, yNest;
    ...
    double flyToNest() {
        int xPos = xNest;
        int yPos = yNest:
        return ( fly( xPos, yPos ) );
    }
    ...
}
```

When we set the values of the local variables in flyToNest(), it has no effect on the values of the instance variables.

The special identifier this refers to the current object; it's often called the "this reference." You can use it any time you need to refer explicitly to the current instance of a class. Often, you don't need to use this because the reference to the current object is implicit; this is the case with using instance variables and methods inside of a class. But we can use this to refer explicitly to instance variables in the object, even if they are shadowed.

The subsequent example shows how we can use this to allow us argument names that shadow instance variable names. This is a fairly common technique, as it saves your having to deliberately make up alternate names. Here's how we could implement our fly() method with shadowed variables:

```
class Bird {
    int xPos, yPos;

    double fly ( int xPos, int yPos ) {
        double distance = Math.sqrt( xPos*xPos + yPos*yPos );
        flap( distance );
        this.xPos = xPos;
        this.yPos = yPos;
        return distance;
    }
    ...
}
```

In this example, the expression `this.xPos` refers to the instance variable `xPos` and assigns it the value of the local variable `xPos`, which would otherwise hide its name. The only reason we need to use `this` in the above example is because we've used argument names that hide our instance variables, and we want to refer to the instance variables.

Static Methods

Static methods (class methods), like static variables, belong to the class and not to an individual instance of the class. What does this mean? Well, first, a static method can access only static members of the class. It doesn't belong to any particular instance, so it can't see any instance variables or call any instance methods. Static methods can be called from instances, just like instance methods, but the important thing is that they can also be used independently of any instance—through the class name itself.

Our `fly()` method uses a static method: `Math.sqrt()`. This method is defined by the `java.lang.Math` class; we'll explore this class in detail in Chapter 7. For now, the important thing to note is that `Math` is the name of a class and not an instance of a `Math` object (you can't even make an instance of `Math`). Because `static` methods can be invoked wherever the class name is available, class methods are closer to normal C-style functions. Static methods are particularly useful for utility methods that perform work that might be useful either independently of instances of the class or in creating instances of the class.

For example, in our `Bird` class we can enumerate all types of birds that can be created:

```
class Bird {
    ...
    static String [] getBirdTypes( ) {
        String [] types;
        // Create list...
        return types;
    }
    ...
}
```

Here we've defined a `static` method `getBirdTypes()` that returns an array of strings containing bird names. We can use `getBirdTypes()` from within an instance of `Bird`, just like an instance method. However, we can also call it from other classes, using the `Bird` class name as a reference:

```
String [] names = Bird.getBirdTypes();
```

Perhaps a special version of the `Bird` class constructor accepts the name of a bird type. We could use this list to decide what kind of bird to create.

Local Variable Initialization

In the `flyToNest()` example, we made a point of initializing the local variables `xPos` and `yPos`. Unlike instance variables, local variables must be initialized before they can be used. It's a compile-time error to try to access a local variable without first assigning it a value:

```
void myMethod() {
    int foo = 42;
    int bar;

    bar += 1;                       // Compile time error

    bar = 99;
    bar += 1;                       // Okay now
}
```

Notice that this doesn't imply local variables have to be initialized when declared, just that the first time they are referenced must be in an assignment. More subtle possibilities arise when making assignments inside of conditionals:

```
void myMethod {
    int foo;

    if ( someCondition ) {
        foo = 42;
        . . .
    }

    foo += 1;                       // Compile time error
                                    // foo may not have been initialized
```

In the above example, `foo` is initialized only if `someCondition` is `true`. The compiler doesn't let you make this wager, so it flags the use of `foo` as an error. We could correct this situation in several ways. We could initialize the variable to a default value in advance or move the usage inside of the conditional. We could also make sure the path of execution doesn't reach the uninitialized variable through some other means, depending on what makes sense for our particular application. For example, we could return from the method abruptly:

```
int foo;
. . .
if ( someCondition ) {
    foo = 42;
    . . .
}
else
    return;

foo += 1;
```

In this case, there's no chance of reaching `foo` in an unused state and the compiler allows the use of `foo` after the conditional.

Why is Java so picky about local variables? One of the most common (and insidious) sources of error in C or C++ is forgetting to initialize local variables, so Java tries to help us out. If it didn't, Java would suffer the same potential irregularities as C or C++.[*]

Argument Passing

Let's consider what happens when you pass arguments to a method. All primitive data types (e.g., `int`, `char`, `float`) are passed by value. Now you're probably used to the idea that reference types (i.e., any kind of object, including arrays and strings) are used through references. An important distinction is that the references themselves (the pointers to these objects) are actually primitive types, and are passed by value too.

Consider the following piece of code:

```
int i = 0;
SomeKindOfObject obj = new SomeKindOfObject();
myMethod( i, obj );
. . .
void myMethod(int j, SomeKindOfObject o) {
. . .
}
```

The first chunk of code calls `myMethod()`, passing it two arguments. The first argument, `i`, is passed by value; when the method is called, the value of `i` is copied into the method's parameter `j`. If `myMethod()` changes the value of `i`, it's changing only its copy of the local variable.

In the same way, a copy of the reference to `obj` is placed into the reference variable `o` of `myMethod()`. Both references refer to the same object, of course, and any changes made through either reference affect the actual (single) object instance, but there are two copies of the pointer. If we change the value of, say, `o.size`, the change is visible through either reference. However, if `myMethod()` changes the reference `o` itself—to point to another object—it's affecting only its copy. In this sense, passing the reference is like passing a pointer in C and *unlike* passing by reference in C++.

---

[*] As with `malloc`'ed storage in C or C++, Java objects and their instance variables are allocated on a heap, which allows them default values once, when they are created. Local variables, however, are allocated on the Java virtual machine stack. As with the stack in C and C++, failing to initialize these could mean successive method calls could receive garbage values, and program execution might be inconsistent or implementation dependent.

What if myMethod() needs to modify the calling method's notion of the obj reference (i.e., make obj reference a different object)? The easy way to do that is to wrap obj inside some kind of object, or even to use this to pass a reference to the calling object. Once we have a reference to the object in which obj lives, modifying it's easy. To see how this works, let's look at another piece of code from an implementation of a linked list:

```
class Element {
    public Element nextElement;

    void addMyselfToList( List list ) {
        list.addToList( this );
    }
}

class List {
    void addToList( Element element ) {
        ...
        element.nextElement = getNextElement();
    }
}
```

Every element in a linked list contains a pointer to the next element in the list. In this code, the Element class represents one element; it includes a method for adding itself to the list. The List class itself contains a method for adding an arbitrary Element to the list. The method addMyselfToList() calls addToList() with the argument this (which is, of course, an Element). addToList() can use the this reference to modify the Element's nextElement instance variable. The same technique can be used to implement callbacks for method invocations.

Method Overloading

Method overloading is the ability to define multiple methods with the same name in a class; when the method is invoked, the compiler picks the correct one based on the arguments passed to the method. This implies, of course, that overloaded methods must have different numbers or types of arguments. In a later section we'll look at method overriding, which occurs when we declare methods with identical signatures in different classes.

Method overloading is a powerful and useful feature. It's another form of polymorphism, sometimes called *parametric polymorphism*. The idea is to create methods that act in the same way on different types of arguments and have what appears to be a single method that operates on any of the types. The Java PrintStream's print() method is a good example of method overloading in action. As you've probably deduced by now, you can print a string representation of just about anything using the expression:

```
System.out.print( argument )
```

The variable `out` is a reference to an object (a `PrintStream`) that defines nine different versions of the `print()` method. They take, respectively, arguments of the following types: `Object`, `String`, `char[]`, `char`, `int`, `long`, `float`, `double`, and `boolean`.

```
class PrintStream {
    void print( Object arg ) { ... }
    void print( String arg ) { ... }
    void print( char [] arg ) { ... }
    ...
}
```

You can invoke the `print()` method with any of these types as an argument, and it's printed in an appropriate way. In a language without method overloading, this would require something more cumbersome, such as a separate method for printing each type of object. Then it would be your responsibility to remember what method to use for each data type.

In the above example, `print()` has been overloaded to support two reference types: `Object` and `String`. What if we try to call `print()` with some other reference type? Say, perhaps, a `Date` object? The answer is that since `Date` is a subclass of `Object`, the `Object` method is selected. When there's not an exact type match, the compiler searches for an acceptable, assignable match. Since `Date`, like all classes, is a subclass of `Object`, a `Date` object can be assigned to a variable of type `Object`. It's therefore an acceptable match, and the `Object` method is selected.

But what if there's more than one possible match? Say, for example, we tried to print a subclass of `String` called `MyString`. (Of course, the `String` class is `final`, so it can't be subclassed, but allow me this brief transgression for purposes of explanation.) `MyString` is assignable to either `String` or to `Object`. Here the compiler makes a determination as to which match is more specific and selects that method. In this case it's the `String` method.

The intuitive explanation is that the `String` class is closer to `MyString` in the inheritance hierarchy. A more rigorous way of specifying it would be to say that a given method is more specific than another method if its arguments are all assignable to the arguments of the second method. In this case, the `String` method is more specific than the `Object` method because type `String` is assignable to type `Object`. The reverse is obviously not true.

If you're paying close attention, you may have noticed I said that the compiler resolves overloaded methods. Method overloading is not something that happens at run-time; this is an important distinction. It means that the selected method is chosen once, when the code is compiled. Once the overloaded method is selected, the choice is fixed until the code is recompiled, even if the class containing the called method is later revised and a more specific overloaded method is added. This is in contrast to overridden (virtual) methods, which are located at run-time and can be found even if they didn't exist when the calling class was compiled. We'll talk about method overriding later in the chapter.

One last note about overloading. In earlier chapters, I've pointed out that Java doesn't support programmer-defined overloaded operators, and that + is the only system-defined overloaded operator. If you've been wondering what an overloaded operator is, I can finally clear up that mystery. In a language like C++, you can customize operators such as + and * to work with objects that you create. For example, you could create a class `Complex` that implements complex numbers, and then overload + to add `Complex` objects and * to multiply complex objects. Some people argue that operator overloading makes for elegant and readable programs, while others say it's just "syntactic sugar" that makes for obfuscated code. The Java designers clearly espoused the later opinion when they chose not to support programmer-defined overloaded operators.

Object Creation

Objects in Java are allocated from a system heap space, much like `malloc`'ed storage in C or C++. Unlike C or C++, however, we needn't manage that memory ourselves. Java takes care of memory allocation and deallocation for you. Java explicitly allocates storage for an object when you create it with the `new` keyword. More importantly, objects are removed by garbage collection when they're no longer referenced.

Constructors

You allocate an object by specifying the `new` operator with an object *constructor*. A constructor is a special method with the same name as its class and no return type. It's called when a new class instance is created, which gives the class an opportunity to set up the object for use. Constructors, like other methods, can accept arguments and can be overloaded:

```
class Date {
    long time;

    Date() {
        time = currentTime();
```

```
        }

        Date( String date ) {
            time = parseDate( date );
        }
        ...
    }
```

In the above example, the class `Date` has two constructors. The first takes no arguments; it's known as the default constructor. Default constructors play a special role in that, if we don't define any constructors for a class, an empty default constructor is supplied for us. The default constructor is what gets called whenever you create an object by calling its constructor with no arguments. Here we have implemented the default constructor so that it sets the instance variable `time` by calling a hypothetical method: `currentTime()`, which resembles the functionality of the real `java.util.Date` class.

The second constructor takes a `String` argument. Presumably, this `String` contains a string representation of the time that can be parsed to set the `time` variable.

Given the constructors above, we create a `Date` object in the following ways:

```
    Date now = new Date();
    Date christmas = new Date("Dec 25, 1997");
```

In each case, Java chooses the appropriate constructor at compile-time based on the rules for overloaded method selection.

If we later remove all references to an allocated object, it'll be garbage collected, as we'll discuss shortly:

```
    christmas = null;              // fair game for the garbage collector
```

Setting the above reference to `null` means it's no longer pointing to the "Dec 25, 1997" object. Unless that object is referenced by another variable, it's now inaccessible and can be garbage collected. Actually, setting `christmas` to any other value would have the same results, but using the value `null` is a clear way to indicate that `christmas` no longer has a useful value.

A few more notes about constructors. Constructors can't be `abstract`, `synchronized`, or `final`. Constructors can, however, be declared with visibility modifiers to control their accessibility. We'll talk in detail about visibility modifiers later in the chapter.

Working with Overloaded Constructors

A constructor can refer to another constructor in the same class or the immediate superclass using special forms of the `this` and `super` references. We'll discuss the first case here, and return to that of the superclass constructor again after we have talked more about subclassing and inheritance.

A constructor can invoke another, overloaded constructor in its class using the reference `this()` with appropriate arguments to select the desired constructor. If a constructor calls another constructor, it must do so as its first statement (we'll explain why in a bit):

```
class Car {
    String model;
    int doors;

    Car( String m, int d ) {
        model = m;
        doors = d;
        // other, complicated setup
        ...
    }

    Car( String m ) {
        this( m, 4 );
    }
    ...
}
```

In the example above, the class `Car` has two overloaded constructors. The first, more explicit one accepts arguments specifying the car's model and its number of doors and uses them to set up the object. We have also provided a simpler constructor that takes just the model as an argument and, in turn, calls the first constructor with a default value of four doors. The advantage of this approach is that you can have a single constructor do all the complicated setup work; other auxiliary constructors simply feed the appropriate arguments to that constructor.

The important point is that the call to `this()` must appear as the first statement in an auxiliary constructor. The syntax is restricted in this way because there's a need to identify a clear chain of command in the calling of constructors. At one end of the chain, Java invokes the constructor of the superclass (if we don't do it explicitly) to ensure that inherited members are initialized properly before we proceed. There's also a point in the chain, just after the constructor of the superclass is invoked, where the initializers of the current class's instance variables are evaluated. Before that point, we can't even reference the instance variables of our class. We'll explain this situation again in complete detail after we have talked about inheritance.

For now, all you need to know is that you can invoke a second constructor only as the first statement of another constructor. In addition, you can't do anything at that point other than pass along arguments of the current constructor. For example, the following is illegal and causes a compile-time error:

```
Car( String m ) {
    int doors = determineDoors();
    this( m, doors );    // Error
}                        // Constructor call must be first statement
```

The simple model name constructor can't do any additional setup before calling the more explicit constructor. It can't even refer to an instance member for a constant value:

```
class Car {
    ...
    final int default_doors = 4;
    ...

    Car( String m ) {
        this( m, default_doors ); // Error
                                  // Referencing uninitialized variable
    }
    ...
}
```

The instance variable `defaultDoors` above is not initialized until a later point in the chain of constructor calls, so the compiler doesn't let us access it yet. Fortunately, we can solve this particular problem by making the identifier `static` as well:

```
class Car {
    ...
    static final int DEFAULT_DOORS = 4;
    ...

    Car( String m ) {
        this( m, DEFAULT_DOORS );  // Okay now
    }
    ...
}
```

The `static` members of our class have been initialized for some time, so it's safe to access them.

Static Code Blocks

It's possible to declare a `static` code block within a class. This code block doesn't belong to any method; instead, it's associated with the class, like a static variable or method. A `static` block initializes `static` class members in the same way a constructor initializes a class instance. In this way, the static parts of a class have complex initialization just like objects:

```
class ColorWheel {
    static Hashtable colors = new Hashtable();

    static {
        colors.put("Red", Color.red );
        colors.put("Green", Color.green );
        colors.put("Blue", Color.blue );
        ...
    }
    ...
}
```

In the above example, the class `ColorWheel` provides a variable `colors` that maps the names of colors to `Color` objects in a `Hashtable`. Because this is a `static` variable, it's available, without duplication, anywhere `ColorWheel` is accessible. The first time the class `ColorWheel` is referenced and loaded, the `static` components of `ColorWheel` are evaluated, in the order they appear in the source. In this case, the `static` code block simply adds elements to the `colors Hashtable`.

Object Destruction

Now that we've seen how to create objects, it's time to talk about their destruction. If you're accustomed to programming in C or C++, you've probably spent time hunting down memory leaks in your code. Java takes care of object destruction for you; you don't have to worry about memory leaks, and you can concentrate on more important programming tasks.

Garbage Collection

Java uses a technique known as *garbage collection* to remove objects that are no longer needed. The garbage collector is Java's grim reaper. It lingers, usually in a low priority thread, stalking objects and awaiting their demise. It finds them, watches them, and periodically counts references to them to see when their time has come. When all references to an object are gone, and it's no longer accessible, the garbage-collection mechanism reclaims it and returns the space to the available pool of resources.

There are many different algorithms for garbage collection; the Java virtual machine architecture doesn't specify a particular scheme. It's worth noting, though, that current implementations of Java use a conservative mark and sweep system. Under this scheme, Java first walks through the tree of all accessible object references and marks them as alive. Then Java scans the heap looking for identifiable objects that aren't so marked. Java finds objects on the heap because they are stored in a characteristic way and have a particular signature of bits in their handles unlikely to be reproduced naturally. This kind of algorithm doesn't suffer from the problem of cyclic references, where detached objects can mutually reference each other and appear alive.

By default, the Java virtual machine is configured to run the garbage collector in a low-priority thread, so that the garbage collector runs periodically to collect stray objects. With the *java* interpreter that comes with the JDK, you can turn off garbage collection by using the −noasyncgc command-line option. If you do this, the garbage collector will be run only if it's requested explicitly or if the Java virtual machine runs out of memory.

A Java application can prompt the garbage collector to make a sweep explicitly by invoking the System.gc() method. An extremely time-sensitive Java application might use this to its advantage by running in an interpreter with asynchronous garbage collection deactivated and scheduling its own cleanup periods. This issue is necessarily implementation dependent, however, because on some platforms, the garbage-collected heap may be implemented in hardware.

Finalization

Before a method is removed by garbage collection, its finalize() method is invoked to give it a last opportunity to clean up its act and free other kinds of resources it may be holding. While the garbage collector can reclaim memory resources, it can't take care of things like closing files and terminating network connections. That's what the finalize() method is for.

An object's finalize() method is guaranteed to be called before the object is garbage collected, but there's no guarantee as to when that will happen. Finalization and collection occur in different phases of the garbage-collection process. A guarantee you do have is that the finalize() method is called only once, even if the finalize() method creates a lingering reference to the object that postpones its garbage collection.

Subclassing and Inheritance

Classes in Java exist in a class hierarchy. A class in Java can be declared as a *subclass* of another class using the extends keyword. A subclass *inherits* variables and methods from its *superclass* and uses them as if they're declared within the subclass itself:

```
class Animal {
    float weight;
    ...
    void eat() {
        ...
    }
    ...
}

class Mammal extends Animal {
    int heartRate;
    // inherits weight
    ...
    void breathe() {
        ...
    }
    // inherits eat()
}
```

In the above example, an object of type `Mammal` has both the instance variable `weight` and the method `eat()`. They are inherited from `Animal`.

A class can extend only one other class. To use the proper terminology, Java allows *single inheritance* of class implementation. Later we'll talk about interfaces, which take the place of *multiple inheritance* as it's primarily used in C++.

A subclass can, of course, be further subclassed. Normally, subclassing specializes or refines a class by adding variables and methods:

```
class Cat extends Mammal {
    boolean longHair;
    // inherits weight and heartRate
    ...
    void purr() {
        ...
    }
    // inherits eat() and breathe()
}
```

The `Cat` class is a type of `Mammal` that is ultimately a type of `Animal`. `Cat` objects inherit all the characteristics of `Mammal` objects and, in turn, `Animal` objects. `Cat` also provides additional behavior in the form of the `purr()` method and the `longHair` variable. We can denote the class relationship in a diagram, as shown in Figure 5–3.

A subclass inherits all members of its superclass not designated as `private`. As we'll discuss shortly, other levels of visibility affect what inherited members of the class can be seen from outside of the class and its subclasses, but at a minimum, a subclass always has the same set of visible members as its parent. For this reason, the type of a subclass can be considered a subtype of its parent, and instances of

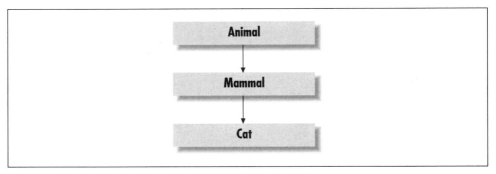

Figure 5–3: A class hierarchy

the subtype can be used anywhere instances of the supertype are allowed. For example:

```
Cat simon = new Cat();
Animal creature = simon;
```

The `Cat simon` in the above example can be assigned to the `Animal` type variable `creature` because `Cat` is a subtype of `Animal`.

Shadowed Variables

In the previous section on methods, we saw that a local variable of the same name as an instance variable hides the instance variable. Similarly, an instance variable in a subclass can shadow an instance variable of the same name in its parent class, as shown in Figure 5–4.

In Figure 5–4, the variable `weight` is declared in three places: as a local variable in the method `foodConsumption()` of the class `Mammal`, as an instance variable of the class `Mammal`, and as an instance variable of the class `Animal`. The actual variable selected depends on the scope in which we are working.

In the above example, all variables were of the same type. About the only reason for declaring a variable with the same type in a subclass is to provide an alternate initializer. A more important use of shadowed variables involves changing their types. We could, for example, shadow an `int` variable with a `double` variable in a subclass that needs decimal values instead of integer values. We do this without changing the existing code because, as its name suggests, when we shadow variables, we don't replace them but instead mask them. Both variables still exist; methods of the superclass see the original variable, and methods of the subclass see the new version. The determination of what variables the various methods see is static and happens at compile-time.

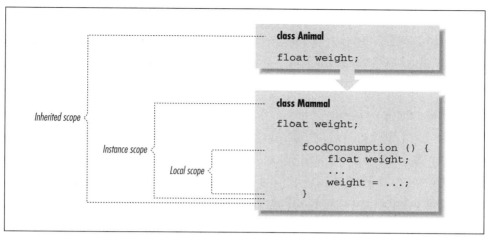

Figure 5–4: The scope of shadowed variables

Here's a simple example:

```
class IntegerCalculator {
    int sum;
    ...
}

class DecimalCalculator extends IntegerCalculator {
    double sum;
    ...
}
```

In this example, we override the instance variable sum to change its type from int to double.[*] Methods defined in the class IntegerCalculator see the integer variable sum, while methods defined in DecimalCalculator see the decimal variable sum. However, both variables actually exist for a given instance of DecimalCalculator, and they can have independent values. In fact, any methods that DecimalCalculator inherits from IntegerCalculator actually see the integer variable sum.

Since both variables exist in DecimalCalculator, we need to reference the variable inherited from IntegerCalculator. We do that using the super reference:

```
int s = super.sum
```

---

[*] Note that a better way to design our calculators would be to have an abstract Calculator class with two subclasses: IntegerCalculator and DecimalCalculator.

Inside of `DecimalCalculator`, the super keyword used in this manner refers to the sum variable defined in the superclass. I'll explain the use of super more fully in a bit.

Another important point about shadowed variables has to do with how they work when we refer to an object by way of a less derived type. For example, we can refer to a `DecimalCalculator` object as an `IntegerCalculator`. If we do so and then access the variable sum, we get the integer variable, not the decimal one:

```
DecimalCalculator dc = new DecimalCalculator();
IntegerCalculator ic = dc;

int s = ic.sum;                    // Accesses IntegerCalculator sum
```

After this detailed explanation, you may still be wondering what shadowed variables are good for. Well, to be honest, the usefulness of shadowed variables is limited, but it's important to understand the concepts before we talk about doing the same thing with methods. We'll see a different and more dynamic type of behavior with method shadowing, or more correctly, *method overriding*.

Overriding Methods

In a previous section, we saw we could declare overloaded methods (i.e., methods with the same name but a different number or type of arguments) within a class. Overloaded method selection works the way I described on all methods available to a class, including inherited ones. This means that a subclass can define some overloaded methods that augment the overloaded methods provided by a superclass.

But a subclass does more than that; it can define a method that has exactly the *same* method signature (arguments and return type) as a method in its superclass. In that case, the method in the subclass *overrides* the method in the superclass and effectively replaces its implementation, as shown in Figure 5–5. Overriding methods to change the behavior of objects is another form of polymorphism: the one most people think of when they talk about the power of object-oriented languages.

In Figure 5–5, `Mammal` overrides the reproduce() method of `Animal`, perhaps to specialize the method for the peculiar behavior of `Mammal`s giving live birth.[*] The `Cat` object's sleeping behavior is overridden to be different from that of a general `Animal`, presumably to accommodate cat naps. The `Cat` class also adds the more unique behaviors of purring and hunting mice.

From what you've seen so far, overridden methods probably look like they shadow methods in superclasses, just as variables do. But overridden methods are actually

* We'll ignore the platypus, which is an obscure nonovoviviparous mammal.

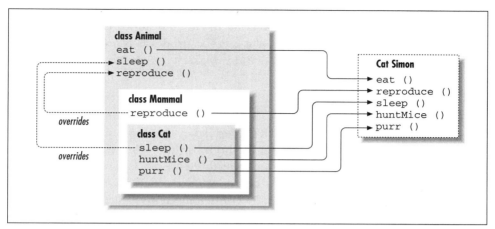

Figure 5–5: Method overriding

more powerful than that. An overridden method in Java acts like a `virtual`
method in C++. When there are multiple implementations of a method in the
inheritance hierarchy of an object, the one in the most derived class always overrides the others, even if we refer to the object by way of a less derived type. In
other words, if we have a `Cat` instance assigned to a variable of the more general
type `Animal` and we call its `sleep()` method, we get the `sleep()` method
implemented in the `Cat` class, not the one in `Animal`:

```
Cat simon = new Cat();
Animal creature = simon;

creature.sleep();              // Accesses Cat sleep();
```

In other respects, the variable `creature` looks like an `Animal`. For example,
access to a shadowed variable would find the implementation in the `Animal` class,
not the `Cat` class. However, because methods are virtual, the appropriate method
in the `Cat` class can be located, even though we are dealing with an `Animal`
object. This means we can deal with specialized objects as if they were more general types of objects and still take advantage of their specialized implementations
of behavior.

Most of what you'll be doing when you're writing a Java applet or application is
overriding methods defined by various classes in the Java API. For example, think
back to the applets we developed in the tutorial in Chapter 2. Almost all of the
methods we implemented for those applets were overridden methods. Recall that
we created a subclass of `Applet` for each of the examples. Then we overrode various methods: `init()` to provide special initialization functionality,
`mouseDrag()` to handle mouse movement, and `paint()` to draw our applet.

A common programming error in Java (at least for me) is to miss and accidentally overload a method when trying to override it. Any difference in the number or type of arguments or the return type of a method produces two overloaded methods instead of a single, overridden method. Make it a habit to look twice when overriding methods.

Overridden methods and dynamic binding

In a previous section, I mentioned that overloaded methods are selected by the compiler at compile-time. Overridden methods, on the other hand, are selected dynamically at run-time. Even if we manage to create an instance of a class our code has never seen (perhaps a new object type loaded from the network) and assign it a more general type variable, overridden methods in the new class will be located and invoked at run-time to replace those that existed when we last compiled our code.

In contrast, if we load a new class that implements an additional, more specific overloaded method, our code will continue to use the implementation it discovered at compile-time. Another effect of this is that casting (i.e., explicitly telling the compiler to treat an object as a type other than its own) affects the selection of overloaded methods, but not overridden methods.

When Java has to dynamically search for overridden methods in subclasses, there's a small performance penalty. In languages like C++, the default is for methods to act like shadowed variables, so you have to explicitly declare the methods you want to be virtual. Java is more dynamic, and the default is for all methods to be virtual. In Java, however, you can go the other direction and explicitly declare methods that can't be overridden; these methods are not subject to dynamic binding and do not suffer in terms of performance. This is done with the `final` modifier. We have seen `final` used with variables to effectively make them constants. When `final` is applied to a method, it means that method can't be overridden (in some sense, its implementation is constant). `final` can also be applied to an entire class, which means the class can't be subclassed.

When the Java compiler is run with the `-O` switch, it performs special optimizations. It can inline `final` methods to improve performance (while slightly increasing the size of the resulting class file). `private` methods, which are effectively `final`, can also be inlined, and `final` classes can benefit from more powerful optimizations.

A more rigorous definition

By now you should have a good, intuitive idea as to how methods are selected from the pool of potentially overloaded and overridden method names of a class. If, however, you are dying for a dry definition, I'll provide one now. If you are satisfied with your understanding, you may wish to skip this little exercise in logic.

In a previous section, I offered an inductive rule for overloaded method resolution. It said that a method is considered more specific than another if its arguments are polymorphically assignable to the arguments of the second method. We can now expand this rule to include the resolution of overridden methods by adding the following condition: to be more specific than another method, the type of the class containing the method must also be assignable to the type of the class holding the second method.

What does that mean? Well, the only classes whose types are assignable are classes in the same inheritance hierarchy. So, what we're talking about now is the set of all methods of the same name in a class or any of its parent or child classes. Since subclass types are assignable to superclass types, but not vice versa, the resolution is pushed, in the way that we expect, down the chain, towards the subclasses. This effectively adds a second dimension to the search, in which resolution is pushed down the inheritance tree towards more refined classes and, simultaneously, towards the most specific overloaded method within a given class.

Static methods

A `static` method in a superclass can be overridden by another `static` method in a subclass, as long as the original method was not declared `final`. However, you can't override a `static` method with a non-`static` method. In other words, you can't hide a `static` method with an instance method.

Exceptions and overridden methods

When we talked about exception handling in Chapter 4, there's one thing I did't mention because it would't have made sense then. An important restriction on overridden methods is that they must adhere to the `throws` clause of the parent's method signature. In other words, if an overridden method throws an exception, the exception must be the type specified by the parent or a subtype of that type.

this and super

The references `this` and `super` make explicit references to the members of the current object or those of a superclass. We have seen `this` used elsewhere to pass a reference to the current object and to refer to shadowed instance variables. The reference `super` is primarily refers to members of a superclass that have been shadowed or overridden:

```
class Animal {
    ...
    void eat( FoodItem f ) {
    }
    ...
}

class Carnivore extends Animal {
    ...
    void eat( FoodItem f ) {
        if ( f instanceof Plant )
            // Complain profusely
        else
            super.eat( f );
    }
    ...
}
```

In the above example, the `Carnivore` class overrides the `Animal` `eat()` method to first check if the hypothetical `FoodItem` object being fed is a type of `Plant` object. If not, it simply calls the (otherwise overridden implementation) in its superclass, using `super`.

`super` prompts the search for the method or variable to begin in the immediate superclass rather than the current class. The method or variable can reside in the immediate superclass, or in a more distant one. The usage of the `super` reference to access overridden methods in a superclass is special; it tells the method resolution system to stop at the superclass. Without `super`, there would be no way to access overridden methods.

Casting

As in C++, a *cast* explicitly tells the compiler to change the apparent type of an object reference. Unlike in C++, casts in Java are checked both at compile- and at run-time to make sure they are legal. Attempting to cast an object to an incompatible type at run-time results in a `ClassCastException`. Only casts between objects in the same inheritance hierarchy (and as we'll see later, to appropriate interfaces) are legal in Java and pass the scrutiny of the compiler and the run-time system.

Casts in Java affect only the treatment of references; they never change the form of the actual object. This is an important rule to keep in mind. You never change the object pointed to by a reference by casting it; you change only the compiler's (or run-time system's) notion of it.

A cast can be used to *narrow* the type of a reference. Often, we'll do this when we have to retrieve an object from a more general type of collection or when it has been previously used as a less derived type. (The prototypical example is using an object in a `Vector` or `Hashtable`, as you'll see in Chapter 7.) Continuing with our `Cat` example:

```
Cat simon = new Cat();
Animal creature = simon;

simon = creature;              // Compile time error, incompatible type

simon = (Cat)creature;         // Okay
```

We can't reassign the reference in `creature` to the variable `simon` even though we know it holds an instance of `Cat`. We have to perform the indicated cast. This is also called *downcasting* the reference.

Note that an implicit cast was performed when we went the other way to *widen* the reference `simon` to type `Animal` during the assignment. In this case, an explicit cast is legal, but superfluous.

If casting seems complicated, here's a simple way to think about it. Basically, you can't lie about what an object is. If you have a `Cat` object, you can cast it to a less derived type (i.e., a type above it in the class hierarchy) such as `Animal` or even `Object`, since all Java classes are a subclass of `Object`. If you have an `Object` you know is a `Cat`, you can downcast the `Object` to be an `Animal` or a `Cat`. However, if you aren't sure if the `Object` is a `Cat` or a `Dog`, you should check it with `instanceof` before you perform the cast. If you get the cast wrong, Java throws a `ClassCastException`.

As I mentioned earlier, casting can affect the selection of compile-time items like variables and overloaded methods, but not the selection of overridden methods. Figure 5–6 shows the difference. As shown in the top half of the diagram, casting the reference `simon` to type `Animal` (widening it) affects the selection of the shadowed variable `weight` within it. However, as the lower half of the diagram indicates, the cast doesn't affect the selection of the overridden method `sleep()`.

Object Construction

When we talked earlier about constructors, we discussed how the special statement `this()` invokes an overloaded constructor upon entry to another constructor. Similarly, the statement `super()` explicitly invokes the constructor of a superclass. Of course, we also talked about how Java makes a chain of constructor calls that includes the superclass's constructor, so why use `super()` explicitly? When Java makes an implicit call to the superclass constructor, it calls the default constructor.

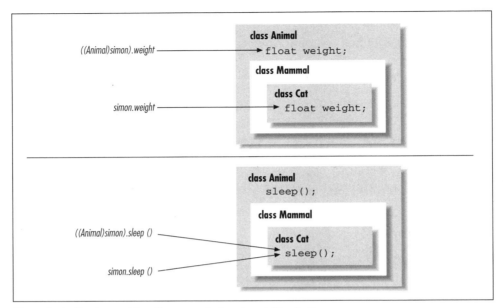

Figure 5–6: Casting and its effect on method and variable selection

So, if we want to invoke a superclass constructor that takes arguments, we have to do so explicitly using super().

If we are going to call a superclass constructor with super(), it must be the first statement of our constructor, just as this() must be the first call we make in an overloaded constructor. Here's a simple example:

```
class Person {
    Person ( String name ) {
        //  setup based on name
        ...
    }
    ...
}

class Doctor extends Person {
    Doctor ( String name, String specialty ) {
        super( name );
        // setup based on specialty
        ...
    }
    ...
}
```

In the this example, we use `super()` to take advantage of the implementation of the superclass constructor and avoid duplicating the code to set up the object based on its name. In fact, because the class `Person` doesn't define a default (no arguments) constructor, we have no choice but to call `super()` explicitly. Otherwise, the compiler would complain that it couldn't find an appropriate default constructor to call. Said another way, if you subclass a class that has only constructors that take arguments, you have to invoke one of the superclass's constructors explicitly from your subclass constructor.

Instance variables of the class are initialized upon return from the superclass constructor, whether that's due to an explicit call via `super()` or an implicit call to the default superclass constructor.

We can now give the full story of how constructors are chained together and when instance variable initialization occurs. The rule has three parts and is applied repeatedly for each successive constructor invoked.

- If the first statement of a constructor is an ordinary statement—i.e., not a call to `this()` or `super()` — Java inserts an implicit call to `super()` to invoke the default constructor of the superclass. Upon returning from that call, Java initializes the instance variables of the current class and proceeds to execute the statements of the current constructor.

- If the first statement of a constructor is a call to a superclass constructor via `super()`, Java invokes the selected superclass constructor. Upon its return, Java initializes the current class's instance variables and proceeds with the statements of the current constructor.

- If the first statement of a constructor is a call to an overloaded constructor via `this()`, Java invokes the selected constructor and upon its return simply proceeds with the statements of the current constructor. The call to the superclass's constructor has happened within the overloaded constructor, either explicitly or implicitly, so the initialization of instance variables has already occurred.

Abstract Methods and Classes

As in C++, a method can be declared with the `abstract` modifier to indicate that it's a prototype, or definition, only. You can't directly use a class that contains an abstract method; you must instead create a subclass that implements the abstract method. An abstract method has no body; it's simply a signature definition followed by a semicolon:

```
abstract vaporMethod( String name );
```

In Java, a class that contains one or more abstract methods must be explicitly declared as an abstract class, also using the `abstract` modifier:

```
abstract class vaporClass {
    ...
    abstract vaporMethod( String name );
    ...
}
```

An abstract class can contain other, non-abstract methods and ordinary variable declarations; however, it can't be instantiated. To be used, it must be subclassed and its abstract methods must be overridden with methods that implement a body. Not all abstract methods have to be implemented in a single subclass, but a subclass that doesn't override all its superclass's abstract methods with actual, concrete implementations must also be declared `abstract`.

Abstract methods provide a rigorous template for creating classes for a specific application. The `java.io.InputStream` class, for example, has a single abstract method called `read()`. Various subclasses of `InputStream` implement `read()` in their own ways to read from their own sources. The rest of the `InputStream` class, however, provides extended functionality built on the simple `read()` method. A subclass of `InputStream` inherits these non-abstract methods that provide functionality based on the simple `read()` method that the subclass implements.

It's often desirable to specify only the prototypes for a whole set of methods and provide no implementation. In C++, this would be a purely abstract class. In Java, you should instead use an *interface*. An interface is like a purely abstract class; it defines a set of methods a class must implement (i.e., the behavior of a class). However, unlike in C++, a class in Java can simply say that it `implements` an interface and go about implementing those methods. As we'll discuss later, a class that implements an interface does doesn't have to inherit from any particular part of the inheritance hierarchy or use a particular implementation.

Packages and Compilation Units

A *package* is a name for a group of related classes. In Chapter 3, we discussed how Java uses package names to locate classes during compilation and at run-time. In this sense, packages are somewhat like libraries; they organize and manage sets of classes. Packages provide more than just source code-level organization though. They also create an additional level of scope for their classes and the variables and methods within them. We'll talk about the visibility of classes in this section. In the next section, we'll discuss the effect that packages have on access to variables and methods between classes.

Compilation Units

The source code for a Java class is called a *compilation unit*. A compilation unit normally contains a single class definition and is named for that class. The definition of a class named `MyClass`, for instance, should appear in a file named *MyClass.java*. For most of us, a compilation unit is just a file with a *.java* extension, but in an integrated development environment, it could be an arbitrary entity. For brevity here, we'll refer to a compilation unit simply as a file.

The division of classes into their own compilation units is important because, as described in Chapter 3, the Java compiler assumes much of the responsibility of a *make* utility. The compiler relies on the names of source files to find and compile dependent classes. It's possible (and common) to put more than one class definition into a single file, but there are some restrictions we'll discuss shortly.

A class is declared to belong to a particular package with the `package` statement. The `package` statement must appear as the first statement in a compilation unit. There can be only one `package` statement, and it applies to the entire file:

```
package mytools.text;

class TextComponent {
    . . .
}
```

In the above example, the class `TextComponent` is placed in the package `mytools.text`.

A Word About Package Names

You should recall from Chapter 3 that package names are constructed in a hierarchical way, using a dot-separated naming convention. Package-name components construct a unique path for the compiler and run-time systems to locate files; however, they don't affect the contents directly in any other way. There is no such thing as a subpackage (the package name space is really flat, not hierarchical) and packages under a particular part of a package hierarchy are related only by association. For example, if we create another package called `mytools.text.poetry` (presumably for text classes specialized in some way to work with poetry), those classes would not be considered part of the `mytools.text` package and would have no special access to its members. In this sense, the package-naming convention can be misleading.

Class Visibility

By default, a class is accessible only to other classes within its package. This means that the class `TextComponent` is available only to other classes in the `mytools.text` package. To be visible elsewhere, a class must be declared as `public`:

```
package mytools.text;

public class TextEditor {
    ...
}
```

The class `TextEditor` can now be referenced anywhere. There can be only a single `public` class defined in a compilation unit; the file must be named for that class.

By hiding unimportant or extraneous classes, a package builds a subsystem that has a well-defined interface to the rest of the world. Public classes provide a facade for the operation of the system and the details of its inner workings can remain hidden, as shown in Figure 5–7. In this sense, packages hide classes in the way classes hide `private` members.

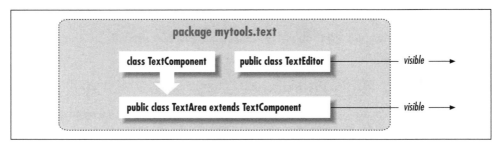

Figure 5–7: Class visibility and packages

Figure 5–7 shows part of the the hypothetical `mytools.text` package. The classes `TextArea` and `TextEditor` are declared `public` and can be used elsewhere in an application. The class `TextComponent` is part of the implementation of `TextArea` and is not accessible from outside of the package.

Importing Classes

Classes within a package can refer to each other by their simple names. However, to locate a class in another package, we have to supply a qualifier. Continuing with the above example, an application refers directly to our editor class by its fully qualified name of `mytools.text.TextEditor`. But we'd quickly grow tired of typing such long class names, so Java gives us the `import` statement. One or more `import` statements can appear at the top of a compilation unit, beneath the `package` statement. The `import` statements list the full names of classes to be used within the file. Like a `package` statement, `import` statements apply to the entire compilation unit. Here's how you might use an `import` statement:

```
package somewhere.else;

import mytools.text.TextEditor;

class MyClass {
    TextEditor editBoy;
    ...
}
```

As shown in the example above, once a class is imported, it can be referenced by its simple name throughout the code. It's also possible to import all of the classes in a package using the * notation:

```
import mytools.text.*;
```

Now we can refer to all `public` classes in the `mytools.text` package by their simple names.

Obviously, there can be a problem with importing classes that have conflicting names. If two different packages contain classes that use the same name, you just have to fall back to using fully qualified names to refer to those classes. Other than the potential for naming conflicts, there's no penalty for importing classes. Java doesn't carry extra baggage into the compiled class files. In other words, Java class files don't contain other class definitions, they only reference them.

The Unnamed Package

A class that is defined in a compilation unit that doesn't specify a package falls into the large, amorphous unnamed package. Classes in this nameless package can refer to each other by their simple names. Their path at compile- and run-time is considered to be the current directory, so package-less classes are useful for experimentation, testing, and brevity in providing examples for books about Java.

Variable and Method Visibility

One of the most important aspects of object-oriented design is data hiding, or *encapsulation*, as it's more precisely known. By treating an object in some respects as a "black box" and ignoring the details of its implementation, we can write stronger, simpler code with components that can be easily reused.

Basic Access Modifiers

By default, the variables and methods of a class are accessible to members of the class itself and other classes in the same package. To borrow from C++ terminology, classes in the same package are `friendly`. We'll call this the default level of visibility. As you'll see as we go on, the default visibility lies in the middle of the range of restrictiveness that can be specified.

The modifiers `public` and `private`, on the other hand, define the extremes. As we mentioned earlier, methods and variables declared as `private` are accessible only within their class. At the other end of the spectrum, members declared as `public` are always accessible, from any class in any package. Of course, the class that contains the methods must also be `public`, as we just discussed. The `public` members of a class should define its most general functionality—what the black box is supposed to do. Figure 5–8 illustrates the three simplest levels of visibility.

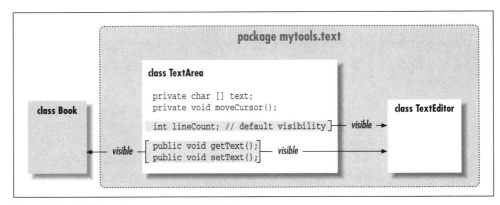

Figure 5–8: Public, private, and default visibility

Figure 5–8 continues with the example from the previous section. Public members in `TextArea` are accessible from anywhere. Private members are not visible from outside the class. The default visibility allows access by other classes in the package.

The `protected` modifier allows special access permissions for subclasses. Contrary to how it might sound, `protected` is slightly less restrictive than the default level of accessibility. In addition to the default access afforded classes in the same package, `protected` members are visible to subclasses of the class, even if they are defined in a different package. If you are a C++ programmer and so used to more restrictive meanings for both the default and `protected` levels of access, this may rub you the wrong way.

We can tighten things up to the more common meaning of `protected` by combining modifiers to get `private protected`.* With `private protected` visibility, members are still accessible to subclasses of the class, but they are invisible to other classes in the package. In other words, adding `private` to `protected` turns off the default access by other classes in the package. Figure 5–9 illustrates the difference between `protected` and `private protected`.

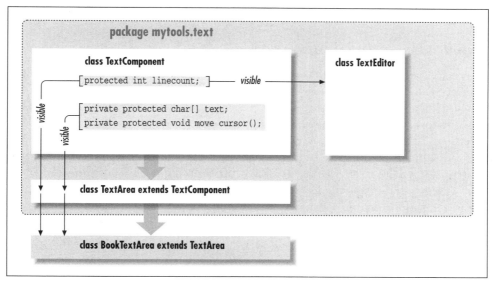

Figure 5–9: Protected and private protected visibility

In Figure 5–9, there are two subclasses of `TextArea`: one inside and one outside the `mytools.text` package. Both the `protected` and `private protected` members of the class are accessible in each subclass; from the point of view of the subclass, they are inherited. However, the `protected` member is also accessible to other classes within the package, while the `private protected` member is not.

Table 5–1 summarizes the levels of visibility available in Java; it runs generally from most restrictive to least. Methods and variables are always visible within a class, so the table doesn't address that issue.

---

* The meaning of the `protected` modifier changed in the Beta2 release of Java, and the `private protected` combination appeared at the same time. They patched some potential security holes, but confused many people.

Table 5–1: Visibility Modifiers

Modifier	Visibility
private	None
private protected	Subclasses only, inside or outside the package
none (default)	Classes in the package
protected	Classes in package and subclasses inside or outside the package
public	All classes

Subclasses and Visibility

There are two important (but unrelated) notes we need to add to the discussion of visibility with regards to class members in subclasses. First, when you override methods of a class in a subclass, it's not possible to reduce their visibility. While it is possible to take a `private` method of a class and override it to be `public` in a subclass, the reverse is not possible. This makes sense when you think about the fact that subtypes have to be usable as instances of their supertype (e.g., a `Mammal` is a type of `Animal`). If we could reduce the visibility of an overridden method, this would be a problem. However, we can reduce the visibility of a variable because it simply results in a shadowed variable. As with all shadowed variables, the two variables are distinct and can have separate visibilities in their different class forms.

The second point is that `protected` variables of a class are visible to its subclasses, but unlike C++, only in objects of the subclass's type or its subtypes. In other words, a subclass can see a `protected` variable from its superclass as an inherited variable, but it can't see the variable in an instance of the superclass itself.

Interfaces

Interfaces are kind of like Boy Scout (or Girl Scout) merit badges. When a scout has learned to build a bird house, he can walk around wearing a little patch with a picture of one on his sleeve. This says to the world, "I know how to build a bird house." Similarly, an *interface* is a list of methods that define some set of behavior for an object. Any class that implements each of the methods listed in the interface can declare that it implements the interface and wear, as its merit badge, an extra type—the interface's type.

Interface types act like class types. You can declare variables to be of an interface type, you can declare arguments of methods to accept interface types, and you can even specify that the return type of a method is an interface type. In each of these cases, what is meant is that any object that implements the interface (i.e., wears the right merit badge) can fill that spot. In this sense, interfaces are orthogonal to the class hierarchy. They cut across the boundaries of what kind of object an item is and deal with it only in terms of what it can do. A class implements as many interfaces as it desires. In this way, interfaces in Java replace the need for multiple inheritance (and all of its messy side effects).

An interface looks like a purely `abstract` class (i.e., a class with only `abstract` methods). You define an interface with the `interface` keyword and list its methods with no bodies:

```
interface Driveable {
    boolean startEngine();
    void stopEngine();
    float accelerate( float acc );
    boolean turn( Direction dir );
}
```

The example above defines an interface called `Driveable` with four methods. It's acceptable, but not necessary, to declare the methods in an interface with the `abstract` modifier, so we haven't used it here. Interfaces define capabilities, so it's common to name interfaces after their capabilities in a passive sense. "Driveable" is a good example; "runnable" and "updatable" would be two more.

Any class that implements all the methods can then declare it implements the interface by using a special `implements` clause in its class definition:

```
class Automobile implements Driveable {
    ...
    boolean startEngine() {
        if ( notTooCold )
            engineRunning = true;
        ...
    }

    void stopEngine() {
        engineRunning = false;
    }

    float accelerate( float acc ) {
        ...
    }

    boolean turn( Direction dir ) {
        ...
    }
    ...
}
```

The class `Automobile` implements the methods of the `Driveable` interface and declares itself `Driveable` using an `implements` clause.

As shown in Figure 5–10, another class, such as `LawnMower`, can also implement the `Driveable` interface. The figure illustrates the `Driveable` interface being implemented by two different classes. While it's possible that both `Automobile` and `Lawnmower` could derive from some primitive kind of vehicle, they don't have to in this scenario. This is a significant advantage of interfaces over standard multiple inheritance as implemented in C++.

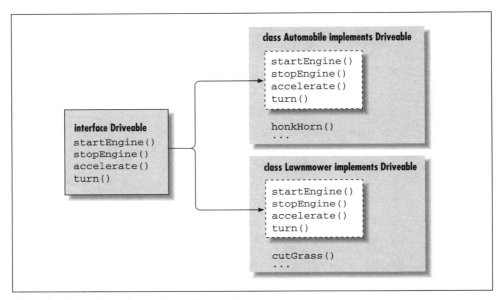

Figure 5–10: Implementing the Driveable interface

After declaring the interface, we have a new type, `Driveable`. We can declare variables of type `Driveable` and assign them any instance of a `Driveable` object:

```
Automobile auto = new Automobile();
Lawnmower mower = new Lawnmower();
Driveable vehicle;

vehicle = auto;
vehicle.startEngine();
vehicle.stopEngine();
...
vehicle = mower;
vehicle.startEngine();
vehicle.stopEngine();
```

Both `Automobile` and `Lawnmower` implement `Driveable` and can be considered of that type.

Interfaces as Callbacks

Interfaces can be used to implement callbacks in Java. A *callback* is a situation where you'd like to pass a reference to some behavior and have another object invoke it later. In C or C++, this is prime territory for function pointers; in Java, we'll use interfaces instead.

Consider two classes: a `TickerTape` class that displays data and a `TextSource` class that provides an information feed. We'd like our `TextSource` to send any new text data. We could have `TextSource` store a reference to a `TickerTape` object, but then we could never use our `TextSource` to send data to any other kind of object. Instead, we'd have to proliferate subclasses of `TextSource` that dealt with different types. A more elegant solution is to have `TextSource` store a reference to an interface type, `TextUpdateable`:

```
interface TextUpdateable {
    receiveText( String text );
}

class TickerTape implements TextUpdateable {
    TextSource source;

    init() {
        source = new TextSource( this );
        ...
    }

    public receiveText( String text ) {
        scrollText( text ):
    }
    ...
}

class TextSource {
    TextUpdateable receiver;

    TextSource( TextUpdateable r ) {
        receiver = r;
    }

    private sendText( String s ) {
        receiver.receiveText( s );
    }
    ...
}
```

The only thing `TextSource` really cares about is finding the right method to invoke to send text. Thus, we can list that method in an interface called

TextUpdateable and have our TickerTape implement the interface. A TickerTape object can then be used anywhere we need something of the type TextUpdateable. In this case, the TextSource constructor takes a TextUpdateable object and stores the reference in an instance variable of type TextUpdateable. Our TickerTape object simply passes a reference to itself as the callback for text updates, and the source can invoke its receiveText() method as necessary.

Interface Variables

Although interfaces allow us to specify behavior without implementation, there's one exception. An interface can contain constant variable identifiers; these identifiers appear in any class that implements the interface. This functionality allows for predefined parameters that can be used with the methods:

```
interface Scaleable {
    static final int BIG = 0, MEDIUM = 1, SMALL = 2;

    void setScale( int size );
}
```

The Scaleable interface defines three integers: BIG, MEDIUM, and SMALL. All variables defined in interfaces are implicitly final and static; we don't have to use the modifiers here but, for clarity, we recommend you do so.

A class that implements Scaleable sees these variables:

```
class Box implements Scaleable {

    void setScale( int size ) {
        switch( size ) {
            case BIG:
                . . .
            case MEDIUM:
                . . .
            case SMALL:
                . . .
        }
    }
    . . .
}
```

Interfaces and Packages

Interfaces behave like classes within packages. An interface can be declared public to make it visible outside of its package. Under the default visibility, an interface is visible only inside of its package. There can be only one public interface declared in a compilation unit.

Subinterfaces

An interface can extend another interface, just as a class can extend another class. Such an interface is called a *subinterface*.

```
interface DynamicallyScaleable extends Scaleable {
    void changeScale( int size );
}
```

The interface DynamicallyScaleable extends our previous Scaleable interface and adds an additional method. A class that implements DynamicallyScaleable must implement all methods of both interfaces.

The Object and Class Classes

java.lang.Object is the mother of all objects; it's the primordial class from which all other classes are ultimately derived. Methods defined in Object are therefore very important because they appear in every instance of any class, throughout all of Java. At last count, there were nine public methods in Object. Five of these are versions of wait() and notify() that are used to synchronize threads on object instances, as we'll discuss in Chapter 6. The remaining four methods are used for basic comparison, conversion, and administration.

Every object has a toString() method that is called when it's to be represented as a text value. PrintStream objects use toString() to print data, as discussed in Chapter 8. toString() is also used when an object is referenced in a string concatenation. Here are some examples:

```
MyObj myObject = new MyObj();
Answer theAnswer = new Answer();

System.out.println( myObject );
String s = "The answer is: " + theAnswer ;
```

To be friendly, a new kind of object should override toString() and implement its own version that provides appropriate printing functionality. Two other methods, equals() and hashCode(), may also require specialization when you create a new class.

Equality

equals() compares whether two objects are equivalent. Precisely what that means for a particular class is something that you'll have to decide for yourself. Two String objects, for example, are considered equivalent if they hold precisely the same characters in the same sequence:

```
String userName = "Joe";
...
if ( userName.equals( suspectName ) )
    arrest( userName );
```

Note that using `equals()` is not the same as:

```
if ( userName == suspectName )              // Wrong!
```

The above code tests to see if the two `String` objects are the same object, which is sufficient but not necessary for them to be equivalent objects.

A class should override the `equals()` method if it needs to implement its own notion of equality. If you have no need to compare objects of a particular class, you don't need to override `equals()`.

Watch out for accidentally overloading `equals()` when you mean to override it. `equals()` takes an `Object` as an argument and returns a `boolean` value. While you'll probably want to check only if an object is equivalent to an object of its own type, in order to properly override `equals()`, the method should accept a generic `Object` as its argument. Here's an example of implementing `equals()`:

```
class Sneakers extends Shoes {
    public boolean equals( Object arg ) {
        if ( (arg != null) && (arg instanceof Sneakers) ) {
            // Now compare arg with this to check equivalence
            // If comparison is okay...
            return true;
        }
        return false;
    }
    ...
}
```

A `Sneakers` object can now be properly compared by any current or future Java classes. If we had instead used a `Sneakers` type object as the argument to `equals()`, all would be well for classes that reference our objects as `Sneakers`, but methods that simply use `Shoes` would not see the overloaded method and would compare `Sneakers` against other `Sneakers` improperly.

Hashcodes

The `hashCode()` method returns an integer that is a hashcode for a class instance. A hashcode is like a signature for an object; it's an arbitrary-looking identifying number that is (with important exceptions) generally different for different instances of the class. Hashcodes are used in the process of storing objects in a `Hashtable`, or a similar kind of collection. The hashcode is essentially an index into the collection. See Chapter 7 for a complete discussion of `Hashtable` objects and hashcodes.

The default implementation of hashCode() in Object assigns each object instance a unique number to be used as a hashcode. If you don't override this method when you create a new class, each instance of the class will have a unique hashcode. This is sufficient for most objects. However, if the class has a notion of equivalent objects, then you should probably override hashCode() so that equivalent objects are given the same hashcode.

java.lang.Class

The last method of Object we need to discuss is getClass(). This method returns a reference to the Class object that produced the object instance.

A good measure of the complexity of an object-oriented language is the degree of abstraction of its class structures. We know that every object in Java is an instance of a class, but what exactly is a class? In C++, objects are formulated by and instantiated from classes, but classes are really just artifacts of the compiler. Thus, you see only classes mentioned in C++ source code, not at run-time. By comparison, classes in Smalltalk are real, run-time entities in the language that are themselves described by "meta-classes" and "meta-class classes." Java strikes a happy medium between these two languages with what is, effectively, a two-tiered system that uses Class objects.

Classes in Java source code are represented at run-time by instances of the java.lang.Class class. There's a Class object for every class you use; this Class object is responsible for producing instances for its class. This may sound overwhelming, but you don't have to worry about any of it unless you are interested in loading new kinds of classes dynamically at run-time.

We can get the Class associated with a particular object with the getClass() method. One thing we can do with the Class object is to ask for the name of the object's class:

```
String s = "Boofa!";
Class strClass = s.getClass();
System.out.println( strClass.getName() ); // prints "java.lang.String"
```

Another thing that we can do with a Class is to ask it to produce a new instance of its type of object. Continuing with the above example:

```
try {
    String s2 = (String)strClass.newInstance();
}
catch ( InstantiationException e ) { ... }
catch ( IllegalAccessException e ) { ... }
```

newInstance() has a return type of Object, so we have to cast it to a reference of the appropriate type. A couple of problems can occur here. An InstantiationException indicates we're trying to instantiate an abstract class or an interface. IllegalAccessException is a more general exception that indicates we can't access a constructor for the object. Note that newInstance() can create only an instance of a class that has an accessible default constructor. There's no way for us to pass any arguments to a constructor.

All this becomes more meaningful when we add the capability to look up a Class by name. forName() is a static method of Class that returns a Class object given its name as a String:

```
try {
    Class sneakersClass = Class.forName("Sneakers");
}
catch ( ClassNotFoundException e ) { ... }
```

A ClassNotFoundException is thrown if the class can't be located.

Combining the above tools, we have the power to load new kinds of classes dynamically. When combined with the power of interfaces, we can use new data types by name in our applications:

```
interface Typewriter {
    void typeLine( String s );
    ...
}

class Printer implements Typewriter {
    ...
}

class MyApplication {
    ...
    String outputDeviceName = "Printer";

    try {
        Class newClass = Class.forName( outputDeviceName );
        Typewriter device = (Typewriter)newClass.newInstance();
        ...
        device.typeLine("Hello...");
    }
    catch ( Exception e ) {
}
```

Inside Arrays

At the end of Chapter 4, I mentioned that arrays have a place in the Java class hierarchy, but I didn't give you any details. Now that we've discussed the object-oriented aspects of Java, I can give you the whole story.

Array classes live in a parallel Java class hierarchy under the Object class. If a class is a direct subclass of Object, then an array class for that base type also exists as a direct subclass of Object. Arrays of more derived classes are subclasses of the corresponding array classes. For example, consider the following class types:

```
class Animal { ... }
class Bird extends Animal { ... }
class Penguin extends Bird { ... }
```

Figure 5–11 illustrates the class hierarchy for arrays of these classes.

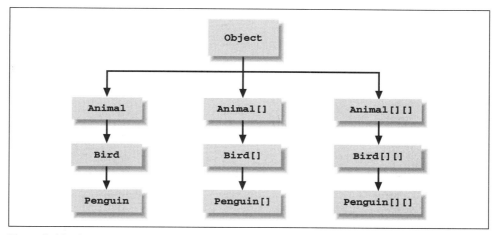

Figure 5–11: Arrays in the Java class hierarchy

Arrays of the same dimension are related to one another in the same manner as their base type classes. In our example, Bird is a subclass of Animal, which means that the Bird[] type is a subtype of Animal[]. In the same way a Bird object can be used in place of an Animal object, a Bird[] array can be assigned to an Animal[] array:

```
Animal [][] animals;
Bird [][] birds = new Bird [10][10];
birds[0][0] = new Bird();

// make animals and birds reference the same array object
animals = birds;
System.out.println( animals[0][0] );                    // prints Bird
```

Because arrays are part of the class hierarchy, we can use `instanceof` to check the type of an array:

```
if ( birds instanceof Animal[][] )                  // yes
```

An array is a subtype of `Object` and can therefore be assigned to `Object` type variables:

```
Object something;
something = animals;
```

Since Java knows the actual type of all objects, you can also cast back if appropriate:

```
animals = (Animal [][])something;
```

Under unusual circumstances, Java may not be able to check the types of objects you place into arrays at compile-time. In those cases, it's possible to receive an `ArrayStoreException` if you try to assign the wrong type of object to an array element. Consider the following:

```
class Dog { ... }
class Poodle extends Dog { ... }
class Chihuahua extends Dog { ... }

Dog [] dogs;
Poodle [] poodles = new Poodle [10];

dogs = poodles;

dogs[3] = new Chihuahua();      // Run-time error, ArrayStoreException
```

Both `Poodle` and `Chihuahua` are subclasses of `Dog`, so an array of `Poodle` objects can therefore be assigned to an array of `Dog` objects, as I described previously. The problem is that an object assignable to an element of an array of type `Dog[]` may not be assignable to an element of an array of type `Poodle`. A `Chihuahua` object, for instance, can be assigned to a `Dog` element because it's a subtype of `Dog`, but not to a `Poodle` element.[*]

---

[*] In some sense this could be considered a tiny hole in the Java type system. It doesn't occur elsewhere in Java, only with arrays. This is because array objects exhibit *covariance* in overriding their assignment and extraction methods. Covariance allows array subclasses to override methods with arguments or return values that are subtypes of the overridden methods, where the methods would normally be overloaded or prohibited. This allows array subclasses to operate on their base types with type safety, but also means that subclasses have different capabilities than their parents, leading to the problem shown above. The Java design team is aware of this hole and is working on a solution.

6

Threads

Threads have been around for some time, but few programmers have actually worked with them. There is even some debate over whether or not the average programmer can use threads effectively. In Java, working with threads can be easy and productive. In fact, threads provide the only way to effectively handle a number of tasks. So it's important that you become familiar with threads early in your exploration of Java.

Threads are integral to the way Java works. We've already seen that an applet's `paint()` method isn't called by the applet itself, but by another thread within the interpreter. At any given time, there may be many such background threads, performing activities in parallel with your application. In fact, it's easy to get a half dozen or more threads running in an applet without even trying, simply by requesting images, updating the screen, playing audio, and so on. But these things happen behind the scenes; you don't normally have to worry about them. In this chapter, we'll talk about writing applications that create and use their own threads explicitly.

Introducing Threads

Conceptually, a thread is a flow of control within a program. A thread is similar to the more familiar notion of a process, except that multiple threads within the same application share much of the same state—in particular, they run in the same address space. It's not unlike a golf course, which can be used by many players at the same time. Sharing the same address space means that threads share instance variables, but not local variables, just like players share the golf course, but not personal things like clubs and balls.

Multiple threads in an application have the same problems as the players sharing a golf course: in a word, synchronization. Just as you can't have two sets of players blindly playing the same green at the same time, you can't have several threads trying to access the same variables without some kind of coordination. Someone is bound to get hurt. A thread can reserve the right to use an object until it's finished with its task, just as a golf party gets exclusive rights to the green until it's done. And a thread that is more important can raise its priority, asserting its right to play through.

The devil is in the details, or course, and those details have historically made threads difficult to use. Java makes creating, controlling, and coordinating threads simple. When creating a new thread is the best way to accomplish some task, it should be as easy as adding a new component to your application.

It is common to stumble over threads when you first look at them, because creating a thread exercises many of your new Java skills all at once. You can avoid confusion by remembering there are always two players involved in running a thread: a Java language object that represents the thread itself and an arbitrary target object that contains the method the thread is to execute. Later, you will see that it is possible to play some sleight of hand and combine these two roles, but that special case just changes the packaging, not the relationship.

The Thread Class and the Runnable Interface

A new thread is born when we create an instance of the `java.lang.Thread` class. The `Thread` object represents a real thread in the Java interpreter and serves as a handle for controlling and synchronizing its execution. With it, we can start the thread, stop the thread, or suspend it temporarily. The constructor for the `Thread` class accepts information about where the thread should begin its execution. Conceptually, we would like to simply tell it what method to run, but since there are no pointers to methods in Java, we can't specify one directly. Instead, we have to take a short detour and use the `Runnable` interface to create an object that contains a "runnable" method.

An object that wants to serve as the target of a `Thread` can declare that it has an appropriate executable method by implementing the `java.lang.Runnable` interface. `Runnable` defines a single, general-purpose method:

```
public interface Runnable {
  abstract public void run();
}
```

Every thread begins its life by executing a `run()` method in a particular object. `run()` is a rather mundane method that can hold an arbitrary body of code. It is `public`, takes no arguments, has no return value, and is not allowed to throw any exceptions.

Any class can contain an appropriate run() method, simply by declaring that it implements the Runnable interface. An instance of this class is then a runnable object that can serve as the target of a new Thread. In this way, we can effectively run a method in any object we want.

Creating and starting threads

A newly born Thread remains idle until we give it a figurative slap on the bottom by calling its start() method. The thread then wakes up and proceeds to execute the run() method of its target object. start() can be called only once in the lifetime of a Thread. Once a thread starts, it continues running until the target object's run() method completes, or we call the thread's stop() method to kill the thread permanently. A little later, we will look at some other methods you can use to control the thread's progress while it is running.

Now let's look at an example. The following class, Animation, implements a run() method to drive its drawing loop:

```
class Animation implements Runnable {
    ...
    public void run() {

        while ( true ) {
            // Draw Frames
            ...
            repaint();
        }
    }
}
```

To use it, we create a Thread object with an instance of Animation as its target object, and invoke its start() method. We can perform these steps explicitly, as in the following:

```
Animation happy = new Animation("Mr. Happy");
Thread myThread = new Thread( happy );
myThread.start();
...
```

Here we have created an instance of our Animation class and passed it as the argument to the constructor for myThread. When we call the start() method, myThread begins to execute Animation's run() method. Let the show begin!

The above situation is not terribly object oriented. More often, we want an object to handle its own thread, as shown in Figure 6-1.

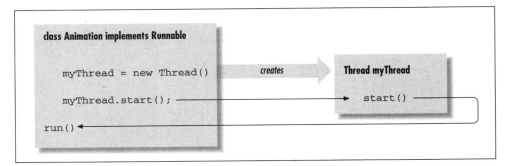

Figure 6–1: Interaction between Animation and its Thread

Figure 6–1 depicts a Runnable object that creates and starts its own Thread. We can have our Animation class perform these actions in its constructor:

```
class Animation implements Runnable {

    Thread myThread;

    Animation (String name) {
        myThread = new Thread( this );
        myThread.start();
    }
    . . .
```

In this case, the argument we pass to the Thread constructor is this, the current object instance. We keep the Thread reference in the instance variable myThread, in case we want to stop the show, or exercise some other kind of control.

A natural born thread

The Runnable interface lets us make an arbitrary object the target of a thread, as we did above. This is the most important, general usage of the Thread class. In most situations where you need to use threads, you'll create a class that implements the Runnable interface. I'd be remiss, however, if I didn't show you the other technique for creating a thread. Another design option is to make our target class a subclass of a type that is already runnable. The Thread class itself implements the Runnable interface; it has its own run() method we can override to make it do something useful:

```
class Animation extends Thread {
    . . .

    public void run() {
        while (true ) {
            // Draw Frames
```

```
        . . .
        repaint();
      }
   }
}
```

The skeleton of our `Animation` class above looks much the same as before, except that our class is now a kind of `Thread`. To go along with this scheme, the default (empty) constructor of the `Thread` class makes itself the default target. That is, by default, the `Thread` executes its own `run()` method when we call the `start()` method, as shown in Figure 6–2. Note that our subclass must override the `run()` method in the `Thread` class because `Thread` simply defines an empty `run()` method.

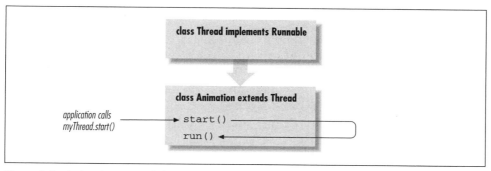

Figure 6–2: Animation as a subclass of Thread

Now we create an instance of `Animation` and call its `start()` method:

```
Animation bouncy = new Animation("Bouncy");
bouncy.start();
```

Alternatively, we can have the `Animation` object start itself when it is created, as before:

```
class Animation extends Thread {

    Animation (String name) {
        start();
    }
    . . .
```

Here our `Animation` object just calls its own `start()` method when it is created.

Subclassing `Thread` probably seems like a convenient way to bundle a `Thread` and its target `run()` method. However, as always, you should let good object-oriented design dictate how you structure your classes. In most cases, a specific run() method is probably closely related to the functionality of a particular class in your application, so you should implement run() in that class. This technique has the added advantage of allowing run() to access any private variables and methods it might need in the class.

If you subclass Thread to implement a thread, you are saying you need a new type of object that is a kind of Thread. While there is something unnaturally satisfying about making an object primarily concerned with performing a single task (like animation), the actual situations where you'll want to create a subclass of Thread should be rather rare. If you find you're subclassing Thread left and right, you may want to examine whether you are falling into the design trap of making objects that are simply glorified functions.

Controlling Threads

We have seen the start() method used to bring a newly created Thread to life. Three other methods let us control a Thread's execution: stop(), suspend(), and resume(). None of these methods take any arguments; they all operate on the current thread object. The stop() method complements start(); it destroys the thread. start() and stop() can be called only once in the life of a Thread. By contrast, the suspend() and resume() methods can be used to arbitrarily pause and then restart the execution of a Thread.

Often, for simple tasks, it is easy enough to throw away a thread when we want to stop it and simply create a new one when want to proceed again. suspend() and resume() can be used in situations where the Thread's setup is very expensive. For example, if creating the thread involves opening a socket and setting up some elaborate communication, it probably makes more sense to use suspend() and resume() with this thread.

Another common need is to put a thread to sleep for some period of time. Thread.sleep() is a static method of the Thread class that causes the currently executing thread to delay for a specified number of milliseconds:

```
try {
    Thread.sleep ( 1000 );
}
catch ( InterruptedException e ) {
}
```

Thread.sleep() throws an InterruptedException if it is interrupted by another Thread.* When a thread is asleep, or otherwise blocked on input of some

---

* The Thread class contains an interrupt() method to allow one thread to interrupt another thread, but this functionality is not implemented in Java 1.0.

kind, it doesn't consume CPU time or compete with other threads for processing. We'll talk more about thread priority and scheduling later.

A Thread's Life

A `Thread` continues to execute until one of the following things happens:

- It returns from its target `run()` method
- It's interrupted by an uncaught exception
- Its `stop()` method is called

So what happens if the `run()` method for a thread never terminates, and the application that started the thread never calls its `stop()` method? The answer is that the thread lives on, even after the application that created it has finished. This means we have to be aware of how our threads eventually terminate, or an application can end up leaving orphaned threads that unnecessarily consume resources.

In many cases, what we really want is to create background threads that do simple, periodic tasks in an application. The `setDaemon()` method can be used to mark a `Thread` as a daemon thread that should be killed and discarded when no other application threads remain. Normally, the Java interpreter continues to run until all threads have completed. But when daemon threads are the only threads still alive, the interpreter will exit.

Here's a devilish example of using daemon threads:

```
class Devil extends Thread {

    Devil() {
        setDaemon( true );
        start();
    }

    public void run() {
        // Perform evil tasks
        ...
    }
}
```

In the above example, the `Devil` thread sets its daemon status when it is created. If any `Devil` threads remain when our application is otherwise complete, Java kills them for us. We don't have to worry about cleaning them up.

Daemon threads are primarily useful in standalone Java applications and in the implementation of the Java system itself, but not in applets. Since an applet runs inside of another Java application, any daemon threads it creates will continue to live until the controlling application exits—probably not the desired effect.

Threading Applets

Applets are embeddable Java applications that are expected to be able to start and stop themselves on command. Unlike threads, applets can be started and stopped any number of times. A Java-enabled Web browser normally starts an applet when the applet is displayed and stops it when the user moves to another page or scrolls the applet out of view. In general, we would like an applet to cease its nonessential activity when it is stopped, and resume it when started again. (See Chapter 10 for a complete discussion of applets).

In this section, we will build `UpdateApplet`, a simple base class for an `Applet` that maintains a `Thread` to automatically update its display at regular intervals. `UpdateApplet` handles the basic starting and stopping behavior for us, as shown below.

```
public class UpdateApplet extends java.applet.Applet
    implements Runnable {

    private Thread updateThread;
    int updateInterval = 1000;

    public void run() {
        while ( true ) {
            try {
                Thread.sleep( updateInterval );
            }
            catch (InterruptedException e ) { }

            repaint();
        }
    }

    public void start() {
        if ( updateThread == null ) {
            updateThread = new Thread(this);
            updateThread.start();
        }
    }

    public void stop() {
        if ( updateThread != null ) {
            updateThread.stop();
            updateThread = null;
        }
    }
}
```

UpdateApplet is a Runnable object that alternately sleeps and calls its repaint() method. It has two other public methods: start() and stop(). These are methods of the Applet class we are overriding; do not confuse them with the similarly named methods of the Thread class. These start() and stop() methods are called by the Java environment to tell the applet when it should and should not be running.

UpdateApplet illustrates an environmentally friendly way to deal with threads in a simple applet. UpdateApplet kills its thread each time the applet is stopped and recreates it if the applet is restarted. When UpdateApplet's start() method is called, we first check to make sure there is no currently executing updateThread. We then create one to begin our execution. When our applet is subsequently stopped, we kill the thread by invoking its stop() method and throw away the reference by setting it to null. Setting updateThread to null serves both to allow the garbage collector to clean up the dead Thread object, and to indicate to UpdateApplet's start() method that the thread is gone.

In truth, an Applet's start() and stop() methods are guaranteed to be called in sequence. As a result, we shouldn't have to check for the existence of updateThread in start() (it should always be null). However, it's good programming practice to perform the test. If we didn't, and for some reason stop() were to fail at its job, we might inadvertently start a lot of threads.

With UpdateApplet doing all of the work for us, we can now create the world's simplest clock applet with just a few lines of code. Figure 6–3 shows our Clock. (This might be a good one to run on your Java wrist watch.).

```
public class Clock extends UpdateApplet {
    public void paint( java.awt.Graphics g ) {
        g.drawString( new java.util.Date().toString(), 10, 25 );
    }
}
```

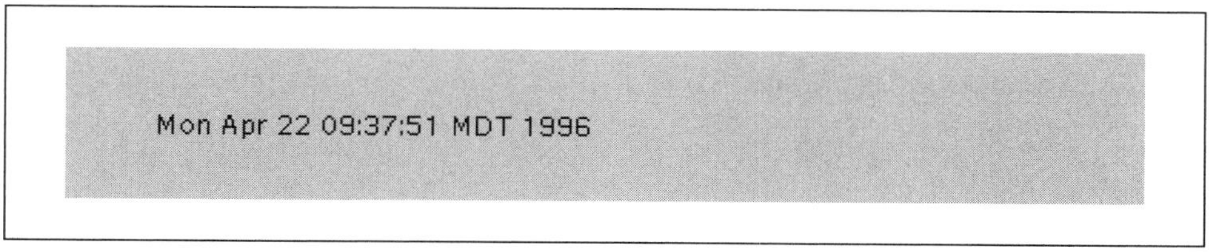

Mon Apr 22 09:37:51 MDT 1996

Figure 6–3: The clock applet

The java.util.Date().toString() sequence simply creates a string that contains the current time; we'll see where this code comes from in Chapter 7.

Our `Clock` applet provides a good example of a simple thread; we don't mind throwing it away and subsequently rebuilding it if the user should happen to wander on and off of our Web page a few times. But what if the task that our thread handles isn't so simple? What if, for instance, we have to open a socket and establish a connection with another system? One solution is to use `Thread`'s `suspend()` and `resume()` methods, as I'll show you momentarily.

Now if you've been wondering why we've been using `stop()` to kill the thread, rather than using the `suspend()` and `resume()` methods all along, here's the explanation you've been waiting for. The problem with applets is that we have no control over how a user navigates Web pages. For example, say a user scrolls our applet out of view, and we use `suspend()` to suspend the applet. Now we have no way of ensuring that the user will bring the applet back into view before moving on to another page. And actually, the same situation would occur if the user simply moves on to another page and never comes back.

If we call `suspend()`, we'd really like to make sure we call `resume()` at a later date, or we'll end up leaving the thread hanging in permanent suspense. But we have no way of knowing if the applet will ever be restarted, so just putting a call to `resume()` in the applet's `start()` method won't work. Leaving the suspended thread around forever might not hurt us, but it's not good programming practice to be wasteful. What we need is a way to guarantee we can clean up our mess if the applet is never used again. What to do?

There is a solution for this dilemma, but in many cases, like with our simple `Clock`, it's just easier to use `stop()`, with a subsequent call to `start()` if necessary. In cases where it is expensive to set up and tear down a thread, we could make the following modifications to `UpdateApplet`:

```
public void start() {
    if ( updateThread == null ) {
        updateThread = new Thread(this);
        updateThread.start();
    }
    else
        updateThread.resume();
}

public void stop() {
    updateThread.suspend();
}

public void destroy() {
    if ( updateThread != null ) {
        updateThread.stop();
        updateThread = null;
    }
}
```

These modifications change `UpdateApplet` so that it suspends and restarts its `updateThread`, rather than killing and recreating it. The new `start()` method creates the thread and calls `start()` if `updateThread` is `null`; otherwise it assumes that the thread has been suspended, so it calls `resume()`. The applet's `stop()` method simply suspends the thread by calling `suspend()`.

What's new here is the `destroy()` method. This is another method that `UpdateApplet` inherits from the `Applet` class. The method is called by the Java environment when the applet is going to be removed (often from a cache). It provides a place where we can free up any resources the applet is holding. This is the perfect place to cut the suspense and clean up after our thread. In our `destroy()` method, we check to see that the thread exists, and if it does, we call `stop()` to kill it and set its reference to `null`.

Synchronization

Every thread has a life of its own. Normally, a thread goes about its business without any regard for what other threads in the application are doing. Threads may be time-sliced, which means they can run in arbitrary spurts and bursts as directed by the operating system. On a multiprocessor system, it is even possible for many different threads to be running simultaneously on different CPUs. This section is about coordinating the activities of two or more threads, so they can work together and not collide in their use of the same address space.

Java provides a few simple structures for synchronizing the activities of threads. They are all based on the concept of *monitors*, a widely used synchronization scheme developed by C.A.R. Hoare. You don't have to know the details about how monitors work to be able to use them, but it may help you to have a picture in mind.

A monitor is essentially a lock. The lock is attached to a resource that many threads may need to access, but that should be accessed by only one thread at a time. It's not unlike a public restroom at a gas station. If the resource is not being used, the thread can acquire the lock and access the resource. By the same token, if the restroom is unlocked, you can enter and lock the door. When the thread is done, it relinquishes the lock, just as you unlock the door and leave it open for the next person. However, if another thread already has the lock for the resource, all other threads have to wait until the current thread finishes and releases the lock, just as if the restroom is locked when you arrive, you have to wait until the current occupant is done and unlocks the door.

Fortunately, Java makes the process of synchronizing access to resources quite easy. The language handles setting up and acquiring locks; all you have to do is specify which resources require locks.

Serializing Methods

The most common need for synchronization among threads in Java is to serialize their access to some resource, namely an object. In other words, synchronization makes sure only one thread at a time can perform certain activities that manipulate an object. In Java, every object has a lock associated with it. To be more specific, every class and every instance of a class has its own lock. The synchronized keyword marks places where a thread must acquire the lock before proceeding.

For example, say we implemented a SpeechSynthesizer class that contains a say() method. We don't want multiple threads calling say() at the same time or we wouldn't be able to understand anything being said. So we mark the say() method as synchronized, which means that a thread has to acquire the lock on the SpeechSynthesizer object before it can speak:

```
class SpeechSynthesizer {

    synchronized void say( String words ) {
        // Speak
    }
}
```

Because say() is an instance method, a thread has to acquire the lock on the particular SpeechSynthesizer instance it is using before it can invoke the say() method. When say() has completed, it gives up the lock, which allows the next waiting thread to acquire the lock and run the method. Note that it doesn't matter whether the thread is owned by the SpeechSynthesizer itself or some other object; every thread has to acquire the same lock, that of the SpeechSynthesizer instance. If say() were a class (static) method instead of an instance method, we could still mark it as synchronized. But in this case as there is no instance object involved, the lock would be on the class object itself.

Often, you want to synchronize multiple methods of the same class, so that only one of the methods modifies or examines parts of the class at a time. All static synchronized methods in a class use the same class object lock. By the same token, all instance methods in a class use the same instance object lock. In this way, Java can guarantee that only one of a set of synchronized methods is running at a time. For example, a SpreadSheet class might contain a number of instance variables that represent cell values, as well as some methods that manipulate the cells in a row:

```
class SpreadSheet {

    int cellA1, cellA2, cellA3;

    synchronized int sumRow() {
        return cellA1 + cellA2 + cellA3;
    }

    synchronized void setRow( int a1, int a2, int a3 ) {
        cellA1 = a1;
        cellA2 = a2;
        cellA3 = a3;
    }
    ...
}
```

In this example, both methods setRow() and sumRow() access the cell values. You can see that problems might arise if one thread were changing the values of the variables in setRow() at the same moment another thread was reading the values in sumRow(). To prevent this, we have marked both methods as synchronized. When threads are synchronized, only one will be run at a time. If a thread is in the middle of executing setRow() when another thread calls sumRow(), the second thread waits until the first one is done executing setRow() before it gets to run sumRow(). This synchronization allows us to preserve the consistency of the SpreadSheet. And the best part is that all of this locking and waiting is handled by Java; it's transparent to the programmer.

In addition to synchronizing entire methods, the synchronized keyword can be used in a special construct to guard arbitrary blocks of code. In this form it also takes an explicit argument that specifies the object for which it is to acquire a lock:

```
synchronized ( myObject ) {
    // Functionality that needs to be synced
    ...
}
```

The code block above can appear in any method. When it is reached, the thread has to acquire the lock on myObject before proceeding. In this way, we can have methods (or parts of methods) in different classes synchronized the same as methods in the same class.

A synchronized method is, therefore, equivalent to a method with its statements synchronized on the current object. Thus:

```
synchronized void myMethod () {
    ...
}
```

is equivalent to:

```
void myMethod () {
    synchronized ( this ) {
        ...
    }
}
```

wait() and notify()

With the `synchronized` keyword, we can serialize the execution of complete methods and blocks of code. The `wait()` and `notify()` methods of the `Object` class extend this capability. Every object in Java is a subclass of `Object`, so every object inherits these methods. By using `wait()` and `notify()`, a thread can give up its hold on a lock at an arbitrary point, and then wait for another thread to give it back before continuing. All of the coordinated activity still happens inside of synchronized blocks, and still only one thread is executing at a given time.

By executing `wait()` from a synchronized block, a thread gives up its hold on the lock and goes to sleep. A thread might do this if it needs to wait for something to happen in another part of the application, as you'll see shortly. Later, when the necessary event happens, the thread that is running it calls `notify()` from a block synchronized on the same object. Now the first thread wakes up and begins trying to acquire the lock again.

When the first thread manages to reacquire the lock, it continues from the point it left off. However, the thread that waited may not get the lock immediately (or perhaps ever). It depends on when the second thread eventually releases the lock, and which thread manages to snag it next. Note also, that the first thread won't wake up from the `wait()` unless another thread calls `notify()`. There is an overloaded version of `wait()`, however, that allows us to specify a timeout period. If another thread doesn't call `notify()` in the specified period, the waiting thread automatically wakes up.

Let's look at a simple scenario to see what's going on. In the following example, we'll assume there are three threads—one waiting to execute each of the three synchronized methods of the `MyThing` class. We'll call them the `waiter`, `notifier`, and `related` threads, respectively. Here's a code fragment to illustrate:

```
class MyThing {

    synchronized void waiterMethod() {
        // Do some stuff

        // Now we need to wait for notifier to do something
        wait();

        // Continue where we left off
```

```
    }

    synchronized void notifierMethod() {
        // Do some stuff

        // Notify waiter that we've done it
        notify();

        // Do more things
    }

    synchronized void relatedMethod() {
        // Do some related stuff
    }
```

Let's assume `waiter` gets through the gate first and begins executing `waiter-Method()`. The two other threads are initially blocked, trying to acquire the lock for the `MyThing` object. When `waiter` executes the `wait()` method, it relinquishes its hold on the lock and goes to sleep. Now there are now two viable threads waiting for the lock. Which thread gets it depends on several factors, including chance and the priorities of the threads. (We'll discuss thread scheduling in the next section).

Let's say that `notifier` is the next thread to acquire the lock, so it begins to run. `waiter` continues to sleep and `related` languishes, waiting for its turn. When `notifier` executes the call to `notify()`, Java prods the `waiter` thread, effectively telling it something has changed. `waiter` then wakes up and rejoins `related` in vying for the `MyThing` lock. Note that it doesn't actually receive the lock; it just changes from saying "leave me alone" to "I want the lock."

At this point, `notifier` still owns the lock and continues to hold it until it leaves its synchronized method (or perhaps executes a `wait()` itself). When it finally completes, the other two methods get to fight over the lock. `waiter` would like to continue executing `waiterMethod()` from the point it left off, while `unrelated`, which has been patient, would like to get started. We'll let you choose your own ending for the story.

For each call to `notify()`, Java wakes up just one method that is asleep in a `wait()` call. If there are multiple threads waiting, Java picks the first thread on a first-in, first-out basis. The `Object` class also provides a `notifyAll()` call to wake up all waiting threads. In most cases, you'll probably want to use `notifyAll()` rather than `notify()`. Keep in mind that `notify()` really means "Hey, something related to this object has changed. The condition you are waiting for may have changed, so check it again." In general, there is no reason to assume only one thread at a time is interested in the change or able to act upon it. Different threads might look upon whatever has changed in different ways.

Often, our `waiter` thread is waiting for a particular condition to change and we will want to sit in a loop like the following:

```
...
while ( condition != true )
    wait();
...
```

Other synchronized threads call `notify()` or `notifyAll()` when they have modified the environment so that `waiter` can check the condition again. This is the civilized alternative to polling and sleeping, as you'll see the following example.

The Message Passer

Now we'll illustrate a classic interaction between two threads: a `Producer` and a `Consumer`. A producer thread creates messages and places them into a queue, while a consumer reads them out and displays them. To be realistic, we'll give the queue a maximum depth. And to make things really interesting, we'll have our consumer thread be lazy and run much slower than the producer. This means that `Producer` occasionally has to stop and wait for `Consumer` to catch up. The example below shows the `Producer` and `Consumer` classes.

```
import java.util.Vector;

class Producer extends Thread {
    static final int MAXQUEUE = 5;
    private Vector messages = new Vector();

    public void run() {
        try {
            while ( true ) {
                putMessage();
                sleep( 1000 );
            }
        }
        catch( InterruptedException e ) { }
    }

    private synchronized void putMessage()
        throws InterruptedException {

        while ( messages.size() == MAXQUEUE )
            wait();
        messages.addElement( new java.util.Date().toString() );
        notify();
    }

    // Called by Consumer
    public synchronized String getMessage()
        throws InterruptedException {
```

```
            notify();
            while ( messages.size() == 0 )
                wait();
            String message = (String)messages.firstElement();
            messages.removeElement( message );
            return message;
        }
    }

class Consumer extends Thread {
    Producer producer;

    Consumer(Producer p) {
        producer = p;
    }

    public void run() {
        try {
            while ( true ) {
                String message = producer.getMessage();
                System.out.println("Got message: " + message);
                sleep( 2000 );
            }
        }
        catch( InterruptedException e ) { }
    }

    public static void main(String args[]) {
        Producer producer = new Producer();
        producer.start();
        new Consumer( producer ).start();
    }
}
```

For convenience, we have included a main() method that runs the complete example in the Consumer class. It creates a Consumer that is tied to a Producer and starts the two classes. You can run the example as follows:

```
% java Consumer
```

The output is the time-stamp messages created by the Producer:

```
Got message: Sun Dec 19 03:35:55 CST 1996
Got message: Sun Dec 19 03:35:56 CST 1996
Got message: Sun Dec 19 03:35:57 CST 1996
...
```

The time stamps initially show a spacing of one second, although they appear every two seconds. Our Producer runs faster than our Consumer. Producer would like to generate a new message every second, while Consumer gets around to reading and displaying a message only every two seconds. Can you see how long it will take the message queue to fill up? What will happen when it does?

Let's look at the code. We are using a few new tools here. Producer and Consumer are subclasses of Thread. It would have been a better design decision to have Producer and Consumer implement the Runnable interface, but we took the slightly easier path and subclassed Thread. You should find it fairly simple to use the other technique; you might try it as an exercise.

The Producer and Consumer classes pass messages through an instance of a java.util.Vector object. We haven't discussed the Vector class yet, but you can think of this one as a queue where we add and remove elements in first-in, first-out order. See Chapter 7 for more information about the Vector class.

The important activity is in the synchronized methods: putMessage() and getMessage(). Although one of the methods is used by the Producer thread and the other by the Consumer thread, they both live in the Producer class because they have to be synchronized on the same object to work together. Here they both implicitly use the Producer object's lock. If the queue is empty, the Consumer blocks in a call in the Producer, waiting for another message.

Another design option would implement the getMessage() method in the Consumer class and use a synchronized code block to explicitly synchronize on the Producer object. In either case, synchronizing on the Producer is important because it allows us to have multiple Consumer objects that feed on the same Producer.

putMessage()'s job is to add a new message to the queue. It can't do this if the queue is already full, so it first checks the number of elements in messages. If there is room, it stuffs in another time stamp. If the queue is at its limit however, putMessage() has to wait until there's space. In this situation, putMessage() executes a wait() and relies on the consumer to call notify() to wake it up after a message has been read. Here we have putMessage() testing the condition in a loop. In this simple example, the test probably isn't necessary; we could assume that when putMessage() wakes up, there is a free spot. However, this test is another example of good programming practice. Before it finishes, putMessage() calls notify() itself to prod any Consumer that might be waiting on an empty queue.

getMessage() retrieves a message for the Consumer. It enters a loop like the Producer's, waiting for the queue to have at least one element before proceeding. If the queue is empty, it executes a wait() and expects the producer to call notify() when more items are available. Notice that getMessage() makes its own unconditional call to notify(). This is a somewhat lazy way of keeping the Producer on its toes, so that the queue should generally be full. Alternatively, getMessage() might test to see if the queue had fallen below a low water mark before waking up the producer.

Now let's add another `Consumer` to the scenario, just to make things really interesting. Most of the necessary changes are in the `Consumer` class; the example below shows the code for the modified class.

```
class Consumer extends Thread {
    Producer producer;
        String name;

    Consumer(String name, Producer producer) {
        this.producer = producer;
        this.name = name;
    }

    public void run() {
        try {
            while ( true ) {
                String message = producer.getMessage();
                System.out.println(name + " got message: " + message);
                sleep( 2000 );
            }
        }
        catch( InterruptedException e ) { }
    }

    public static void main(String args[]) {
        Producer producer = new Producer();
        producer.start();

        // Start two this time
        new Consumer( "One", producer ).start();
        new Consumer( "Two", producer ).start();
    }
}
```

The `Consumer` constructor now takes a string name, to identify each consumer. The `run()` method uses this name in the call to `println()` to identify which consumer received the message.

The only modification to make in the `Producer` code is to change the call to `notify()` in `putMessage()` to a call to `notifyAll()`. Now, instead of the consumer and producer playing tag with the queue, we can have many players waiting on the condition of the queue to change. We might have a number of consumers waiting for a message, or we might have the producer waiting for a consumer to take a message. Whenever the condition of the queue changes, we prod all of the waiting methods to reevaluate the situation by calling `notifyAll()`. Note, however, that we don't need to change the call to `notify()` in `getMessage()`. If a `Consumer` thread is waiting for a message to appear in the queue, it's not possible for the `Producer` to be simultaneously waiting because the queue is full.

Here is some sample output when there are two consumers running, as in the
`main()` method shown above:

```
One got message: Wed Mar 20 20:00:01 CST 1996
Two got message: Wed Mar 20 20:00:02 CST 1996
One got message: Wed Mar 20 20:00:03 CST 1996
Two got message: Wed Mar 20 20:00:04 CST 1996
One got message: Wed Mar 20 20:00:05 CST 1996
Two got message: Wed Mar 20 20:00:06 CST 1996
One got message: Wed Mar 20 20:00:07 CST 1996
Two got message: Wed Mar 20 20:00:08 CST 1996
...
```

We see nice, orderly alternation between the two consumers, as a result of the calls
to `sleep()` in the various methods. Interesting things would happen, however, if
we were to remove all of the calls to `sleep()` and let things run at full speed. The
threads would compete and their behavior would depend on whether or not the
system is using time slicing. On a time-sliced system, there should be a fairly random distribution between the two consumers, while on a non-time-sliced system, a
single consumer could monopolize the messages. And since you're probably wondering about time slicing, let's talk about thread priority and scheduling.

Scheduling and Priority

Java makes certain guarantees as to how its threads are scheduled. Every thread
has a priority value. If, at any time, a thread of a higher priority than the current
thread becomes runnable, it preempts the lower priority thread and begins executing. By default, threads at the same priority are scheduled round robin, which
means once a thread starts to run, it continues until it does one of the following:

Sleeps
  Calls `Thread.sleep()` or `wait()`

Waits for lock
  Waits for a lock in order to run a synchronized method

Blocks on I/O
  Blocks, for example, in a `xread()` or an `accept()` call

Explicitly yields control
  Calls `yield()`

Terminates
  Completes its target method or is terminated by a `stop()` call

This situation looks something like what's shown in Figure 6–4.

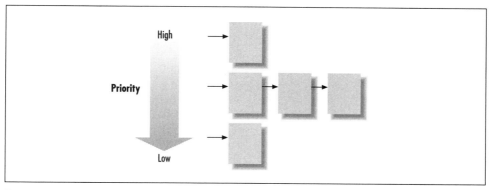

Figure 6–4: Priority preemptive, round robin scheduling

Java leaves certain aspects of scheduling up to the implementation.[*] The main point here is that some, but not all, implementations of Java use time slicing on threads of the same priority.[†] In a time-sliced system, thread processing is chopped up, so that each thread runs for a short period of time before the context is switched to the next thread, as shown in Figure 6–5.

Higher priority threads still preempt lower priority threads in this scheme. The addition of time slicing mixes up the processing among threads of the same priority; on a multiprocessor machine, threads may even be run simultaneously. Unfortunately, this feature can lead to differences in your application's behavior.

Since Java doesn't guarantee time slicing, you shouldn't write code that relies on this type of scheduling; any software you write needs to function under the default round-robin scheduling. But if you're wondering what your particular flavor of Java does, try the following experiment:

```
class Thready {
    public static void main( String args [] ) {
        new MyThread("Foo").start();
        new MyThread("Bar").start();
    }
}
```

---

[*] This implementation-dependent aspect of Java isn't a big deal, since it doesn't hurt for an implementation to add time slicing on top of the default round-robin scheduling. It's actually not hard to create a time-slicing effect by simply having a high-priority thread sleeping for a specified time interval. Every time it wakes up, it interrupts a lower-priority thread and causes processing to shift round robin to the next thread.

[†] As of Java Release 1.0, Sun's Java Interpreter for the Windows 95 and Windows NT platforms uses time slicing, as does the Netscape Navigator Java environment. Sun's Java 1.0 for the Solaris UNIX platforms doesn't.

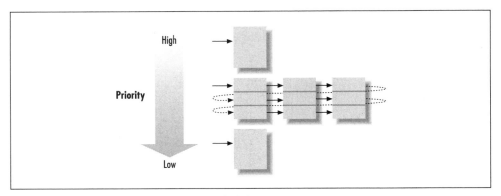

Figure 6–5: Priority preemptive, time-sliced scheduling

```
class MyThread extends Thread {
    String message;

    MyThread ( String message ) {
        this.message = message;
    }

    public void run() {
        while ( true )
            System.out.println( message );
    }
}
```

The Thready class starts up two MyThread objects. Thready is a thread that goes into a hard loop (very bad form) and prints its message. Since we don't specify a priority for either thread, they both inherit the priority of their creator, so they have the same priority. When you run this example, you will see how your Java implementation does it scheduling. Under a round-robin scheme, only "Foo" should be printed; "Bar" never appears. In a time-slicing implementation, you should occasionally see the "Foo" and "Bar" messages alternate.

Priorities

Now let's change the priority of the second thread:

```
class Thready {
    public static void main( String args [] ) {
        new MyThread("Foo").start();

        Thread bar = new MyThread("Bar");
        bar.setPriority( Thread.NORM_PRIORITY + 1 );
        bar.start();
    }
}
```

As you might expect, this changes how our example behaves. Now you may see a few "Foo" messages, but "Bar" should quickly take over and not relinquish control, regardless of the scheduling policy.

Here we have used the `setPriority()` method of the `Thread` class to adjust our thread's priority. The `Thread` class defines three standard priority values, as shown in Table 6–1.

Table 6–1: Thread Priority Values

Value	Definition
MIN_PRIORITY	Minimum priority
NORM_PRIORITY	Normal priority
MAX_PRIORITY	Maximum priority

If you need to change the priority of a thread, you should use one of these values or a close relative value. But let me warn you against using `MAX_PRIORITY` or a close relative value; if you elevate many threads to this priority level, priority will quickly become meaningless. A slight increase in priority should be enough for most needs. For example, specifying `NORM_PRIORITY + 1` in our example is enough to beat out our other thread.

Yielding

As I said earlier, whenever a thread sleeps, waits, or blocks on I/O, it gives up its time slot, and another thread is scheduled. So as long as you don't write methods that use hard loops, all threads should get their due. However, a `Thread` can also give up its time voluntarily with the `yield()` call. We can change our previous example to include a `yield()` on each iteration:

```
class MyThread extends Thread {
    ...

    public void run() {
        while ( true ) {
            System.out.println( message );
            yield();
        }
    }
}
```

Now you should see "Foo" and "Bar" messages alternating one for one. If you have threads that perform very intensive calculations, or otherwise eat a lot of CPU time, you might want to find an appropriate place for them to yield control occasionally. Alternatively, you might want to drop the priority of your intensive thread, so that more important processing can proceed around it.

In this chapter:
- *Strings*
- *Math Utilities*
- *Dates*
- *Vectors and Hashtables*
- *Properties*
- *The Security Manager*

7

Basic Utility Classes

If you've been reading this book sequentially, you've read all about the core Java language constructs, including the object-oriented aspects of the language and the use of threads. Now it's time to shift gears and talk about the Java Application Programming Interface (API), the collection of classes that comes with every Java implementation. The Java API encompasses all the public methods and variables in the classes that comprise the eight core Java packages, listed in Table 7–1. This table also lists the chapters in this book that describe each of the packages.

Table 7–1: Packages of the Java API

Package	Contents	Chapter(s)
java.lang	Basic language classes	4, 5, 6, 7
java.io	Input and output	8
java.util	Utilities and collections classes	7
java.net	Sockets and URLs	9
java.applet	The applet API	10
java.awt	The Abstract Windowing Toolkit	10, 11
java.awt.image	AWT image classes	11

As you can see in Table 7–1, we've already examined some of the classes in java.lang in earlier chapters on the core language constructs. Starting with this chapter, we'll throw open the Java toolbox and begin examining the rest of the classes in the API.

We'll begin our exploration with some of the fundamental language classes in java.lang, including strings and math utilities. Figure 7–1 shows the class hierarchy of the java.lang package.

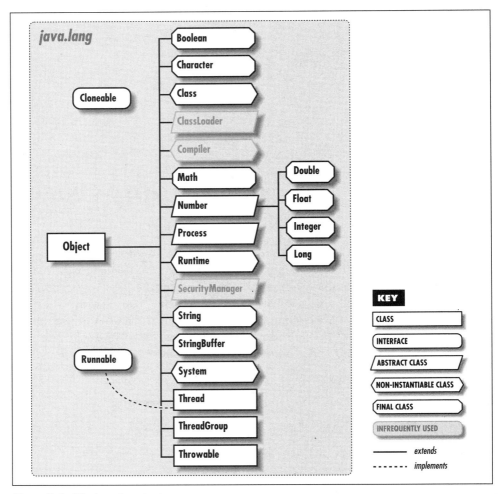

Figure 7–1: The java.lang package

We cover some of the classes in `java.util`, such as classes that support date and time values, random numbers, vectors, and hashtables. Figure 7–2 shows the class hierarchy of the `java.util` package.

Strings

In this section, we take a closer look at the Java `String` class (or more specifically, `java.lang.String`). Because strings are used so extensively throughout Java (or any programming language, for that matter), the Java `String` class has quite a bit of functionality. We'll test drive most of the important features, but before you

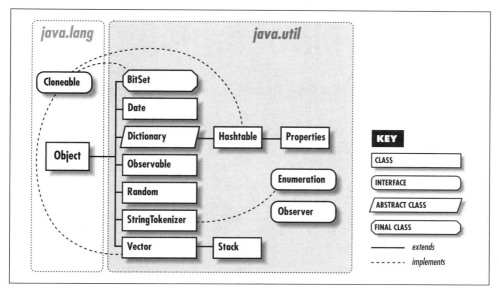

Figure 7–2: The java.util package

go off and write a complex parser or regular expression library, you should probably refer to a Java class reference manual for additional details.

Strings are immutable; once you create a `String` object, you can't change its value. Operations that would otherwise change the characters or the length of a string instead return a new `String` object that copies the needed parts of the original. Because of this feature, strings can be safely shared. Java makes an effort to consolidate identical strings and string literals in the same class into a shared string pool.

String Constructors

To create a string, assign a double-quoted constant to a `String` variable:

```
String quote = "To be or not to be";
```

Java automatically converts the string literal into a `String` object. If you're a C or C++ programmer, you may be wondering if `quote` is null-terminated. This question doesn't make any sense with Java strings. The `String` class actually uses a Java character array internally. It's `private` to the `String` class, so you can't get at the characters and change them. As always, arrays in Java are real objects that know their own length, so `String` objects in Java don't require special terminators (not even internally). If you need to know the length of a `String`, use the `length()` method:

```
int length = quote.length();
```

Strings can take advantage of the only overloaded operator in Java, the + operator, for string concatenation. The following code produces equivalent strings:

```
String name = "John " + "Smith";
String name = "John ".concat("Smith");
```

Literal strings can't span lines in Java source files, but we can concatenate lines to produce the same effect:

```
String poem =
    "'Twas brillig, and the slithy toves\n" +
    "   Did gyre and gimble in the wabe:\n" +
    "All mimsy were the borogoves,\n" +
    "   And the mome raths outgrabe.\n";
```

Of course, embedding lengthy text in source code should now be a thing of the past, given that we can retrieve a `String` from anywhere on the planet via a URL. In Chapter 9, we'll see how to do things like:

```
String poem =
    (String) new URL
        ("http://server/~dodgson/jabberwocky.txt").getContent();
```

In addition to making strings from literal expressions, we can construct a `String` from an array of characters:

```
char [] data = { 'L', 'e', 'm', 'm', 'i', 'n', 'g' };
String lemming = new String( data );
```

Or from an array of bytes:

```
byte [] data = { 65, 66, 67 };
String abc = new String(data, 0);
```

The second argument to the `String` constructor for byte arrays is an integer. It's used to fill the high bytes of the string's Unicode character representation. Unless you know something about Unicode, you probably want this value to be zero.

Strings from Things

We can get the string representation of most things with the static `String.valueOf()` method. Various overloaded versions of this method give us string values for all of the primitive types:

```
String one = String.valueOf( 1 );
String two = String.valueOf( 2.0f );
String notTrue = String.valueOf( false );
```

All objects in Java have a `toString()` method, inherited from the `Object` class (see Chapter 5). For class-type references, `String.valueOf()` invokes the object's `toString()` method to get its string representation. If the reference is `null`, the result is the literal string "null":

```
String date = String.valueOf( new Date() );
System.out.println( date );
// Sun Dec 19 05:45:34 CST 1999

date = null;
System.out.println( date );
// null
```

Things from Strings

Producing primitives like numbers from `String` objects is not a function of the `String` class. For that we need the primitive wrapper classes; they are described in the next section on the `Math` class. The wrapper classes provide `valueOf()` methods that produce an object from a `String`, as well as corresponding methods to retrieve the value in various primitive forms. Two examples are:

```
int i = Integer.valueOf("123").intValue();
double d = Double.valueOf("123.0").doubleValue();
```

In the above code, the `Integer.valueOf()` call yields an `Integer` object that represents the value 123. An `Integer` object can provide its primitive value in the form of an `int` with the `intValue()` method.

The `charAt()` method of the `String` class lets us get at the characters of a `String` in an array-like fashion:

```
String s = "Newton";

for ( int i = 0; i < s.length(); i++ )
    System.out.println( s.charAt( i ) );
```

This code prints the characters of the string one at a time. Alternatively, we can get the characters all at once with `toCharArray()`. Here's a way to save typing a bunch of single quotes:

```
char [] abcs = "abcdefghijklmnopqrstuvwxyz".toCharArray();
```

Comparisons

Just as in C, you can't compare strings for equality with "==" because as in C, strings are actually references. If your Java compiler doesn't happen to coalesce multiple instances of the same string literal to a single string pool item, even the expression `"foo" == "foo"` will return `false`. Comparisons with <, >, <=, and >= don't work at all, because Java can't convert references to integers.

Use the `equals()` method to compare strings:

```
String one = "Foo";

char [] c = { 'F', 'o', 'o' };
String two = new String ( c );

if ( one.equals( two ) )                // yes
```

An alternate version, `equalsIgnoreCase()`, can be used to check the equivalence of strings in a case-insensitive way:

```
String one = "FOO";
String two = "foo";

if ( one.equalsIgnoreCase( two ) )      // yes
```

The `compareTo()` method compares the lexical value of the `String` against another `String`. It returns an integer that is less than, equal to, or greater than zero, just like the C routine `strcmp()`:

```
String abc = "abc";
String def = "def";
String num = "123";

if ( abc.compareTo( def ) < 0 )         // yes

if ( abc.compareTo( abc ) == 0 )        // yes

if ( abc.compareTo( num ) > 0 )         // yes
```

On some systems, the behavior of lexical comparison is complex, and obscure alternative character sets exist. Java avoids this problem by comparing characters strictly by their position in the Unicode specification.

Searching

The `String` class provides several methods for finding substrings within a string. The `startsWith()` and `endsWith()` methods compare an argument `String` with the beginning and end of the `String`, respectively:

```
String url = "http://foo.bar.com/";
if ( url.startsWith("http:") )
    // do HTTP
```

Overloaded versions of `indexOf()` search for the first occurrence of a character or substring:

```
int i = abcs.indexOf( 'p' );           // i = 15
int i = abcs.indexOf( "def" );         // i = 3
```

Correspondingly, overloaded versions of `lastIndexOf()` search for the last occurrence of a character or substring.

Editing

A number of methods operate on the `String` and return a new `String` as a result. While this is useful, you should be aware that creating lots of strings in this manner can affect performance. If you need to modify a string often, you should use the `StringBuffer` class, as I'll discuss shortly.

`trim()` is a useful method that removes leading and trailing white space (i.e., carriage return, newline, and tab) from the `String`:

```
String abc = "   abc   ";
abc = abc.trim();                       // "abc"
```

In the above example, we have thrown away the original `String` (with excess white space), so it will be garbage collected.

The `toUpperCase()` and `toLowerCase()` methods return a new `String` of the appropriate case:

```
String foo = "FOO".toLowerCase();
String FOO = foo.toUpperCase();
```

`substring()` returns a specified range of characters. The starting index is inclusive; the ending is exclusive:

```
String abcs = "abcdefghijklmnopqrstuvwxyz";
String cde = abcs.substring(2, 5);       // "cde"
```

String Method Summary

Many people complain when they discover the Java `String` class is `final` (i.e., it can't be subclassed). There is a lot of functionality in `String`, and it would be nice to be able to modify its behavior directly. Unfortunately, there is also a serious need to optimize and rely on the performance of `String` objects. As I discussed in Chapter 5, the Java compiler can optimize `final` classes by inlining methods when appropriate. The implementation of `final` classes can also be trusted by classes that work closely together, allowing for special cooperative optimizations. If you want to make a new string class that uses basic `String` functionality, use a `String` object in your class and provide methods that delegate method calls to the appropriate `String` methods.

Table 7–2 summarizes the methods provided by the `String` class.

Table 7–2: String Methods

Method	Functionality
charAt()	Gets at a particular character in the string
compareTo()	Compares the string with another string
concat()	Concatenates the string with another string
copyValueOf()	Returns a string equivalent to the specified character array
endsWith()	Checks if the string ends with a suffix
equals()	Compares the string with another string
equalsIgnoreCase()	Compares the string with another string and ignores case
getBytes()	Copies characters from the string into a byte array
getChars()	Copies characters from the string into a character array
hashCode()	Returns a hashcode for the string
indexOf()	Searches for the first occurrence of a character or substring in the string
intern()	Fetches a unique instance of the string from a global shared string pool
lastIndexOf()	Searches for the last occurrence of a character or substring in a string
length()	Returns the length of the string
regionMatches()	Checks whether a region of the string matches the specified region of another string
replace()	Replaces all occurrences of a character in the string with another character
startsWith()	Checks if the string starts with a prefix
substring()	Returns a substring from the string
toCharArray()	Returns the array of characters from the string
toLowerCase()	Converts the string to uppercase
toString()	Converts the string to a string
toUpperCase()	Converts the string to lowercase
trim()	Removes the leading and trailing white space from the string
valueOf()	Returns a string representation of a value

java.lang.StringBuffer

The `java.lang.StringBuffer` class is a growable buffer for characters. It's an efficient alternative to code like the following:

```
String ball = "Hello";
ball = ball + " there.";
ball = ball + " How are you?";
```

The above example repeatedly produces new `String` objects. This means that the character array must be copied over and over, which can adversely affect performance. A more economical alternative is to use a `StringBuffer` object and its `append()` method:

```
StringBuffer ball = new StringBuffer("Hello");
ball.append(" there.");
ball.append(" How are you?");
```

The `StringBuffer` class actually provides a number of overloaded `append()` methods, for appending various types of data to the buffer.

We can get a `String` from the `StringBuffer` with its `toString()` method:

```
String message = ball.toString();
```

`StringBuffer` also provides a number of overloaded `insert()` methods for inserting various types of data at a particular location in the string buffer.

The `String` and `StringBuffer` classes cooperate, so that even in this last operation, no copy has to be made. The string data is shared between the objects, unless and until we try to change it in the `StringBuffer`.

So, when should you use a `StringBuffer` instead of a `String`? If you need to keep adding characters to a string, use a `StringBuffer`; it's designed to efficiently handle such modifications. You'll still have to convert the `StringBuffer` to a `String` when you need to use any of the methods in the `String` class. You can print a `StringBuffer` directly using `System.out.println()` because `println()` calls the `toString()` for you.

Another thing you should know about `StringBuffer` methods is that they are thread-safe, just like all public methods in the Java API. This means that any time you modify a `StringBuffer`, you don't have to worry about another thread coming along and messing up the string while you are modifying it. If you recall our discussion of synchronization in Chapter 6, you know that being thread-safe means that only one thread at a time can change the state of a `StringBuffer` instance.

On a final note, I mentioned earlier that strings take advantage of the single overloaded operator in Java, +, for concatenation. You might be interested to know that the compiler uses a `StringBuffer` to implement concatenation. Consider the following expression:

```
String foo = "To " + "be " + "or";
```

This is equivalent to:

```
String foo = new
   StringBuffer().append("To ").append("be ").append("or").toString();
```

This kind of chaining of expressions is one of the things operator overloading hides in other languages.

java.util.StringTokenizer

A common programming task involves parsing a string of text into words or "tokens" that are separated by some set of delimiter characters. The `java.util.StringTokenizer` class is a utility that does just this. The following example reads words from the string `text`:

```
String text = "Now is the time for all good men (and women)...";
StringTokenizer st = new StringTokenizer( text );

while ( st.hasMoreTokens() )  {
    String word = st.nextToken();
    ...
}
```

First, we create a new `StringTokenizer` from the `String`. We invoke the `has-MoreTokens()` and `nextToken()` methods to loop over the words of the text. By default, we use white space (i.e., carriage return, newline, and tab) as delimiters.

The `StringTokenizer` implements the `java.util.Enumeration` interface, which means that `StringTokenizer` also implements two more general methods for accessing elements: `hasMoreElements()` and `nextElement()`. These methods are defined by the `Enumeration` interface; they provide a standard way of returning a sequence of values, as we'll discuss a bit later. The advantage of `nextToken()` is that it returns a `String`, while `nextElement()` returns an `Object`. The `Enumeration` interface is implemented by many items that return sequences or collections of objects, as you'll see when we talk about hashtables and vectors later in the chapter. Those of you who have used the C `strtok()` function should appreciate how useful this object-oriented equivalent is.

You can also specify your own set of delimiter characters in the `StringTokenizer` constructor, using another `String` argument to the constructor. Any combination of the specified characters is treated as the equivalent of white space for tokenizing:

```
text = "http://foo.bar.com/";
tok = new StringTokenizer( text, "/:" );

if ( tok.countTokens() < 2 )                 // bad URL

String protocol = tok.nextToken();           // protocol = "http"
String host = tok.nextToken();               // host = "foo.bar.com"
```

The example above parses a URL specification to get at the protocol and host components. The characters "/" and ":" are used as separators. The `countTokens()` method provides a fast way to see how many tokens will be returned by `nextToken()`, without actually creating the `String` objects.

An overloaded form of nextToken() accepts a string that defines a new delimiter set for that and subsequent reads. And finally, the StringTokenizer constructor accepts a flag that specifies that separator characters are to be returned individually as tokens themselves. By default, the token separators are not returned.

Math Utilities

Java supports integer and floating-point arithmetic directly. Higher-level math operations are supported through the java.lang.Math class. Java provides wrapper classes for all primitive data types, so you can treat them as objects if necessary. Java also provides the java.util.Random class for generating random numbers.

Java handles errors in integer arithmetic by throwing an ArithmeticException:

```
int zero = 0;

try {
    int i = 72 / zero;
}
catch ( ArithmeticException e ) {        // division by zero
}
```

To generate the error in the above example, we created the intermediate variable zero. The compiler is somewhat crafty and would have caught us if we had blatantly tried to perform a division by zero.

Floating-point arithmetic expressions, on the other hand, don't throw exceptions. Instead, they take on the special out-of-range values shown in Table 7–3.

Table 7–3: Special Floating-Point Values

Value	Mathematical representation
POSITIVE_INFINITY	1.0/0.0
NEGATIVE_INFINITY	-1.0/0.0
NaN	0.0/0.0

The following example generates an infinite result:

```
double zero = 0.0;
double d = 1.0/zero;

if ( d == Double.POSITIVE_INFINITY )
    System.out.println( "Division by zero" );
```

The special value NaN indicates the result is "not a number." The value NaN has the special distinction of not being equal to itself (NaN != NaN). Use Float.isNaN() or Double.isNaN() to test for NaN.

java.lang.Math

The java.lang.Math class serves as Java's math library. All its methods are static and used directly; you can't instantiate a Math object. We use this kind of degenerate class when we really want methods to approximate normal functions in C. While this tactic defies the principles of object-oriented design, it makes sense in this case, as it provides a means of grouping some related utility functions in a single class. Table 7–4 summarizes the methods in java.lang.Math.

Table 7–4: Methods in java.lang.Math

Method	Argument type(s)	Functionality
Math.abs(a)	int, long, float, double	Absolute value
Math.acos(a)	double	Arc cosine
Math.asin(a)	double	Arc sine
Math.atan(a)	double	Arc tangent
Math.atan2(a,b)	double	Converts rectangular to polar coordinates
Math.ceil(a)	double	Smallest whole number greater than or equal to a
Math.cos(a)	double	Cosine
Math.exp(a)	double	Exponential number to the power of a
Math.floor(a)	double	Largest whole number less than or equal to a
Math.log(a)	double	Natural logarithm of a
Math.max(a, b)	int, long, float, double	Maximum
Math.min(a, b)	int, long, float, double	Minimum
Math.pow(a, b)	double	a to the power of b
Math.random()	None	Random number generator
Math.rint(a)	double	Converts double value to integral value in double format
Math.round(a)	float, double	Rounds
Math.sin(a)	double	Sine
Math.sqrt(a)	double	Square root
Math.tan(a)	double	Tangent

`log()`, `pow()`, and `sqrt()` can throw an `ArithmeticException`. `abs()`, `max()`, and `min()` are overloaded for all the scalar values, `int`, `long`, `float`, or `double`, and return the corresponding type. Versions of `Math.round()` accept either `float` or `double` and return `int` or `long` respectively. The rest of the methods operate on and return `double` values:

```
double irrational = Math.sqrt( 2.0 );
int bigger = Math.max( 3, 4 );
long one = Math.round( 1.125798 );
```

For convenience, `Math` also contains the `static final double` values `E` and `PI`:

```
double circumference = diameter * Math.PI;
```

Wrappers for Primitive Types

In languages like Smalltalk, numbers and other simple types are objects, which makes for an elegant language design, but has trade-offs in efficiency and complexity. By contrast, there is a schism in the Java world between class types (i.e., objects) and primitive types (i.e., numbers, characters, and boolean values). Java accepts this trade-off simply for efficiency reasons. When you're crunching numbers you want your computations to be lightweight; having to use objects for primitive types would seriously affect performance. For the times you want to treat values as objects, Java supplies a wrapper class for each of the primitive types, as shown in Table 7–5.

Table 7–5: Primitive Type Wrappers

Primitive	Wrapper
`boolean`	`java.lang.Boolean`
`char`	`java.lang.Char`
`byte`	`java.lang.Byte`
`short`	`java.lang.Short`
`int`	`java.lang.Integer`
`long`	`java.lang.Long`
`float`	`java.lang.Float`
`double`	`java.lang.Double`

An instance of a wrapper class encapsulates a single value of its corresponding type. It's an immutable object that serves as a container to hold the value and let us retrieve it later. You can construct a wrapper object from a primitive value or from a `String` representations of the value. The following code is equivalent:

```
Float pi = new Float( 3.14 );
Float pi = new Float( "3.14" );
```

Wrapper classes throw a `NumberFormatException` when there is an error in parsing from a string:

```
try {
    Double bogus = new Double( "huh?" );
}
catch ( NumberFormatException e ) {       // bad number
}
```

You should arrange to catch this exception if you want to deal with it. Otherwise, since it's a subclass of `RuntimeException`, it will propagate up the call stack and eventually cause a run-time error if not caught.

Sometimes you'll use the wrapper classes simply to parse the `String` representation of a number:

```
String sheep = getParameter("sheep");
int n = new Integer( sheep ).intValue();
```

Here we are retrieving the value of the `sheep` parameter. This value is returned as a `String`, so we need to convert it to a numeric value before we can use it. Every wrapper class provides methods to get primitive values out of the wrapper; we are using `intValue()` to retrieve an `int` out of `Integer`. Since parsing a `String` representation of a number is such a common thing to do, the `Integer` and `Long` classes also provide the `static` methods `Integer.parseInt()` and `Long.parseLong()` that read a `String` and return the appropriate type. So the second line above is equivalent to:

```
int n = Integer.parseInt( sheep );
```

All wrappers provide access to their values in various forms. You can retrieve scalar values with the methods `doubleValue()`, `floatValue()`, `longValue()`, and `intValue()`:

```
Double size = new Double ( 32.76 );

double d = size.doubleValue();
float f = size.floatValue();
long l = size.longValue();
int i = size.intValue();
```

The above code is equivalent to the primitive `double` value cast to the various types. For convenience, the `Double`class and all of the other wrapper classes provide casting functionality.

Another common use of wrappers occurs when we have to treat a primitive value as an object in order to place it in a list or other structure that operates on objects. As you'll see shortly, a `Vector` is an extensible array of `Objects`. We can can use wrappers to hold numbers in a `Vector`, along with other objects:

```
Vector myNumbers = new Vector();

Integer thirtyThree = new Integer( 33 );
myNumbers.addElement( thirtyThree );
```

Here we have created an `Integer` wrapper so that we can insert the number into the `Vector` using `addElement()`. Later, we when are taking elements back out of the `Vector`, we can get the number back out of the `Integer` as follows:

```
Integer theNumber = (Integer)myNumbers.firstElement();
int n = theNumber.intValue();              // n = 33
```

Random Numbers

You can use the `java.util.Random` class to generate random values. It's a pseudo-random number generator that can be initialized with a 48-bit seed.[*] The default constructor uses the current time as a seed, but if you want a repeatable sequence, specify your own seed with:

```
long seed = mySeed;
Random rnums = new Random( seed );
```

This code creates a random-number generator. Once you have a generator, you can ask for random values of various types using the methods listed in Table 7–6.

Table 7–6: Random Number Methods

Method	Range
nextInt()	-2147483648 to 2147483647
nextLong()	-9223372036854775808 to 9223372036854775807
nextFloat()	-1.0 to 1.0
nextDouble()	-1.0 to 1.0

By default, the values are uniformly distributed. You can use the `nextGaussian()` method to create a Gaussian distribution of `double` values, with a mean of 0.0 and a standard deviation of 1.0.

The `static` method `Math.random()` retrieves a random `double` value. This method initializes a `private` random-number generator in the `Math` class, using

---

[*] The generator uses a linear congruential formula. See *The Art of Computer Programming*, Volume 2 "Semi-numerical Algorithms," by Donald Knuth (Addison-Wesley).

the default `Random` constructor. So every call to `Math.random()` corresponds to a call to `nextDouble()` on that random number generator.

Dates

Working with dates and times without the proper tools can be a chore.[*] The `java.util.Date` class is a utility that encapsulates all of the hard work for you. An instance of `Date` represents a particular date and time. It provides methods for setting and retrieving its components and comparing itself with another time.

The default constructor creates a `Date` object set to the current time, as determined by the local system clock:

```
Date now = new Date();
System.out.println( now );          // Wed Feb 14 06:02:30 CST 1997
```

As you can see, the time reflects the localized time in your time zone.

Alternately, a `Date` can be constructed for an arbitrary time. Two constructors let us specify the time by components:

```
// Midnight year/month/day localized
Date aDate = Date (year, month, day);

// Precise time and date localized
Date orDate = Date (year, month, day, hour, minute, second);

// 6:02:30, Valentine's day, 1989, local time zone
Date vday = Date (89, 1, 14, 6, 2, 30);
```

Years are specified as the number of years since 1900. All other values begin counting with zero, except for day-of-the-month, which starts counting with one. Hence, in the last example, we used 1 to specify "February." January is month 0. Refer to Table 7–7 below for valid ranges.

`Date` is useful because it accepts an out-of-range value and normalizes it by adjusting other date components. For instance:

```
Date whatDay = Date (89, 1, 44);        // Day = 44  -> Mar 16, 1989
```

The spurious 44 day value causes the month to roll over from February to March. Best of all, a `Date` can be constructed from a string representation:

```
Date aDate = new Date( "Dec 19, 1997" );  // Midnight, Dec 19th 1997
Date bDate = new Date( "19 Dec 1997" );
```

---

[*] For a wealth of information about time and world time keeping conventions, see *http://tycho.usno.navy.mil/*, the U.S. Navy Directorate of Time.

Many variations of common syntax are acceptable, but the most standard (and the one I recommend) is the format specified by the IETF:

```
Date aDate = new Date( "Fri, 19 Dec 1997 13:30:00" );
Date bDate = new Date( "Fri, 19 Dec 1997 13:30:00 CST" );
```

U.S. time-zone designations are accepted, but you can also specify a time zone relative to GMT:

```
Date aDate = new Date( "Fri, 19 Dec 1997 19:30:00 GMT+0600")
```

Java manages times internally with a UNIX-like `long` time value that represents the number of milliseconds since midnight, January 1, 1970 GMT. Thus a `Date` can be constructed from an actual time (`long`) value:

```
Date bigBang = new Date( 0L );        // Thr Jan 1 00:00:00 GMT 1970
```

When you construct a `Date` for the current time, Java draws the time value from the system clock. This value is available through the `static` method `System.currentTimeMillis()`.

When you set the date and time of a `Date` object, that information is actually converted to the above absolute time format internally. When you later retrieve any portion of the `Date` with a `Date` method or print the date, the value will be localized for the time zone of your system:

```
Date aDate = new Date( "Fri, 19 Dec 1997 13:30:00 EST" );
System.out.println ( aDate );         // Fri Dec 19 12:30:00 CST 1997
```

Table 7–7 summarizes the methods that set and retrieve individual components of a `Date` after it has been created.

Table 7–7: Date Methods

Method	Range of Values
getYear(), setYear()	Years since 1900
getMonth(), setMonth()	Month starting with January [0 – 11]
getDate(), setDate()	Day of month [1 – 31] *(beware, this one is different)*
getDay(), setDay()	Day starting with Sunday [0 – 6]
getHours(), setHours()	Hours staring with midnight [0 – 23]
getMinutes(), setMinutes()	Minutes [0 – 59]
getSeconds(), setSeconds()	Seconds [0 – 59]
getTime(), setTime()	Actual time value (long)

The `Date` class also provides methods for comparing `Date` values. You can compare two `Date` values using the `before()`, `after()`, and `equals()` methods:

```
Date myBirthday, yourBirthday;

if ( myBirthday.before( yourBirthday ) ) // I'm older than you
```

Vectors and Hashtables

Vectors and hashtables are *collection classes*. Each stores a group of objects according to a particular retrieval scheme. Aside from that, they are not particularly closely related things. A *hashtable* is a dictionary; it stores and retrieves objects by a key value. A *vector*, on the other hand, holds an ordered collection of elements. It's essentially a dynamic array. Both of these, however, have more subtle characteristics in common. First, they are two of the most useful aspects of the core Java distribution. Second, they both take full advantage of Java's dynamic nature at the expense of some of its more static type safety.

If you work with dictionaries or associative arrays in other languages, you should understand how useful these classes are. If you are someone who has worked in C or another static language, you should find collections to be truly magical. They are part of what makes Java powerful and dynamic. Being able to work with lists of objects and make associations between them is an abstraction from the details of the types. It lets you think about the problems at a higher level and saves you from having to reproduce common structures every time you need them.

java.util.Vector

A `Vector` is a dynamic array; it can grow to accommodate new items. You can also insert and remove elements at arbitrary positions within it. As with other mutable objects in Java, `Vector` is thread-safe. The `Vector` class works directly with the type `Object`, so we can use them with instances of any kind of class.[*] We can even put different kinds of `Objects` in a `Vector` together; the `Vector` doesn't know the difference.

As you might guess, this is where things get tricky. To do anything useful with an `Object` after we take it back out of a `Vector`, we have to cast it back (narrow) it to its original type. This can be done with safety in Java because the cast is checked at run-time. Java throws a `ClassCastException` if we try to cast an object to the wrong type. However, this need for casting means that your code must remember types or methodically test them with `instanceof`. That is the price we pay for having a completely dynamic collection class that operates on all types.

---

[*] In C++, where classes don't derive from a single `Object` class that supplies a base type and common methods, the elements of a collection would usually be derived from some common collectable class. This forces the use of multiple inheritance and brings its associated problems.

You might wonder if you can subclass `Vector` to produce a class that looks like a `Vector`, but that works on just one type of element in a type-safe way. Unfortunately, the answer is no. We could override `Vector`'s methods to make a `Vector` that rejects the wrong type of element at run-time, but this does not provide any new compile-time, static type safety. In C++, templates provide a safe mechanism for parameterizing types by restricting the types of objects used at compile-time. The keyword `generic` is a reserved word in Java. This means that it's possible that future versions might support C++-style templates, using `generic` to allow statically checked parameterized types.

We can construct a `Vector` with default characteristics and add elements to it using `addElement()` and `insertElement()`:

```
Vector things = new Vector();

String one = "one";
String two = "two";
String three = "three";

things.addElement( one );
things.addElement( three );
things.insertElementAt( two, 1 );
```

`things` now contains three `String` objects in the order "one," "two," and "three". We can retrieve objects by their position with `elementAt()`, `firstElement()`, and `lastElement()`:

```
String s1 = (String)things.firstElement();      // "one"
String s3 = (String)things.lastElement();       // "three"
String s2 = (String)things.elementAt(1);        // "two"
```

We have to cast each `Object` back to a `String` in order to assign it a `String` reference. `ClassCastException` is a type of `RuntimeException`, so we can neglect to guard for the exception if we are feeling confident about the type we are retrieving. Often, as in this example, you'll just have one type of object in the `Vector`. If we were unsure about the types of objects we were retrieving, we would want to be prepared to catch the `ClassCastException` or test the type explicitly with the `instanceof` operator.

We can search for an item in a `Vector` with the `indexOf()` method:

```
int i = things.indexOf( three );                // i = 2
```

`indexOf()` returns a value of –1 if the object is not found. As a convenience, we can also use `contains()` simply to test for the presence of the object.

Finally, removeElement() removes a specified Object from the Vector:

```
things.removeElement( two );
```

The element formerly at position three now becomes the second element.

The size() method reports the number of objects currently in the Vector. You might think of using this to loop through all elements of a Vector, using elementAt() to get at each element. This works just fine, but there is a more general way to operate on a complete set of elements like those in a Vector.

java.util.Enumeration

The java.util.Enumeration interface can be used by any sort of set to provide serial access to its elements. An object that implements the Enumeration interface presents two methods: nextElement() and hasMoreElements(). nextElement() returns an Object type, so it can be used with any kind of collection. As with taking objects from a Vector, you need to know or determine what the objects are and cast them to the appropriate types before using them.

Enumeration is useful because any type of object can implement the interface and then use it to provide access to its elements. If you have an object that handles a set of values, you should think about implementing the Enumeration interface. Simply provide a hasMoreElements() test and a nextElement() iterator and declare that your class implements java.util.Enumeration. One advantage of an Enumeration is that you don't have to provide all values up front; you can provide each value as it's requested with nextElement(). And since Enumeration is an interface, you can write general routines that operate on all of the elements Enumeration.

An Enumeration does not guarantee the order in which elements are returned, however, so if order is important you don't want to use an Enumeration. You can iterate through the elements in an Enumeration only once; there is no way to reset it to the beginning or move backwards through the elements.

A Vector returns an Enumeration of its contents when we call the elements() method:

```
Enumeration e = things.elements();

while ( e.hasMoreElements() ) {
    String s = (String)e.nextElement();
    System.out.println( s ):
}
```

The above code loops three times, as call `nextElement()`, to fetch our strings. The actual type of object returned by `elements()` is a `VectorEnumeration`, but we don't have to worry about that. We can always refer to an `Enumeration` simply by its interface.

Note that `Vector` does not implement the `Enumeration` interface. If it did, that would put a serious limitation on `Vector` because we could cycle through the elements in it only once. That's clearly not the purpose of a `Vector`, which is why `Vector` instead provides a method that returns an `Enumeration`.

java.util.Hashtable

As I said earlier, a hashtable is a dictionary, similar to an associative array. A hashtable stores and retrieves elements with key values; they are very useful for things like caches and minimalist databases. When you store a value in a hashtable, you associate a key with that value. When you need to look up the value, the hashtable retrieves it efficiently using the key. The name hashtable itself refers to how the indexing and storage of elements is performed, as we'll discuss shortly. First I want to talk about how to use a hashtable.

The `java.util.Hashtable` class implements a hashtable that, like `Vector`, operates on the type `Object`. A `Hashtable` stores an element of type `Object` and associates it with a key, also of type `Object`. In this way, we can index arbitrary types of elements using arbitrary types as keys. As with `Vector`, casting is generally required to narrow objects back to their original type after pulling them out of a hashtable.

A `Hashtable` is quite easy to use. We can use the `put()` method to store items:

```
Hashtable dates = new Hashtable();

dates.put( "christmas", new Date( "25 Dec 1997" ) );
dates.put( "independence", new Date( "4 Jul 1997" ) );
dates.put( "groundhog", new Date( "2 Feb 1997" ) );
```

First we create a new `Hashtable`. Then we add three `Date` objects to it, using `String` objects as keys. The key is the first argument to `put()`; the value is the second. Only one value can be stored per key. If we try to store a second object under a key that already exists in the `Hashtable`, the old element is booted out and replaced by the new one. The return value of the `put()` method is normally `null`, but if the call to `put()` results in replacing an element, the method instead returns the old stored `Object`.

We can now use the `get()` method to retrieve each of the above dates by name, using the `String` key by which it was indexed:

```
Date d = (Date)dates.get( "christmas" );
```

The get() method returns a null value if no element exists for the given key. The cast is required to narrow the returned object back to type Date. I hope you can see the advantage of using a Hashtable over a regular array. Each value is indexed by a key instead of a simple number, so unlike a simple array, we don't have to remember where each Date is stored.

Once we've put a value in a Hashtable, we can take it back out with the remove() method, again using the key to access the value:

```
dates.remove("christmas");
```

We can test for the existence of a key with containsKey():

```
if ( dates.containsKey( "groundhog" ) ) {      // yes
```

Just like with a Vector, we're dealing with a set of items. Actually, we're dealing with two sets: keys and values. The Hashtable class has two methods, keys() and elements(), for getting at these sets. The keys() method returns an Enumeration of the keys for all of the elements in the Hashtable. We can use this Enumeration to loop through all of the keys:

```
for (Enumeration e = dates.keys(); e.hasMoreElements(); ) {
    String key = (String)e.nextElement();
    ...
}
```

Similarly, elements() provides an Enumeration of the elements themselves.

Hashcodes and key values

If you've used a hashtable before, you've probably guessed that there's more going on behind the scenes than I've let on so far. An element in a hashtable is not associated with its key by identity, but by something called a *hashcode*. Every object in Java has an identifying hashcode value determined by its hashCode() method, which is inherited from the Object class. When you store an element in a hashtable, the hashcode of the key object registers the element internally. Later, when you retrieve the item, that same hashcode looks it up efficiently.

A hashcode is usually a random-looking integer value based on the contents of an object, so it's different for different instances of a class. Two objects that have different hashcodes serve as unique keys in a hashtable; each object can reference a different stored object. Two objects that have the same hashcode value, on the other hand, appear to a hashtable as the same key. They can't coexist as keys to different objects in the hashtable.

Generally, we want our object instances to have unique hash codes, so we can put arbitrary items in a hashtable and index them with arbitrary keys. The default `hashCode()` method in the `Object` class simply assigns each object instance a unique number to be used as a hashcode. If a class does not override this method, each instance of the class will have a unique hashcode. This is sufficient for most objects.

However, it's also useful to allow equivalent objects to serve as equivalent keys. `String` objects provide a good example of this case. Although Java does its best to consolidate them, a literal string that appears multiple times in Java source code is often represented by different `String` objects at run-time. If each of these `String` objects has a different hash code, even though the literal value is the same, we could not use strings as keys in a hashtable, like we did the in above examples.

The solution is to ensure that equivalent `String` objects return the same hash-code value so that they can act as equivalent keys. The `String` class overrides the default `hashCode()` method so that equivalent `String` objects return the same hash code, while different `String` objects have unique hashcodes. This is possible because `String` objects are immutable; the contents can't change, so neither can the hashcode.

A few other classes in the Java API also override the default `hashCode()` method in order to provide equivalent hashcodes for equivalent objects. For example, each of the primitive wrapper classes provides a `hashCode()` method for this purpose. Other objects likely to be used as hashtable keys, such as `Color`, `Date`, `File`, and `URL`, also implement their own `hashCode()` methods.

So now maybe you're wondering when you need to override the default `hash-Code()` method in your objects. If you're creating a class to use for keys in a hashtable, think about whether the class supports the idea of "equivalent objects." If so, you should implement a `hashCode()` method that returns the same hash-code value for equivalent objects.

To accomplish this, you need to define the hashcode of an object to be some suitably complex and arbitrary function of the contents of that object. The only criterion for the function is that it should be almost certain to provide different values for different contents of the object. Because the capacity of an integer is limited, hashcode values are not guaranteed to be unique. This limitation is not normally a problem though, as there are 2^{32} possible hashcodes to choose from. The more sensitive the hashcode function is to small differences in the contents the better. A hashtable works most efficiently when the hashcode values are as randomly and evenly distributed as possible. As an example, you could produce a hashcode for a `String` object by adding the character values at each position in the string and multiplying the result by some number, producing a large random-looking integer.

java.util.Dictionary

`java.util.Dictionary` is the `abstract` superclass of `Hashtable`. It lays out the basic `get()`, `put()`, and `remove()` functionality for dictionary-style collections. You could derive other types of dictionaries from this class. For example, you could implement a dictionary with a different storage format, such as a binary tree.

Properties

The `java.util.Properties` class is a specialized hashtable for strings. Java uses the `Properties` object to replace the environment variables used in other programming environments. You can use a `Properties` table to hold arbitrary configuration information for an application in an easily accessible format. The `Properties` object can also load and store information using streams (see Chapter 8 for information on streams).

Any string values can be stored as key/value pairs in a `Properties` table. However, the convention is to use a dot-separated naming hierarchy to group property names into logical structures, as is done with X resources on UNIX systems.[*] The `java.lang.System` class provides system-environment information in this way, through a system `Properties` table I'll describe shortly.

Create an empty `Properties` table and add `String` key/value pairs just as with any `Hashtable`:

```
Properties props = new Properties();
props.put("myApp.xsize", "52");
props.put("myApp.ysize", "79");
```

Thereafter, you can retrieve values with the `getProperty()` method:

```
String xsize = props.getProperty( "myApp.xsize" );
```

If the named property doesn't exist, `getProperty()` returns `null`. You can get an `Enumeration` of the property names with the `propertyNames()` method:

```
for ( Enumeration e = props.propertyNames(); e.hasMoreElements; ) {
    String name = e.nextElement();
    ...
}
```

---

[*] Unfortunately, this is just a naming convention right now, so you can't access logical groups of properties as you can with X resources.

Default Values

When you create a `Properties` table, you can specify a second table for default property values:

```
Properties defaults;
...
Properties props = new Properties( defaults );
```

Now when you call `getProperty()`, the method searches the default table if it doesn't find the named property in the current table. An alternative version of `getProperty()` also accepts a default value; this value is returned if the property is not found in the current list or in the default list:

```
String xsize = props.getProperty( "myApp.xsize", "50" );
```

Loading and Storing

You can save a `Properties` table to an `OutputStream` using the `save()` method. The property information is output in flat ASCII format. Continuing with the above example, output the property information to `System.out` as follows:

```
props.save( System.out, "Application Parameters" );
```

As we'll discuss in Chapter 8, `System.out` is a standard output stream similar to C's `stdout`. We could also save the information to a file by using a `FileOutput-Stream` as the first argument to `save()`. The second argument to `save()` is a `String` that is used as a header for the data. The above code outputs something like the following to `System.out`:

```
#Application Parameters
#Mon Feb 12 09:24:23 CST 1997
myApp.ysize=79
myApp.xsize=52
```

The `load()` method reads the previously saved contents of a `Properties` object from an `InputStream`:

```
FileInputStream fin;
...
Properties props = new Properties()
props.load( fin );
```

The `list()` method is useful for debugging. It prints the contents to an `Out-putStream` in a format that is more human-readable but not retrievable by `load()`.

System Properties

The `java.lang.System` class provides access to basic system environment information through the `staticSystem.getProperty()` method. This method returns a `Properties` table that contains system properties. System properties take the place of environment variables in other programming environments.

Table 7–8 summarizes system properties that are guaranteed to be defined in any Java environment.

Table 7–8: System Properties

System Property	Meaning
`java.vendor`	Vendor-specific string
`java.vendor.url`	URL of vendor
`java.version`	Java version
`java.home`	Java installation directory
`java.class.version`	Java class version
`java.class.path`	The class path
`os.name`	Operating-system name
`os.arch`	Operating-system architecture
`os.version`	Operating-system version
`file.separator`	File separator (such as "/" or "\")
`path.separator`	Path separator (such as ":" or ";")
`line.separator`	Line separator (such as "\n" or "\r\n")
`user.name`	User account name
`user.home`	User's home directory
`user.dir`	Current working directory

Applets are, by current Web browser conventions, prevented from reading the following properties: `java.home`, `java.class.path`, `user.name`, `user.home`, and `user.dir`. As you'll see in the next section, these restrictions are implemented by a `SecurityManager` object.

The Security Manager

As I described in Chapter 1, a Java application's access to system resources, such as the display, the filesystem, threads, external processes, and the network, can be controlled at a single point with a *security manager*. The class that implements this functionality in the Java API is the `java.lang.SecurityManager` class.

An instance of the `SecurityManager` class can be installed once, and only once, in the life of the Java run-time environment. Thereafter, every access to a fundamental system resource is filtered through specific methods of the `SecurityManager` object by the core Java packages. By installing a specialized `SecurityManager`, we can implement arbitrarily complex (or simple) security policies for allowing access to individual resources.

When the Java run-time system starts executing, it's in a wide-open state until a `SecurityManager` is installed. The "null" security manager grants all requests, so the Java virtual environment can perform any activity with the same level of access as other programs running under the user's authority. If the application that is running needs to ensure a secure environment, it can install a `SecurityManager` with the `staticSystem.setSecurityManager()` method. For example, a Java-enabled Web browser like Netscape Navigator installs a `SecuritytyManager` before it runs any Java applets.

`java.lang.SecurityManager` must be subclassed to be used. This class does not actually contain any `abstract` methods; it's `abstract` as an indication that its default implementation is not very useful. By default, each security method in `SecurityManager` is implemented to provide the strictest level of security. In other words, the default `SecurityManager` simply rejects all requests.

The following example, `MyApp`, installs a trivial subclass of `SecurityManager` as one of its first activities:

```
class FascistSecurityManager extends SecurityManager { }

public class MyApp {
    public static void main( Strings [] args ) {
        System.setSecurityManager( new FascistSecurityManager() );
        // No access to files, network, windows, etc.
        ...
    }
}
```

In the above scenario, `MyApp` does little aside from reading from `System.in` and writing to `System.out`. Any attempts to read or write files, access the network, or even open a window, results in a `SecurityException` being thrown.

After this draconian `SecurityManager` is installed, it's impossible to change the `SecurityManager` in any way. The security of this feature is not dependent on the `SecurityManager`; you can't replace or modify the `SecurityManager` under any circumstances. The upshot of this is that you have to install one that handles all your needs up front.

To do something more useful, we can override the methods that are consulted for access to various kinds of resources. Table 7–9 lists some of the more important access methods. You should not normally have to call these methods yourself, although you could. They are called by the core Java classes before granting particular types of access.

Table 7–9: SecurityManager Methods

Method	Can I ... ?
checkAccess(Thread g)	Access this thread?
checkExit(int status)	Execute a System.exit()?
checkExec(String cmd)	exec() this process?
checkRead(String file)	Read a file?
checkWrite(String file)	Write a file?
checkDelete(String file)	Delete a file?
checkConnect(String host, int port)	Connect a socket to a host?
checkListen(int port)	Create a server socket?
checkAccept(String host, int port)	Accept this connection?
checkPropertyAccess(String key)	Access this system property?
checkTopLevelWindow(Object window)	Create this new top-level window?

All these methods, with the exception of checkTopLevelWindow(), simply return to grant access. If access is not granted, they throw a SecurityException. checkTopLevelWindow() returns a boolean value. A value of true indicates the access is granted; a value of false indicates the access is granted with the restriction that the new window should provide a warning border that serves to identify it as an untrusted window.

Let's implement a silly SecurityManager that allows only files beginning with the name *foo* to be read:

```
class  FooFileSecurityManager extends SecurityManager {

    public void checkRead( String s ) {
        if ( !s.startsWith("foo") )
            throw new SecurityException("Access to non-foo file: " +
                s + " not allowed." );
    }
}
```

Once the FooFileSecurityManager is installed, any attempt to read a filename other than *foo** from any class will fail and cause a SecurityException to be thrown. All other security methods are inherited from SecurityManager, so they are left at their default restrictiveness.

All restrictions placed on applets by an applet-viewer application are enforced through a SecurityManager, which allows untrusted code loaded from over the network to be executed safely. The restrictions placed on applets are currently fairly harsh. As time passes and security considerations related to applets are better understood and accepted, the applet API will hopefully become more powerful and allow forms of persistence and access to designated public information.

8

Input/Output Facilities

In this chapter, we'll continue our exploration of the Java API by looking at many of the classes in the `java.io` package. These classes support a number of forms of input and output; I expect you'll use them often in your Java applications. Figure 8–1 shows the class hierarchy of the `java.io` package.

We'll start by looking at the stream classes in `java.io`; these classes are all subclasses of the basic `InputStream` and `OutputStream` classes. Then we'll examine the `File` class and discuss how you can interact with the filesystem using classes in `java.io`.

Streams

All fundamental I/O in Java is based on *streams*. A stream represents a flow of data, or a channel of communications with (at least conceptually) a writer at one end and a reader at the other. When you are working with terminal input and output, reading or writing files, or communicating through sockets in Java, you are using a stream of one type or another. So you can see the forest without being distracted by the trees, I'll start by summarizing the different types of streams.

`InputStream/OutputStream`
> Abstract classes that define the basic functionality for reading or writing an unstructured sequence of bytes. All other kinds of streams in Java are built on top of the basic `InputStream` and `OutputStream`.

`DataInputStream/DataOutputStream`
> Specialized stream filters that add the ability to read and write simple data types like numeric primitive and `String` objects.

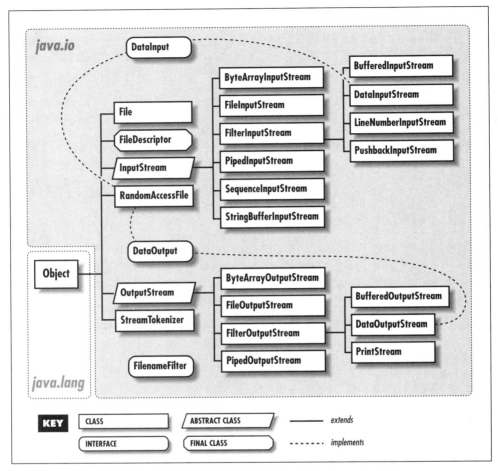

Figure 8–1: The java.io package

BufferedInputStream/BufferedOutputStream
Specialized stream filters that incorporate buffering for additional efficiency.

PrintStream
A specialized stream filter that helps with printing text.

PipedInputStream/PipedOutputStream
"Double-ended" streams that always occur in pairs. Data written into a Piped-OutputStream is read from its corresponding PipedInputStream.

`FileInputStream/FileOutputStream`
>   Implementations of `InputStream` and `OutputStream` that read from and
>   write to files on the local filesystem.

Streams in Java are one-way streets. The `java.io.InputStream` and `java.io.OutputStream` classes represent the ends of a simple stream, as shown in Figure 8–2. For bidirectional conversations, we use one of each type of stream.

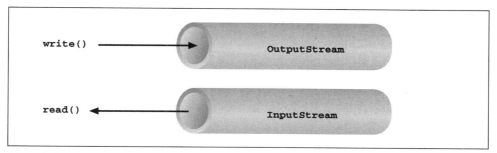

Figure 8–2: Basic InputStream and OutputStream functionality

`InputStream` and `OutputStream` are `abstract` classes that define the lowest-level interface for all streams. They contain methods for reading or writing an unstructured flow of byte-level data. Because these classes are abstract, you can never create a "pure" input stream or output. Java implements subclasses of these for activities like reading and writing files, and communicating with sockets. Because all streams inherit the structure of `InputStream` or `OutputStream`, the various kinds of streams can be used interchangeably. For example, a method often takes an `InputStream` as an argument. This means the method accepts any subclass of `InputStream`. Specialized types of streams can also be layered to provide higher-level functionality, such as buffering or handling larger data types.

We'll discuss all of the interesting stream types in this section, with the exception of `FileInputStream` and `FileOutputStream`. We'll postpone the discussion of file streams until the next section, where we'll cover issues involved with accessing the filesystem in Java.

Terminal I/O

The prototypical example of an `InputStream` object is the standard input of a Java application. Like `stdin` in C or `cin` in C++, this object reads data from the program's environment, which is usually a terminal window or a command pipe. The `java.lang.System` class, a general repository for system-related resources, provides a reference to standard input in the `static` variable `in`. `System` also provides objects for standard output and standard error in the `out` and `err` variables, respectively. The following example shows the correspondence:

```
InputStream stdin = System.in;
OutputStream stdout = System.out;
OutputStream stderr = System.err;
```

This example hides the fact that `System.out` and `System.err` aren't really `OutputStream` objects, but more specialized and useful `PrintStream` objects. I'll explain these later, but for now we can reference out and err as `Output-Stream` objects, since they are a kind of `OutputStream` by inheritance.

We can read a single byte at a time from standard input with the `InputStream`'s `read()` method. If you look closely at the API, you'll see that the `read()` method of the base `InputStream` class is actually an `abstract` method. What lies behind `System.in` is an implementation of `InputStream`, so it's valid to call `read()` for this stream:

```
try {
    int val = System.in.read();
    ...
}
catch ( IOException e ) {
}
```

As is the convention in C, `read()` provides a byte of information, but its return type is `int`. A return value of −1 indicates a normal end of stream has been reached; you'll need to test for this condition when using the simple `read()` method. If an error occurs during reading, an `IOException` is thrown. All basic input and output stream commands can throw an `IOException`, so you should arrange to catch and handle them as appropriate for your application.

To retrieve the value as a byte, perform the cast:

```
byte b = (byte) val;
```

Of course, you'll need to check for the end-of-stream condition before you perform the cast. An overloaded form of `read()` fills a byte array with as much data as possible up to the limit of the array size and returns the number of bytes read:

```
byte [] bity = new byte [1024];
int got = System.in.read( bity );
```

We can also check the number of bytes available for reading on an `InputStream` with the `available()` method. Once we have that information, we can create an array of exactly the right size:

```
int waiting = System.in.available();
if ( waiting > 0 ) {
    byte [] data = new byte [ waiting ];
    System.in.read( data );
    ...
}
```

InputStream provides the skip() method as a way of jumping over a number of bytes. Depending on the implementation of the stream and if you aren't interested in the intermediate data, skipping bytes may be more efficient than reading them. The close() method shuts down the stream and frees up any associated system resources. It's a good idea to close a stream when you are done using it.

Stream Wrappers

What if we want to do more than read and write a mess of bytes? The java.io.FilterInputStream and java.io.FilterOutputStream classes provide the basis for building streams that wrap other streams and add new features. A filtered stream takes an InputStream or OutputStream in its constructor; it delegates calls to the underlying stream while doing some additional processing of its own. The FilterInputStream and FilterOutputStream classes themselves aren't useful; they must be subclassed and specialized to create a new type of filtering operation. For example, specialized wrapper streams like DataInputStream and DataOutputStream provide additional methods for reading and writing various data types.

As we said, when you create an instance of a filtered stream, you specify an InputStream or OutputStream in the constructor. The specialized stream wraps an additional layer of functionality around the other stream, as shown in Figure 8–3. Because filtered streams themselves are subclasses of the fundamental InputStream and OutputStream types, stream filters can be layered on top of each other to provide different combinations of features.

Data streams

DataInputStream and DataOutputStream are filtered streams that let you read or write strings and primitive data types that comprise more than a single byte. DataInputStream and DataOutputStream implement the DataInput and DataOutput interfaces, respectively. These interfaces define the methods required for streams that read strings and Java primitive types in a machine-independent manner.

You can construct a DataInputStream from an InputStream and then use a method like readLine() to read a string of data:

```
DataInputStream dis = new DataInputStream( System.in );
String line = dis.readLine();
```

The above example wraps the standard input stream in a DataInputStream and uses it to read a line of text. readLine() reads bytes up to a carriage return, newline, or combination thereof.

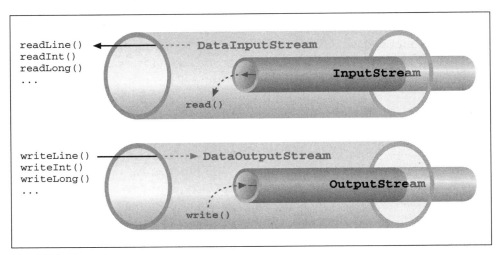

Figure 8–3: Layered streams

Here's how to use `readInt()` to read an integer value from the stream:

```
int i = dis.readInt();
```

`readInt()` reads four bytes of binary information from the stream and turns them into a 32-bit integer. All `DataInputStream` methods that read primitive types also read binary information.

If you want to parse a human-readable string into an integer, you need to get the appropriate string of text (perhaps using `readLine()`) and convert the `String` into an integer:

```
String text = dis.readLine();
int i = Integer.parseInt( text );
```

The techniques for handling strings in this manner are described in Chapter 7.

The `DataOutputStream` class provides write methods that correspond to the read methods in `DataInputStream`. For example, `writeInt()` writes an integer in binary format to the underlying output stream.

The `readUTF()` and `writeUTF()` methods of `DataInputStream` and `DataOutputStream` read and write a Java `String` of Unicode characters using the UTF-8 "transformation format." UTF-8 is an ASCII-compatible encoding of Unicode characters commonly used for the transmission and storage of Unicode text.[*]

---

[*] Check out the URL *http://www.stonehand.com/unicode/standard/utf8.html* for more information on UTF-8.

We can use a `DataInputStream` with any kind of input stream, whether it be from a file, a socket, or standard input. The same applies to using a `DataOutputStream`, or, for that matter, any other specialized streams in `java.io`.

Buffered streams

The `BufferedInputStream` and `BufferedOutputStream` classes add a data buffer of a specified size to the stream path. A buffer can increase efficiency by reducing the number of physical read or write operations that correspond to `read()` or `write()` method calls. You create a buffered stream with an appropriate input or output stream and a buffer size. Furthermore, you can wrap another stream around a buffered stream so that it benefits from the buffering. Here's a simple buffered input stream:

```
BufferedInputStream bis = new BufferedInputStream(myInputStream, 4096);
...
bis.read();
```

In this example, we specify a buffer size of 4096 bytes. If we leave off the size of the buffer in the constructor, a reasonably sized one is chosen for us. On our first call to `read()`, `bis` tries to fill the entire 4096-byte buffer with data. Thereafter, calls to `read()` retrieve data from the buffer until it's empty.

A `BufferedOutputStream` works in a similar way. Calls to `write()` store the data in a buffer; data is actually written only when the buffer fills up. You can also use the `flush()` method to wring out the contents of a `BufferedOutputStream` before the buffer is full.

Some input streams like `BufferedInputStream` support the ability to mark a location in the data and later reset the stream to that position. The `mark()` method sets the return point in the stream. It takes an integer value that specifies the number of bytes that can be read before the stream gives up and forgets about the mark. The `reset()` method returns the stream to the marked point; any data read after the call to `mark()` is read again.

This functionality is especially useful when you are reading the stream in a parser. You may occasionally fail to parse a structure and so must try something else. In this situation, you can have your parser generate an error (a homemade `ParseException`) and then reset the stream to the point before it began parsing the structure:

```
BufferedInputStream input;
...
try {
    input.mark( MAX_DATA_STRUCTURE_SIZE );
    return( parseDataStructure( input ) );
}
```

```
catch ( ParseException e ) {
    input.reset();
    ...
}
```

Print streams

Another useful filtered stream is `java.io.PrintStream`. This class provides a suite of overloaded `print()` methods that turn their arguments into strings and push them out the stream. A complementary set of `println()` methods adds a newline to the end of the strings. The `System.out` and `System.err` streams are `PrintStream` objects; you have already seen such streams strewn throughout this book:

```
System.out.print("Hello world...\n");
System.out.println("Hello world...");
System.out.println( "The answer is: " + 17 );
System.out.println( 3.14 );
```

The `PrintStream` class doesn't handle Unicode; it discards the top eight bits of all 16-bit Unicode characters. Thus, a `PrintStream` can display only Latin-1 (ISO8859-1) characters.

When you create a `PrintStream` object, you can pass an additional `boolean` value to the constructor. If this value is `true`, the `PrintStream` automatically performs a `flush()` on the `OutputStream` each time it sends a newline:

```
boolean autoFlush = true;
PrintStream p = new PrintStream( myOutputStream, autoFlush );
```

When this technique is used with a buffered output stream, it corresponds to the behavior of terminals and ttys that send data line by line.

One important difference between `PrintStream` and other streams is that if there is an error, none of its methods throw an `IOException`. Instead, if we are interested, we can check for errors with the `checkError()` method:

```
System.out.println( reallyLongString );
if ( System.out.checkError() )                    // Uh oh
```

Pipes

Normally, our applications are directly involved with one side of a given stream at a time. `PipedInputStream` and `PipedOutputStream`, however, let us create two sides of a stream and connect them together, as shown in Figure 8–4. This provides a stream of communication between threads, for example.

To create a pipe, we use both a `PipedInputStream` and a `PipedOutput-Stream`. We can simply choose a side and then construct the other side using the first as an argument:

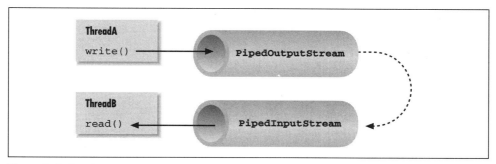

Figure 8–4: Piped streams

```
PipedInputStream pin = new PipedInputStream();
PipedOutputStream pout = new PipedOutputStream( pin );
```

Alternatively:

```
PipedOutputStream pout = new PipedOutputStream( );
PipedInputStream pin = new PipedInputStream( pout );
```

In each of these examples, the effect is to produce an input stream, `pin`, and an output stream, `pout`, that are connected. Data written to `pout` can then be read by `pin`. It is also possible to create the `PipedInputStream` and the `PipedOutputStream` separately, and then connect them with the `connect()` method.

Once the two ends of the pipe are connected, use the two streams as you would other input and output streams. You can use `read()` to read data from the `PipedInputStream` and `write()` to write data to the `PipedOutputStream`. If the internal buffer of the pipe fills up, the writer blocks and waits until more space is available. Conversely, if the pipe is empty, the reader blocks and waits until some data is available. Internally, the blocking is implemented with `wait()` and `notifyAll()`, as described in Chapter 6.

One advantage to using piped streams is that they provide stream functionality in our code, without compelling us to build new, specialized streams. For example, we can use pipes to create a simple logging facility for our application. We can send messages to the logging facility through an ordinary `PrintStream`, and then it can do whatever processing or buffering is required before sending the messages off to their ultimate location. The following example shows the skeleton of our logging facility:

```java
import java.io.*;

class LoggerDaemon extends Thread {
    PipedInputStream in = new PipedInputStream();

    LoggerDaemon() {
        setDaemon( true );
        start();
    }

    public void run() {
        DataInputStream din = new DataInputStream( in );
        String s;

        try {
            while ( (s = din.readLine()) != null ) {
                // process line of data
                // ...
            }
        }
        catch (IOException e ) { }
    }

    PrintStream getStream() throws IOException {
        return new PrintStream( new PipedOutputStream( in ) );
    }
}

class myApplication {
    public static void main ( String [] args ) throws IOException {
        PrintStream out = new LoggerDaemon().getStream();

        out.println("Application starting...");
        // ...
        out.println("Warning: does not compute!");
        // ...
    }
}
```

LoggerDaemon is a daemon thread, so it will die when our application exits. LoggerDaemon reads strings from its end of the pipe, the `PipedInputStream` input. LoggerDaemon also provides a method, `getStream()`, that returns a `PipedOutputStream` that is connected to its input stream. Simply create a new LoggerDaemon and fetch the output stream to begin sending messages.

In order to read strings with the `readLine()` method, LoggerDaemon wraps a `DataInputStream` around its `PipedInputStream`. For convenience, it also presents its `PipedOutputStream` as a `PrintStream`, rather than a simple `OutputStream`.

One advantage of implementing `LoggerDaemon` with pipes is that we can log messages as easily as we write text to a terminal or any other stream. In other words, we can use all our normal tools and techniques. Another advantage is that the processing happens in another thread, so we can go about our business while the processing takes place.

There is nothing stopping us from connecting more than two piped streams. For example, we could chain multiple pipes together to perform a series of filtering operations. We could also funnel data from multiple `PipedOutputStream` objects to a single `PipedInputStream`.

Strings to Streams and Back

The `StringBufferInputStream` class is another useful stream class. The stream is created from a `String`; `StringBufferInputStream` essentially wraps stream functionality around a `String`. Here's how to use a `StringBufferInputStream`:

```
String data = "There once was a man from Nantucket...";
StringBufferInputStream sbis = new StringBufferInputStream( data );

byte T = sbis.read();
byte h = sbis.read();
byte e = sbis.read();
```

The `StringBufferInputStream` class is useful when you want to read data in a `String` as if it were coming from a stream, such as a file, pipe, or socket. For example, suppose you create a parser that expects to read tokens from a stream. But you want to provide a method that also parses a big string. You can easily add one using `StringBufferInputStream`.

Turning things around, the `ByteArrayOutputStream` class lets us write to a growable array of bytes through an output stream. The internal array grows as necessary to accommodate the data. In the following examples, we create a `ByteArrayOutputStream` and wrap it in a `PrintStream` for convenience:

```
ByteArrayOutputStream buffer = new ByteArrayOutputStream();
PrintStream out = new PrintStream( buffer );

out.println("A moose once bit my sister.");
out.println("No, really!");

String results = buffer.toString();
```

First we print a few lines to the output stream, to give it some data, then retrieve the results as a string with the `toString()` method. Alternately, we could get the results as a byte array with the `toByteArray()` method.

The `ByteArrayOutputStream` class is useful if you want to capture the output of something that normally sends output to a stream, such as a file or the console. A `PrintStream` wrapped around a `ByteArrayOutputStream` competes with `StringBuffer` as the easiest way to construct large strings piece by piece. While using a `StringBuffer` is more efficient, `PrintStream` provides more functionality than the normal `append()` method used by `StringBuffer`.

rot13InputStream

Before we leave streams, let's try our hand at making one of our own. I mentioned earlier that specialized stream wrappers are built on top of the `FilterInput-Stream` and `FilterOutputStream` classes. It's quite easy to create our own subclass of `FilterInputStream` that can be wrapped around other streams to add new functionality.

The following example, `rot13InputStream`, performs a *rot13* operation on the bytes that it reads. *rot13* is a trivial algorithm that shifts alphanumeric letters to make them not quite human-readable; it's cute because it's symmetric. That is, to "un-rot13" some text, simply *rot13* it again. We'll use the `rot13InputStream` class again in the `crypt` protocol handler example in Chapter 9, so we've put the class in the `example.io` package to facilitate reuse. Here's our `rot13InputStream` class:

```
package example.io;
import java.io.*;

public class rot13InputStream extends FilterInputStream {

    public rot13InputStream ( InputStream i ) {
        super( i );
    }

    public int read() throws IOException {
        return rot13( in.read() );
    }

    private int rot13 ( int c ) {
        if ( (c >= 'A') && (c <= 'Z') )
            c=(((c-'A')+13)%26)+'A';
        if ( (c >= 'a') && (c <= 'z') )
            c=(((c-'a')+13)%26)+'a';
        return c;
    }
}
```

The `FilterInputStream` needs to be initialized with an `InputStream`; this is the stream to be filtered. We provide an appropriate constructor for the `rot13InputStream` class and invoke the parent constructor with a call to `super()`. `FilterInputStream` contains a protected instance variable, `in`, where it stores the stream reference and makes it available to the rest of our class.

The primary feature of a `FilterInputStream` is that it overrides the normal `InputStream` methods to delegate calls to the `InputStream` in the variable `in`. So, for instance, a call to `read()` simply turns around and calls `read()` on `in` to fetch a byte. An instance of `FilterInputStream` itself could be instantiated from an `InputStream`; it would pass its method calls on to that stream and serve as a pass-through filter. To make things interesting, we can override methods of the `FilterInputStream` class and do extra work on the data as it passes through.

In our example, we have overridden the `read()` method to fetch bytes from the underlying `InputStream`, `in`, and then perform the *rot13* shift on the data before returning it. Note that the `rot13()` method shifts alphabetic characters, while simply passing all other values, including the end of stream value (`-1`). Our subclass now acts like a *rot13* filter. All other normal functionality of an `Input-Stream`, like `skip()` and `available()` is unmodified, so calls to these methods are answered by the underlying `InputStream`.

Files

Unless otherwise restricted, a Java application can read and write to the host filesystem with the same level of access as the user who runs the Java interpreter. Java applets and other kinds of networked applications can, of course, be restricted by the `SecurityManager` and cut off from these services. We'll discuss applet access at the end of this section. First, let's take a look at the tools for basic file access.

Working with files in Java is still somewhat problematic. The host filesystem lies outside of Java's virtual environment, in the real world, and can therefore still suffer from architecture and implementation differences. Java tries to mask some of these differences by providing information to help an application tailor itself to the local environment; I'll mention these areas as they occur.

java.io.File

The `java.io.File` class encapsulates access to information about a file or directory entry in the filesystem. It gets attribute information about a file, lists the entries in a directory, and performs basic filesystem operations like removing a file or making a directory. While the `File` object handles these tasks, it doesn't provide direct access for reading and writing file data; there are specialized streams for that purpose.

File constructors

You can create an instance of `File` from a `String` pathname as follows:

```
File fooFile = new File( "/tmp/foo.txt" );
File barDir = new File( "/tmp/bar" );
```

You can also create a file with a relative path like:

```
File f = new File( "foo" );
```

In this case, Java works relative to the current directory of the Java interpreter. You can determine the current directory by checking the `user.dir` property in the `System Properties` list (`System.getProperty("user.dir")`).

An overloaded version of the `File` constructor lets you specify the directory path and filename as separate `String` objects:

```
File fooFile = new File( "/tmp", "foo.txt" );
```

With yet another variation, you can specify the directory with a `File` object and the filename with a `String`:

```
File tmpDir = new File( "/tmp" );
File fooFile = new File ( tmpDir, "foo.txt" );
```

None of the `File` constructors throw any exceptions. This means the object is created whether or not the file or directory actually exists; it isn't an error to create a `File` object for an nonexistent file. You can use the `exists()` method to find out whether the file or directory exists.

Path localization

One of the reasons that working with files in Java is problematic is that pathnames are expected to follow the conventions of the local filesystem. Java's designers intend to provide an abstraction that deals with most system-dependent filename features, such as the file separator, path separator, device specifier, and root directory. Unfortunately, not all of these features are implemented in the current version.

On some systems, Java can compensate for differences such as the direction of the file separator slashes in the above string. For example, in the current implementation on Windows platforms, Java accepts paths with either forward slashes or backslashes. However, under Solaris, Java accepts only paths with forward slashes.

Your best bet is to make sure you follow the filename conventions of the host filesystem. If your application is just opening and saving files at the user's request, you should be able to handle that functionality with the `java.awt.FileDialog` class. This class encapsulates a graphical file-selection dialog box. The methods of the `FileDialog` take care of system-dependent filename features for you.

If your application needs to deal with files on its own behalf, however, things get a little more complicated. The File class contains a few static variables to make this task easier. File.separator defines a String that specifies the file separator on the local host (e.g., "/" on UNIX systems and "\" on Windows systems), while File.separatorChar provides the same information in character form. File.pathSeparator defines a String that separates items in a path (e.g., ":" on UNIX systems; ";" on Windows systems); File.pathSeparatorChar provides the information in character form.

You can use this system-dependent information in several ways. Probably the simplest way to localize pathnames is to pick a convention you use internally, say "/", and do a String replace to substitute for the localized separator character:

```
// We'll use forward slash as our standard
String path = "mail/1995/june/merle";
path = path.replace('/', File.separatorChar);
File mailbox = new File( path );
```

Alternately, you could work with the components of a pathname and built the local pathname when you need it:

```
String [] path = { "mail", "1995", "june", "merle" };

StringBuffer sb = new StringBuffer(path[0]);
for (int i=1; i< path.length; i++)
    sb.append( File.separator + path[i] );

File mailbox = new File( sb.toString() );
```

One thing to remember is that Java interprets the backslash character (\) as an escape character when used in a String. To get a backslash in a String, you have to use "\\".

File methods

Once we have a valid File object, we can use it to ask for information about the file itself and to perform standard operations on it. A number of methods let us ask certain questions about the File. For example, isFile() returns true if the File represents a file, while isDirectory() returns true if it's a directory. isAbsolute() indicates whether the File has an absolute or relative path specification.

The components of the File pathname are available through the following methods: getName(), getPath(), getAbsolutePath(), and getParent(). getName() returns a String for the filename without any directory information; getPath() returns the directory information without the filename. If the File has an absolute path specification, getAbsolute() returns that path. Otherwise it returns the relative path appended to the current working directory. getParent() returns the parent directory of the File.

We can get the modification time of a file or directory with lastModified(). This time value is not useful as an absolute time; you should use it only to compare two modification times. We can also get the size of the file in bytes with length(). Here's a fragment of code that prints some information about a file:

```
File fooFile = new File( "/tmp/boofa" );

String type = fooFile.isFile() ? "File " : "Directory ";
String name = fooFile.getName();
long len = fooFile.length();
System.out.println(type + name + ", " + len + " bytes " );
```

If the File object corresponds to a directory, we can list the files in the directory with the list() method:

```
String [] files = fooFile.list();
```

list() returns an array of String objects that contains filenames. (You might expect that list() would return an Enumeration instead of an array, but it doesn't.)

If the File refers to a nonexistent directory, we can create the directory with mkdir() or mkdirs(). mkdir() creates a single directory; mkdirs() creates all of the directories in a File specification. Use renameTo() to rename a file or directory and delete() to delete a file or directory. Note that File doesn't provide a method to create a file; creation is handled with a FileOutputStream as we'll discuss in a moment.

Table 8–1 summarizes the methods provided by the File class.

Table 8–1: File Methods

Method	Return type	Description
canRead()	boolean	Is the file (or directory) readable?
canWrite()	boolean	Is the file (or directory) writable?
delete()	boolean	Deletes the file (or directory)
exists()	boolean	Does the file (or directory) exist?
getAbsolutePath()	String	Returns the absolute path of the file (or directory)
getName()	String	Returns the name of the file (or directory)
getParent()	String	Returns the name of the parent directory of the file (or directory)
getPath()	String	Returns the path of the file (or directory)

Table 8–1: File Methods (continued)

Method	Return type	Description
isAbsolute()	boolean	Is the filename (or directory name) absolute?
isDirectory()	boolean	Is the item a directory?
isFile()	boolean	Is the item a file?
lastModified()	long	Returns the last modification time of the file (or directory)
length()	long	Returns the length of the file
list()	String []	Returns a list of files in the directory
mkdir()	boolean	Creates the directory
mkdirs()	boolean	Creates all directories in the path
renameTo(File dest)	boolean	Renames the file (or directory)

File Streams

Java provides two specialized streams for reading and writing files in the filesystem: `FileInputStream` and `FileOutputStream`. These streams provide the basic `InputStream` and `OutputStream` functionality applied to reading and writing the contents of files. They can be combined with the filtered streams described earlier to work with files in the same way we do other stream communications.

Because `FileInputStream` is a subclass of `InputStream`, it inherits all standard `InputStream` functionality for reading the contents of a file. `FileInput-Stream` provides only a low-level interface to reading data, however, so you'll typically wrap another stream like a `DataInputStream` around the `FileInput-Stream`.

You can create a `FileInputStream` from a `String` pathname or a `File` object:

```
FileInputStream foois = new FileInputStream( fooFile );
FileInputStream passwdis = new FileInputStream( "/etc/passwd" );
```

When you create a `FileInputStream`, Java attempts to open the specified file. Thus, the `FileInputStream` constructors can throw a `FileNotFoundException` if the specified file doesn't exist, or an `IOException` if some other I/O error occurs. You should be sure to catch and handle these exceptions in your code. When the stream is first created, its `available()` method and the `File` object's `length()` method should return the same value. Be sure to call the `close()` method when you are done with the file.

The following class, ListIt, is a small utility that displays the contents of a file or directory to standard output:

```java
import java.io.*;

class ListIt {
    public static void main ( String args[] ) throws Exception {
        File file =  new File( args[0] );

        if ( !file.exists() || !file.canRead() ) {
            System.out.println( "Can't read " + file );
            return;
        }

        if ( file.isDirectory() ) {
            String [] files = file.list();
            for (int i=0; i< files.length; i++)
                System.out.println( files[i] );
        }
        else
            try {
                FileInputStream fis = new FileInputStream ( file );
                byte [] data = new byte [ fis.available() ];
                fis.read( data );
                System.out.write( data );
            }
            catch ( FileNotFoundException e )
                System.out.println( "File Disappeared" );
    }
}
```

ListIt constructs a File object from its first command-line argument and tests the File to see if it exists and is readable. If the File is a directory, ListIt prints the names of the files in the directory. If File is a plain file, ListIt allocates an array large enough to hold the data and then reads the data and prints it.

FileOutputStream is a subclass of OutputStream, so it inherits all the standard OutputStream functionality for writing to a file. Just like FileInput-Stream though, FileOutputStream provides only a low-level interface to writing data. You'll typically wrap another stream like a DataOutputStream or a PrintStream around the FileOutputStream to provide higher-level functionality. You can create a FileOutputStream from a String pathname or a File object. Unlike FileInputStream however, the FileOutputStream constructors don't throw a FileNotFoundException. If the specified file doesn't exist, the FileOutputStream creates the file. The FileOutputStream constructors can throw an IOException if some other I/O error occurs, so you still need to handle this exception.

If the specified file does exist, the `FileOutputStream` opens it for writing. When you actually call a `write()` method, the new data overwrites the current contents of the file. If you need to append data to an existing file, you should use a `RandomAccessFile`, as I'll discuss shortly.

The following example reads a line of data from standard input and writes it to the file */tmp/foo.txt*:

```
String s = new DataInputStream( System.in ).readLine();

File out = new File( "/tmp/foo.txt" );
if ( out.canWrite() ) {
    FileOutputStream fos = new FileOutputStream ( out );
    PrintStream pfos = new PrintStream( fos )
    pfos.println( s );
}
```

Notice how we have wrapped a `PrintStream` around the `FileOutputStream` to facilitate writing the data. To be a good filesystem citizen, you need to call the `close()` method when you are done with the `FileOutputStream`.

java.io.RandomAccessFile

The `java.io.RandomAccessFile` class provides the ability to read and write data from or to any specified location in a file. `RandomAccessFile` implements both the `DataInput` and `DataOutput` interfaces, so you can use it to read and write strings and Java primitive types. In other words, `RandomAccessFile` defines the same methods for reading and writing data as `DataInputStream` and `DataOutputStream`. However, because the class provides random, rather than sequential, access to file data, it's not a subclass of either `InputStream` or `OutputStream`.

You can create a `RandomAccessFile` from a `String` pathname or a `File` object. The constructor also takes a second `String` argument that specifies the mode of the file. Use "r" for a read-only file or "rw" for a read-write file. Here's how to create a simple database to keep track of user information:

```
try {
    RandomAccessFile users = new RandomAccessFile( "Users", "rw" );
    ...
}
catch (IOException e) {
}
```

When you create a `RandomAccessFile` in read-only mode, Java tries to open the specified file. If the file doesn't exist, `RandomAccessFile` throws an

IOException. If, however, you are creating a RandomAccessFile in read-write mode, the object creates the file if it doesn't exist. The constructor can still throw an IOException if some other I/O error occurs, so you still need to handle this exception.

After you have created a RandomAccessFile, call any of the normal reading and writing methods, just as you would with a DataInputStream or DataOutput-Stream. If you try to write to a read-only file, the write method throws an IOException.

What makes a RandomAccessFile special is the seek() method. This method takes a long value and uses it to set the location for reading and writing in the file. You can use the getFilePointer() method to get the current location. If you need to append data on the end of the file, use length() to determine that location. You can write or seek beyond the end of a file, but you can't read beyond the end of a file. The read methods throws a EOFException if you try to do this.

Here's an example of writing some data to our user database:

```
users.seek( userNum * RECORDSIZE );
users.writeUTF( userName );
users.writeInt( userID );
```

One caveat to notice with this example is that we need to be sure that the String length for userName, along with any data that comes after it, fits within the boundaries of the record size.

Applets and Files

For security reasons, applets are not permitted to read and write to arbitrary places in the filesystem. The ability of an applet to read and write files, as with any kind of system resource, is under the control of the SecurityManager object installed by the application that is running the applet, such as an applet viewer or Java-enabled Web browser. All filesystem access must first pass the scrutiny of the SecurityManager. With that in mind, applet-viewer applications are free to implement their own schemes for what, if any, access an applet may have.

For example, Sun's HotJava Web browser allows applets to have access to specific files designated by the user in an access-control list. Netscape Navigator, on the other hand, currently doesn't allow applets any access to the filesystem.

It isn't unusual to want an applet to maintain some kind of state information on the system where it's running. But for a Java applet that is restricted from access to the local filesystem, the only option is to store data over the network on its server. Although, at the moment, the Web is a relatively static, read-only environment, applets have at their disposal powerful, general means for communicating data over networks, as you'll see in Chapter 9. The only limitation is that, by convention, an applet's network communication is restricted to the server that launched it. This limits the options for where the data will reside.

There are no built-in mechanisms for persistence in the core Java distribution. The only means of writing data to a server in Java is through a network socket. In Chapter 9 we'll look at building networked applications with sockets in detail. With the tools of that chapter it's possible to build powerful client/server applications.

9

Network Programming

The network is the soul of Java. Most of what is new and exciting about Java centers around the potential for new kinds of dynamic, networked applications. This chapter discusses the `java.net` package, which contains classes for communications and working with networked resources. These classes fall into two categories: the sockets API and classes for working with Uniform Resource Locators (URLs). Figure 9–1 shows all of the classes in `java.net`.

Java's sockets interface provides access to the standard network protocols used for communications between hosts on the Internet. Sockets are the mechanism underlying all other kinds of portable networked communications. Your processes can use sockets to communicate with a server or peer applications on the Net, but you have to implement your own application-level protocols for handling and interpreting the data. Higher-level functionality, like remote procedure calls and distributed objects, are implemented with sockets.

The Java URL classes provide an API for accessing well-defined networked resources, like documents and applications on servers. The classes use an extensible set of prefabricated protocol and content handlers to perform the necessary communication and data conversion for accessing URL resources. With URLs, an application can fetch a complete file or database record from a server on the network with just a few lines of code. Applications like Web browsers, which deal with networked content, use the URL class to simplify the task of network programming. They also take advantage of the dynamic nature of Java, which allows handlers for new types of URLs to be added on the fly. As new types of servers and new formats for content evolve, additional URL handlers can be supplied to retrieve and interpret the data without modifying the original application.

In this chapter, I'll try to provide some practical and realistic examples of Java network programming using both APIs. Sadly, the current state of affairs is

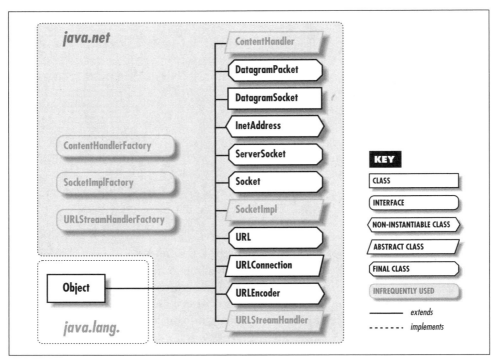

Figure 9–1: The java.net package

disappointing. The real release of HotJava isn't available, and Netscape Navigator imposes many restrictions on what you can do. In addition, a few standards that we need haven't been defined. Nevertheless, you can use all of Java's networking capabilities to build your own free-standing applications. I'll point out the shortcomings with Netscape Navigator and the standards scene as I go along.

Sockets

Sockets are a low-level programming interface for networked communications. They send streams of data between applications that may or may not be on the same host. Sockets originated in BSD UNIX and are, in other languages, hairy and complicated things with lots of small parts that can break off and choke little children. The reason for this is that most sockets APIs can be used with almost any kind of underlying network protocol. Since the protocols that transport data across the network can have radically different features, the socket interface can be quite complex. (For a discussion of sockets in general, see *UNIX Network Programming*, by Richard Stevens (Prentice-Hall)).

Java supports a simplified object-oriented interface to sockets that makes network communications considerably easier. If you have done network programming using sockets in C or another structured language, you should be pleasantly surprised at how simple things can be when objects encapsulate the gory details. If this is the first time you've come across sockets, you'll find that talking to another application can be as simple as reading a file or getting user input. Most forms of I/O in Java, including network I/O, use the stream classes described in Chapter 8. Streams provide a unified I/O interface; reading or writing across the Internet is similar to reading or writing a file on the local system.

Java provides different kinds of sockets to support two distinct classes of underlying protocols. In this first section, we'll look at Java's `Socket` class, which uses a *connection-oriented* protocol. A connection-oriented protocol gives you the equivalent of a telephone conversation; after establishing a connection, two applications can send data back and forth; the connection stays in place even when no one is talking. The protocol ensures that no data is lost and that it always arrives in order. In the next section we'll look at the `DatagramSocket` class, which uses a *connectionless* protocol. A connectionless protocol is more like the postal service. Applications can send short messages to each other, but no attempt is made to keep the connection open between messages, to keep the messages in order, or even to guarantee that they arrive.

In theory, just about any protocol family can be used underneath the socket layer: Novell's IPX, Apple's AppleTalk, even the old ChaosNet protocols. But this isn't a theoretical world. In practice, there's only one protocol family people care about on the Internet, and only one protocol family Java supports: the Internet protocols, IP. The `Socket` class speaks TCP, and the `DatagramSocket` class speaks UDP, both standard Internet protocols. These protocols are available on any system that is connected to the Internet.

Clients and Servers

When writing network applications, it's common to talk about clients and servers. The distinction is increasingly vague, but the side that initiates the conversation is usually the *client*. The side that accepts the request to talk is usually the *server*. In the case where there are two peer applications using sockets to talk, the distinction is less important, but for simplicity we'll use the above definition.

For our purposes, the most important difference between a client and a server is that a client can create a socket to initiate a conversation with a server application at any time, while a server must prepare to listen for incoming conversations in advance. The `java.net.Socket` class represents a single side of a socket

connection on either the client or server. In addition, the server uses the
`java.net.ServerSocket` class to wait for connections from clients. An application acting as a server creates a `ServerSocket` object and waits, blocked in a call
to its `accept()` method, until a connection arrives. When it does, the `accept()`
method creates a `Socket` object the server uses to communicate with the client. A
server carries on multiple conversations at once; there is only a single `Server-
Socket`, but one active `Socket` object for each client, as shown in Figure 9–2.

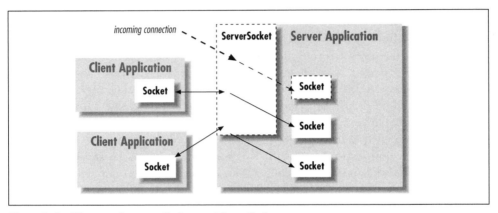

Figure 9–2: Clients and servers, Sockets and ServerSockets

A client needs two pieces of information to locate and connect to another server
on the Internet: a hostname (used to find the host's network address) and a port
number. The port number is an identifier that differentiates between multiple
clients or servers on the same host. A server application listens on a prearranged
port while waiting for connections. Clients select the port number assigned to the
service they want to access. If you think of the host computers as hotels and the
applications as guests, then the ports are like the guests' room numbers. For one
guest to call another, he or she must know the other party's hotel name and room
number.

Clients

A client application opens a connection to a server by constructing a `Socket` that
specifies the hostname and port number of the desired server:

```
try {
    Socket sock = new Socket("wupost.wustl.edu", 25);
}
catch ( UnknownHostException e ) {
    System.out.println("Can't find host.");
}
catch ( IOException e ) {
```

```
    System.out.println("Error connecting to host.");
}
```

This code fragment attempts to connect a Socket to port 25 (the SMTP mail service) of the host *wupost.wustl.edu*. The client handles the possibility that the hostname can't be resolved (UnknownHostException) and that it might not be able to connect to it (IOException).

As an alternative to using a hostname, you can provide a string version of the host's IP address:

```
Socket sock = new Socket("128.252.120.1", 25);     // wupost.wustl.edu
```

Once a connection is made, input and output streams can be retrieved with the Socket getInputStream() and getOutputStream() methods. The following (rather arbitrary and strange) conversation illustrates sending and receiving some data with the streams. Refer to Chapter 8 for a complete discussion of working with streams.

```
try {
    Socket server = new Socket("foo.bar.com", 1234);
    InputStream in = server.getInputStream();
    OutputStream out = server.getOutputStream();

    // Write a byte
    out.write(42);

    // Say "Hello" (send newline delimited string)
    PrintStream pout = new PrintStream( out );
    pout.println("Hello!");

    // Read a byte
    Byte back = in.read();

    // Read a newline delimited string
    DataInputStream din = new DataInputStream( in );
    String response = din.readLine();

    server.close();
}
catch (IOException e ) { }
```

In the exchange above, the client first creates a Socket for communicating with the server. The Socket constructor specifies the server's hostname (*foo.bar.com*) and a prearranged port number (1234). Once the connection is established, the client writes a single byte to the server using the OutputStream's write() method. It then wraps a PrintStream around the OutputStream in order to send text more easily. Next, it performs the complementary operations, reading a byte from the server using InputStream's read() and then creating a DataInputStream from which to get a string of text. Finally, it terminates the connection with the close() method. All these operations have the potential to generate IOExceptions; the catch clause is where our application would deal with these.

Servers

After a connection is established, a server application uses the same kind of Socket object for its side of the communications. However, to accept a connection from a client, it must first create a ServerSocket, bound to the correct port. Let's recreate the previous conversation from the server's point of view:

```
// Meanwhile, on foo.bar.com...
try {
    ServerSocket listener = new ServerSocket( 1234 );

    while ( !finished ) {
        Socket aClient = listener.accept();      // wait for connection

        InputStream in = aClient.getInputStream();
        OutputStream out = aClient.getInputStream();

        // Read a byte
        Byte importantByte = in.read();

        // Read a string
        DataInputStream din = new DataInputStream( in );
        String request = din.readLine();

        // Write a byte
        out.write(43);

        // Say "Goodbye"
        PrintStream pout = new PrintStream( out );
        pout.println("Goodbye!");

        aClient.close();
    }

    listener.close();

}
catch (IOException e ) { }
```

First, our server creates a ServerSocket attached to port 1234. On some systems there are rules about what ports an application can use. Port numbers below 1024 are usually reserved for system processes and standard, well-known services, so we pick a port number outside of this range. The ServerSocket need be created only once. Thereafter we can accept as many connections as arrive.

Next we enter a loop, waiting for the `accept()` method of the `ServerSocket` to return an active `Socket` connection from a client. When a connection has been established, we perform the server side of our dialog, then close the connection and return to the top of the loop to wait for another connection. Finally, when the server application wants to stop listening for connections altogether, it calls the `close()` method of the `ServerSocket`.[*]

As you can see, this server is single-threaded; it handles one connection at a time; it doesn't call `accept()` to listen for a new connection until it's finished with the current connection. A more realistic server would have a loop that accepts connections concurrently and passes them off to their own threads for processing. (Our tiny HTTP daemon in a later section will do just this.)

Sockets and security

The examples above presuppose the client has permission to connect to the server, and that the server is allowed to listen on the specified socket. This is not always the case. Specifically, applets and other applications run under the auspices of a `SecurityManager` that can impose arbitrary restrictions on what hosts they may or may not talk to, and whether they can listen for connections. The security policy imposed by the current version of Netscape Navigator allows applets to open socket connections only to the host that served them. That is, they can talk back only to the server from which their class files were retrieved. Applets are not allowed to open server sockets themselves.

Now, this doesn't meant an applet can't cooperate with its server to communicate with anyone, anywhere. A server could run a proxy that lets the applet communicate indirectly with anyone it likes. What the current security policy prevents is malicious applets roaming around inside corporate firewalls. It places the burden of security on the originating server, and not the client machine. Restricting access to the originating server limits the usefulness of "trojan" applications that do annoying things from the client side. You won't let your proxy mail bomb people, because you'll be blamed.

The DateAtHost Client

Many networked workstations run a time service that dispenses their local clock time on a well-known port. This was a precursor of NTP, the more general Network Time Protocol. In the next example, `DateAtHost`, we'll make a specialized subclass of `java.util.Date` that fetches the time from a remote host instead of

---

[*] A somewhat obscure security feature in TCP/IP specifies that if a server socket actively closes a connection while a client is connected, it may not be able to bind (attach itself) to the same port on the server host again for a period of time (the maximum time to live of a packet on the network). It's possible to turn off this feature, and it's likely that your Java implementation will have done so.

initializing itself from the local clock. (See Chapter 7 for a complete discussion of the Date class.)

DateAtHost connects to the time service (port 37) and reads four bytes representing the time on the remote host. These four bytes are interpreted as an integer representing the number of seconds since the turn of the century. DateAtHost converts this to Java's variant of the absolute time (milliseconds since January 1, 1970, a date that should be familiar to UNIX users) and then uses the remote host's time to initialize itself:

```
import java.net.Socket;
import java.io.*;

public class DateAtHost extends java.util.Date {
    static int timePort = 37;
    static final long offset = 2208988800L; // Seconds from century to
                                            // Jan 1, 1970 00:00 GMT

    public DateAtHost( String host ) throws IOException {
        this( host, timePort );
    }

    public DateAtHost( String host, int port ) throws IOException {
        Socket sock = new Socket( host, port );
        DataInputStream din =
            new DataInputStream(sock.getInputStream());
        int time = din.readInt();
        sock.close();

        setTime( (((1L << 32) + time) - offset) * 1000 );
    }
}
```

That's all there is to it. It's not very long, even with a few frills. We have supplied two possible constructors for DateAtHost. Normally we'll use the first, which simply takes the name of the remote host as an argument. The second, overloaded constructor specifies the hostname and the port number of the remote time service. (If the time service were running on a nonstandard port, we would use the second constructor to specify the alternate port number.) This second constructor does the work of making the connection and setting the time. The first constructor simply invokes the second (using the this() construct) with the default port as an argument. Supplying simplified constructors that invoke their siblings with default arguments is a common and useful technique.

The second constructor opens a socket to the specified port on the remote host. It creates a DataInputStream to wrap the input stream and then reads a 4-byte integer using the readInt() method. It's no coincidence the bytes are in the right order. Java's `DataInputStream` and `DataOutputStream` classes work with the bytes of integer types in *network byte order* (most significant to least significant). The time protocol (and other standard network protocols that deal with binary data) also uses the network byte order, so we don't need to call any conversion routines. (Explicit data conversions would probably be necessary if we were using a nonstandard protocol, especially when talking to a non-Java client or server.) After reading the data, we're finished with the socket, so we close it, terminating the connection to the server. Finally, the constructor initializes the rest of the object by calling `Date`'s `setTime()` method with the calculated time value.[*]

The `DateAtHost` class can work with a time retrieved from a remote host almost as easily as `Date` is used with the time on the local host. The only additional overhead is that we have to deal with the possible `IOException` that can be thrown by the `DateAtHost` constructor:

```
try {
    Date d = new DateAtHost( "sura.net" );
    System.out.println( "The time over there is: " + d );
    int hours = d.getHours();
    int minutes = d.getMinutes();
    ...
}
catch ( IOException e ) { }
```

This example fetches the time at the host *sura.net* and prints its value. It then looks at some components of the time using the `getHours()` and `getMinutes()` methods of the `Date` class.

The TinyHttpd Server

Have you ever wanted your very own Web server? Well, you're in luck. In this section, we're going to build `TinyHttpd`, a minimal but functional HTTP daemon. `TinyHttpd` listens on a specified port and services simple HTTP "get file" requests. They look something like this:

```
GET /path/filename [optional stuff]
```

Your Web browser sends one or more such as lines for each document it retrieves. Upon reading the request, the server tries to open the specified file and send its contents. If that document contains references to images or other items to be displayed inline, the browser continues with additional `GET` requests. For best performance (especially in a time-slicing environment), `TinyHttpd` services each

---

[*] The conversion first creates a long value, which is the unsigned equivalent of the integer `time`. It subtracts an offset to make the time relative to the epoch (January 1, 1970) rather than the century, and multiples by 1000 to convert to milliseconds.

request in its own thread. Therefore, `TinyHttpd` can service several requests concurrently.

Over and above the limitations imposed by its simplicity, `TinyHttpd` suffers from the limitations imposed by the fickleness of filesystem access, as discussed in Chapter 8. It's important to remember that file pathnames are still architecture dependent—as is the concept of a filesystem to begin with. This example should work, as is, on UNIX and DOS-like systems, but may require some customizations to account for differences on other platforms. It's possible to write more elaborate code that uses the environmental information provided by Java to tailor itself to the local system. (Chapter 8 gives some hints about how to do this).

WARNING

This example will serve files from your host without protection. Don't try this at work.

Now, without further ado, here's `TinyHttpd`:

```
import java.net.*;
import java.io.*;
import java.util.*;

public class TinyHttpd {
    public static void main( String argv[] ) throws IOException {
        ServerSocket ss = new ServerSocket(Integer.parseInt(argv[0]));
        while ( true )
            new TinyHttpdConnection( ss.accept() );
    }
}

class TinyHttpdConnection extends Thread {
    Socket sock;
    TinyHttpdConnection ( Socket s ) {
        sock = s;
        setPriority( NORM_PRIORITY - 1 );
        start();
    }

    public void run() {
        try {
            OutputStream out = sock.getOutputStream();
            String req =
                new DataInputStream(sock.getInputStream()).readLine();
            System.out.println( "Request: "+req );

            StringTokenizer st = new StringTokenizer( req );
            if ( (st.countTokens() >= 2) &&
                 st.nextToken().equals("GET") ) {
                if ( (req = st.nextToken()).startsWith("/") )
                    req = req.substring( 1 );
```

```
            if ( req.endsWith("/") || req.equals("") )
                req = req + "index.html";

            try {
                FileInputStream fis = new FileInputStream ( req );
                byte [] data = new byte [ fis.available() ];
                fis.read( data );
                out.write( data );
            }
            catch ( FileNotFoundException e )
                new PrintStream( out ).println("404 Not Found");
        } else
            new PrintStream( out ).println( "400 Bad Request" );

        sock.close();
    }
    catch ( IOException e )
        System.out.println( "I/O error " + e );
}
}
```

Compile `TinyHttpd` and place it in your class path. Go to a directory with some interesting documents and start the daemon, specifying an unused port number as an argument. For example:

```
% java TinyHttpd 1234
```

You should now be able to use your Web browser to retrieve files from your host. You'll have to specify the nonstandard port number in the URL. For example, if your hostname is *foo.bar.com*, and you started the server as above, you could reference a file as in:

```
http://foo.bar.com:1234/welcome.html
```

`TinyHttpd` looks for files relative to its current directory, so the pathnames you provide should be relative to that location. Retrieved some files? Al'righty then, let's take a closer look.

`TinyHttpd` is comprised of two classes. The public `TinyHttpd` class contains the `main()` method of our standalone application. It begins by creating a `ServerSocket`, attached to the specified port. It then loops, waiting for client connections and creating instances of the second class, a `TinyHttpdConnection` thread, to service each request. The `while` loop waits for the `ServerSocket` `accept()` method to return a new `Socket` for each client connection. The `Socket` is passed as an argument to construct the `TinyHttpdConnection` thread that handles it.

`TinyHttpdConnection` is a subclass of `Thread`. It lives long enough to process one client connection and then dies. `TinyHttpdConnection`'s constructor does three things. After saving the `Socket` argument for its caller, it adjusts its own priority and then invokes `start()` to bring its `run()` method to life. By lowering its priority to `NORM_PRIORITY-1` (just below the default priority), we ensure that the threads servicing established connections won't block `TinyHttpd`'s main thread from accepting new requests. (On a time-slicing system, this is less important.)

The body of `TinyHttpdConnection`'s `run()` method is where all the magic happens. First, we fetch an `OutputStream` for talking back to our client. The second line reads the `GET` request from the `InputStream` into the variable `req`. This request is a single newline-terminated `String` that looks like the `GET` request we described earlier. Since this is the only time we read from this socket, it's hard to resist the urge to be terse. Alternatively, we could break that statement into three steps: getting the `InputStream`, creating the `DataInputStream` wrapper, and reading the line. The three-line version is certainly more readable and should not be noticeably slower.

We then parse the contents of `req` to extract a filename. The next few lines are a brief exercise in string manipulation. We create a `StringTokenizer` and make sure there are at least two tokens. Using `nextToken()`, we take the first token and make sure it's the word `GET`. (If both conditions aren't met, we have an error.) Then we take the next token (which should be a filename), assign it to `req`, and check whether it begins with "/". If so, we use `substring()` to strip the first character, giving us a filename relative to the current directory. If it doesn't begin with "/", the filename is already relative to the current directory. Finally, we check to see if the requested filename looks like a directory name (i.e., ends in slash) or is empty. In these cases, we append the familiar default filename *index.html*.

Once we have the filename, we try to open the specified file and load its contents into a large byte array. (We did something similar in the `ListIt` example in Chapter 8.) If all goes well, we write the data out to client on the `OutputStream`. If we can't parse the request or the file doesn't exist, we wrap our `OutputStream` with a `PrintStream` to make it easier to send a textual message. Then we return an appropriate HTTP error message. Finally, we close the socket and return from `run()`, removing our `Thread`.

Taming the daemon

The biggest problem with `TinyHttpd` is that there are no restrictions on the files it can access. With a little trickery, the daemon will happily send any file in your filesystem to the client. It would be nice if we could restrict TinyHttpd to files that are in the current directory, or a subdirectory. To make the daemon safer, let's add a security manager. I discussed the general framework for security managers in Chapter 7. Normally, a security manager is used to prevent Java code downloaded over the Net from doing anything suspicious. However, a security manager will serve nicely to restrict file access in a self-contained application.

Here's the code for the security manager class:

```
import java.io.*;

class TinyHttpdSecurityManager extends SecurityManager {

    public void checkAccess(Thread g) { };
    public void checkListen(int port) { };
    public void checkLink(String lib) { };
    public void checkPropertyAccess(String key) { };
    public void checkAccept(String host, int port) { };
    public void checkWrite(FileDescriptor fd) { };
    public void checkRead(FileDescriptor fd) { };

    public void checkRead( String s ) {
        if ( new File(s).isAbsolute() || (s.indexOf("..") != -1) )
            throw new
                SecurityException("Access to file : "+s+" denied.");
    }
}
```

The heart of this security manager is the checkRead() method. It checks two things: it makes sure that the pathname we've been given isn't an absolute path, which could name any file in the filesystem; and it makes sure the pathname doesn't have a double dot (..) in it, which refers to the parent of the current directory. With these two restrictions, we can be sure (at least on a UNIX or DOS-like filesystem) that we have restricted access to only subdirectories of the current directory. If the pathname is absolute or contains "..", checkRead() throws a SecurityException.

The other do-nothing method implementations—e.g., checkAccess()—allow the daemon to do its work without interference from the security manager. If we don't install a security manager, the application runs with no restrictions. However, as soon as we install any security manager, we inherit implementations of many "check" routines. The default implementations won't let you do anything; they just throw a security exception as soon as they are called. We have to open holes so the daemon can do its own work; it still has to accept connections, listen on sockets, create threads, read property lists, etc. Therefore, we override the default checks with routines that allow these things.

Now you're thinking, isn't that overly permissive? Not for this application; after all, TinyHttpd never tries to load foreign classes from the Net. The only code we are executing is our own, and it's assumed we won't do anything dangerous. If we were planning to execute untrusted code, the security manager would have to be more careful about what to permit.

Now that we have a security manager, we must modify TinyHttpd to use it. Two changes are necessary: we must install the security manager and catch the security exceptions it generates. To install the security manager, add the following code at the beginning of TinyHttpd's main() method:

```
System.setSecurityManager( new TinyHttpdSecurityManager() );
```

To catch the security exception, add the following catch clause after FileNot-FoundException's catch clause:

```
catch ( SecurityException e )
    new PrintStream( out ).println( "403 Forbidden" );
```

Now the daemon can't access anything that isn't within the current directory or a subdirectory. If it tries to, the security manager throws an exception and prevents access to the file. The daemon then returns a standard HTTP error message to the client.

TinyHttpd still has room for improvement. First, it consumes a lot of memory by allocating a huge array to read the entire contents of the file all at once. A more realistic implementation would use a buffer and send large amounts of data in several passes. TinyHttpd also fails to deal with simple things like directories. It wouldn't be hard to add a few lines of code (again, refer to the ListIt example in Chapter 8) to read a directory and generate linked HTML listings like most Web servers do.

Datagram Sockets

TinyHttpd used a Socket to create a connection to the client using the TCP protocol. In that example, TCP itself took care of data integrity; we didn't have to worry about data arriving out of order or incorrect. Now we'll take a walk on the wild side. We'll build an applet that uses a java.net.DatagramSocket, which uses the UDP protocol. A datagram is sort of like a "data telegram": it's a discrete chunk of data transmitted in one packet. Unlike the previous example, where we could get a convenient OutputStream from our Socket and write the data as if writing to a file, with a DatagramSocket we have to work one datagram at a time. (Of course, the TCP protocol was taking our OutputStream and slicing the data into packets, but we didn't have to worry about those details).

UDP doesn't guarantee that the data will get through. If the data do get through, they may not arrive in the right order; it's even possible for duplicate datagrams to arrive. Using UDP is something like cutting the pages out of the encyclopedia, putting them into separate envelopes, and mailing them to your friend. If your friend wants to read the encyclopedia, it's his or her job to put the pages in order. If some pages got lost in the mail, your friend has to send you a letter asking for replacements.

Obviously, you wouldn't use UDP to send a huge amount of data. But it's significantly more efficient than TCP, particularly if you don't care about the order in which messages arrive, or whether the data arrive at all. For example, in a database lookup, the client can send a query; the server's response itself constitutes an acknowledgment. If the response doesn't arrive within a certain time, the client can send another query. It shouldn't be hard for the client to match responses to its original queries. Some important applications that use UDP are the Domain Name System (DNS) and Sun's Network Filesystem (NFS).

The HeartBeat Applet

In this section we'll build a simple applet, `HeartBeat`, that sends a datagram to its server each time it's started and stopped. (See Chapter 10 for a complete discussion of the `Applet` class.) We'll also build a simple standalone server application, `Pulse`, that receives that datagrams and prints them. By tracking the output, you could have a crude measure of who is currently looking at your Web page at any given time. This is an ideal application for UDP: we don't want the overhead of a TCP socket, and if datagrams get lost, it's no big deal.

First, the `HeartBeat` applet:

```
import java.net.*;
import java.io.*;

public class HeartBeat extends java.applet.Applet {
    String myHost;
    int myPort;

    public void init() {
        myHost = getCodeBase().getHost();
        myPort = Integer.parseInt( getParameter("myPort") );
    }

    private void sendMessage( String message ) {
        try {
            byte [] data = new byte [ message.length() ];
            message.getBytes(0, data.length, data, 0);
            InetAddress addr = InetAddress.getByName( myHost );
            DatagramPacket pack =
                new DatagramPacket(data, data.length, addr, myPort);
```

```
                    DatagramSocket ds = new DatagramSocket();
                    ds.send( pack );
                    ds.close();
                }
            catch ( IOException e )
                System.out.println( e );
        }

    public void start() {
        sendMessage("Arrived");
    }
    public void stop() {
        sendMessage("Departed");
    }
}
```

Compile the applet and include it in an HTML document with an `<applet>` tag:

```
<applet height=10 width=10 code=HeartBeat>
    <param name="myPort" value="1234">
</applet>
```

The `myPort` parameter should specify the port number on which our server application listens for data.

Next, the server-side application, `Pulse`:

```
import java.net.*;
import java.io.*;

public class Pulse {
    public static void main( String [] argv ) throws IOException {

        DatagramSocket s =
            new DatagramSocket(Integer.parseInt(argv[0]));
        while ( true ) {
            DatagramPacket packet = new DatagramPacket(new byte
                                            [1024], 1024);
            s.receive( packet );
            String message = new String(packet.getData(), 0, 0,
                                    packet.getLength());
            System.out.println( "Heartbeat from: " +
                packet.getAddress().getHostName() + " - " + message );
        }
    }
}
```

Compile `Pulse` and run it on your Web server, specifying a port number as an argument:

```
% java Pulse 1234
```

The port number should be the same as that you used in the `myPort` parameter of the `<applet>` tag for `HeartBeat`.

Now, pull up the Web page in your browser. You won't see anything there (a better application might do something visual as well), but you should get a blip from the `Pulse` application. Leave the page and return to it a few times. Each time the applet is started or stopped, it sends a message:

```
Heartbeat from: foo.bar.com - Arrived
Heartbeat from: foo.bar.com - Departed
Heartbeat from: foo.bar.com - Arrived
Heartbeat from: foo.bar.com - Departed
...
```

Cool, eh? Just remember the datagrams are not guaranteed to arrive (although it's unlikely you'll see them fail) and it's possible that you could miss an arrival or a departure. Now let's look at the code.

HeartBeat

HeartBeat overrides the `init()`, `start()`, and `stop()` methods of the `Applet` class, and implements one private method of its own, `sendMessage()`, that sends a datagram. `HeartBeat` begins its life in `init()`, where it determines the destination for its messages. It uses the `Applet getCodeBase()` and `getHost()` methods to find the name of its originating host, and fetches the correct port number from the `myPort` parameter of the HTML tag. After `init()` has finished, the `start()` and `stop()` methods are called whenever the applet is started or stopped. These methods merely call `sendMessage()` with the appropriate message.

`sendMessage()` is responsible for sending a `String` message to the server as a datagram. It takes the text as an argument, constructs a datagram packet containing the message, and then sends the datagram. All of the datagram information, including the destination and port number, are packed into a `java.net.DatagramPacket` object. The `DatagramPacket` is like an addressed envelope, stuffed with our bytes. After the `DatagramPacket` is created, `sendMessage()` simply has to open a `DatagramSocket` and send it.

The first four lines of `sendMessage()` build the `DatagramPacket`:

```
try {
    byte [] data = new byte [ message.length() ];
    message.getBytes(0, data.length, data, 0);
    InetAddress addr = InetAddress.getByName( myHost );
    DatagramPacket pack =
        new DatagramPacket(data, data.length, addr, myPort );
```

First, the contents of `message` are placed into an array of bytes called `data`. Next a `java.net.InetAddress` object is created from the name `myHost`. An

`InetAddress` simply holds the network address information for a host in a special format. We get an `InetAddress` object for our host by using the static `get-ByName()` method of the `InetAddress` class. (We can't construct an `InetAddress` object directly.) Finally, we call the `DatagramPacket` constructor with four arguments: the byte array containing our data, the length of the data, the destination address object, and the port number.

The remaining lines construct a default client `DatagramSocket` and call its `send()` method to transmit the `DatagramPacket`; after sending the datagram, we close the socket:

```
DatagramSocket ds = new DatagramSocket();
ds.send( pack );
ds.close();
```

Two operations throw a type of `IOException`: the `InetAd-dress.getByName()` lookup and the `DatagramSocket send()`. `InetAd-dress.getByName()` can throw an `UnknownHostException`, which is a type of `IOException` that indicates that the host name can't be resolved. If `send()` throws an `IOException`, it implies a serious client side problem in talking to the network. We need to catch these exceptions; our `catch` block simply prints a message telling us that something went wrong. If we get one of these exceptions, we can assume the datagram never arrived. However, we can't assume the converse. Even if we don't get an exception, we still don't know that the host is actually accessible or that the data actually arrived; with a `DatagramSocket`, we never find out.

Pulse

The `Pulse` server corresponds to the `HeartBeat` applet. First, it creates a `Data-gramSocket` to listen on our prearranged port. This time, we specify a port number in the constructor; we get the port number from the command line as a string (`argv[0]`) and convert it to an integer with `Integer.parseInt()`. Note the difference between this call to the constructor and the call in `HeartBeat`. In the server, we need to listen for incoming datagrams on a prearranged port, so we need to specify the port when creating the `DatagramSocket`. In the client, we need only to send datagrams, so we don't have to specify the port in advance; we build the port number into the `DatagramPacket` itself.

Second, `Pulse` creates an empty `DatagramPacket` of a fixed size to receive an incoming datagram. This alternative constructor for `DatagramPacket` takes a byte array and a length as arguments. As much data as possible is stored in the byte array when it's received. (A practical limit on the size of a UDP datagram is 8K.) Finally, `Pulse` calls the `DatagramSocket`'s `receive()` method to wait for a packet to arrive. When a packet arrives, its contents are printed.

As you can see, working with `DatagramSocket` is slightly more tedious than working with `Socket`s. With datagrams, it's harder to spackle over the messiness of the socket interface. However, the Java API rather slavishly follows the UNIX interface, and that doesn't help. I don't see any reason why we have to prepare a datagram to hand to `receive()` (at least for the current functionality); `receive()` ought to create an appropriate object on its own and hand it to us, saving us the effort of building the datagram in advance and unpacking the data from it afterwards. It's easy to imagine other conveniences; perhaps we'll have them in a future release.

Working with URLs

A URL points to an object on the Internet. It's a collection of information that identifies an item, tells you where to find it, and specifies a method for communicating with it or retrieving it from its source. A URL refers to any kind of information source. It might point to static data, such as a file on a local filesystem, a Web server, or an FTP archive; or it can point to a more dynamic object such as a news article on a news spool or a record in a WAIS database. URLs can even refer to less tangible resources such as Telnet sessions and mailing addresses.

A URL is usually presented as a string of text, like an address.[*] Since there are many different ways to locate an item on the Net, and different mediums and transports require different kinds of information, there are different formats for different kinds of URLs. The most common form specifies three things: a network host or server, the name of the item and its location on that host, and a protocol by which the host should communicate:

```
protocol://hostname/location/item
```

protocol is an identifier such as "http," "ftp," or "gopher"; *hostname* is an Internet hostname; and the *location* and *item* components form a path that identifies the object on that host. Variants of this form allow extra information to be packed into the URL, specifying things like port numbers for the communications protocol and fragment identifiers that reference parts inside the object.

We sometimes speak of a URL that is relative to a base URL. In that case we are using the base URL as a starting point and supplying additional information. For example, the base URL might point to a directory on a Web server; a relative URL might name a particular file in that directory.

---

[*] The term URL was coined by the Uniform Resource Identifier (URI) working group of the IETF to distinguish URLs from the more general notion of Uniform Resource Names or URNs. URLs are really just static addresses, whereas URNs would be more persistent and abstract identifiers used to resolve the location of an object anywhere on the Net. URLs are defined in RFC 1738 and RFC 1808.

The URL class

A URL is represented by an instance of the `java.net.URL` class. A URL object manages all information in a URL string and provides methods for retrieving the object it identifies. We can construct a URL object from a URL specification string or from its component parts:

```
try {
    URL aDoc = new URL( "http://foo.bar.com/documents/homepage.html" );
    URL sameDoc =
        new URL("http","foo.bar.com","documents/homepage.html");
}
catch ( MalformedURLException e ) { }
```

The two URL objects above point to the same network resource, the *homepage.html* document on the server *foo.bar.com*. Whether or not the resource actually exists and is available isn't known until we try to access it. At this point, the URL object just contains data about the object's location and how to access it. No connection to the server has been made. We can examine the URL's components with the `getProtocol()`, `getHost()`, and `getFile()` methods. We can also compare it to another URL with the `sameFile()` method. `sameFile()` determines if two URLs point to the same resource. It can be fooled, but `sameFile` does more than compare the URLs for equality; it takes into account the possibility that one server may have several names, and other factors.

When a URL is created, its specification is parsed to identify the protocol component. If the protocol doesn't make sense, or if Java can't find a protocol handler for it, the URL constructor throws a `MalformedURLException`. A protocol handler is a Java class that implements the communications protocol for accessing the URL resource. For example, given an "http" URL, Java prepares to use the HTTP protocol handler to retrieve documents from the specified server.

Stream Data

The most general way to get data back from URL is to ask for an `InputStream` from the URL by calling `openStream()`. If you're writing an applet that will be running under Netscape, this is about your only choice. In fact, it's a good choice if you want to receive continuous updates from a dynamic information source. The drawback is that you have to parse the contents of an object yourself. Not all types of URLs support the `openStream()` method; you'll get an `UnknownService-Exception` if yours doesn't.

The following code reads a single line from an HTML file:

```
try {
    URL url = new URL("http://server/index.html");
    DataInputStream dis = new DataInputStream( url.openStream() );
    String line = dis.readLine();
```

We ask for an `InputStream` with `openStream()`, and wrap it in a `DataInput-Stream` to read a line of text. Here, because we are specifying the "http" protocol in the URL, we still require the services of an HTTP protocol handler. As we'll discuss more in a bit, that brings up some questions about what handlers we have available to us and where. This example partially works around those issues because no content handler is involved; we read the data and interpret it as a content handler would. However, there are even more limitations on what applets can do right now. For the time being, if you construct URLs relative to the applet"s `codeBase()`, you should be able to use them in applets as in the above example. This should guarantee that the needed protocol is available and accessible to the applet. Again, we'll discuss the more general issues a bit later.

Getting the Content as an Object

`openStream()` operates at a lower level than the more general content-handling mechanism implemented by the URL class. We showed it first because, until some things are settled, you'll be limited as to when you can use URLs in their more powerful role. When a proper content handler is available to Java (currently, only if you supply one with your standalone application), you'll be able to retrieve the object the URL addresses as a complete object, by calling the URL's `getContent()` method. `getContent()` initiates a connection to the host, fetches the data for you, determines the data's MIME type, and invokes a content handler to turn the data into a Java object.

For example: given the URL *http://foo.bar.com/index.html*, a call to `getContent()` uses the HTTP protocol handler to receive the data and the HTML content handler to turn the data into some kind of object. A URL that points to a plain-text file would use a text-content handler that might return a `String` object. A GIF file might be turned into an `Image` object for display, using a GIF content handler. If we accessed the GIF file using an "ftp" URL, Java would use the same content handler, but would use the FTP protocol handler to receive the data.

`getContent()` returns the output of the content handler. Now we're faced with a problem: exactly what did we get? Since the content handler can return almost anything, the return type of `getContent()` is `Object`. Before doing anything meaningful with this `Object`, we must cast it into some other data type that we can work with. For example, if we expect a `String`, we'll cast the result of `get-Content()` to a `String`:

```
String content;

try
    content = (String)myURL.getContent();
catch ( Exception e ) { }
```

Of course, we are presuming we will in fact get a `String` object back from this URL. If we're wrong, we'll get a `ClassCastException`. Since it's common for servers to be confused (or even lie) about the MIME types of the objects they serve, it's wise to catch that exception (it's a subclass of `RuntimeException`, so catching it is optional) or to check the type of the returned object with the `instanceof` operator:

```
if ( content instanceof String ) {
    String s = (String)content;
    ...
```

Various kinds of errors can occur when trying to retrieve the data. For example, `getContent()` can throw an `IOException` if there is a communications error; `IOException` is not a type of `RuntimeException`, so we must catch it explicitly, or declare the method that calls `getContent()` can throw it. Other kinds of errors can happen at the application level: some knowledge of how the handlers deal with errors is necessary.

For example, consider a URL that refers to a nonexistent file on an HTTP server. When requested, the server probably returns a valid HTML document that consists of the familiar "404 Not Found" message. An appropriate HTML content handler is invoked to interpret this, and might return it as it would any other HTML object. At this point, there are several alternatives, depending entirely on the content handler's implementation. It might return a `String` containing the error message; it could also conceivably return some other kind of object or throw a specialized subclass of `IOException`. To find out that an error occurred, the application may have to look directly at the object returned from `getContent()`. After all, what is an error to the application may not be an error as far as the protocol or content handlers are concerned. "404 Not Found" isn't an error at this level; it's a perfectly valid document.

Another type of error occurs if a content handler that understands the data's MIME type isn't available. In this case, `getContent()` invokes a minimal content handler used for data with an unknown type, and returns the data as a raw `InputStream`. A sophisticated application might specialize this behavior to try to decide what to do with the data on its own.

The `openStream()` and `getContent()` methods both implicitly create a connection to the remote URL object. For some applications, it may be necessary to use the `openConnection()` method of the URL to interact directly with the protocol handler. `openConnection()` returns a URLConnection object, which represents a single, active connection to the URL resource. We'll examine URL-Connections further when we start writing protocol handlers.

Web Browsers and Handlers

The content- and protocol-handler mechanisms I've introduced can be used by any application that accesses data via URLs. This mechanism is extremely flexible; to handle a URL, you need only the appropriate protocol and content handlers. To extend a Java-built Web browser so that it can handle new and specialized kinds of URLs, you need only supply additional content and protocol handlers. Furthermore, Java's ability to load new classes over the Net means that the handlers don't even need to be a part of the browser. Content and protocol handlers could be downloaded over the Net, from the same site that supplies the data, and used by the browser. If you wanted to supply some completely new data type, using a completely new protocol, you could make your data file plus a content handler and a protocol handler available on your Web server; anyone using a Web browser built in Java would automatically get the appropriate handlers whenever they access your data. In short, Java lets you build automatically extendible Web browsers; instead of being a gigantic do-everything application, the browser becomes a lightweight scaffold that dynamically incorporates extensions as needed. Figure 9–3 shows the conceptual operation of a content handler; Figure 9–4 does the same for a protocol handler.

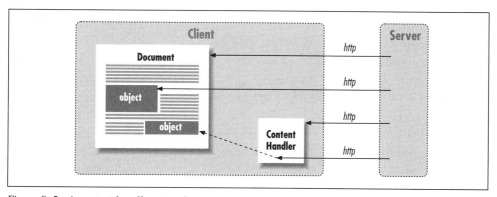

Figure 9–3: A content handler at work

Sun's HotJava was the first browser to demonstrate these features. When HotJava encounters a type of content or a protocol it doesn't understand, it searches the

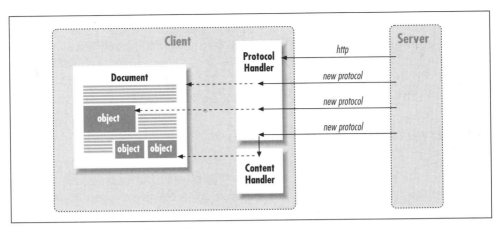

Figure 9–4: A protocol handler at work

remote server for an appropriate handler class. HotJava also interprets HTML data as a type of content; that is, HTML isn't a privileged data type built into the browser. HTML documents use the same content- and protocol-handler mechanisms as other data types.

Unfortunately, a few nasty flies are stuck in this ointment. Content and protocol handlers are part of the Java API: they're an intrinsic part of the mechanism for working with URLs. However, specific content and protocol handlers aren't part of the API; the `ContentHandler` class and the two classes that make up protocol handlers, `URLStreamHandler` and `URLConnection`, are all abstract classes. They define what an implementation must provide, but they don't actually provide an implementation. This is not as paradoxical as it sounds. After all, the API defines the `Applet` class, but doesn't include any specific applets. Likewise, the standard Java classes don't include content handlers for HTML, GIF, MPEG, or other common data types. Even this isn't a real problem, although a library of standard content handlers would be useful. (JDK provides some content and protocol handlers in the `sun.net.www.content` and `sun.net.www.protocol` packages, but these are undocumented and subject to change.) There are two real issues here:

- There isn't any standard that tells you what kind of object the content handler should return. I danced around the issue just above, but it's a real problem. It's common sense that GIF data should be turned into an `Image` object, but at the moment, that's an application-level decision. If you're writing your own application and your own content handlers, that isn't an issue: you can make any decision you want. But if you're writing content handlers that interface to arbitrary Web browsers, you need a standard that defines what the browser expects. You can use the `sun.net` classes to make a guess, but a real standard hasn't been worked out yet.

- There isn't any standard that tells you where to put content and protocol handlers so that an application (like a Web browser) can find them. Again, you can make application-level decisions about where to place your own handlers, but that doesn't solve the real problem: we want our content and protocol handlers to be usable by any browser. It's possible to make an educated guess about what the standard will be, but it's still a guess.

The next release of Sun's HotJava Web browser should certainly take full advantage of handlers,[*] but current versions of Netscape Navigator do not. When the next release of HotJava appears, it may resolve these questions, at least on a de facto basis. (It would certainly be in Sun's interest to publish some kind of standard as soon as possible.) Although we can't tell you what standards will eventually evolve, we can discuss how to write handlers for standalone applications. When the standards issues are resolved, revising these handlers to work with HotJava and other Web browsers should be simple.

The most common Java-capable platform, Netscape Navigator, doesn't use the content- and protocol-handler mechanisms to render Net resources. It's a classic monolithic application: knowledge about certain kinds of objects, like HTML and GIF files, is built-in. It can be extended via a plug-in mechanism, but plug-ins aren't portable (they're written in C) and can't be downloaded dynamically over the Net. Applets running in Netscape can use a limited version of the URL mechanism, but the browser imposes many restrictions. As I said earlier, you can construct URLs relative to the applet's code base, and use the `openStream()` method to get a raw input stream from which to read data, but that's it. For the time being, you can't use your own content or protocol handlers to work with applets loaded over the Net. Allowing this would be a simple extension, even without content- and protocol-handler support integrated into Netscape itself. We can only hope they add this support soon.

Writing a Content Handler

`getContent()` invokes a content handler whenever it's called to retrieve an object at some URL. The content handler must read the flat stream of data produced by the URL's protocol handler (the data read from the remote source), and construct a well-defined Java object from it. By "flat," I mean that the data stream

---

[*] Downloadable handlers will be part of HotJava 1.0, though they are not supported by the "pre-beta 1" release. The current release *does* support local content and protocol handlers. HotJava 1.0 also promises additional classes to support network applications.

the content handler receives has no artifacts left over from retrieving the data and processing the protocol. It's the protocol handler's job to fetch and decode the data before passing it along. The protocol handler's output is your data, pure and simple.

The roles of content and protocol handlers do not overlap. The content handler doesn't care how the data arrives, or what form it takes. It's concerned only with what kind of object it's supposed to create. For example, if a particular protocol involves sending an object over the network in a compressed format, the protocol handler should do whatever is necessary to unpack it before passing the data on to the content handler. The same content handler can then be used again with a completely different protocol handler to construct the *same* type of object received via a *different* transport mechanism.

Let's look at an example. The following lines construct a URL that points to a GIF file on an FTP archive and attempt to retrieve its contents:

```
try {
    URL url = new URL ("ftp://ftp.wustl.edu/graphics/gif/a/apple.gif");
    Image img = (Image)url.getContent();
    ...
```

When we construct the URL object, Java looks at the first part of the URL string (i.e., everything prior to the colon) to determine the protocol and locate a protocol handler. In this case, it locates the FTP protocol handler, which is used to open a connection to the host and transfer data for the specified file.

After making the connection, the URL object asks the protocol handler to identify the resource's MIME type.[*] It does this through a variety of means, but in this case it probably just looks at the filename extension (*.gif*) and determines that the MIME type of the data is image/gif. The protocol handler then looks for the content handler responsible for the image/gif type, and uses it to construct the right kind of object from the data. The content handler returns an Image object, which getContent() returns to us as an Object; we cast this Object back to the Image type so we can work with it.

In an upcoming section, we'll build a simple content handler. To keep things as simple as possible, our example will produce text as output; the URL's getContent() method will return this as a String object.

---

[*] MIME stands for Multipurpose Internet Mail Extensions. It's a standard design to facilitate multimedia email, but has become more widely used as a way to specify the treatment of data contained in a document.

Locating Content Handlers

As I said earlier, there's no standard yet for where content handlers should be located. However, we're writing code now and need to know what package to place our class files in. In turn, this determines where to place the class files in the local filesystem. Because we are going to write our own standalone application to use our handler, we'll place our classes in a package in our local class path and tell Java where they reside. However, we will follow the naming scheme that's likely to become the standard. If other applications expect to find handlers in different locations (either locally or on servers), you'll simply have to repackage your class files according to their naming scheme and put them in the correct place.

Package names translate to path names when Java is searching for a class. This holds for locating content-handler classes as well as other kinds of classes. For example, on a UNIX- or DOS-based system, a class in a package named `net.www.content` would live in a directory with *net/www/content/* as part of its pathname. To allow Java to find handler classes for arbitrary new MIME types, content handlers are organized into packages corresponding to the basic MIME type categories. The handler classes themselves are then named after the specific MIME type. This allows Java to map MIME types directly to class names.

According to the scheme we'll follow, a handler for the `image/gif` MIME type is called `gif` and placed in a package called `net.www.content.image`. The fully qualified name of the class would then be `net.www.content.image.gif`, and it would be located in the file *net/www/content/image/gif.class*, somewhere in the local class path or on a server. Likewise, a content handler for the `video/mpeg` MIME type would be called `mpeg` and there would be an *mpeg.class* file located (again, on a UNIX-/DOS-like filesystem) in a *net/www/content/video/* directory somewhere in a local class path or on a server.

Many MIME type names include a dash (-), which is illegal in a class name. You should convert dashes and other illegal characters into underscores when building Java class and package names. Also note that there are no capital letters in the class names. This violates the coding convention used in most Java source files, in which class names start with capital letters. However, capitalization is not significant in MIME type names, so it's simpler to name the handler classes accordingly. Table 9–1 shows how some typical MIME types are converted to package and class names.[*]

---

[*] The "pre-beta 1" release of HotJava has a temporary solution that is compatible with the convention described here. In the HotJava *properties* file, add the line:

```
java.content.handler.pkgs=net.www.content
```

Table 9–1: Converting MIME Types to Class and Package Names

MIME type	Package name	Class name	Class location
`image/gif`	`net.www.content.image`	`gif`	*net/www/content/image/*
`image/jpeg`	`net.www.content.image`	`jpeg`	*net/www/content/image/*
`text/html`	`net.www.content.text`	`html`	*net/www/content/text/*

The application/x-tar Handler

In this section, we'll build a simple content handler that reads and interprets *tar* (tape archive) files. *tar* is an archival format widely used in the UNIX-world to hold collections of files, along with their basic type and attribute information.[*] A *tar* file is similar to a ZIP file, except that it's not compressed. Files in the archive are stored sequentially, in flat text or binary with no special encoding. In practice, *tar* files are usually compressed for storage using an application like UNIX *compress* or GNU *gzip* and then named with a filename extension like *.tar.gz* or *.tgz*.

Most Web browsers, upon retrieving a *tar* file, prompt the user with a **File Save** dialog. The assumption is that if you are retrieving an archive, you probably want to save it for later unpacking and use. We would like to instead implement a *tar* content handler that allows an application to read the contents of the archive and give us a listing of the files that it contains. In itself, this would not be the most useful thing in the world, because we would be left with the dilemma of how to get at the archive's contents. However, a more complete implementation of our content handler, used in conjunction with an application like a Web browser, could generate output that lets us select and save individual files within the archive.

The code that fetches the *.tar* file and lists its contents looks like this:

```
try {
    URL listing =
        new URL("http://somewhere.an.edu/lynx/lynx2html.tar");
    String s = (String)listing.getContents();
    System.out.println( s );
    . . .
```

We'll produce a listing similar to the UNIX *tar* application's output:

```
Tape Archive Listing:

0      Tue Sep 28 18:12:47 CDT 1993 lynx2html/
14773 Tue Sep 28 18:01:55 CDT 1993 lynx2html/lynx2html.c
470    Tue Sep 28 18:13:24 CDT 1993 lynx2html/Makefile
172    Thu Apr 01 15:05:43 CST 1993 lynx2html/lynxgate
```

---

[*] There are several slightly different versions of the *tar* format. This content handler understands the most widely used variant.

```
3656   Wed Mar 03 15:40:20 CST 1993 lynx2html/install.csh
490    Thu Apr 01 14:55:04 CST 1993 lynx2html/new_globals.c
...
```

Our content handler dissects the file to read the contents and generate the listing. The URL's getContent() method returns that information to our application as a String object.

First we must decide what to call our content handler and where to put it. The MIME-type hierarchy classifies the *tar* format as an "application type extension." Its proper MIME type is then application/x-tar. Therefore, our handler belongs to the net.www.content.application package, and goes into the class file *net/www/content/application/x_tar.class*. Note that the name of our class is x_tar, rather than x-tar; you'll remember the dash is illegal in a class name so, by convention, we convert it to an underscore.

Here's the code for the content handler; compile it and place it in the *net/www/content/application/* package, somewhere in your class path:

```java
package net.www.content.application;

import java.net.*;
import java.io.*;
import java.util.Date;

public class x_tar extends ContentHandler {
    static int
        RECORDLEN = 512,
        NAMEOFF = 0, NAMELEN = 100,
        SIZEOFF = 124, SIZELEN = 12,
        MTIMEOFF = 136, MTIMELEN = 12;

    public Object getContent(URLConnection uc) throws IOException {
        InputStream is = uc.getInputStream();
        StringBuffer output =
            new StringBuffer( "Tape Archive Listing:\n\n" );
        byte [] header = new byte[RECORDLEN];
        int count = 0;

        while ( (is.read(header) == RECORDLEN) &&
                (header[NAMEOFF] != 0) ) {

            String name =
                new String(header, 0, NAMEOFF, NAMELEN).trim();
            String s = new String(header, 0, SIZEOFF, SIZELEN).trim();
            int size = Integer.parseInt(s, 8);
            s = new String(header, 0, MTIMEOFF, MTIMELEN).trim();
            long l = Integer.parseInt(s, 8);
            Date mtime = new Date( l*1000 );

            output.append( size + " " + mtime + " " + name + "\n" );
```

```
                count += is.skip( size ) + RECORDLEN;
                if ( count % RECORDLEN != 0 )
                    count += is.skip ( RECORDLEN - count % RECORDLEN);
            }

        if ( count == 0 )
            output.append("Not a valid TAR file\n");

        return( output.toString() );
    }
}
```

The ContentHandler class

Our x_tar handler is a subclass of the abstract class java.net.Content-Handler. Its job is to implement one method: getContent(), which takes as an argument a special "protocol connection" object and returns a constructed Java Object. The getContent() method of the URL class ultimately uses this get-Content() method when we ask for the contents of the URL.

The code looks formidable, but most of it's involved with processing the details of the *tar* format. If we remove these details, there isn't much left:

```
    public class x_tar extends ContentHandler {

        public Object getContent( URLConnection uc ) throws IOException {
            // get input stream
            InputStream is = uc.getInputStream();

            // read stream and construct object
            // ...

            // return the constructed object
            return( output.toString() );
        }
    }
```

That's really all there is to a content handler; it's relatively simple.

The URLConnection

The java.net.URLConnection object that getContent() receives represents the protocol handler's connection to the remote resource. It provides a number of methods for examining information about the URL resource, such as header and type fields, and for determining the kinds of operations the protocol supports. However, its most important method is getInputStream(), which returns an InputStream from the protocol handler. Reading this InputStream gives you the raw data for the object the URL addresses. In our case, reading the InputStream feeds x_tar the bytes of the *tar* file it's to process.

Constructing the object

The majority of our `getContent()` method is devoted to interpreting the stream of bytes of the *tar* file and building our output object: the `String` that lists the contents of the *tar* file. Again, this means that this example involves the particulars of reading *tar* files, so you shouldn't fret too much about the details.

After requesting an `InputStream` from the `URLConnection`, `x_tar` loops, gathering information about each file. Each archived item is preceded by a header that contains attribute and length fields. `x_tar` interprets each header and then skips over the remaining portion of the item. It accumulates the results (the file listings) in a `StringBuffer`. (See Chapter 7 for a discussion of `String-Buffer`.) For each file, we add a line of text listing the name, modification time, and size. When the listing is complete, `getContent()` returns the `String-Buffer` as a `String` object.

The main `while` loop continues as long as it's able to read another header record, and as long as the record's "name" field isn't full of ASCII null values. (The *tar* file format calls for the end of the archive to be padded with an empty header record, although most *tar* implementations don't seem to do this.) The `while` loop retrieves the name, size, and modification times as character strings from fields in the header. The most common *tar* format stores its numeric values in octal, as fixed-length ASCII strings. We extract the strings and use `Integer.parseInt()` to parse them.

After reading and parsing the header, `x_tar` skips over the data portion of the file and updates the variable `count`, which keeps track of the offset into the archive. The two lines following the initial skip account for *tar*'s "blocking" of the data records. In other words, if the data portion of a file doesn't fit precisely into an integral number of blocks of `RECORDLEN` bytes, *tar* adds padding to make it fit.

Whew. Well, as I said, the details of parsing *tar* files are not really our main concern here. But `x_tar` does illustrate a few tricks of data manipulation in Java.

It may surprise you that we didn't have to provide a constructor; our content handler relies on its default constructor. We don't need to provide a constructor because there isn't anything for it to do. Java doesn't pass the class any argument information when it creates an instance of it. You might suspect that the `URLConnection` object would be a natural thing to provide at that point. However, when you are calling the constructor of a class that is loaded at run-time, you can't pass it any arguments, as we discussed in Chapter 5.

Using our new handler

When I began this discussion of content handlers, I showed a brief example of how our x_tar content handler would work for us. We need to make a few brief additions to that code in order to use our new handler and fetch URLs that point to *.tar* files. Since we're writing a standalone application, we're not only responsible for writing handlers that obey the package/class naming scheme we described earlier; we are also responsible for making our application use the naming scheme.

In a standalone application, the mapping between MIME types and content-handler class names is done by a special java.net.ContentHandlerFactory object we must install. The ContentHandlerFactory accepts a String containing a MIME type and returns the appropriate content handler. It's responsible for implementing the naming convention and creating an instance of our handler. Note that you don't need a content-handler factory if you are writing handlers for use by remote applications; a browser like HotJava, that loads content handlers over the Net, has its own content-handler factory.

To make absolutely clear what's happening, we'll provide a simple factory that knows only about our x_tar handler, and install it at the beginning of our application:

```
import java.net.*;
import java.io.*;

class OurContentHandlerFactory implements ContentHandlerFactory {

    public ContentHandler createContentHandler(String mimetype) {
        if ( mimetype.equalsIgnoreCase( "application/x-tar" ) )
            return new net.www.content.application.x_tar();
        else
            return null;
    }
}

public class TarURLTest {
    public static void main (String [] args) throws Exception {

        URLConnection.setContentHandlerFactory(new
                    OurContentHandlerFactory() );

        URL url = new URL( args[0] );
        String s = (String)url.getContent();
        System.out.println( s );
    }
}
```

The class OurContentHandlerFactory implements the ContentHandler-Factory interface. It recognizes the MIME-type application/x-tar and returns a new instance of our `x_tar` handler. `TarURLTest` uses the static method `URLConnection.setContentHandlerFactory()` to install our new `ContentHandlerFactory`. After it's installed, our factory is called every time we retrieve the contents of a URL object. If it returns a `null` value, Java looks for handlers in a default location.[*]

After installing the factory, `TarURLTest` reads a URL from the command line, opens that URL, and lists its contents. Now you have a portable *tar* command that can read its *tar* files from arbitrary locations on the Net. I'll confess that I was lazy about exception handling in this example. Of course, a real application would need to catch and handle the appropriate exceptions; but we already know how to do that.

A final design note. Our content handler returned the *tar* listing as a `String`. I don't want to harp on the point, but this isn't the only option. If we were writing a content handler to work in the context of a Web browser, we might want it to produce some kind of HTML object that might display the listing as hypertext. Again, knowing the right solution requires that we know what kind of object a browser expects to receive, and currently that's undefined.

In the next section, we'll turn the tables and look at protocol handlers. There we'll be building `URLConnection` objects and someone else will have the pleasure of reconstituting the data.

Writing a Protocol Handler

A URL object uses a protocol handler to establish a connection with a server and perform whatever protocol is necessary to retrieve data. For example, an HTTP protocol handler knows how to talk to an HTTP server and retrieve a document; an FTP protocol handler knows how to talk to an FTP server and retrieve a file. All types of URLs use protocol handlers to access their objects. Even the lowly "file" type URLs use a special "file" protocol handler that retrieves files from the local filesystem. The data a protocol handler retrieves is then fed to an appropriate content handler for interpretation.

While we refer to a protocol handler as a single entity, it really has two parts: a `java.net.URLStreamHandler` and a `java.net.URLConnection`. These are both `abstract` classes we will subclass to create our protocol handler. (Note that these are `abstract` classes, not interfaces. Although they contain abstract methods we are required to implement, they also contain many utility methods we can

---

[*] If we don't install a `ContentHandlerFactory` (or later, as we'll see a `URLStreamHandlerFactory` for protocol handlers), Java defaults to searching for a vendor-specific package name. If you have Sun's Java Development Kit, it searches for content handlers in the `sun.net.www.content` package hierarchy and protocol handler classes in the `sun.net.www.protocol` package hierarchy.

use or override.) The URL looks up an appropriate URLStreamHandler, based on the protocol component of the URL. The URLStreamHandler then finishes parsing the URL and creates a URLConnection when it's time to communicate with the server. The URLConnection represents a single connection with a server, and implements the communication protocol itself.

Locating Protocol Handlers

Protocol handlers are organized in a package hierarchy similar to content handlers. Unlike content handlers, which are grouped into packages by the MIME types of the objects that they handle, protocol handlers are given individual packages. Both parts of the protocol handler (the URLStreamHandler class and the URLConnection class) are located in a package named for the protocol they support.

For example, the classes for an FTP protocol handler would be found in the net.www.protocol.ftp package. The URLStreamHandler is placed in this package and given the name Handler; all URLStreamHandlers are named Handler and distinguished by the package in which they reside. The URLConnection portion of the protocol handler is placed in the same package, and can be given any name. There is no need for a naming convention because the corresponding URLStreamHandler is responsible for creating the URLConnection objects it uses. Table 9–2 gives the obvious examples.[*]

Table 9–2: Mapping Protocols into Package and Class Names

Protocol	Package name	URLStreamHandler class name	Handler class location
FTP	net.www.protocol.ftp	Handler	*net/www/protocol/ftp/*
HTTP	net.www.protocol.http	Handler	*net/www/protocol/http/*

URLs, Stream Handlers, and Connections

The URL, URLStreamHandler, URLConnection, and ContentHandler classes work together closely. Before diving into an example, let's take a step back, look at the parts a little more closely, and see how these things communicate. Figure 9–5 shows how these components relate to each other.

---

* The "pre-beta 1" release of HotJava has a temporary solution that is compatible with the convention described here. In the HotJava *properties* file, add the line:

    java.protocol.handler.pkgs=net.www.protocol

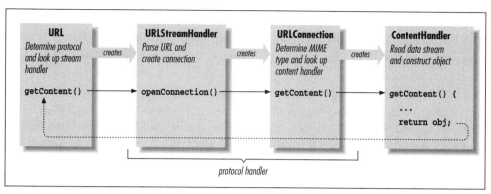

Figure 9–5: The protocol handler machinery

We begin with the URL object, which points to the resource we'd like to retrieve. The URLStreamHandler helps the URL class parse the URL specification string for its particular protocol. For example, consider the following call to the URL constructor:

```
URL url = new URL("protocol://foo.bar.com/file.ext");
```

The URL class parses only the protocol component; later, a call to the URL class' getContent() or openStream() method starts the machinery in motion. The URL class locates the appropriate protocol handler by looking in the protocol-package hierarchy. It then creates an instance of the appropriate URLStreamHandler class.

The URLStreamHandler is responsible for parsing the rest of the URL string, including hostname and filename, and possibly an alternative port designation. This allows different protocols to have their own variations on the format of the URL specification string. Note that this step is skipped when a URL is constructed with the "protocol," "host," and "file" components specified explicitly. If the protocol is straightforward, its URLStreamHandler class can let Java do the parsing and accept the default behavior. For this illustration, we'll assume that the URL string requires no special parsing. (If we use a nonstandard URL with a strange format, we're responsible for parsing it ourselves, as I'll show shortly.)

The URL object next invokes the handler's openConnection() method, prompting the handler to create a new URLConnection to the resource. The URLConnection performs whatever communications are necessary to talk to the resource and begins to fetch data for the object. At that time, it also determines the MIME type of the incoming object data and prepares an InputStream to hand to the appropriate content handler. This InputStream must send "pure" data with all traces of the protocol removed.

The URLConnection also locates an appropriate content handler in the content-handler package hierarchy. The URLConnection creates an instance of a content handler; to put the content handler to work, the URLConnection's getContent() method calls the content handler's getContent() method. If this sounds confusing, it is: we have three getContent() methods calling each other in a chain. The newly created ContentHandler object then acquires the stream of incoming data for the object by calling the URLConnection's getInput-Stream() method. (Recall that we acquired an InputStream in our x_tar content handler.) The content handler reads the stream and constructs an object from the data. This object is then returned up the getContent() chain: from the content handler, the URLConnection, and finally the URL itself. Now our application has the desired object in its greedy little hands.

To summarize, we create a protocol handler by implementing a URLStreamHan-dler class that creates specialized URLConnection objects to handle our proto-col. The URLConnection objects implement the getInputStream() method, which provides data to a content handler for construction of an object. The base URLConnection class implements many of the methods we need; therefore, our URLConnection needs only to provide the methods that generate the data stream and return the MIME type of the object data.

Okay. If you're not thoroughly confused by all that terminology (or even if you are), let's move on to the example. It should help to pin down what all these classes are doing.

The crypt Handler

In this section, we'll build a *crypt* protocol handler. It parses URLs of the form:

```
crypt:type//hostname[:port]/location/item
```

type is an identifier that specifies what kind of encryption to use. The protocol itself is a simplified version of HTTP; we'll implement the GET command and no more. I added the *type* identifier to the URL to show how to parse a nonstandard URL spec-ification. Once the handler has figured out the encryption type, it dynamically loads a class that implements the chosen encryption algorithm and uses it to retrieve the data. Obviously, we don't have room to implement a full-blown public-key encryption algorithm, so we'll use the rot13InputStream class from Chap-ter 8. It should be apparent how the example can be extended by plugging in a more powerful encryption class.

The Encryption class

First, we'll lay out our plug-in encryption class. We'll define an abstract class called CryptInputStream that provides some essentials for our plug-in encrypted protocol. From the `CryptInputStream` we'll create a subclass, `rot13CryptInputStream`, that implements our particular kind of encryption:

```
package net.www.protocol.crypt;
import java.io.*;

abstract class CryptInputStream extends InputStream {
    InputStream in;
    OutputStream talkBack;
    abstract public void set( InputStream in, OutputStream talkBack );
}

class rot13CryptInputStream extends CryptInputStream {

    public void set( InputStream in, OutputStream talkBack ) {
        this.in = new example.io.rot13InputStream( in );
    }
    public int read() throws IOException {
        if ( in == null )
            throw new IOException("No Stream");

        return in.read();
    }
}
```

Our `CryptInputStream` class defines a method called `set()` that passes in the `InputStream` it's to translate. Our `URLConnection` calls `set()` after creating an instance of the encryption class. We need a `set()` method because we want to load the encryption class dynamically, and we aren't allowed to pass arguments to the constructor of a class when it's dynamically loaded. We ran into this same restriction in our content handler. In the encryption class, we also provide an `OutputStream`. A more complex kind of encryption might use the `Output-Stream` to transfer public-key information. Needless to say, *rot13* doesn't, so we'll ignore the `OutputStream` here.

The implementation of `rot13CryptInputStream` is very simple. `set()` just takes the `InputStream` it receives and wraps it with the `rot13InputStream` filter we developed in Chapter 8. `read()` reads filtered data from the `Input-Stream`, throwing an exception if `set()` hasn't been called.

The URLStreamHandler

Next we'll build our `URLStreamHandler` class. The class name is `Handler`; it extends the abstract `URLStreamHandler` class. This is the class the Java URL looks up by converting the protocol name (*crypt*) into a package name

(net.www.protocol.crypt). The fully qualified name of this class is
net.www.protocol.crypt.Handler:

```
package net.www.protocol.crypt;

import java.io.*;
import java.net.*;

public class Handler extends URLStreamHandler {
    String cryptype;

    protected void parseURL(URL u, String spec, int start, int end) {
        int slash = spec.indexOf('/');
        cryptype = spec.substring(start, slash);
        start=slash;
        super.parseURL(u, spec, start, end);
    }

    protected URLConnection openConnection(URL url)
        throws IOException {

        return new CryptURLConnection( url, cryptype );
    }
}
```

Java creates an instance of our URLStreamHandler when we create a URL specifying the *crypt* protocol. Handler has two jobs: to assist in parsing the URL specification strings and to create CryptURLConnection objects when it's time to
open a connection to the host.

Our parseURL() method overrides the parseURL() method in the URL-
StreamHandler class. It's called whenever the URL constructor sees a URL
requesting the *crypt* protocol. For example:

```
URL url = new URL("crypt:rot13//foo.bar.com/file.txt");
```

parseURL() is passed a reference to the URL object, the URL specification string,
and starting and ending indexes that shows what portion of the URL string we're
expected to parse. The URL class has already identified the protocol name, otherwise it wouldn't have found our protocol handler. Our version of parseURL()
retrieves our *type* identifier from the specification, stores it in the variable cryptype, and then passes the rest on to the superclass' parseURL() method to complete the job. To find the encryption type, take everything between the starting
index we were given and the first slash in the URL string. Before calling
super.parseURL(), we update the start index, so that it points to the character
just after the type specifier. This tells the superclass parseURL() we've already
parsed everything prior to the first slash, and it's responsible for the rest.

Before going on, I'll note two other possibilities. If we hadn't hacked the URL string for our own purposes by adding a type specifier, we'd be dealing with a standard URL specification. In this case, we wouldn't need to override `parseURL()`; the default implementation would have been sufficient. It could have sliced the URL into host, port, and filename components normally. On the other hand, if we had created a completely bizarre URL format, we would need to parse the entire string. There would be no point calling `super.parseURL()`; instead, we'd have called the `URLStreamHandler`'s protected method `setURL()` to pass the URL's components back to the URL object.

The other method in our `Handler` class is `openConnection()`. After the URL has been completely parsed, the URL object calls `openConnection()` to set up the data transfer. `openConnection()` calls the constructor for our `URLConnection` with appropriate arguments. In this case, our `URLConnection` object is named `CryptURLConnection`, and the constructor requires the URL and the encryption type as arguments. `parseURL()` picked the encryption type from the URL string and stored it in the `cryptype` variable. `openConnection()` returns a reference to our `URLConnection`, which the URL object uses to drive the rest of the process.

The URLConnection

Finally, we reach the real guts of our protocol handler, the `URLConnection` class. This is the class that opens the socket, talks to the server on the remote host, and implements the protocol itself. This class doesn't have to be public, so you can put it in the same file as the `Handler` class we just defined. We call our class `Crypt-URLConnection`; it extends the abstract `URLConnection` class. Unlike `ContentHandler` and `StreamURLConnection`, whose names are defined by convention, we can call this class anything we want; the only class that needs to know about the `URLConnection` is the `URLStreamHandler`, which we wrote ourselves.

```
class CryptURLConnection extends URLConnection {
    CryptInputStream cis;
    static int defaultPort = 80;

    CryptURLConnection ( URL url, String cryptype )
        throws IOException {

        super( url );
        try {
            String name = "net.www.protocol.crypt." + cryptype
                            + "CryptInputStream";
            cis = (CryptInputStream)Class.forName(name).newInstance();
        }
        catch ( Exception e ) { }
    }
```

```
synchronized public void connect() throws IOException {
    int port;
    if ( cis == null )
        throw new IOException("Crypt Class Not Found");
    if ( (port = url.getPort()) == -1 )
        port = defaultPort;
    Socket s = new Socket( url.getHost(), port );

    // Send the filename in plaintext
    OutputStream server = s.getOutputStream();
    new PrintStream( server ).println( "GET "+url.getFile() );

    // Initialize the CryptInputStream
    cis.set( s.getInputStream(), server );
    connected = true;
}

synchronized public InputStream getInputStream()
    throws IOException {

    if (!connected)
        connect();
    return ( cis );
}

public String getContentType() {
    return guessContentTypeFromName( url.getFile() );
}
}
```

The constructor for our CryptURLConnection class takes as arguments the destination URL and the name of an encryption type. We pass the URL on to the constructor of our superclass, which saves it in a protected url instance variable. We could have saved the URL ourselves, but calling our parent's constructor shields us from possible changes or enhancements to the base class. We use cryptype to construct the name of an encryption class, using the convention that the encryption class is in the same package as the protocol handler (i.e., net.www.protocol.crypt); its name is the encryption type followed by the suffix CryptInputStream.

Once we have a name, we need to create an instance of the encryption class. To do so, we use the static method Class.forName() to turn the name into a Class object and newInstance() to load and instantiate the class. (This is how Java loads the content and protocol handlers themselves.) newInstance() returns an Object; we need to cast it to something more specific before we can work with it. Therefore, we cast it to our CryptInputStream class, the abstract class that rot13CryptInputStream extends. If we implement any additional encryption types as extensions to CryptInputStream and name them appropriately, they will fit into our protocol handler without modification.

We do the rest of our setup in the `connect()` method of the `URLConnection`. There, we make sure we have an encryption class and open a `Socket` to the appropriate port on the remote host. `getPort()` returns `-1` if the URL doesn't specify a port explicitly; in that case we use the default port for an HTTP connection (port 80). We ask for an `OutputStream` on the socket, assemble a `GET` command using the `getFile()` method to discover the filename specified by the URL, and send our request by writing it into the `OutputStream`. (For convenience, we wrap the `OutputStream` with a `PrintStream` and call `println()` to send the message.) We then initialize the `CryptInputStream` class by calling its `set()` method and passing it an `InputStream` from the `Socket` and the `OutputStream`.

The last thing `connect()` does is set the `boolean` variable `connected` to `true`. `connected` is a `protected` variable inherited from the `URLConnection` class. We need to track the state of our connection because `connect()` is a `public` method. It's called by the `URLConnection`'s `getInputStream()` method, but it could also be called by other classes. Since we don't want to start a connection if one already exists, we use `connected` to tell us if this is so.

In a more sophisticated protocol handler, `connect()` would also be responsible for dealing with any protocol headers that come back from the server. In particular, it would probably stash any important information it can deduce from the headers (e.g., MIME type, content length, time stamp) in instance variables, where it's available to other methods. At a minimum, `connect()` strips the headers from the data so the content handler won't see them. I'm being lazy and assuming that we'll connect to a minimal server, like the modified `TinyHttpd` daemon I discuss below, which doesn't bother with any headers.

The bulk of the work has been done; a few details remain. The `URLConnection`'s `getContent()` method needs to figure out which content handler to invoke for this URL. In order to compute the content handler's name, `getContent()` needs to know the resource's MIME type. To find out, it calls the `URLConnection`'s `getContentType()` method, which returns the MIME type as a `String`. Our protocol handler overrides `getContentType()`, providing our own implementation.

The `URLConnection` class provides a number of tools to help determine the MIME type. It's possible that the MIME type is conveyed explicitly in a protocol header; in this case, a more sophisticated version of `connect()` would have stored the MIME type in a convenient location for us. Some servers don't bother to insert the appropriate headers, though, so you can use the method `guessContentTypeFromName()` to examine filename extensions, like *.gif* or *.html*, and

map them to MIME types. In the worst case, you can use guessContentType-
FromStream() to intuit the MIME type from the raw data. The Java developers
call this method "a disgusting hack" that shouldn't be needed, but that is unfortunately necessary "in a world where HTTP servers lie about content types and extensions are often nonstandard." We'll take the easy way out and use the
guessContentTypeFromName() utility of the URLConnection class to determine the MIME type from the filename extension of the URL we are retrieving.

Once the URLConnection has found a content handler, it calls the content handler's getContent() method. The content handler then needs to get an
InputStream from which to read the data. To find an InputStream, it calls the
URLConnection's getInputStream() method. getInputStream() returns
an InputStream from which its caller can read the data after protocol processing
is finished. It checks whether a connection is already established; if not, it calls
connect() to make the connection. Then it returns a reference to our Crypt-
InputStream.

A final note on getting the content type: if you read the documentation, it's clear
that the Java developers had some ideas about how to find the content type. The
URLConnection's default getContentType() calls getHeaderField(),
which is presumably supposed to extract the named field from the protocol headers (it would probably spit back information connect() had stored in protected
variables). The problem is there's no way to implement getHeaderField() if
you don't know the protocol, and since the Java developers were designing a general mechanism for working with protocols, they couldn't make any assumptions.
Therefore, the default implementation of getHeaderField() returns null;
you have to override it to make it do anything interesting. Why wasn't it an abstract
method? I can only guess, but making getHeaderField() abstract would have
forced everyone building a protocol handler to implement it, whether or not they
actually needed it.

The application

We're almost ready to try out a crypt URL! We still need an application (a mini-
browser, if you will) to use our protocol handler, and a server to serve data with
our protocol. If HotJava were available, we wouldn't need to write the application
ourselves; in the meantime, writing this application will teach us a little about how
a Java-capable browser works. Our application is similar to the application we
wrote to test the x_tar content handler.

Because we're working in a standalone application, we have to tell Java how to find
our protocol-handler classes. Java relies on a java.net.URLStreamHandler-

Factory object to take a protocol name and return an instance of the appropriate handler. The `URLStreamHandlerFactory` is very similar to the `ContentHandlerFactory` we saw earlier. We'll provide a trivial implementation that knows only our particular handler. Again, if we were using our protocol handler with HotJava, this step would not be necessary; HotJava has its own stream-handler factory that tells it where to find handlers. To get HotJava to read files with our new protocol, we'd only have to put our protocol handler in the right place. (Note too, that an applet running in HotJava can use any of the methods in the URL class and therefore can use the content- and protocol-handler mechanism; applets would also rely on HotJava's stream-handler and content-xhandler factories.)

Here's our `StreamHandlerFactory` and sample application:

```
import java.net.*;

class OurURLStreamHandlerFactory implements URLStreamHandlerFactory {
    public URLStreamHandler createURLStreamHandler(String protocol) {
        if ( protocol.equalsIgnoreCase("crypt") )
            return new net.www.protocol.crypt.Handler();
        else
            return null;
    }
}

class CryptURLTest {
    public static void main( String argv[] ) throws Exception {

        URL.setURLStreamHandlerFactory(
            new OurURLStreamHandlerFactory());

        URL url = new URL("crypt:rot13//foo.bar.com:1234/myfile.txt");
        System.out.println( url.getContent() );
    }
}
```

The `CryptURLTest` class installs our factory and reads a document via the new "crypt:rot13" URL. (In the example, we have assumed that a *rot13* server is running on port 1234 on the host *foo.bar.com.*) When the `CryptURLTest` application calls the URL's `getContent()` method, it automatically finds our protocol handler, which decodes the file.

`OurURLStreamHandlerFactory` is really quite simple. It implements the URL-StreamHandlerFactory interface, which requires a single method called `createURLStreamHandler()`. In our case, this method checks whether the protocol's name is *crypt*; if so, the method returns an instance of our encryption protocol handler, `net.www.protocol.crypt.Handler`. For any other protocol name, it returns `null`. If we were writing a browser and needed to implement a more general factory, we would compute a class name from the protocol name, check to see if that class exists, and return an instance of that class.

The server

We still need a *rot13* server. Since the *crypt* protocol is nothing more than HTTP with some encryption added, we can make a *rot13* server by modifying one line of the `TinyHttpd` server we developed earlier, so that it spews its files in *rot13*. Just change the line that reads the data from the file:

```
f.read( data );
```

To instead read through a `rot13InputStream`:

```
new example.io.rot13InputStream( f ).read( data );
```

I assume you placed the `rot13InputStream` example in a package called `example.io`, and that it's somewhere in your class path. Now recompile and run the server. It automatically encodes the files before sending them; our sample application decodes them on the other end.

I hope that this example and the rest of this chapter have given you some food for thought. Content and protocol handlers are among the most exciting ideas in Java. It's unfortunate that we have to wait for future releases of HotJava and Netscape to take full advantage of them. In the meantime, you can experiment and implement your own applications.

10

The Abstract Windowing Toolkit

The Abstract Windowing Toolkit (AWT), or "another windowing toolkit," as some people affectionately call it, provides a large collection of classes for building a GUI in Java. With AWT, you can create windows, draw, work with images, and use components like buttons, scrollbars, and pull-down menus. The classes that comprise the AWT are part of the `java.awt` package.

For our purposes, AWT is divided into two large chunks: a user-interface chunk that provides the buttons, check boxes, text-input areas, and other user-interface components; and a graphics chunk that handles drawing and image rendering. In this chapter, we'll talk about the user-interface components; in the next, we'll cover images (and throw in audio for good measure). We don't cover the full functionality of AWT in this book; that would easily require a book by itself. Instead, we'll cover the basics of the tools you are most likely to use, and we'll hint at what can be done with some of the more advanced features. Figure 10–1 shows the user interface portion of the `java.awt` package.

As its name suggests, AWT is an abstraction. Its classes and functionality are the same for all Java implementations, so Java applications built with AWT should work the same way on all platforms. For example, the same code works under Windows NT/95, the X Window System, and the Macintosh. To achieve platform independence, AWT uses interchangeable toolkits that call the host windowing system to create user-interface components, thus shielding your application code from the details of the environment it's running in. Let's say you ask AWT to create a button. When your application or applet runs, a toolkit appropriate to the environment

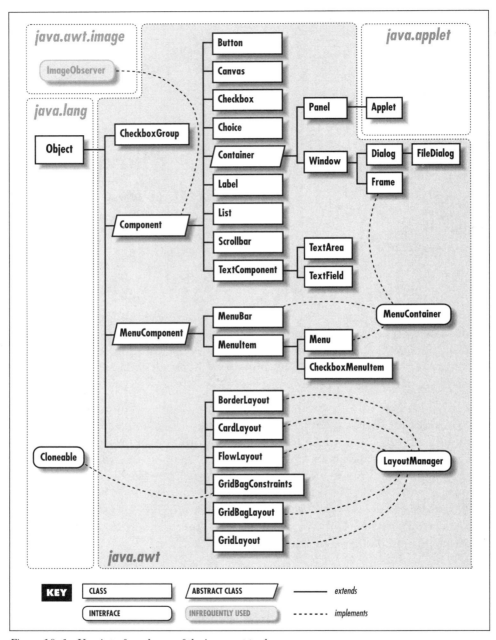

Figure 10–1: User-interface classes of the java.awt package.

renders the button appropriately: on Windows, you'll get a button that looks like other Windows buttons; on a Macintosh, you'll get a Mac button; and so on.

Working with user-interface components in AWT is meant to be easy. The low-level (native) GUI toolkits are admittedly complex, but you won't have to work with them directly unless you want to port AWT to a new platform or provide an alternative "look and feel" for the built-in components. When building a user interface for your application, you'll be working with prefabricated components. It's easy to assemble a collection of user-interface components (buttons, text areas, etc.), and arrange them inside containers to build complex layouts. You can also use simple components such as building blocks for making entirely new kinds of interface gadgets that are completely portable and reusable.

AWT uses layout managers to arrange components inside containers and control their sizing and positioning. Layout manages define a strategy for arranging components instead of relying on absolute positioning. For example, you can define a user interface with a collection of buttons and text areas, and be reasonably confident it will always display correctly. It doesn't matter that Windows, UNIX, and the Macintosh render your buttons and text areas differently; the layout manager still positions them sensibly with respect to each other.

Unfortunately, the reality is that most of the complaints about the first release of Java center around AWT. AWT is very different from what many people are used to and lacks some of the features other GUI environments provide (at least for now). It's also true that most of the bugs in current implementations of Java lie in the AWT toolkits. As bugs are fixed and developers become accustomed to AWT, I expect the number of complaints to diminish. But for the time being, expect to see some rough edges.

GUI Concepts in Java

Most of this chapter contains examples of using various classes in the `java.awt` package. But before we dive into those examples, we need to spend a bit of time talking about the concepts AWT uses for creating and handling user interfaces. This material should get you up to speed on GUI concepts, and how they are used in Java.

Components

A component is the fundamental user-interface object in Java. Everything you see on the display in a Java application is an AWT component. This includes things like windows, drawing canvases, buttons, checkboxes, scrollbars, lists, menus, and text fields. To be used, a component is normally placed in a container. Containers group components, arrange them for display, and sometimes associate them with a particular display device. All components are derived from the abstract `java.awt.Component` class, as you saw in Figure 10–1. For example, the `Button` class is a subclass of the `Component` class, which is derived directly from `Object`.

For the sake of simplicity, we can split the functionality of the `Component` class into two categories: appearance and behavior. The `Component` class contains methods and variables that control an object's general appearance. This includes basic attributes such as whether or not it's visible, its current size and location, and certain common graphical defaults like font and color. The `Component` class also contains methods implemented by specific subclasses to produce the actual graphics the object displays. When a component is first displayed, it's associated with a particular display device. The `Component` class encapsulates access to its display area on that device. This includes methods for accessing graphics and for working with off-screen drawing buffers for the display.

By a `Component`'s behavior, we usually mean the way it responds to user-driven events. When the user performs an action (like pressing the mouse button) within a component's display area, an AWT thread delivers an event to the component by invoking an event-handling methods. Common events are classified by type of activity (e.g., mouse click, mouse movement, key press) and then passed to one of several specific event-handling methods. Subclasses can receive events by overriding these methods individually, or by intercepting all events in a single method, before they are classified.

Components pass certain responsibilities on to the container objects in which they reside. Instead of handling an event itself, a component may pass it to its container and allow the container to handle the event. A component also informs its container when it does something that might affect other components in the container, such as changing its size or visibility. The container then knows it needs to be laid out again.

Containers in Java are themselves a kind of component. Because all components share this structure, container objects can manage and arrange `Component` objects without knowing what they are and what they are doing. Components can be swapped and replaced with new versions easily, and combined into composite user-interface objects that can be treated as individual components. This lends itself well to building larger, reusable user-interface items.

Peers

We have just described a nice system in which components govern their own appearance, and events are delivered to the components to consume or redirect as they see fit. Unfortunately, getting data out to a display medium and receiving events from input devices involve crossing the line from Java to the real world. The real world is a nasty place full of architecture dependence, local peculiarities, and strange physical devices like mice, trackballs, and power gloves.

At some level, our components will have to talk to objects that contain native methods to interact with the host operating system. To keep this interaction as clean and well-defined as possible, Java uses a set of *peer* interfaces. A peer interface lets a pure Java language component use its corresponding real component—the peer object—in the user environment. You won't generally deal directly with peer interfaces or the objects behind them; peer handling is encapsulated within the Component class. It's important to understand the process, though, because it imposes some limitations on what you can do with components.

For example, when a component such as a Button is first created and displayed on the screen, the Component class asks an AWT Toolkit class to create a corresponding peer object, as shown in Figure 10–2. The Toolkit is a *factory* that knows how to create objects in the native display system; Java uses factories as an additional level of abstraction that separates the implementation of an object from its functionality. The Toolkit object contains methods for making instances of each type of component peer. As a developer, you never work with a native user interface directly. Toolkit objects can be swapped and replaced to provide new implementations of the components without affecting the rest of Java.

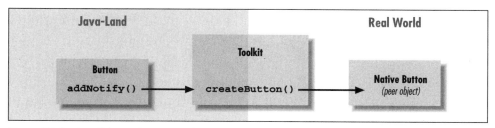

Figure 10–2: A toolkit creating a peer object

Figure 10–2 shows a Toolkit producing a peer object for a Button. When you add a button to a container, the container calls the Button's addNotify() method. In turn, addNotify() calls the Toolkit's createButton() method to make the Button's peer object in the real display system. Thereafter, the component class keeps a reference to the peer object and calls the peer's methods directly.

The `java.awt.peer` package, shown in Figure 10–3, parallels the `java.awt` package and contains an interface for each type of component. For example, the `Button` component has a `ButtonPeer` interface, which defines the capabilities of a button.

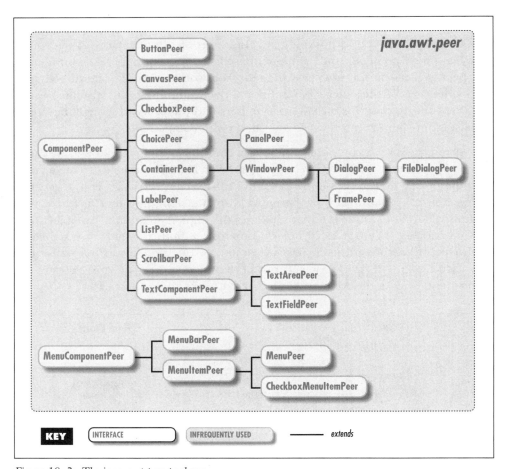

Figure 10–3: The java.awt.peer package

The peer objects themselves can be built in whatever way is necessary, using a combination of Java methods and native methods. A Java-land button doesn't know or care how the real-world button is implemented or what additional capabilities it may have; it knows only about the existence of the methods defined in the `ButtonPeer` interface. Figure 10–4 shows a call to the `setLabel()` method of a `Button` object, which results in a call to the corresponding `setLabel()` method of the native button object.

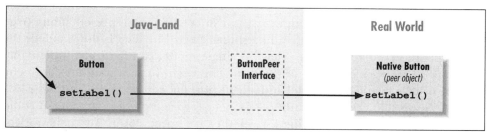

Figure 10–4: Invoking a method in the peer interface

In this case, the only action a button peer must perform is set its label; `setLabel()` is the only method in the `ButtonPeer` interface. How the native button acts, responds to user input, etc. is entirely up to it. It might turn green when pressed or play a sound. The component in Java-land has no control over these aspects of the native button's behavior, which has important implications. It means that AWT can use native components from whatever platform it resides on. It also means, however, that a lot of a component's functionality is locked away where we can't get to it. We'll see that we can intercept events before the peer object has a chance to act on them, but we usually can't change the object's basic behavior.

A component gets its peer when it's added to a container. Containers are associated with display devices, and hence `Toolkit` objects, and thus control the process of peer creation. This ought to mean you can't ask certain questions about a component before it's placed in a container. For example, you shouldn't be able to ask about a component's size until the component knows how it's being displayed. Java's developers apparently thought this restriction too onerous, so container-less components are associated with a default toolkit that answers such questions. In practice, the default toolkit is usually able to provide the right answer. Problems would arise if different containers had different toolkits, but this feature isn't part of the current implementation.[*]

Before we continue our discussion of GUI concepts, I want to make a brief aside and talk about the Model/View/Controller (MVC) framework. MVC is a method of building reusable components that logically separates the structure, representation, and behavior of a component into separate pieces. MVC is primarily concerned with building user-interface components, but the basic ideas can be applied to many design issues; its principles can be seen throughout Java. Java doesn't implement all of MVC, whose origins are in Smalltalk, but MVC's influence is apparent throughout the language.

---

[*] Multiple-toolkit environments are an interesting and potentially useful possibility. For example, such a toolkit might let you open a display on a remote console, or create a display with a different "look and feel" from the default. So far, there aren't any multiple-toolkit environments, but they should certainly exist before too long.

The fundamental idea behind MVC is the separation of the data model for an item from its presentation. For example, we can draw different representations (e.g., bar graphs, pie charts) of the data in a spreadsheet. The data is the "model"; the particular representation is the "view." A single model can have many views that show different representations of the data. The behavior of a user-interface component usually changes its model and affects how the component is rendered as a view. If we were to create a button component for example, its data model could be as simple as a `boolean` value for whether it's up or down. The behavior for handling mouse-press events would alter the model and the display would examine that data when it draws the on-screen representation.

MVC is also central to the way in which Java works with graphics, as you'll see in Chapter 11. Image information from a producer, such as a graphics engine or video stream, is distributed to consumers that can represent different views of the data. Consumers register with a producer and receive updates when the image has changed.

The factory concept used by the `Toolkit` objects is related to MVC; factories use Java interfaces to separate the implementation of an object from its behavior. An object that implements an interface doesn't have to fit into a particular class structure; it needs only to provide the methods defined by the interface. Thus, an AWT `Toolkit` is a factory that produces native user-interface components that correspond to Java components. The native components don't need to match AWT's class structure, provided they implement the appropriate interface.

Painting and updating

Components can be asked to draw themselves at any time. In a more procedural programming environment, you might expect a component would be involved in drawing only when first created or when it changes its appearance. In Java, components act in a way that is more closely tied to the underlying behavior of the display environment. For example, when you obscure a component with a window and then reexpose it, an AWT thread asks the component to redraw itself.

AWT asks a component to redraw itself by calling its `paint()` method. `paint()` may be called at any time, but in practice, it's called when the object is first made visible, whenever it changes its appearance, and whenever some tragedy in the display system messes up its area. Because `paint()` can't make any assumptions about why it was called, it must redraw the component's entire display.

However, redrawing the whole component is unnecessary if only a small part changes. In this case, you'd like to specify what part of the component has changed, and redraw that part alone. Painting a large portion of the screen is time consuming, and can cause flickering that is especially annoying if you're redrawing the object frequently, as with animation. When a component realizes it needs to redraw itself, it asks AWT to schedule a call to its `update()` method. `update()` might do some additional drawing of its own, but often, it simply defines a clipping region—by calling `clipRect()`—to limit the extent of the painted area and then calls `paint()` explicitly. A simple component doesn't have to implement its own `update()` method, but that doesn't mean the method doesn't exist. In this case, the component gets a default version of `update()` that simply clears the component's area and calls `paint()`.

A component never calls its `update()` method directly. Instead, when a component requires redrawing, it schedules a call to `update()` by calling `repaint()`. The `repaint()` method asks AWT to schedule the component for repainting. At some point in the future, a call to `update()` occurs. AWT is allowed to manage these requests in whatever way is most efficient. If there are too many requests to handle, or if there are multiple requests for the same component, AWT can schedule a single call to `update()`. Therefore, you can't predict exactly when `update()` will be called in response to a `repaint()`; all you can expect is that it happens at least once. Another form of `repaint()` allows you to specify a time period within which you would like an update, giving the system more flexibility in scheduling the request. An application could use this method to govern its refresh rate.

Both `paint()` and `update()` take a single argument: a `Graphics` object. The `Graphics` object represents the component's graphics context. It corresponds to the area of the screen on which the component can draw, and provides the methods for performing primitive drawing and image manipulation. We'll look at the `Graphics` class in detail in Chapter 11.

All components paint and update themselves using this mechanism. However, you really care about it only when doing your own drawing, and in practice, you should be drawing only on `Canvas` and `Panel` objects (an `Applet` is a kind of `Panel`). Other kinds of objects, like buttons and scrollbars, have lots of behavior built in to their peers. You could draw on one of these objects, but unless you specifically catch the appropriate events and redraw (which could get complicated), your handiwork is likely to disappear. `Canvas` and `Panel` objects exist purely to give you the satisfaction of drawing on them. By itself, a `Canvas` has no outward appearance; it takes up space and has a background color, but otherwise, it's empty. By subclassing `Canvas` and adding your own code, you can create a more complicated object like a graph canvas or a flying toaster. We'll see an example of subclassing `Canvas` later in the chapter. A `Panel` is like a `Canvas`, but it's also a `Container`, so that it can hold other user interface components.

Events

Events are created by the host environment and delivered to a component by its event-handling methods. When an event handler is called, it's passed an `Event` object and possibly some extra arguments. The `Event` contains variables that identify the type of event and where it came from.

There are two levels at which a component might handle an event. The `handleEvent()` method of the `Component` class handles events at a low level; this method is called for every event of any kind that is delivered to the object. The default implementation of `handleEvent()` categorizes the event and passes it off to one of several helper methods, which are conveniences to make event handling easier. When an event arrives, it contains a lot of information about who produced it, and when and where it happened. It's not hard to get this information directly from the event and take action based on the information.

But just the same, it's convenient to have separate methods for different event types, so that events can be handled at a higher level. Subclasses of `Component` can override specific methods for discrete mouse events such as `mouseDown()` and `mouseUp()`, for keyboard `keyDown()` and `keyUp()` strokes, for focus changes, and for general "action" events that correspond to things like button presses and menu choices.

If you have a component that is interested in many different kinds of events, you might find it convenient to override `handleEvent()` itself. When you override an event handler, keep in mind that these methods should be lightweight. An event handler should do as little as possible (e.g., set a few variables) and return, letting some other part of the application do the real work. If an event handler does too much, the application will seem unresponsive and sluggish; the event-handling thread will spend its time doing computation, rather than responding to user input.

A component or container that overrides a particular event-handling method doesn't necessarily have to handle that event. It can look at the event and decide whether to respond to it or allow it to be passed on. An event handler returns the `boolean` value `true` to indicate it has handled the event; in this case, the event is consumed. If the handler decides that isn't interested in the event, it should return `false`; in this case, the event is passed to its container. Since a `Container` is also a `Component`, it has an identical set of event handling methods, and it, too, can pass the event up the chain to its container if it's not interested. Ultimately, if neither the component nor any of its parent containers is interested in an event, it is finally passed to the component's peer object. Most events are simply eaten up by peer objects. Figure 10–5 illustrates the process by which an event is produced by the environment and passed to a component. The dashed lines indicate the potential for the event to be passed on, in turn, to the component's container object, or eventually, its peer.

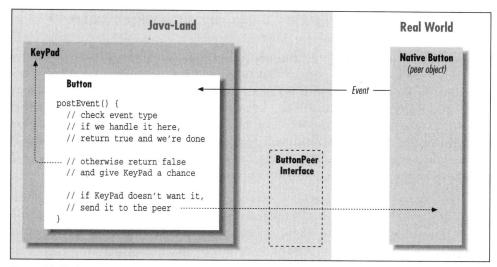

Figure 10–5: Event handling

I have implied that `handleEvent()` is the first method invoked for an event. Actually, events are first delivered to the `postEvent()` method of the `Component` class. The default behavior of `postEvent()` is to implement the scheme I described above. It calls the component's `handleEvent()` method, giving it an opportunity to take the event. If the component doesn't want the event, it invokes its big brother, the `postEvent()` method of the enclosing container class. Failing that, it hands the event to the peer object. It's important to know about `postEvent()` because later we'll want to build user-interface components that generate their own events. These components deliver events by calling `postEvent()` directly.

Focus please

In order to receive keyboard events, a component has to have the *focus*. The component with the focus is simply the currently selected input component. It receives all keyboard event information until the focus changes. A component can ask for keyboard focus with the `Component`'s `getFocus()` method. Text components like `TextField` and `TextArea` do this automatically whenever you click the mouse in their area. A component receives updates on its focus status through "got focus" and "lost focus" events. If you want to create your own text-oriented component, you can override the gotFocus() and lostFocus() methods to catch these. If your component has focus, you might use these methods to change the shape of a cursor.

Containers

Now that you understand components and events, containers should be easy. A container is a kind of component that holds and manages other components. If you look back to Figure 10–1, you can see the part of the java.awt class hierarchy that descends from Container. A Frame object is a top-level window on your display. Frame is derived from Window, which is pretty much the same, but lacks a border. Panel is a generic container element used to group components in Frames and other Panels. The Applet class is a kind of Panel; as a Panel, an Applet has the ability to contain other user-interface components.

A container has the same methods as other components, including the graphical and event-handling methods. A container also maintains a list of "child" components. The add() method of the Container class adds a component to the container. Thereafter, this component is arranged in the container's layout and displayed. As I said before, unhandled events from the child component are also passed to the container, where they can be handled.

Layout managers

A *layout manager* is an object that controls the placement and sizing of components within the display area of a container. A layout manager is like a window manager in a display system; it controls where the components go and how big they are. Every container has a default layout manager, but you can easily install a new one by calling the setLayout() method.

AWT comes with a few layout managers that implement common layout schemes. The default layout manager for a Panel is a FlowLayout, which tries to place objects at their preferred size from left to right and top to bottom in the container. The default for a Frame is a BorderLayout, which places a limited number of objects at named locations like "North," "South," and "Center." Another layout manager, the GridLayout, arranges components in a rectangular grid.

As I mentioned above, you normally call add() to add a component to a container. There are two overloaded versions of add(); which one you use depends on which layout manager is in effect. Most of the time, you'll use the version of add() that takes a single Component as an argument. However, if you're using a BorderLayout, you need to specify where to put the new Component. In this case, you'll need to call the two-argument version of add() like this:

```
add("North", newComponent)
```

This line of code adds `newComponent` to the container in the "North" position. Other layout managers, namely `CardLayout` and `GridBagLayout`, also require you to use this version of `add()`.

validate() and layout()

A layout manager arranges the components in a container only when asked to. Several things can mess up a container after it's initially laid out:

- Changing its size

- Resizing or moving one of its child components

- Adding, showing, removing, or hiding a child component

Any of these actions causes the container to be marked invalid. Saying that a container is invalid simply means it needs to have its child components readjusted by its layout manager. This is accomplished by calling the `Container`'s `validate()` method. `validate()` then calls the `Container`'s `layout()` method, which asks the layout manager to do its job. In addition, `validate()` also notes that the `Container` has been fixed (i.e., it's valid again) and looks at each child component of the container, recursively validating any that are also messed up.

So if you have an applet that contains a small `Panel`—say a keypad holding some buttons—and you change the size of the `Panel` by calling its `resize()` method, you should also call `validate()` on the applet. The applet's layout manager may then reposition or resize the keypad within the applet. It also automatically calls `validate()` for the keypad, so that it can rearrange its buttons to fit inside its new area.

There are two things you should note. First, all components, not just containers, maintain a notion of when they are valid or invalid. But most components (e.g., buttons) don't do anything special when they're validated. Next, child components are validated only if they are invalid. That means that if you have an invalid component nested inside a valid component and you validate a container above them both, the invalid component will never be reached.[*] This behavior seems highly counterintuitive; you naturally expect `validate()` to validate all components nested underneath. Ultimately, the reasoning behind `validate()`'s behavior is to limit the amount of time it takes to validate containers and to give you more control over what is rearranged and when.

---

[*] In Java 1.0.2, the semantics of `invalidate()` have changed so this situation shouldn't occur.

Applets

If you've been waiting for an applet discussion, here it is. An `Applet` is basically a `Panel` with an attitude; Figure 10–6 shows the classes in the `java.applet` package. An `Applet` expects to be embedded in a document and used in a viewing environment that provides it with special resources. In all other respects, however, applets are just ordinary `Panel` objects. Like a `Panel`, an `Applet` can contain user-interface components and implement all the basic drawing and event-handling capabilities of the `Component` class. We can draw on an `Applet` by overriding its `paint()` method; we can respond to events in the `Applet`'s display area by providing the appropriate event-handling methods. The additional structure applets have helps them interact with the viewer environment.

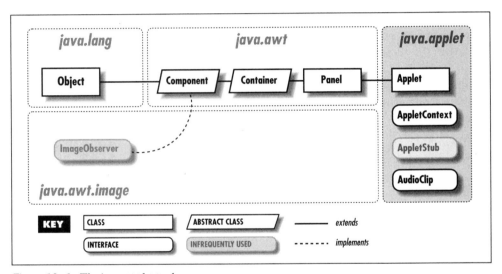

Figure 10–6: The java.applet package

Applet Control

The `Applet` class contains four methods an applet can override to help it through its life cycle. The `init()`, `start()`, `stop()`, and `destroy()` methods are called by an applet viewer, such as a Web browser, to influence an applet's behavior. `init()` is called once, after the applet is instantiated. The `init()` method is where you perform basic setup like parsing parameters, building a user interface, and loading resources. Given what we've said about object-oriented design, you might expect the `Applet`'s constructor would be the right place for such initialization. In fact, the constructor is called before the applet has access to certain resources, like information about its environment. Therefore, an applet doesn't supply a constructor; it always uses the default constructor for the `Applet` class. You should do your initialization in the `init()` method.

The `start()` method is called whenever the applet becomes visible; it shouldn't be a surprise then that the `stop()` method is called whenever the applet becomes invisible. For example, `start()` is called when the applet is first displayed, such as when it scrolls onto the screen; `stop()` is called if the applet scrolls off the screen or the viewer leaves the document. `start()` is called to tell the applet it should be active. An applet may want to start threads, animate, or otherwise perform useful (or annoying) activity. `stop()` is called to let the applet know it should go dormant. Applets should cease CPU-intensive or wasteful activity when they are stopped and resume it when (and if) they are restarted. However, there's no requirement that an invisible applet stop computing; in some applications, it may be useful for the applet to continue running in the background. Just be considerate of your user, who doesn't want an invisible applet dragging down system performance.

Finally, the `destroy()` method is called to give the applet a final chance to clean up before it's removed—some time after the call to `stop()`. For example, an applet might want to close down suspended communications channels or remove graphics frames. Exactly when `destroy()` is called depends on the applet viewer; Netscape Navigator calls `destroy()` just prior to deleting the applet from its cache. This means that although an applet can cling to life after being told to `stop()`, how long it can go on is unpredictable. If you want to maintain your applet as the user progresses through other activities, consider putting it in an HTML frame.

Viewer Environment Resources

An applet needs to communicate with its applet viewer. For example, it needs to find out about the HTML document in which it appears. An applet also needs to ask the viewer to get images, audio clips, and other items; it may even need to ask the viewer about other applets on the same HTML page in order to communicate with them. To communicate with their environment, applets use the `AppletStub` and `AppletContext` interface objects. Unless you're writing a browser or some other application that loads and runs applets, you'll never have to implement these interfaces, but you should know they exist.

An applet can find where it lives with the `getDocumentBase()` and `getCode-Base()` methods. `getDocumentBase()` returns the base URL of the document in which the applet appears; `getCodeBase()` returns the base URL of the

Applet's class file. An applet can use these to construct relative URLs from which to load other resources like data, images, and sound. The following example uses getDocumentBase() to construct a URL and load a properties-configuration file. (See Chapter 7 for a discussion of properties.)

```
Properties props = new Properties();
try
    props.load(
        new URL(getDocumentBase(), "appletConfig.props").openStream());
catch ( IOException e ) { }
```

We'll see other examples of using getDocumentBase() and getCodeBase() when we start working with images.

An applet can also retrieve parameters from the parameter tags associated with the <applet> tag in the HTML document. Use the the getParameter() method to retrieve parameters:

```
String imageName = getParameter( "imageName" );
try
    int numberOfSheep = Integer.parseInt(getParameter( "sheep" ));
catch ( NumberFormatException e ) { }
```

The getImage() method asks for an image from the viewer environment. The image may be pulled from a cache or loaded asynchronously when later used. The getAudioClip() method, similarly, retrieves sound clips. It's worth noting that an applet could open its own connection to the server and retrieve images or sounds directly. However, using getImage() and getAudioClip() is preferable because they take advantage of the browser's cache.

An applet can query the viewer to find what applets are running alongside it. To get an enumeration of references to other accessible applets, call getApplets(). To get a reference to an applet by name (i.e., the name given in the HTML <applet> tag), call getApplet():

```
DancingApplet sibling = getApplet(" Fred ");
if ( sibling != null )
    sibling.dance();
```

Note that to use getApplet(), an applet must know the cooperating applet's name in advance. If you don't have a reference to the applet, or the applet's name, you can still invoke a static method of the applet's class:

```
DancingApplet.setAllDancers( DancingApplet.DISCO );
```

It's up to the browser to define the scope of applet references; you can assume that other applets loaded through documents with the same base URL as your applet are accessible, but applets in other documents are not.

Two other methods pass applet requests to the viewer. The status line is a blurb of text that usually appears somewhere in the viewer's display, indicating a current activity. An applet can request that some text be placed in the status line with the `showStatus()` call. An applet can also request the viewer show a new document URL. To do this, the applet makes a call to the `AppletContext` directly. Get a reference to the `AppletContext` with the `getAppletContext()` method. The whole process could look something like:

```
getAppletContext().showDocument( url );
```

`url` is a URL object for the displayed page. An overloaded version of `showDocument()` has an additional `String` argument to direct the display to a particular Netscape Navigator frame. Both `showStatus()` and `showDocument()` requests may be ignored by a cold-hearted viewer or Web browser.

Using Components and Containers

User-interface objects are derived from the `Component` class; subclasses implement methods to define their own behavior. We'll talk about specific components in `java.awt` and provide examples of their use shortly. But first, I want to talk about how to get components to work together to perform useful tasks.

For purposes of this discussion, we'll divide the basic components in `java.awt` into two categories: *functional* components and *building-block* components. Functional components are objects like buttons, scrollbars, menus, and text fields; they have some obvious interactive behavior, such as depressing, sliding, listing, or editing. Building-block components don't do much on their own; instead they let you combine functional components in useful ways. The two building-block components we'll be using most often are the `Frame` and `Panel` objects.

When working with a functional component, you're more interested in the results of its job than the details. If you add a `Button` to your application, you probably want to know when it's pushed, although you probably don't care about precisely where it was pushed or how long it took to push it. When they are used, many functional components send a generic event called ACTION_EVENT. These events are passed to the component's `action()` method. For example, buttons send action events when pushed, checkboxes do so when checked, and text-entry fields do when you hit RETURN. Many of our simple examples catch action events. Other kinds of events provide more detailed information and require more context to use. These include mouse movement and button events and events generated by individual key strokes.

Smart Components

An event can be handled by a component itself or one of its containers; the choice depends on how unique the item is. If we have a component that does something special or complicated, we might design it to handle its own events. In this case we are building a smart component. To handle events in a smart component, we subclass the component and override the event-handling methods we are interested in. In the following example, `PressMeButton` is an example of a smart button that handles its own events:

```
import java.awt.*;
public class PressMe extends java.applet.Applet {
    public void init() {
        add ( new PressMeButton() );
    }
}

class PressMeButton extends Button {
    PressMeButton() {
        setLabel("Press Me!");
    }
    public boolean action(Event e, Object arg) {
        System.out.println("Thanks man.");
        return true;
    }
}
```

Here we have created a subclass of `Button` called `PressMeButton`. The button's constructor is nothing special; it just sets a label. The interesting part of `Press-MeButton` is its `action()` method, which overrides the `Button` class' `action()` method. By overriding `action()`, the `PressMeButton` says it wants to handle its own action events. When the button is pressed, an event-handling thread calls `action()`, which prints a message on the Java console. The `PressMe` applet that uses our button does one thing; it creates a new instance of `PressMe-Button` and calls `add()` to add the button to its layout.

Can we further subclass `PressMeButton`? Yes, but it's probably not a good idea. We could override `action()`, but that's where all `PressMeButton`'s functionality is located. Therefore, your new version of `action()` would have to invoke the superclass' method or reimplement it. This is not a particularly robust design— and in a more complicated situation, might be next to impossible. We can improve on this situation a little by overriding the lower-level event-handling method, but that skirts the issue. The only way to make truly drop-in replacement components is by working with the `Toolkit`.

Smart Containers

If you are building a user interface with a lot of simple components, you'll probably want to arrange the components in a container and let it handle the events. In this case you are building a smart container. Recall that a `Container` has exactly the same event-handling methods as a component because containers are themselves a kind of `Component`. We can therefore subclass a container object to override the appropriate event-handling methods and receive events generated by its components.

`Frame` and `Panel` objects are kinds of `Containers`. A `Frame` is a separate, top-level window on your display. A `Panel` is a generic container that groups components inside of `Frames` and other `Panels`. We can subclass `Panel` or `Frame` and override methods to handle events generated by its children. The following example creates a kind of `Panel` called a `KeyPad` that holds a configurable number of `Button` components, as shown in Figure 10–7. `KeyPad` handles the action events that occur when buttons are pressed.

```java
import java.awt.*;

public class Keys extends java.applet.Applet {
    public void init() {
        add ( new KeyPad( 16 ) );
        resize(preferredSize());
    }
}
class KeyPad extends Panel {
    KeyPad ( int n ) {
        int s = (int)Math.sqrt(n);
        setLayout( new GridLayout(s, s) );
        for (int i=0; i<n; i++)
            add( new Button( Integer.toString(i) ) );
    }

    public boolean action(Event e, Object arg) {
        System.out.println("Button "+arg+" pressed");
        return true;
    }
}
```

The constructor for our `KeyPad` object takes an integer, n, that specifies the number of keys. `KeyPad` makes n `Button` components and adds them to itself. We use a `GridLayout` to arrange the buttons in a familiar pattern. The constructor decides how many buttons are in each row of the keypad and installs a new `Grid-Layout` object as the layout manager for our `Panel`. (We'll talk about the details of using various layout managers later.) We tell `GridLayout` how many rows and columns of components we'd like, and it does its best to arrange them accordingly. (If there are too many or too few buttons, the layout manager finds a way to

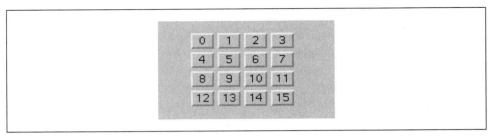

Figure 10–7: The KeyPad applet

accommodate them.) We loop, creating the n Button objects and calling the
add() method to add them to our keypad.

When we create each button, we label it with a number; the Button constructor
takes a string for the button's label. When one of the buttons is pushed, it generates an action event that's eventually passed to its container object, our KeyPad.
The action() event-handling method is invoked with two parameters: the event
and an argument from the object that caused it. A Button object sends its label as
the argument of its event, so we can use arg to print a message saying which button was pushed. Note that it makes a lot more sense to build a smart keypad than a
collection of smart buttons, particularly if you consider what a real keypad application would have to do. In a more realistic keypad, we might keep track of the key
presses and use them to construct a number or a string. You could implement
these features with a set of smart buttons, but it's more natural to put the intelli-
gence in the keypad.

Because KeyPad is a kind of Panel and Panel is ultimately derived from Component, we can add KeyPad to other container objects. This is precisely what
happens when we add an instance of it to our Keys applet; recall that an Applet
is a kind of Panel itself. KeyPad is therefore a new kind of user-interface component that we could use as part of a larger user interface.

So, how would KeyPad talk to the rest of the user interface? Suppose we have an
Enter key: how would it send its results? One of two ways, most likely. We could
design KeyPad to call a method in another object when something important
happens (i.e., a callback). To be more modular and component-like though, Key-
Pad could generate its own events and send them to its container, just like other
components. We'll see an example of this technique later in the chapter when we
create another kind of component.

Components can be disabled to reject user input. A disabled component is usually
indicated by "ghosting" its appearance; for instance, you could lower the contrast
or change its color. To see the effect, try making the following change to our Key-
Pad example:

```
public boolean void action(Event e, Object arg) {
    ((Component)e.target).disable();
    return true;
}
```

Now, instead of printing a value when a button is pressed, KeyPad disables the button: each button can be pressed only once. You can also disable an entire container. Disabling a Panel, for instance, disables all the components it contains.

Who Sent That Event?

Practically speaking, the first thing you need to do in an event handler is figure out exactly who sent you the event. For the PressMeButton it was easy because there was only one object to worry about. We overrode the action() event-handling method of the PressMeButton object itself. Since it contained no other components within it, we could make the assumption that the only action events it would receive were those that occurred when PressMeButton itself was pressed.

More often, you'll be putting components in containers, so you'll have to be more selective about where the event actually came from. In our KeyPad example, we use the arg parameter to distinguish which button was pressed and print our message. We could, just as easily, have used this information to do another, more complicated activity based on which button was pushed. Different kinds of objects send different information in the event arg field. Refer to class documentation (or experimentation) to see what information different objects stuff into the events they send.

If you're writing a large application, you may have dozens of buttons, checkboxes, scrollbars, and text areas to worry about. You can always get needed information by looking at the target variable of the Event object sent to the event handler. target is a reference to the object that sent the event. Sometimes it's sufficient simply to know what kind of object sent the event; for example, if you have only one scrollbar in your container. In that case, you can use the instanceof operator to test target for various types:

```
handleEvent(Event e) {
    if ( e.target instanceof Scrollbar ) {
        ...
    }
    ...
```

If you have more than one kind of object in your container, you need to do more work. If you have references to the various components lying around, you should use the == operator to test the identity of the object:

```
action(Event e, Object arg) {
    if ( e.target == myLeftScrollbar ) {
        . . .
    }
    . . .
```

It's often better to be safe than sorry. You should try to be specific when testing your events and return `false` whenever you receive an unexpected event; this return value allows the event to be passed to other handlers, which may be expecting it. This extra care pays off when you suddenly have to add some new functionality to your interface. We'll opt for brevity in our examples and test only when it's absolutely necessary, but you shouldn't emulate this coding style.

Text Components

Now let's look at the specific components in `java.awt` you can use in your GUIs. AWT gives us two basic text components: `TextArea` is a multiline text editor with vertical and horizontal scrollbars; `TextField` is a simple, single-line text editor. The following applet, `TextBox`, creates a `TextArea` and ties it to a `TextField`, as you can see in Figure 10–8. Lines entered in the `TextField` are added to the `TextArea`'s display. Try it out. You may have to click your mouse in the `TextField` to give it focus before typing in it. If you enter more than 10 lines, you can test drive the scrollbar.

Figure 10–8: The TextBox applet

```
import java.awt.*;

public class TextBox extends java.applet.Applet {
    TextArea area;
    TextField field;
    int ROWS = 10, COLS = 20;

    public void init() {
        setLayout( new BorderLayout() );
        Panel p = new Panel();
        p.add( area = new TextArea( ROWS, COLS ));
        add( "North", p );
        area.setFont( new Font("TimesRoman",Font.BOLD,18) );
        area.setText("Howdy!\n");

        p = new Panel();
        p.add( field = new TextField( COLS ));
        add( "Center", p );
        resize(preferredSize());
    }

    public boolean action( Event e, Object arg ) {
        if ( e.target instanceof TextField ) {
            String s = area.getText() + arg + "\n";
            area.setText( s );
            field.setText("");
            return true;
        }
        return false;
    }
}
```

TextBox is exceedingly simple; we've done a few things to make it more interesting. First, we set the applet's layout manager to BorderLayout. We use Border-Layout to position the TextArea above the TextField. We also put the TextArea and TextField inside their own Panel objects so they can maintain their own sizes, rather than let the BorderLayout stretch them around. We also change the size of the text area by giving it a bigger font using Component's set-Font() method; fonts are discussed in Chapter 11.

Here are the details of how we create the TextArea and TextField and put them in Panel objects. First, we create a Panel and then we create a TextArea with the specified number of rows and columns and add it to the Panel with p.add(). Then we add the Panel itself to the applet with add("North",p); this places the Panel in the BorderLayout's "North" position. Next we do the same with a TextField, adding it to another Panel and adding that Panel to the BorderLayout in the "Center" position.

Hitting RETURN in the `TextField` generates an action event, and that's where the fun begins. We handle the event in the `action()` method of our container, the `TextBox` applet. First, we check to make sure the event came from our `TextField`. (We are going to ignore any events generated by the `TextArea`.) Then we use the `getText()` and `setText()` methods to manipulate the text the user has typed. These methods can be used for both `TextField` and `TextArea`, because these components are derived from the `TextComponent` class, and therefore have some common functionality.

First, the event handler calls `area.getText()` to read the text from our `TextArea`. It then sticks whatever has been typed into the `TextField` onto the end of this text; the current contents of the `TextField` is available in the `arg` argument to `action()`. We then use `area.setText()` to display the entire text in the `TextArea`, and `field.setText()` to clear the `TextField` for new input.

By default, `TextField` and `TextArea` are editable; you can type and edit in both text components. They can be changed to output-only areas with the `setEditable()` method. Both text components also support *selections*. A selection is a subset of text that is highlighted for copying and pasting in your windowing system. You select text by dragging the mouse over it; you can then copy and paste it into other text windows. You can get the selected text explicitly with `getSelectedText()`.

Menus and Choices

A `Menu` is a standard, pull-down menu with a fixed name. Menus can hold other menus as submenu items, letting you implement complex menu structures. Menus come with several restrictions; they must be attached to a menu bar, and the menu bar can be attached only to a `Frame` (or another menu). You can't stick a `Menu` at an arbitrary position within a container. A top-level `Menu` has a name that is always visible in the menu bar.

A `Choice` is an item that lets you choose from a selection of alternatives. If this sounds like a menu, you're right. Choices are free-spirited relatives of menus. A `Choice` item can be positioned anywhere, in any kind of container. It looks something like a button, with the current selection as its label. When you press the mouse button on a choice, it unfurls to show possible selections.

Both menus and choices send action events when an item is selected. We'll create a little example that illustrates choices and menus and demonstrates how to work with the events they generate. Since a `Menu` has to be placed in the menu bar of a

Frame, we'll take this opportunity to show off a Frame object as well. Dinner-Menu pops up a window containing a **Food** choice and a menu of **Utensils**, as shown in Figure 10–9. DinnerMenu prints a message for each selection; choosing **Quit** from the menu removes the window. Give it a try.

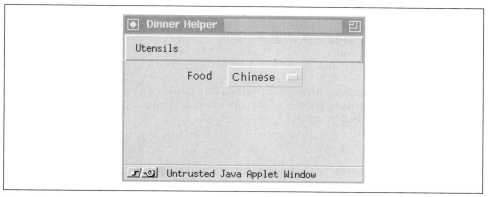

Figure 10–9: The DinnerMenu applet

```
import java.awt.*;

public class DinnerMenu extends java.applet.Applet {
    public void init() {
        Frame f = new DinnerFrame();
        f.show();
    }
}

class DinnerFrame extends Frame {
    DinnerFrame() {
        setTitle("Dinner Helper");
        setLayout( new FlowLayout() );
        add( new Label("Food") );

        Choice c = new Choice ();
        c.addItem("Chinese");
        c.addItem("Italian");
        c.addItem("American");
        add( c );

        Menu m = new Menu("Utensils");
        m.add(new MenuItem("Fork"));
        m.add(new MenuItem("Knife"));
        m.add(new MenuItem("Spoon"));
        Menu subMenu = new Menu("hybrid");
        subMenu.add(new MenuItem("Spork"));
        subMenu.add(new MenuItem("Spife"));
        subMenu.add(new MenuItem("Knork"));
        m.add(subMenu);
```

```
        m.add("Quit");
        MenuBar mb = new MenuBar();
        mb.add(m);
        setMenuBar(mb);

        resize(200, 200);
    }

    public boolean action(Event e, Object arg) {
        if ( arg.equals("Quit") ) {
            dispose();
            return true;
        }
        if ( e.target instanceof Choice ) {
            System.out.println("Food: "+arg);
            return true;
        }


        if ( e.target instanceof Menu ) {
            System.out.println("Utensil: "+arg);
            return true;
        }
        return false;
    }
}
```

Yes, I know. **Quit** doesn't belong in the **Utensils** menu. If it's driving you crazy, you can go back and add a **File** menu as an exercise when we're through.

So what do we have? Well, we've created a new kind of component called `Din-nerFrame` that implements our palette of dinner options. We do our set-up work in the `DinnerFrame` constructor. `DinnerFrame` sets the name on its titlebar with `setTitle()`. The constructor also handles a few other miscellaneous details, such as setting the layout manager that places things side by side in the display area and later, resizes itself.

We make an instance of `Choice` and add three options to it with its `addItem()` method. `Choice` options are simple `String` objects. When one is picked, we get an action event with an argument that specifies the selected option name. We can also examine the currently selected item at any time with the `Choice`'s `getSe-lectedItem()` method. As with any component, we display the `Choice` by adding it to our applet's layout with `add()`.

The `Menu` has a few more moving parts. A `Menu` holds `MenuItem` objects. A simple `MenuItem` just has a `String` as a label. It sends this as an argument in an action event when it's selected. We can set its font with `setFont()`. We can also turn it on or off with `enable()` and `disable()`; these methods control whether the `MenuItem` is available or not. A `Menu` object is itself a kind of `MenuItem`, and this allows us to use a menu as a submenu in another menu.

We construct the Menu with its name and call its add() method to give it three new MenuItem objects. Next, we repeat this process to make a new Menu object, subMenu, and add it as the fourth option. Its name appears as the menu item along with a little arrow, indicating it's a submenu. When it's selected, the sub-Menu menu pops up to the side and we can select from it. Finally, we add one last simple menu item, to serve as a **Quit** option.

Now that we have the menu; to use it, we have to insert it in in a menu bar. A MenuBar holds Menu objects. We create a MenuBar and set it as the menu bar for DinnerFrame with the Frame.setMenuBar() method. We can then add our menu to it with MenuBar.add():

```
MenuBar mb = new MenuBar();
mb.add(m);
setMenuBar(mb);
```

Suppose our applet didn't have its own frame? Where could we put our menu? Ideally, you'd like the applet to be able to add a menu to the top-level menu bar of the Web browser or applet viewer. Unfortunately, at the time of this writing, there is no standard for doing so. (There are obvious security considerations in allowing an applet to modify its viewer.)

One final note about the DinnerMenu example. Any time you use a Frame, and thus create a new top-level window, you should add the following event-handling code:

```
public boolean handleEvent( Event e ) {
    if ( e.id == Event.WINDOW_DESTROY ) {
        dispose();
        return true;
    }
    ...
}
```

This code handles the window-destroy event that can be generated by various window managers (e.g., **Close** from the window menu). By calling dispose(), we indicate the window is no longer needed, so that it can release its window-system resources.

Checkboxes

A Checkbox is a labeled toggle button. A group of such toggle buttons can be made mutually exclusive by tethering them together with a CheckboxGroup object. By now you're probably well into the swing of things and could easily master the Checkbox on your own. We'll throw out an example to illustrate a different way of dealing with the state of components and to show off a few more things about containers.

A Checkbox sends action events when it's pushed, just like other buttons. In our last example, we caught the action events from our choice and menu selections and worked with them when they happened. For something like a checkbox, we might want to be lazy and check on the state of the buttons only at some later time, such as when the user commits an action. It's like filling out a form; you can change your choices until you submit the form.

The following applet, DriveThrough, lets us check off selections on a fast food menu, as shown in Figure 10–10. DriveThrough prints the results when we press the **Place Order** button.

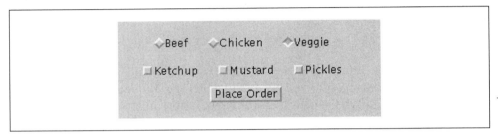

Figure 10–10: The DriveThrough applet

```java
import java.awt.*;

public class DriveThrough extends java.applet.Applet {
    Panel condimentsPanel = new Panel();
    CheckboxGroup entreeGroup = new CheckboxGroup();

    public void init() {
        condimentsPanel.add( new Checkbox("Ketchup"));
        condimentsPanel.add( new Checkbox("Mustard"));
        condimentsPanel.add( new Checkbox("Pickles"));

        Checkbox c;
        Panel entreePanel = new Panel();
        entreePanel.add( c = new Checkbox("Beef") );
        c.setCheckboxGroup( entreeGroup );
        entreePanel.add( c = new Checkbox("Chicken") );
        c.setCheckboxGroup( entreeGroup );
        entreePanel.add( c = new Checkbox("Veggie") );
        c.setCheckboxGroup( entreeGroup );
        entreeGroup.setCurrent( c );

        Panel orderPanel = new Panel();
        orderPanel.add( new Button("Place Order") );

        setLayout( new GridLayout(3, 1) );
        add( entreePanel );
        add( condimentsPanel );
        add( orderPanel );
```

```
        resize( preferredSize() );
    }

    public boolean action ( Event e, Object o ) {
        if ( !(e.target instanceof Button) )
            return false;

        Checkbox c = entreeGroup.getCurrent();
            System.out.println( c.getLabel() + " sandwich" );

        Component [] components = condimentsPanel.getComponents();
        for (int i=0; i< components.length; i++)
            if ( (c = (Checkbox)components[i]).getState() )
                System.out.println( "With " + c.getLabel() );
        System.out.println("Thank you, drive through...");
        return true;
    }
}
```

DriveThrough lays out two panels, each containing three checkboxes. The checkboxes in the entreePanel are tied together through a single Checkbox-Group object. We call their setCheckboxGroup() methods to point them at a single CheckboxGroup object that manages and makes them mutually exclusive. The CheckboxGroup object is an odd animal. One expects it to be a container or a component, but it isn't; it's simply a helper object that coordinates the functionality of the Checkbox objects. Because a CheckboxGroup isn't a container, it doesn't have an add() method. To put a checkbox into a group, you call the setCheckboxGroup() method of the Checkbox class.

Once a set of checkboxes have been placed in a checkbox group, only one of the boxes may be checked at a time. In this applet, the checkbox group forces you to choose a beef, chicken, or veggie entree, but not more than one. The condiment choices, however, aren't in a checkbox group, so you can request ketchup, mustard, and pickles on your chicken sandwich.

When the **Place Order** button is pushed, we would like to gather the information in the checkboxes and print it. We could have saved references to them in a number of ways; this example demonstrates two. First, we find out which entree was selected. To do so, call the CheckboxGroup with getCurrent(). getCurrent() returns the selected Checkbox; we use getLabel() to extract the entree's name.

To find out which condiments were selected, we use a more complicated procedure. The problem is that condiments aren't mutually exclusive, so we don't have the convenience of a CheckboxGroup. Instead, we ask the condiments Panel for a list of its components. The getComponent() method returns an array of references to the container's child components. We'll use this to loop over the components and print the results. We cast each element of the array back to Checkbox, and call its getState() to see if the button is on or off. Remember that if we were dealing with different types of components, we could determine what kind of component we had with the instanceof operator.

Using a Canvas

The Canvas object can be used as a simple drawing area. Canvas is different from the functional components we've looked at so far: it doesn't have any default functionality. The Canvas is a blank slate that implements whatever functionality we want. We can override the paint() method of a Canvas to draw, display information, and generate graphics. To accomplish something interactive, we can catch low-level events like mouse movement and key presses within the Canvas's area and implement some interesting behavior. We can build just about any kind of user-interface item in this way. In fact, it might be considerably easier to build a new kind of button from scratch out of a Canvas than to subclass the real Button class; a functional component like a button has a lot of built in behavior that can't be changed easily. We'll demonstrate this technique later.

The following example extends Canvas to make a BullsEyeArea component. Whenever your mouse roams inside the BullsEyeArea, little concentric circles start following it around, as shown in Figure 10–11.

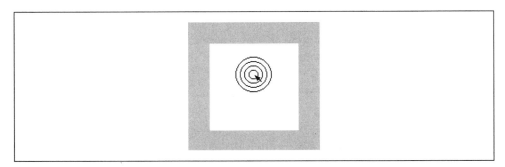

Figure 10–11: The BullsEye applet

```
import java.awt.*;

public class BullsEye extends java.applet.Applet {
    public void init() {
        add( new BullsEyeArea(100, 100) );
    }
}

class BullsEyeArea extends Canvas {
```

```
        int xpos, ypos, radius=20, rings=4;

        BullsEyeArea( int w, int h ) {
            resize( w, h );
            setBackground( Color.white );
        }
        public boolean mouseMove( Event e, int x, int y ) {
            xpos=x; ypos=y;
            repaint();
            return true;
        }
        public void paint( Graphics g ) {
            for (int i=0; i<rings; i++) {
                int r = radius - radius/rings*i;
                g.drawOval( xpos-r, ypos-r, r*2, r*2);
            }
        }
    }
```

BullsEyeArea takes a width and a height as arguments in its constructor and resizes itself to those dimensions. We can call resize() from anywhere there is a reference to the component, so we could have left the size out of the constructor and had our applet set the size of the component after creating it. The constructor also sets the default background color to white.

To do its job, BullsEyeArea overrides two methods of the Canvas class: mouseMove() and paint(). Whenever the mouse moves within its area, an event is delivered to mouseMove(). Our mouseMove() saves the latest coordinates of the mouse position into the instance variables xpos and ypos. It then calls repaint() to schedule an update of the display and returns true to indicate the event was handled. A short time later, an AWT thread calls the default update() method, which clears the Canvas's area and calls our paint() method. paint() then draws some circles centered around the new xpos and ypos coordinates.

Note that paint() method is called asynchronously, in response to our repaint() request. We can tell it what to draw only indirectly. We put the necessary information somewhere accessible; in this case, in instance variables of the BullsEyeArea class. In a sense, the xpos and ypos coordinates are a model that represents the position of the mouse. Our paint() method then looks at this model and renders a view of the it—the little bullseye pattern. This is, in general, how things get drawn in AWT.

Because paint() is called asynchronously and it accesses instance variables that are shared by the mouseMove() method, it would be appropriate to declare that both paint() and mouseMove() are synchronized. Making these methods synchronized would prevent `mouseMove()` from modifying the position while `paint()` is redrawing the bull's eye. In this simple example, however, it's not really necessary; if `mouseMove()` and `paint()` collide, the only consequence is that the bull's eye is drawn in a slightly incorrect position.

In more complex applications, you should be careful about synchronization. However, in more complex applications, the stakes are also higher. Synchronization has side effects. In this case, the event-handling thread (which calls `mouseMove()`) might get stuck waiting for `paint()` to return; by nature, `paint()` might take a long time. The position of the bull's eye would track the mouse more accurately, but might lag behind; the application would be slow and unresponsive. A good solution to this problem would be to isolate the code that sets and reads `xpos` and `ypos` in two private methods, and synchronize those methods. By doing so, we prevent that the event-handling thread from getting stuck waiting for a lengthy `paint()` operation.

Using Scrollbars

Now we'll turn to a more interesting and useful example. `ScrollMe` demonstrates the basics of how to use scrollbar components. It displays a section of a large image and allows the user to pan around within it using horizontal and vertical scrollbars, as shown in Figure 10–12.

Figure 10–12: The ScrollMe applet

`ScrollMe` is a fairly long example (60+ lines) because we have structured the applet in a more realistic way. `ScrollMe` makes use of two specialized components within it. One is a kind of `Canvas` that displays the image; the other is a kind of `Container` that glues together the image canvas and the two scroll bars.

I'll warn you up front that `ScrollMe` has some deficiencies. One problem is that we are going to be displaying an image in this example, but we have not yet discussed working with images; that will come in the next chapter. We'll therefore try to keep the image messiness to a minimum.

Another concession is that our scrollbars are somewhat dumb. They have a simple, fixed range that represents the area to be scrolled. In a better implementation, our scrollbars would be more dynamic. They should pop up only when needed and scale themselves to reflect the size of the scrollable area in proportion to the visible area. The problem is that we can't find out the size of an image until it has been loaded, and we can't compute ideal sizes for the scrollbars until we know how big the image is. There is nothing terribly complex about making fancy scrollbars; it just requires more code. You should find it straightforward to add these niceties after you know how to work with images.

Now let's dive into the code for `ScrollMe`:

```java
import java.awt.*;

public class ScrollMe extends java.applet.Applet {

    public void init() {
        Image img = getImage( getCodeBase(), getParameter("img") );
        setLayout( new GridLayout( 1, 1 ) );
        add( new ImageScroller( img ) );
    }
}

class ImageScroller extends Panel {
    int steps = 50, pagestep = 25;
    ScrollableImageCanvas canvas;

    ImageScroller ( Image img ) {
        setLayout( new BorderLayout() );
        Scrollbar vs = new Scrollbar( Scrollbar.VERTICAL,
                                      0, pagestep, 0, steps );
        Scrollbar hs = new Scrollbar( Scrollbar.HORIZONTAL,
                                      0, pagestep, 0, steps );
        canvas = new ScrollableImageCanvas( img, hs, vs );
        add( "Center", canvas );
        add( "South", hs );
        add( "East", vs );
    }

    public boolean handleEvent ( Event e ) {
        switch( e.id ) {
```

```
            case Event.SCROLL_LINE_UP:
            case Event.SCROLL_LINE_DOWN:
            case Event.SCROLL_PAGE_UP:
            case Event.SCROLL_PAGE_DOWN:
            case Event.SCROLL_ABSOLUTE:
                canvas.repaint();
                return true;
        }
        return false;
    }
}

class ScrollableImageCanvas extends Canvas {
    Image img;
    Scrollbar vscroll, hscroll;

    ScrollableImageCanvas ( Image img, Scrollbar hscroll,
                                        Scrollbar vscroll ) {
        this.img = img;
        this.hscroll = hscroll;
        this.vscroll = vscroll;
    }

    public void update( Graphics g ) {
        paint( g );
    }
    public void paint( Graphics g ) {
        if ( ! prepareImage( img, this ) )
            return;

        int x = - (img.getWidth( this )
                    - size().width)/hscroll.getMaximum()
                    * hscroll.getValue();
        int y = - (img.getHeight( this )
                    - size().height)/vscroll.getMaximum()
                    * vscroll.getValue();
        g.drawImage( img, (x<0)?0:x, (y<0)?0:y, this );
    }
}
```

Don't panic if you see some unfamiliar things; we'll explain them as we go along.

We have created two new components for use by our ScrollMe applet. ScrollableImageCanvas is a Canvas that knows how to display an image. If the image is too large for it to hold, it consults the values of two Scrollbar objects to decide what portion to draw. Another new component, ImageScroller, is a Panel that holds a ScrollableImageCanvas along with the two Scrollbar objects it requires. It arranges them on the display and handles the events that are generated when the scrollbars move by prompting the ScrollableImageCanvas to repaint itself. ImageScroller is a smart panel that manages the image canvas and the two scrollbars. Another approach would have been to create specialized smart `Scrollbar` objects that would catch their own events and know how to call the object they were controlling when they were changed.

So, what do our new components do? Let's start at the top and work our way down. The `ScrollMe` applet itself is very simple; it does all of its work in `init()`. First it acquires an `Image` object with a call to `getImage()`. It then specifies a `GridLayout` layout manager with a single (one-by-one) area. (Never fear, we'll be getting to our discussion of layout managers quite soon now.) Finally, `ScrollMe` adds the `ImageScroller` to the applet. I chose a `GridLayout` because it resizes components to fill the entire area available to them. Because we specified a one-by-one layout, the `GridLayout` allocates the applet's entire area to the `ImageScroller` and resizes `ImageScroller` to fill the applet.

Next comes the `ImageScroller` object itself. `ImageScroller` takes a reference to our `Image` in its constructor. It creates the necessary `Scrollbar` objects and the `ScrollableImageCanvas`, and glues them together with a `BorderLayout`; this layout manager makes it easy to position the scrollbars alongside the image. It's worth asking why we used a `BorderLayout` here and a degenerate (one-by-one) `GridLayout` in the applet itself; couldn't the applet use a `BorderLayout` to accomplish the same thing with less work? Yes, but by putting the `BorderLayout` into `ImageScroller`, we've made a reusable component; we can easily add `ImageScroller` objects wherever we wish.

The `handleEvent()` method of `ImageScroller` doesn't do much; its only active job is to catch the events from the scrollbars and prompt the canvas to repaint itself as necessary. Scrollbars can generate several different kinds of events depending on how they're used; we handle the events created when the user scrolls up or down by a single line, a page, or by moving the bar to an absolute position. In each case, we simply call the `repaint()` method of the `ScrollableImageCanvas` to have it repaint itself.

The `Scrollbar` constructor requires special attention. It takes several arguments. The first is an identifier that specifies whether we want a horizontal or a vertical scrollbar. Next are the scrollbar's initial value, page size, and the scrollbar's minimum and maximum values. The page size is the number of steps occupied by the visible portion of the area that's scrolled; it's the amount the scrollbar's value changes when the scrollbar is paged up or down. We have arbitrarily decided that the range for our scrollbar is 50 steps; the page size is half that. Again, in a better implementation, the range and page size would be determined dynamically, based on the size of the image and the area allotted to it. Ideally, there should be some correspondence between the steps of the scrollbar and the area of the image: a larger range for a large span of image to be scrolled.

ScrollableImageCanvas is a specialized Canvas that looks at the value of the scrollbars and displays a portion of our image. It needs access to three objects: two scrollbar components and the image we're displaying. Our image is the Image object we retrieved with the applet's getImage() method. The objects were all passed to the ScrollableImageCanvas when we called its constructor.

The rest is very simple. The only oddity is the first line of our paint() method. The call to prepareImage() ensures that the data for the image we are about to draw is ready. As you'll see in Chapter 11, Java may delay loading the image until it's actually needed. prepareImage() checks to see if the image is complete and kicks the browser to fetch it if it hasn't started yet. If the image isn't ready yet, paint() returns without displaying anything.

It takes only three lines of code to draw the image. The first two lines compute where to place the image, based on the image's size, the canvas's size, and the position of the scrollbars. (If we're executing this code, the image must have loaded, so we can use img.getWidth() and img.getHeight() to find the image's size.) All we're really doing is reading the value of the scrollbars, computing some x and y coordinates, and splatting the image out onto the screen. Conveniently, the parts of the image that fall outside the ScrollableImageCanvas disappear; by choosing the right x and y coordinates, we draw just the part of the image that we want to see. To read the Scrollbar, we use the getMaximum() method to find out its maximum possible value; getValue() finds its current value.

drawImage() does the actual display. It takes a reference to our image object, the coordinates, and a reference to the container itself (this), which serves as an image observer. (We'll discuss image observers in Chapter 11; for now, take this on faith.) We fiddle with the coordinates in the call to drawImage() to prevent strange behavior if the image is smaller than the canvas.

One last detail: we overrode update(), which normally clears the graphics area to its background color before calling paint(). In this case, erasing the old image before painting the new one is wasted effort, so we supply an update() method that simply calls paint().

Building a New Component

So far, we've made several new kinds of components, but we haven't used them in a very component-like fashion. Most of our new components have had a narrow mission in life, and communicated directly with other parts of our applications through references. Our ScrollableImageCanvas example relied on an ImageScroller for its setup and repainting. The ImageScroller itself was self-contained, but wouldn't be all that useful on its own. What would we do if we wanted `ImageScroller` to allow the user to make a selection? How would we report that to our applet? One obvious way would be to provide it with a callback and have it tap us on the shoulder when it was ready. A nicer approach, however, would be to have `ImageScroller` mimic the native AWT components and send action events when it's used.

The following example creates a new component called `PictureButton`. `PictureButton` looks at least somewhat button-like and generates action events when pressed. The `PressIt` applet is passed the events in its `action()` method, just as with any other button, and prints a message each time it's pressed.

```java
import java.awt.*;

public class PressIt extends java.applet.Applet {
    Image img;
    public void init() {
        img = getImage( getCodeBase(), getParameter("img") );
        PictureButton pb = new PictureButton( img );
        pb.resize( 50, 50 );
        add ( pb );
    }

    public boolean action(Event e, Object arg) {
        if ( arg == img )
            System.out.println("Picture Button pressed!");
        return true;
    }
}

class PictureButton extends Canvas {
    int edge = 3;
    Image img;
    boolean pressed = false;

    PictureButton(Image i) {
        img = i;
        setBackground( Color.white );
    }

    public void paint( Graphics g ) {
        int off =  pressed ? 0 : edge;
        g.drawImage( img, off, off, size().width-edge,
                                    size().height-edge, this );
    }
    public boolean mouseDown( Event e, int x, int y ) {
        pressed = true;
        repaint();
        return true;
    }
    public boolean mouseUp( Event e, int x, int y ) {
        pressed = false;
```

```
        repaint();
        Event event = new Event( this, Event.ACTION_EVENT, img );
        getParent().postEvent( event );
        return true;
    }
}
```

Okay, so it's not beautiful. Maybe you'd like to return to this example after we've talked more about images and perform some fancier shading. Feel free.

The important thing about the `PictureButton` is the way it communicates with the rest of the applet. The communication takes place in the `mouseUp()` method. Whenever `mouseUp()` is called, we create a new `Event`. The event constructor takes three arguments: the object sending the event (`this`), which lets the recipient figure out who sent the event; the event's type (`ACTION_EVENT`); and an arbitrary object that can be anything we think useful (in this case, a reference to the image that's displayed on the button). To send the event, we call the recipient's `postEvent()` method. We want to send our event to the button's container (the applet), so we use `getParent()` to get a reference.

The container's `postEvent()` method is the nerve center of its event dispatch mechanism; from there, our event is handed off to `handleEvent()` and `action()`. Note that all this takes place in AWT's event-handling thread, which started the process by calling `mouseUp()`. However, we could call `postEvent()` from any part of an applet or application. Event handlers shouldn't assume they will always be called by a particular thread.

Dialogs

A `Dialog` is a top-level `Window` that can be *modal*. A modal window is one that seizes the attention of the user by staying in the foreground and grabbing all input, until it is satisfied. `Dialog` objects are useful for pop-up messages and queries or important user-driven decisions. We'll do a quick example of a `Dialog` window and then take a look at `FileDialog`, a subclass of `Dialog` that provides an easy-to-use file-selector component.

Queries

The following example, `YesNo`, is a simple `Dialog` box that prompts the user with a question and provides **Yes** and **No** buttons, as shown in Figure 10–13. We can wait for a response to the dialog by calling its `answer()` method, which blocks until the user responds.

```
import java.awt.*;

class YesNo extends Dialog {
```

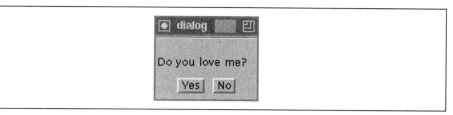

Figure 10–13: The YesNo dialog

```java
private boolean yes = false;

YesNo( Frame frame, String question ) {
    super(frame, true);
    add( "Center", new Label(question) );
    Panel yn = new Panel();
    yn.add( new Button("Yes"));
    yn.add( new Button("No"));
    add("South", yn);
    pack();
}

synchronized public boolean answer() {
    try
        wait();
    catch (InterruptedException e) { }
    return yes;
}

synchronized public boolean action( Event e, Object arg) {
    if ( ((String)arg).equals("Yes") )
        yes = true;

    notifyAll();
    dispose();
    return true;
}

public static void main(String[] s) {
    Frame f = new Frame();
    f.add( "Center", new Label("I'm the application") );
    f.pack();
    f.show();

    YesNo query = new YesNo( f, "Do you love me?");
    query.show();
    if ( query.answer() == true )
        System.out.println("She loves me...");
    else
        System.out.println("She loves me not...");
}
}
```

Our YesNo class extends Dialog and does most of its basic set up in its constructor. Our first task is to pass some set-up information to the constructor of the Dialog class with a call to super(). Here we are invoking the Dialog constructor that takes two parameters: a parent Frame object and a boolean value that specifies whether the Dialog is to act modal or not. Since a Dialog is really a top-level window, we have to tell it explicitly who is to serve as its parent container with the Frame argument. The parent Frame receives uncaught events from the Dialog.[*] The default layout for a Dialog window is BorderLayout, which is convenient for arranging our message and the **Yes** and **No** buttons.

The remainder of the Dialog-related code gets the response. We have synchronized the standard action() method and a new public method, answer(). A call to answer() performs a wait() and blocks until the action() method receives a button press and wakes it up with a notifyAll(). We also dispose() of the Dialog after the question has been answered.

We have included a main() in our Dialog so that you can test drive the class in an application. All we do there is create a parent frame (which is somewhat useless to us in this context), create the query, and display it with show(). We then wait breathlessly for a response from the answer() method and act accordingly.

File Selection

A FileDialog is a standard, file-selection box. As with other AWT components, most of FileDialog is implemented in the native part of the AWT toolkit, so it looks and acts like a standard file selector on your platform.

Now selecting files all day can be pretty boring without a greater purpose, so we'll exercise the FileDialog in a mini-editor application. Editor provides a text area in which we can load and work with files. We'll stop just shy of the capability to save and let you fill in the blanks (with a few caveats). The FileDialog created by Editor is shown in Figure 10–14.

```java
import java.awt.*;
import java.io.*;

class Editor extends Frame {
    TextArea textArea = new TextArea();

    Editor() {
        super("Editor");
        setLayout( new BorderLayout() );
        add("Center", textArea);
        Menu menu = new Menu ("File");
        menu.add ( new MenuItem ("Load") );
```

---

[*] No longer true in 1.0.2.

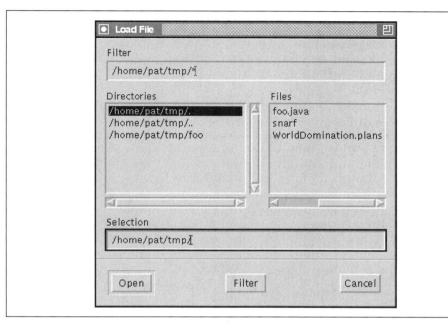

Figure 10–14: A FileDialog

```
        menu.add ( new MenuItem ("Save") );
        menu.add ( new MenuItem ("Quit") );
        MenuBar menuBar = new MenuBar();
        menuBar.add ( menu );
        setMenuBar( menuBar );
        pack();
    }

    public boolean action( Event event, Object obj ) {
        if ( ((String)obj).equals("Quit") )
            dispose();
        else if ( ((String)obj).equals("Load") )
            loadFile();
        else if ( ((String)obj).equals("Save") )
            saveFile();

        return true;
    }

    private void loadFile () {
        FileDialog fd = new FileDialog( this, "Load File",
            FileDialog.LOAD );
        fd.show();
        String file = fd.getFile();
        if ( file == null ) // Cancel
            return;
```

```
        try {
            FileInputStream fis = new FileInputStream ( fd.getFile() );
            byte [] data = new byte [ fis.available() ];
            fis.read( data );
            textArea.setText( new String( data, 0 ) );
        } catch ( IOException e )
            textArea.setText( "Could not load file..." );
    }

    private void saveFile() {
        FileDialog fd = new FileDialog( this, "Save File",
            FileDialog.SAVE );
        fd.show();
        // Save file data...
    }

    public static void main(String[] s) {
        new Editor().show();
    }
}
```

Editor is a Frame that lays itself out with a TextArea and a pull-down menu. From the pull-down **File** menu, we can opt to **Load**, **Save**, or **Quit**. The action() method catches the events associated with these menu selections and takes the appropriate action.

The interesting parts of Editor are the private methods loadFile() and saveFile(). loadFile() creates a new FileDialog with three parameters: a parent frame (just as with in the previous Dialog example), a title, and a directive parameter. This parameter should be one of the static identifiers LOAD or SAVE, which tells the dialog whether to load or save a file.

A FileDialog does its work when the its show() method is called. Unlike most components, its show() method blocks the caller until it completes its job; the file selector then disappears. After that, we can retrieve the designated filename with the FileDialog's getFile() method.[*] In loadFile(), we use a fragment of code from Chapter 8 to get the contents of the named file. We then add the contents to the TextArea with setText(). You can use loadFile() as a roadmap for the unfinished saveFile() method, but it would be prudent to add the standard safety precautions. For example, you could use the previous YesNo example to prompt the user before overwriting an existing file.

---

[*] Under Windows 95, the current implementation of FileDialog appends a "*.*" to filenames if they do not have a trailing extension name. It's unclear whether this is a bug or a feature.

Layout Managers

A layout manager is an object that arranges the child components of a container, as shown in Figure 10–15. It moves and resizes components within the container's display area according to a particular layout scheme. The layout manager's job is to fit the components into the available area, while maintaining the proper spatial relationships between the components. AWT comes with a few standard layout managers for common arrangements; you can make your own layout manager if you have special requirements.

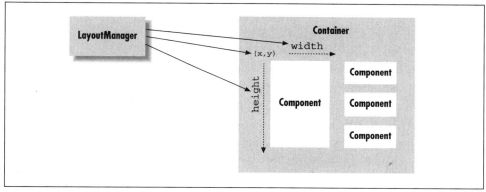

Figure 10–15: LayoutManager at work

Every container has a default layout manager; therefore, when you make a new container, it comes with a `LayoutManager` object of the appropriate type. You can install a new layout manager at any time with the `setLayout()` method. Below, we set the layout manager of a container to `BorderLayout`:

```
setLayout ( new BorderLayout() );
```

Notice that we call the `BorderLayout` constructor, but we don't even save a reference to the layout manager. This is typical; once you have installed a layout manager, it does its work behind the scenes, interacting with the container. You rarely call the layout manager's methods directly, so you don't need a reference; the only exceptions are for `CardLayout` and `GridBagLayout`. However, you do need to know what the layout manager is going to do with your components as you work with them.

As I explained earlier, the `LayoutManager` is consulted whenever the container is validated, to reorganize the contents. It does its job by calling the `move()` and `resize()`—or, alternatively `reshape()`—methods of the individual child components to arrange them in the container's display area. This happens the first time a container is shown, and thereafter whenever the container's `validate()` method is called. Containers that are a subclass of the `Window` class (which include `Frame`) are automatically revalidated whenever they are packed or resized. Calling `pack()` sets the window's size to the preferred size of its components.

Every component has two important pieces of information used by the layout manager in placing and sizing it: a preferred size and a minimum size. These are reported by the `preferredSize()` and `minimumSize()` methods of the `Component` class, respectively. For example, a plain `Button` object can be resized to any proportions. However, the button's designer can provide a preferred size for a good-looking button. The layout manager might use this size when there are no other constraints, or it might ignore it, depending on its scheme. Now, if we give the button a label, the button may need a minimum size in order to display itself properly. The layout manager might show more respect for the button's minimum size and guarantee that it has at least that much space.

The preferred size of a `Container` object has the same meaning as for any other type of component. However, since a `Container` may hold its own components and want to arrange them in its own layout, its preferred size is a function of its own layout manager. The layout manager is therefore involved in both sides of the issue. It asks the components in its container for their preferred (or minimum) sizes in order to arrange them. Based on those values it also calculates the preferred size that is reported by its own container to the container above it.

When a layout manager is called to arrange its components, it's working within a fixed area. It begins by looking at its container's dimensions, and the preferred or minimum sizes of the child components. It then doles out screen area and sets the sizes of components according to its scheme. You can override the `minimumSize()` and `preferredSize()` methods of a component, but you should do this only if you are actually specializing the component, and it has new needs. If you find yourself fighting with a layout manager because it's changing the size of one of your components, you are probably using the wrong kind of layout manager or not composing your interface properly. Remember that it's possible to use a number of `Panel` objects in a given display, where each one has its own `LayoutManager`. Try breaking down the problem: place related components in their own `Panel` and then arrange the panels in the container. You can accomplish a lot by using composite layouts.

Flow Layouts

`FlowLayout` is a simple layout manager that tries to arrange components with their preferred sizes, from left to right and top to bottom in the display. A `FlowLayout` can have a specified justification of LEFT, CENTER, or RIGHT, and a fixed horizontal and vertical padding. By default, a flow layout uses CENTER justification, meaning that all components are centered within the area allotted to them. `FlowLayout` is the default for `Panel` components like `Applet`.

The following applet adds five buttons to the default `FlowLayout`; the result is shown in Figure 10–16.

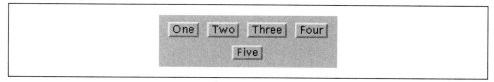

Figure 10–16: A flow layout

```
import java.awt.*;

public class Flow extends java.applet.Applet {
    public void init() {
        // Default for Applet is FlowLayout
        add( new Button("One") );
        add( new Button("Two") );
        add( new Button("Three") );
        add( new Button("Four") );
        add( new Button("Five") );
    }
}
```

If the applet is small enough, some of the buttons spill over to a second or third row.

Grid Layouts

`GridLayout` arranges components into a fixed number of rows and columns. The components are arbitrarily resized to fit in the resulting areas; their minimum and preferred sizes are consequently ignored. `GridLayout` is most useful for arranging containers like `Panels`. Use it to divide your area into rectangular regions.

`GridLayout` takes the number of rows and columns in its constructor. If you subsequently give it too many objects to manage, it adds extra columns to make the objects fit. You can also set the number of rows or columns to zero, which means that you don't care how many elements the layout manager packs in that dimension. For example, GridLayout(2,0) requests a layout with two rows and an unlimited number of columns; if you put ten components into this layout, you'll get two rows of five columns each.

The following applet sets a GridLayout with three rows and two columns as its layout manager; the results are shown in Figure 10–17.

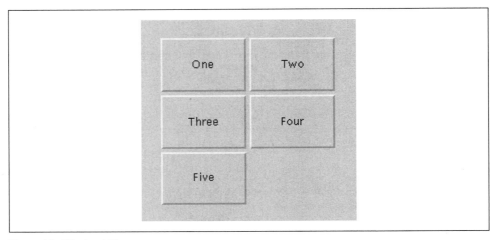

Figure 10–17: A grid layout

```
import java.awt.*;

public class Grid extends java.applet.Applet {
    public void init() {
        setLayout( new GridLayout( 3, 2 ));
        add( new Button("One") );
        add( new Button("Two") );
        add( new Button("Three") );
        add( new Button("Four") );
        add( new Button("Five") );
    }
}
```

The five buttons are laid out, in order, from left to right, top to bottom, with one empty spot.

Border Layouts

BorderLayout is a little more interesting. It tries to arrange objects in one of five geographical locations: "North," "South," "East," "West," and "Center," possibly with some padding between. BorderLayout is the default layout for Window and Frame objects. Because each component is associated with a direction, Border-Layout can manage at most five components; it squashes or stretches those components to fit its constraints. As we'll see in the second example, this means that you often want to have BorderLayout manage sets of components in their own panels.

When we add a component to a border layout, we need to specify both the component and the position at which to add it. To do so, we use an overloaded version of the add() method that takes an additional String argument. This additional argument specifies the position and is passed to the layout manager when the new component is added. Normally the LayoutManager is not consulted until it's asked to lay out the components.

The following applet sets a BorderLayout layout and adds our five buttons again, named for their locations; the result is shown in Figure 10–18.

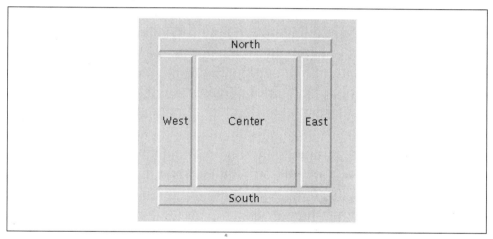

Figure 10–18: A border layout

```
import java.awt.*;

public class Border extends java.applet.Applet {
    public void init() {
        setLayout( new java.awt.BorderLayout() );
        add("North", new Button("North") );
        add("East", new Button("East") );
        add("South", new Button("South") );
        add("West", new Button("West") );
        add("Center", new Button("Center") );
    }
}
```

So, how exactly is the area divided up? Well, the objects at "North" and "South" get their preferred height and are expanded to fill the full area horizontally. "East" and "West" components on the other hand, get their preferred width, and are expanded to fill the remaining area between "North" and "South" vertically. Finally, the "Center" object takes all of the rest of the space. As you can see in Figure 10–18, our buttons get distorted into awkward shapes.

What if we don't want BorderLayout messing with the sizes of our components? One option would be to put each button in its own Panel. The default layout for a Panel is FlowLayout, which respects the preferred size of components. The preferred sizes of the panels are effectively the preferred sizes of the buttons, but if the panels are stretched, they won't pull their buttons with them. Border2 illustrates this approach as shown in Figure 10–19.

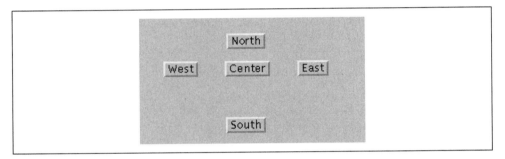

Figure 10–19: Another border layout

```
import java.awt.*;

public class Border2 extends java.applet.Applet {
    public void init() {
        setLayout( new BorderLayout() );
        Panel p = new Panel();
        p.add(new Button("East") );
        add("East", p);
        p = new Panel();
        p.add(new Button("West") );
        add("West", p);
        p = new Panel();
        p.add(new Button("North") );
        add("North", p);
        p = new Panel();
        p.add(new Button("South") );
        add("South", p);
        p = new Panel();
        p.add(new Button("Center") );
        add("Center", p);
    }
}
```

In this example, we create a number of panels, put our buttons inside the panels, and put the panels into the applet, which has the BorderLayout manager. Now, the Panel for the "Center" button soaks up the extra space that comes from the BorderLayout. Each Panel's FlowLayout centers the button in the panel and uses the button's preferred size. This version of the applet has a lot of unused space. If we wanted, we could get rid of the extra space by resizing the applet:

```
resize( preferredSize() );
```

Card Layouts

CardLayout is a special layout manager for creating the effect of a stack of cards. Instead of arranging all of the container's components, it displays only one at a time. You would use this kind of layout to implement a hypercard stack or a Windows-style set of configuration screens. When you add a component to the layout, you use the two-argument version of add(); the extra argument is an arbitrary string that serves as the card's name:

```
add("netconfigscreen", myComponent);
```

To bring a particular card to the top of the stack, call the CardLayout's show() method with two arguments: the parent Container and the name of the card you want to show. There are also methods like first(), last(), next(), and previous() for working with the stack of cards. These methods take a single argument: the parent Container. Here's a simple example:

```
import java.awt.*;

public class main extends java.applet.Applet {
        CardLayout cards = new CardLayout();

        public void init() {
                setLayout( cards );
                add("one", new Button("one") );
                add("two", new Button("two") );
                add("three", new Button("three") );
        }

        public boolean action( Event e, Object arg) {
                cards.next( this );
                return true;
        }
}
```

We add three buttons to the layout and cycle through them as they are pressed. In a more realistic example, we would build a group of panels, each of which might implement some part of a complex user interface, and add those panels to the layout. Each panel would have its own layout manager. The panels would be resized to fill the entire area available (i.e., the area of the `Container` they are in), and their individual layout managers would arrange their internal components.

Other Layouts

We've covered the basic layout managers; with them, you should be able to create just about any user interface you like. However, there are a few additional layout managers that may be helpful in special situations.

`GridBagLayout` is a very flexible layout manager that allows arbitrary relative and weighted placing and various types of constrained sizing. According to some, `GridBagLayout` is the layout manager of choice; it slices, dices, and generally does just about anything you want. Seriously, `GridBagLayout` arranges components in a two-dimensional grid. Its primary advantage is that it also lets you set weighted constraints on how items fill unused areas: how they grow and stretch when a window is resized.

However, `GridBagLayout`s have their problems. They came on the scene late and appear to suffer from the pressure of a rushed development schedule. In my opinion, `GridBagLayout` is ugly both in model and implementation. It's excessively complex and, once you get passed the simplest situations, hard to get working correctly. You can accomplish almost everything you want by nesting panels with other layout managers inside each other. If you look back through this chapter, you'll see some simple examples of composite layouts; it's up to you and your imagination to determine how far composite layouts can take you.

That's not all, folks. If you want to experiment with layout managers that are undocumented, may change, and may not be available on all platforms, look in the `sun.awt` classes. You'll find a `HorizBagLayout`, a `VerticalBagLayout`, and a `VariableGridLayout`. Furthermore, public-domain layout managers of all descriptions are beginning to appear on the Net; keep your eye on Gamelan and the other Java archives.

What About Absolute Positioning?

It's possible to set the layout manager to `null`: no layout control. You might do this to position an object on the display at some absolute coordinates. This is almost never the right approach. Components might have different minimum sizes on different platforms, and your interface would not be very portable.

The following applet doesn't use a layout manager, and works with absolute coordinates instead:

```java
import java.awt.*;

public class MoveButton extends java.applet.Applet {
    Button button = new Button("I Move");

    public void init() {
        setLayout( null );
        add( button );
        button.resize( button.preferredSize() );
        button.move( 20, 20);
    }

    public boolean mouseDown( Event e, int x, int y ) {
        button.move( x, y );
        return ( true );
    }

}
```

Click in the applet area, outside of the button, to move the button to a new location. If you are running the example in an external viewer, try resizing the window and note that the button stays at a fixed position relative to the display origin.

In this chapter:
- *Basic Drawing*
- *Fonts*
- *Images*
- *Drawing Techniques*
- *Image Processing*
- *Working with Audio*

11

Drawing and Images

If you've read the last chapter and seen the examples in the tutorial in Chapter 2, then you've probably picked up the basics of how graphical operations are performed in Java. Up to this point, we have done some simple drawing and even displayed an image or two. In this chapter, we will finally give graphics programming its due and go into depth about drawing techniques and the tools for working with images in Java.

Basic Drawing

The classes you'll use for drawing come from the `java.awt` package, as shown in Figure 11–1.

An instance of the `java.awt.Graphics` class is called a *graphics context*. It represents a drawable surface such as a component's display area or an off-screen image buffer. A graphics context provides methods for performing all basic drawing operations on its area, including the painting of image data. We call the `Graphics` object a graphics context because it also holds contextual information about the drawing area. This information includes parameters like the drawing area's clipping region, painting color, transfer mode, and text font. If you consider the drawing area to be a painter's canvas, you might think of a graphics context as an easel that holds a set of tools and marks off the work area.

There are four ways you normally acquire a `Graphics` object. Roughly, from most common to least, they are:

- From AWT, as the result of a painting request. In this case, AWT acquires a new graphics context for the appropriate area and passes it to your component's `paint()` or `update()` method.

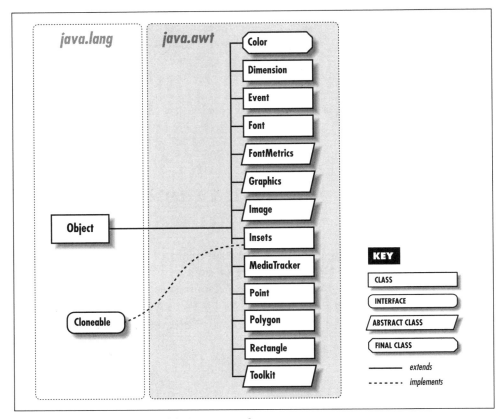

Figure 11–1: Graphics classes of the java.awt package

- Directly from an off-screen image buffer. In this case, we ask the image buffer for a graphics context directly. We'll use this when we discuss techniques like double buffering.

- By copying an existing Graphics object. Duplicating a graphics object can be useful for more elaborate drawing operations; different copies of a Graphics object draw into the same area on the screen, but can have different attributes and clipping regions.

- Directly from an on-screen component. It's possible to ask a component to give you a Graphics object for its display area. However, this is almost always a mistake; if you feel tempted to do this, think about why you're trying to circumvent the normal paint()/repaint() mechanism.

Each time a component's update() or paint() method is called, AWT provides the component with a new Graphics object for drawing in the display area. This means that attributes we set during one painting session, such as drawing color or clipping region, are reset the next time `paint()` or `update()` is called. (Each call to `paint()` starts with a tidy new easel.) For the most common attributes, like foreground color, background color, and font, we can set defaults in the component itself. Thereafter, the graphics contexts for painting in that component come with those properties initialized appropriately.

If we are working in a component's `update()` method, we can assume our on-screen artwork is still intact, and we need only to make whatever changes are needed to bring the display up to date. One way to optimize drawing operations in this case is by setting a clipping region, as we'll see shortly. If our `paint()` method is called, however, we have to assume the worst and redraw the entire display.

Drawing Methods

Methods of the `Graphics` class operate in a standard coordinate system. The origin of a newly created graphics context is the top left pixel of the component's drawing area, as shown in Figure 11–2.

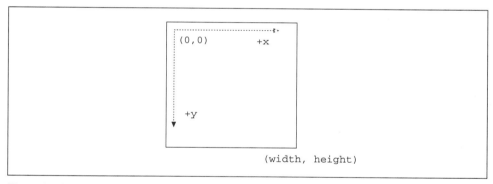

Figure 11–2: Graphics coordinate system

The diagram above illustrates the default coordinate system. The point with coordinates of the width and height of the drawing area lies just outside the visible area at the bottom right corner. The coordinate system can be translated (shifted) with the `translate()` method to specify a new point as the origin.

The drawable area of the graphics context can be clipped to a smaller region with the `clipRect()` method. Clipping can be used only to reduce the drawing area, not to expand it; you can't undo the clipping of an area. If you need to work with more than one clipping region, you can create a copy of the original graphics context with its `create()` method.

The basic drawing and painting methods should be familiar to you if you've done
any graphical programming. The following applet, `TestPattern`, exercises most
of the simple shape drawing commands; it's shown in Figure 11–3.

Figure 11–3: The TestPattern applet

```
import java.awt.*;

public class TestPattern extends java.applet.Applet {
    int theta = 45;

    public void paint( Graphics g ) {
        int appWidth = size().width;
        int appHeight = size().height;
        int width = appWidth/2;
        int height = appHeight/2;
        int x = (appWidth - width)/2;
        int y = (appHeight- height)/2;

        int [] polyXs = { 0, appWidth/2, appWidth, appWidth/2 };
        int [] polyYs = { appHeight/2, 0, appHeight/2, appHeight };
        Polygon poly = new Polygon( polyXs, polyYs, 4 );

        g.setColor( Color.black );
        g.fillRect( 0, 0, size().width, size().height );
        g.setColor( Color.yellow );
        g.fillPolygon( poly );
        g.setColor( Color.red );
        g.fillRect( x, y, width, height );
        g.setColor( Color.green );
        g.fillOval( x, y, width, height );
        g.setColor( Color.blue );
        int delta = 90;
```

```
        g.fillArc( x, y, width, height, theta, delta );
        g.setColor( Color.white );
        g.drawLine( x, y, x+width, x+height );
    }

    public boolean mouseDown(Event e, int x, int y ) {
        theta = (theta + 10) % 360;
        repaint();
        return true;
    }
```

TestPattern draws a number of simple shapes and responds to mouse clicks by rotating the filled arc and repainting. Compile it and give it a try. If you click repeatedly on the applet, you may notice that everything flashes when it repaints. TestPattern is not very intelligent about redrawing; we'll examine some better techniques in the upcoming section on drawing techniques.

With the exception of fillArc() and fillPolygon(), each method takes a simple x, y coordinate for the top left corner of the shape and a width and height for its size. We have picked values that draw the shapes centered, at half the width and height of the applet.

The most interesting shape we've have drawn is the Polygon, a yellow diamond. A Polygon object is specified by two arrays that contain the x and y coordinates of each vertex. In our example, the coordinates of the points in the polygon are (polyx[0], polyy[0]), (polyx[1], polyy[1]), and so on. There are simple drawing methods in the Graphics class that take two arrays and draw or fill the polygon, but we chose to create a Polygon object and draw it instead. The reason is that the Polygon object has some useful utility methods that we might want to use later. A Polygon can, for instance, give you its bounding box and tell you if a given point lies within its area.

The fillArc() method requires six integer arguments. The first four specify the bounding box for an oval—just like the fillOval() method. The final two arguments specify what portion of the oval we want to draw, as a starting angle and an offset. Both the starting angle and the offset are specified in degrees. Zero degrees is at three o'clock; a positive angle is clockwise. For example, to draw the right half of a circle, you might call:

```
    g.fillArc(0, 0, radius * 2, radius * 2, -90, 180);
```

Table 11–1 shows the shape-drawing methods of the Graphics class. As you can see, for each of the fill() methods in the example, there is a corresponding draw() method that renders the shape as an unfilled line drawing.

Table 11–1: Shape Drawing Methods in the Graphics Class

Method	Description
draw3DRect()	Draws a highlighted, 3D rectangle
drawArc()	Draws an arc
drawLine()	Draws a line
drawOval()	Draws an oval
drawPolygon()	Draws a polygon
drawRect()	Draws a rectangle
drawRoundRect()	Draws a rounded-corner rectangle
fill3DRect()	Draws a filled, highlighted, 3D rectangle
fillArc()	Draws a filled arc
fillOval()	Draws a filled oval
fillPolygon()	Draws a filled polygon
fillRect()	Draws a filled rectangle
fillRoundRect()	Draws a filled, rounded-corner rectangle

There are a few important drawing methods missing from Table 11–1. For example, the drawString() method, which draws text, and the drawImage() method, which draws an image. We'll discuss these methods in detail in later sections.

Colors

The TestPattern applet fills its shapes with a number of colors, using the set-Color() method of the Graphics object. setColor() sets the current color in the graphics context, so we set it to a different color before each drawing operation. But where do these color values come from?

The java.awt.Color class handles color in Java. A Color object describes a single color. You can create a Color by specifying the red, green, and blue values of the color, either as integers between 0 and 255 or as floating-point values between 0.0 and 1.0. You can also use getColor() to look up a color name in the system properties table, as described in Chapter 7. getColor() takes a String color property name, retrieves the integer value from the Properties list, and returns the Color object that corresponds to that color.

The Color class also defines a number of static final color values; these are what we used in the TestPattern example. These constants, such as Color.black and Color.red, provide a convenient set of basic colors for your drawings.

Fonts

Text fonts in Java are represented by instances of the `java.awt.Font` class. A Font object is constructed from a font name, style identifier, and a point size. We can create a `Font` at any time, but it's meaningful only when applied to a particular component on a given display device. Here are a few fonts:

```
Font timesFont = new Font("TimesRoman", Font.PLAIN, 12);
Font courierFont = new Font("Courier", Font.BOLD, 18);
```

The font name is a string that identifies a font family. The following five font names should be available on all platforms:

- Dialog
- Helvetica
- TimesRoman
- Courier
- Symbol

The font name is mapped to an actual font on the local platform. Working with fonts is another area in which Java is still rife with platform dependencies, but if you stick to these font names, you should be able to create portable applications.

You can also use the `static` method `Font.getFont()` to look up a font name in the system properties list. `getFont()` takes a `String` font property name, retrieves the font name from the `Properties` table, and returns the `Font` object that corresponds to that font.

The Font class defines three `static` style identifiers: PLAIN, BOLD, and ITALIC. You can use these values on all fonts. The point size determines the size of the font on a display. If a given point size isn't available, Font substitutes a default size.[*]

You can retrieve information about a Font with a number of routines. For example, `getName()` returns the font name `String`, while `getFamily()` returns the font family. Use `getSize()` and `getStyle()` to retrieve the point size and style, respectively.

A Font object is used as an argument to the `setFont()` method of a Component or Graphics object. Subsequent text-drawing commands like `drawString()` for that component or in that graphics context use the specified font.

---

[*] There is no straightforward way to determine if a given Font is available at a given point size in the current release of Java. Hopefully Sun will accommodate better Font handling functionality (and perhaps true, portable Fonts) in a future release.

Font Metrics

To get detailed size and spacing information about a font, we can ask for a
`java.awt.FontMetrics` object. Different systems can have different real fonts
available; the available fonts may not match the font you request. Thus, a `Font-`
`Metrics` object presents information about a particular font on a particular system, not general information about a font. For example, if you ask for the metrics
of a nine-point Courier font, what you get isn't some abstract truth about Courier
fonts; you get the metrics of the font that the particular system uses for nine-point
Courier—which may not be nine point or even Courier.

Use the `getFontMetrics()` method for a `Component` to retrieve the `Font-`
`Metrics` for a `Font` as it would appear for that component:

```
public void init() {
    ...
    // Get the metrics for a particular font on this component
    FontMetrics timesMetrics = getFontMetrics( timesFont );
    ...
}
```

The `Graphics` object also has a `getFontMetrics()` method that gets the
`FontMetrics` information for the current font in the graphics context.

```
public void paint( Graphics g ) {
    // Get the metrics for the current font
    FontMetrics fm = g.getFontMetrics();
    ...
}
```

The following applet, `FontShow`, displays a word and draws reference lines showing certain characteristics of its font, as shown in Figure 11–4. Clicking in the
applet toggles the point size between a small and a large value.

```
import java.awt.*;

public class FontShow extends java.applet.Applet {
    static final int LPAD=25;   // Frilly line padding
    boolean bigFont = true;

    public void paint( Graphics g ) {
        String message = getParameter( "word" );
        g.drawRect(0, 0, size().width-1, size().height-1);

        if ( bigFont )
            g.setFont( new Font("Dialog",Font.PLAIN,24) );
        else
            g.setFont( new Font("Dialog",Font.PLAIN,12) );

        FontMetrics metrics = g.getFontMetrics();
        int fontAscent = metrics.getAscent ();
```

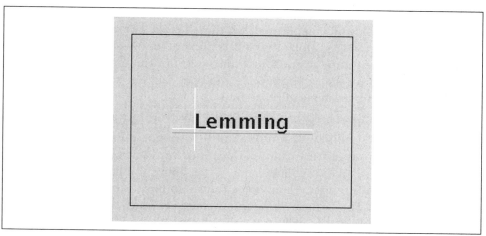

Figure 11–4: The FontShow applet

```
        int fontDescent = metrics.getDescent();
        int messWidth = metrics.stringWidth ( message );
        // Center text
        int startX = size().width/2 - messWidth/2;
        int startY = size().height/2 - fontDescent/2 + fontAscent/2;

        g.drawString(message, startX, startY);

        g.setColor( Color.white );   // Base lines
        g.drawLine( startX-LPAD, startY, startX+messWidth+LPAD,
            startY );
        g.drawLine( startX, startY+ LPAD, startX,
            startY-fontAscent-LPAD );
        g.setColor( Color.green );   // Ascent line
        g.drawLine( startX-LPAD, startY-fontAscent,
                    startX+messWidth+LPAD, startY-fontAscent );
        g.setColor( Color.red );     // Descent line
        g.drawLine( startX-LPAD, startY+fontDescent,
                    startX+messWidth+LPAD, startY+fontDescent );
    }

    public boolean mouseDown( Event e, int x, int y ) {
        bigFont = !bigFont;
        repaint();
        return true;
    }
}
```

Compile FontShow and run it with an applet tag like the following:

```
<applet height=200 width=250 code=FontShow>
    <param name="word" value="Lemming">
</applet>
```

The `word` parameter specifies the text to be displayed.

`FontShow` may look a bit complicated, but there's really not much to it. The bulk of the code is in `paint()`, which simply sets the font, draws our word, and adds a few lines to illustrate some of the font's characteristics (metrics). For fun we also catch mouse clicks (in the `mouseDown()` method) and alternate the font size by setting the `bigFont` variable and repainting.

By default, text is rendered above and to the right of the coordinates specified in the `drawString()` method. If you think of that starting point as the origin of a coordinate system, the axes are called the *baselines*. `FontShow` draws these lines in white. The greatest height the characters stretch above the baseline is called the *ascent* and is shown by a green line. Some fonts also have parts of letters that fall below the baseline. The farthest distance any character reaches below the baseline is called the *descent*. `FontShow` illustrates this with a red line.

We ask for the ascent and descent of our font with the `FontMetrics getMaxAscent()` and `getMaxDescent()` methods. We also ask for the width of our string (when rendered in this font) with the `stringWidth()` method. We use this information to center the word in the display area. To center the word vertically, we average the influence of the ascent and descent.

Table 11–2 provides a short list of methods that return useful font metrics.

Table 11–2: Font Metric Methods

Method	Description
`getFont()`	Font object these metrics describe
`getAscent()`	Height above baseline
`getDescent()`	Depth below baseline
`getLeading()`	Standard vertical spacing between lines
`getHeight()`	Total line height (ascent + descent + leading)
`charWidth(char ch)`	Width of a character
`stringWidth(String str)`	Width of a string
`getWidths()`	The widths of the first 256 characters in this font; returns `int[]`
`getMaxAdvance()`	Maximum character width of any character

Leading space is the padding between lines of text. The `getHeight()` method reports the total height of a line of text, including the leading space.

Images

So far, we've worked with methods for drawing simple shapes and displaying text. For more complex graphics, we'll be working with images. AWT has a powerful set of tools for generating and displaying image data that address the problems of working in a distributed and multithreaded application environment. We'll start with the basics of the `java.awt.Image` class and see how to get an image into an `Applet` and draw it on a display. This job isn't quite as simple as it sounds; the browser might have to retrieve the image from a networked source when we ask for it. Fortunately, if we're just interested in getting the image on the screen whenever it's ready, we can let AWT handle the details for us. Later in this chapter, we'll discuss how to manage image loading ourselves, as well as how to create raw image data and feed it efficiently to the rest of an application.

java.awt.Image

The `java.awt.Image` class represents a view of an image. The view is created from an image source that produces pixel data. Images can be from a static source, such as GIF or JPEG data, or a dynamic one, such as a video stream or a graphics engine.

An applet can ask its viewer to retrieve an image by calling the `getImage()` method. The location of the image to be retrieved is given as a URL, either absolute or relative:

```
class MyApplet extends java.applet.Applet {
    public void init() {
        try {
            // absolute URL
            URL monaURL = new URL(
                "http://myserver/images/mona_lisa.gif");
            Image monaImage = getImage( monaURL );

            // relative URL
            URL imagesBaseURL = new URL(
                "http://myserver/cartoon/images/");
            Image daffyDuckImage = getImage( imagesBaseURL,
                "daffy.gif");
            Image buggsBunnyImage = getImage( imagesBaseURL,
                "buggs.gif");

        }
        catch ( MalformedURLException e ) { }
```

When an applet wants to load its own images, they are usually stored close to the applet itself. We can use `getCodeBase()` to specify a URL relative to the applet's location. If `MyApplet` and *myimage.gif* are at the same base location (i.e., in the same directory on a UNIX or DOS-like system), `MyApplet` can request the image with:

```
Image myImage = getImage( getCodeBase(), "myimage.gif");
```

Once we have an `Image` object, it is drawn into a graphics context with the `draw-Image()` method of the `Graphics` class. The simplest form of `drawImage()` takes four parameters: the `Image` object, the `x`, `y` coordinates at which to draw it, and a reference to a special *image observer* object.

Image Observers

Images in AWT are processed asynchronously, which means Java performs image operations like loading and scaling on its own time. For example, the `getIm-age()` method always returns immediately, even if the image data has to be retrieved over the network from Mars and isn't available yet. In fact, if it's a new image, Java won't even begin to fetch it until we try to use it. The advantage of this technique is that Java can do the work of a powerful, multithreaded image-processing environment for us. However, it also introduces several problems. If Java is loading an image for us, how do we know when it's completely loaded? What if we want to work with the image as it arrives? What if we need to know properties of the image (like its dimensions) before we can start working with it? What if there's an error in loading the image?

These problems are handled by image observers—designated objects that implement the `ImageObserver` interface. All operations that draw or examine `Image` objects return immediately, but they take an image-observer object as a parameter. The `ImageObserver` monitors the image's status and makes information about the image available to the rest of the application. When image data is loaded from its source, an image observer is notified of its progress, including when new pixels are available, when a complete frame of the image is ready, and if there is an error during loading. The image observer also receives attribute information about the image, such as its dimensions and properties, as soon as they are known.

The `drawImage()` method, like other image operations, takes a reference to an `ImageObserver` object as a parameter. `drawImage()` returns a `boolean` value specifying whether or not the image was painted in its entirety. If the image data has not yet been loaded or is only partially available, `drawImage()` paints whatever fraction of the image it can and returns. The image-observer object, however, is registered as being interested in information about the image. It's then called repeatedly as more pixel information is available and again when the entire image is complete. The image observer can do whatever it wants with this information.

Most often it calls `repaint()` to prompt the applet to draw the image again with the updated data; as you should recall, a call to `repaint()` initiates a call to `paint()` to be scheduled. In this way an applet can redraw the image as it arrives, for a progressive loading effect, or wait until the entire image is loaded.

We'll discuss creating image observers a bit later. For now, we can avoid the issue by using a prefabricated image observer. It just so happens that the `Component` class implements the `ImageObserver` interface and provides some simple repainting behavior for us. This means that every component can serve as its own default image observer; we simply pass a reference to our applet (or other component) as the image-observer parameter of a `drawImage()` call. Hence the mysterious `this` we've occasionally seen when working with graphics:

```
class MyApplet extends java.applet.Applet {
    . . .
    public void paint( Graphics g ) {
        drawImage( monaImage, x, y, this );
        . . .
```

Our applet serves as the image observer and calls `repaint()` for us to redraw the image as necessary. If the image arrives slowly, our applet is notified repeatedly, as new chunks become available. As a result, the image appears gradually, as it's loaded. The `awt.image.incrementaldraw` and `awt.image.redrawrate` system properties control this behavior. `redrawrate` limits how often `repaint()` is called; the default value is every 100 milliseconds. `incremental-draw` prevents drawing until the entire image has arrived. By default, this property is set to "true"; set it to "false" to turn off incremental redrawing.

Scaling and Size

Another version of `drawImage()` renders a scaled version of the image:

```
drawImage( monaImage, x, y, x2, y2, this );
```

This draws the entire image within the rectangle formed by the points x, y and x2, y2, scaling as necessary. (Cool, eh?) `drawImage()` behaves the same as before; the image is processed by the component as it arrives and the image observer is notified as more pixel data and the completed image are available.

The `Image getHeight()` and `getWidth()` methods retrieves the dimensions of a loaded image. Since this information may not be available until the image data is completely loaded, both methods also take an `ImageObserver` object as a parameter. If the dimensions aren't yet available, they return values of −1 and notify the observer. We'll see how to deal with these and other problems a bit later. For now, we'll use `Component` as an image observer to get by, and move on to some general painting techniques.

Drawing Techniques

Having learned to walk, let's try a jog. In this section, we'll look at some techniques for doing fast and flicker-free drawing and painting. If you're interested in animation or smooth updating, you should read on.

Drawing operations take time, and time spent drawing leads to delays and imperfect results. Our goal is to minimize the amount of drawing work we do and, as much as possible, to do that work away from the eyes of the user. You'll remember that our `TestPattern` applet had a blinking problem. It blinked because `Test-Pattern` performs several, large, area-filling operations each time its `paint()` method is called. On a very slow system, you might even be able to see each shape being drawn in succession. `TestPattern` could be easily fixed by drawing into an off-screen buffer and then copying the completed buffer to the display. To see how to eliminate flicker and blinking problems, we'll look at an applet that needs even more help.

`TerribleFlicker` illustrates some of the problems of updating a display. Like many animations, it has two parts: a constant background and a changing object in the foreground. In this case, the background is a checkerboard pattern and the object is a small, scaled image we can drag around on top of it, as shown in Figure 11–5. Our first version of `TerribleFlicker` lives up to its name and does a very poor job of updating.

Figure 11–5: The TerribleFlicker applet

```
import java.awt.*;

public class TerribleFlicker extends java.applet.Applet {
    int grid = 10;
    int currentX, currentY;
```

```
        Image img;
        int imgWidth = 60, imgHeight = 60;

        public void init() {
            img = getImage( getCodeBase(), getParameter("img") );
        }

        public void paint( Graphics g ) {
            int w = size().width/grid;
            int h = size().height/grid;
            boolean black = false;
            for ( int y = 0; y <= grid; y++ )
                for ( int x = 0; x <= grid; x++ ) {
                    g.setColor(  (black = !black) ? Color.black :
                        Color.white );
                    g.fillRect( x * w, y * h, w, h );
                }
            g.drawImage( img, currentX, currentY, imgWidth, imgHeight,
                this );
        }
        public boolean mouseDrag( Event e, int x, int y ) {
            currentX=x; currentY=y;
            repaint();
            return true;
        }
    }
```

Try dragging the image; you'll notice both the background and foreground flicker as they are repeatedly redrawn. What is `TerribleFlicker` doing, and what is it doing wrong?

As the mouse is dragged, `TerribleFlicker` keeps track of its position in two instance variables, `currentX` and `currentY`. On each call to `mouseDrag()`, the coordinates are updated, and `repaint()` is called to ask that the display be updated. When `paint()` is called, it looks at some parameters, draws the checkerboard pattern to fill the applet's area, and finally paints a small version of the image at the latest coordinates.

Our first, and biggest, problem is that we are updating, but we have neglected to implement the applet's `update()` method with a good strategy. Because we haven't overridden `update()`, we are getting the default implementation of the `Component update()` method, which looks something like this:

```
// Default implementation of applet update
public void update( Graphics g ) {
    setColor ( backgroundColor );
    fillRect( 0, 0, size().width, size().height );
    paint ( g );
}
```

This method simply clears the display to the background color and calls our `paint()` method. This is almost never the best strategy, but is the only appropriate default for `update()`, which doesn't know how much of the screen we're really going to paint.

Our applet paints its own background, so we can provide a simpler version of `update()` that doesn't bother to clear the display:

```
public void update( Graphics g ) {
    paint( g );
}
```

This applet works better because we have eliminated one large, unnecessary, and (in fact) annoying graphics operation. However, although we have eliminated a `fillRect()` call, we're still doing a lot of wasted drawing. Most of the background stays the same each time it's drawn. You might think of trying to make `paint()` smarter, so that it wouldn't redraw these areas, but remember that `paint()` has to be able to draw the entire scene because it might be called in situations when the display isn't intact. The solution is to have `update()` help out by restricting the area `paint()` can draw.

Clipping

The `clipRect()` method of the `Graphics` class restricts the drawing area of a graphics context to a smaller region. A graphics context normally has an effective clipping region that limits drawing to the entire display area of the component. We can specify a smaller clipping region with `clipRect()`.

How is the drawing area restricted? Well, foremost, drawing operations that fall outside of the clipping region are not displayed. If a drawing operation overlaps the clipping region, we see only the part that's inside. A second effect is that, in a good implementation, the graphics context can recognize drawing operations that fall completely outside the clipping region and ignore them altogether. Eliminating unnecessary operations can save time if we're doing something complex, like filling a bunch of polygons. This doesn't save the time our application spends calling the drawing methods, but the overhead of calling these kinds of drawing methods is usually negligible compared to the time it takes to execute them. (If we were generating an image pixel by pixel, this would not be the case, as the calculations would be the major time sink, not the drawing.)

So we can save time in our applet by having our update method set a clipping region that results in only the affected portion of the display being redrawn. We can pick the smallest rectangular area that includes both the old image position and the new image position, as shown in Figure 11–6. This is the only portion of the display that really needs to change; everything else stays the same.

An arbitrarily smart `update()` could save even more time by redrawing only those regions that have changed. However, the simple clipping strategy we've

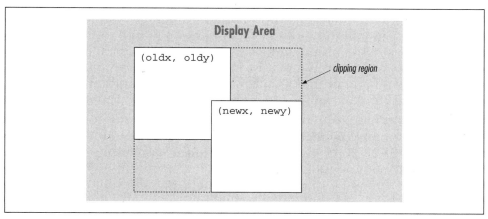

Figure 11–6: Determining the clipping region

implemented here can be applied to many kinds of drawing, and gives quite good performance, particularly if the area being changed is small.

One important thing to note is that, in addition to looking at the new position, our updating operation now has to remember the last position at which the image was drawn. Let's fix our applet so it will use a clipping region. To keep this short and emphasize the changes, we'll take some liberties with design and make our next example a subclass of `TerribleFlicker`. Let's call it `ClippedFlicker`:

```java
import java.awt.*;

public class ClippedFlicker extends TerribleFlicker {
    int nextX, nextY;

    public boolean mouseDrag( Event e, int x, int y ) {
        nextX=x; nextY=y;
        repaint();
        return true;
    }

    void clipToAffectedArea( Graphics g, int oldx, int oldy, int newx,
                        int newy, int width, int height) {
        int x = Math.min( oldx, newx );
        int y = Math.min( oldy, newy );
        int w = ( Math.max( oldx, newx ) + width ) - x;
        int h = ( Math.max( oldy, newy ) + height ) - y;
        g.clipRect( x, y, w, h );
    }

    public void update( Graphics g ) {
        int lastX = currentX, lastY = currentY;
        currentX = nextX; currentY = nextY;
```

```
            clipToAffectedArea( g, lastX, lastY, currentX, currentY,
                                imgWidth, imgHeight );
            paint( g );
        }
    }
```

You should find that `ClippedFlicker` is significantly faster, though it still flickers. We'll make one more change in the next section to eliminate that.

So, what have we changed? First, we've overridden `mouseDrag()` so that instead of setting the current coordinates of the image, it sets another set of coordinates called `nextX` and `nextY`. These are the coordinates at which we'll display the image the next time we draw it.

`update()` now has the added responsibility of taking the next position and making it the current position, by setting the `currentX` and `currentY` variables. This effectively decouples `mouseDrag()` from our painting routines. We'll discuss why this is advantageous in a bit. `update()` then uses the current and next coordinates to set a clipping region on the `Graphics` object before handing it off to `paint()`.

We have created a new, `private` method to help it do this. `clipToAffectedArea()` takes as arguments the new and old coordinates and the width and height of the image. It determines the bounding rectangle as shown in Figure 11-6, then calls `clipRect()` to set the clipping region. As a result, when `paint()` is called, it draws only the affected area of the screen.

So, what's the deal with `nextX` and `nextY`? By making `update()` keep track of the next, current, and last coordinates separately, we accomplish two things. First, we always have an accurate view of where the last image was drawn and second, we have decoupled where the next image will be drawn from `mouseDrag()`.

It's important to decouple painting from `mouseDrag()` because there isn't necessarily a one-to-one correspondence between calls to `repaint()` and subsequent calls by AWT to our `update()` method. This isn't a defect; it's a feature that allows AWT to schedule and consolidate painting requests. Our concern is that our `paint()` method may be called at arbitrary times while the mouse coordinates are changing. This is not necessarily bad. If we are trying to position our object, we probably don't want the display to be redrawn for every intermediate position of the mouse. It would slow down the dragging unnecessarily.

If we were concerned about getting every single change in the mouse's position, we would have two options. We could either do some work in the `mouseDrag()` method itself, or put our events into some kind of queue. We'll see an example of the first solution in our `DoodlePad` example a bit later. The latter solution would mean circumventing AWT's own event-scheduling capabilities and replacing them with our own, and we don't want to take on that responsibility.

Double Buffering

Now let's get to the most powerful technique in our toolbox: *double buffering*. Double buffering is a technique that fixes our flickering problems completely. It's easy to do and gives us almost flawless updates. We'll combine it with our clipping technique for better performance, but in general you can use double buffering with or without clipping.

Double buffering our display means drawing into an off-screen buffer and then copying our completed work to the display in a single painting operation, as shown in Figure 11–7. It takes the same amount of time to draw a frame, but double buffering instantaneously updates our display when it's ready.

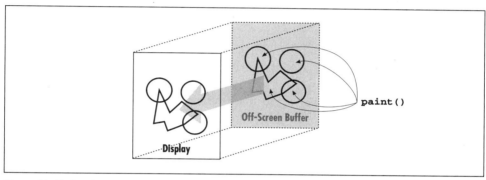

Figure 11–7: Double buffering

We can get this effect by changing just a few lines of our `ClippedFlicker` applet. Modify `update()` to look like the following, and add the new `offScrImg` instance variable as shown:

```
...
Image offScrImg;

public void update( Graphics g ) {
    if ( offScrImg == null )
        offScrImg = createImage( size().width, size().height );

    Graphics og = offScrImg.getGraphics();

    int lastX = currentX, lastY = currentY;
    currentX = nextX; currentY = nextY;
    clipToAffectedArea( og, lastX, lastY, currentX, currentY,
    imgWidth,
        imgHeight );
    clipToAffectedArea( g, lastX, lastY, currentX, currentY, imgWidth,
        imgHeight );
    paint( og );
```

```
        g.drawImage(offScrImg, 0, 0, this);
        og.dispose();
    }
    ...
```

Now, when you drag the image, you shouldn't see any flickering. The update rate should be about the same as in the previous example (or marginally slower), but the image should move from position to position without noticeable repainting.

So, what have we done this time? Well, the new instance variable, `offScrImg`, is our off-screen buffer. It is a drawable `Image` object. We can get an off-screen `Image` for a component with the `createImage()` method. `createImage()` is similar to `getImage()`, except that it produces an empty image area of the specified size. We can then use the off-screen image like our standard display area by asking it for a graphics context with the `Image` `getGraphics()` method. After we've drawn into the off-screen image, we can copy that image back onto the screen with `drawImage()`.

The biggest change to the code is that we now pass `paint()` the graphics context of our off-screen buffer, rather than that of the on-screen display. `paint()` is now drawing on `offScrImg`; it's our job to copy the image to the display when it's done. This might seem a little suspicious to you, as we are now using `paint()` in two capacities. AWT calls `paint()` whenever it's necessary to repaint our entire applet and passes it an on-screen graphics context. When we update ourselves, however, we call `paint()` to do its work on our off-screen area and then copy that image onto the screen from within `update()`.

Note that we're still clipping. In fact, we're clipping both the on-screen and off-screen buffers. Off-screen clipping has the same benefits we described earlier: AWT should be able to ignore wasted drawing operations. On-screen clipping minimizes the area of the image that gets drawn back to the display. If your display is fast, you might not even notice the savings, but it's an easy optimization, so we'll take advantage of it.

We create the off-screen buffer in `update()` because it's a convenient and safe place to do so. We have to ask for a new graphics context for the off-screen buffer with each call to `update()`; every update operation requires a different clipping region, and the old clipping region can't be undone. Therefore, we can't save the off-screen graphics context between calls. Note that we could save a copy of the graphics context and duplicate it with `create()` for each call. Also, note that our image observer probably won't be called, since `drawImage()` isn't doing anything nasty like scaling, and the image itself is always available.

The dispose() method of the Graphics class allows us to deallocate the graphics context explicitly when we are through with it. This is simply an optimization. It may provide some performance improvement when doing heavy drawing. We could allow garbage collection to reclaim the unused objects; however, the garbage collection process might be hampered if we are doing intense calculations or lots of repainting.

Off-Screen Drawing

In addition to serving as buffers for double buffering, off-screen images are useful for saving complex, hard-to-produce, background information. We'll look at a simple example: the "doodle pad." DoodlePad is a simple drawing tool that lets us scribble by dragging the mouse, as shown in Figure 11–8. It draws into an off-screen image; its paint() method simply copies the image to the display area.

Figure 11–8: The DoodlePad applet

```
import java.awt.*;

public class DoodlePad extends java.applet.Applet {
    DrawPad dp;
    public void init() {
        setLayout( new BorderLayout() );
        add( "Center", dp = new DrawPad() );
        Panel p = new Panel();
        p.add( new Button("Clear") );
        add( "South", p );
    }
    public boolean action( Event e, Object o ) {
```

```
            dp.clear();
            return true;
        }
    }

class DrawPad extends Canvas {
    Image drawImg;
    Graphics drawGr;
    int xpos, ypos, oxpos, oypos;

    DrawPad() {
        setBackground( Color.white );
    }
    public boolean mouseDrag( Event e, int x, int y ) {
        xpos=x; ypos=y;
        if ( drawGr != null )
            drawGr.drawLine( oxpos, oypos, oxpos=xpos, oypos=ypos );
        repaint();
        return true;
    }
    public boolean mouseDown( Event e, int x, int y ) {
        oxpos=x; oypos=y;
        return true;
    }
    public void update( Graphics g ) {
        paint(g);
    }
    public void paint( Graphics g ) {
        if ( drawImg == null ) {
            drawImg = createImage( size().width, size().height );
            drawGr = drawImg.getGraphics();
        }
        g.drawImage(drawImg, 0, 0, null);
    }
    public void clear() {
        drawImg.getGraphics().clearRect(0, 0, size().width,
            size().height);
        repaint();
    }
}
```

Give it a try. Draw a nice moose, or a sunset. I just drew a lovely cartoon of Bill Gates. If you make a mistake, hit the **Clear** button and start over.

The parts should be familiar by now. We have made a type of Canvas called DrawPad. The new DrawPad component handles mouseDrag() movement events by drawing lines into an off-screen image and calling repaint() to update the display. DrawPad's paint() method simply does a drawImage() to copy the off-screen drawing area to the display. In this way, DrawPad saves our sketch information.

What is unusual about `DrawPad` is that it does some drawing outside of `paint()` or `update()`. In our clipping example, we talked about decoupling `update()` and `mouseDrag()`; we were willing to discard some mouse movements in order to save some updates. In this case, we want to let the user scribble with the mouse, so we should respond to every mouse movement. Therefore, we do our work in `mouseDrag()` itself. As a rule, we should be careful about doing heavy work in event-handling methods because we don't want to interfere with other tasks the AWT thread is performing. In this case, our line-drawing operation should not be a burden, and our primary concern is getting as close a coupling as possible between the mouse-movement events and the sketch on the screen.

`mouseDrag()` draws lines into the off-screen buffer. It maintains a set of old coordinates, to be used as a starting point for the next line segment. We override our `mouseDown()` method to reset the old coordinates to the current mouse position whenever the user picks up and moves to a new location. Finally, `DrawPad` provides a `clear()` method that clears the off-screen buffer and calls `repaint()` to update the display. The `DoodlePad` applet ties the `clear()` method to an appropriately labeled button through its `action()` method.

What if we wanted to do something with the image after the user has finished scribbling on it? Well, as we'll see in the next section, we could get the pixel data for the image from its `ImageProducer` object and work with that. It wouldn't be hard to create a save facility that stores the pixel data and reproduces it later. Think about how you might go about creating a networked "bathroom wall" where people could scribble on your Web pages.

Image Processing

Up to this point, we've confined ourselves to working with the high-level drawing commands of the `Graphics` class and using images in a hands-off mode. In this section, we'll clear up some of the mystery surrounding images and see how they are produced and used. The classes in the `java.awt.image` package handle image processing; Figure 11–9 shows the classes in this package.

First, we'll return to our discussion about image observers and see how we can get more control over image data as it's processed asynchronously by native AWT components. Then we'll open the hood and have a look at image production. If you're interested in creating sophisticated graphics, such as rendered images or video displays, this is the information you've been waiting for.

Objects that work with image data fall into one of three categories: image-data producers, image-data consumers, and image-status observers. Image producers implement the `ImageProducer` interface. They create pixel data and distribute it to one or more consumers. Image consumers implement a corresponding

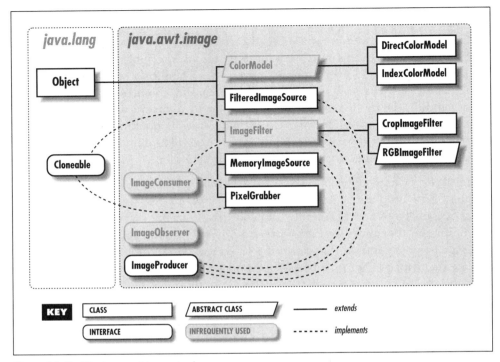

Figure 11–9: The java.awt.image package

ImageConsumer interface. They eat the pixel data and do something useful with it, such as display it on screen or analyze its contents. Image observers, as I mentioned earlier, implement the ImageObserver interface. They are effectively nosy neighbors of image consumers that watch as the image data arrives.

Image producers generate the information that defines each pixel of an image. A pixel has both a color and a transparency; the transparency specifies how pixels underneath the image show through. Image producers maintain a list of registered consumers for the image and send them this pixel data in one or more passes, as the pixels are generated. Image producers give the consumers other kinds of information as well, such as the image's dimensions. The producer also notifies the consumer when it has reached a boundary of the image. For a static image, such as GIF or JPEG data, the producer signals when the entire image is complete, and production is finished. For a video source or animation, the image producer could generate a continuous stream of pixel data and mark the end of each frame.

An image producer delivers pixel data and other image-attribute information by invoking methods in its consumers, as shown in Figure 11–10. This diagram illustrates an image producer sending pixel data to three consumers by invoking their setPixels() methods.

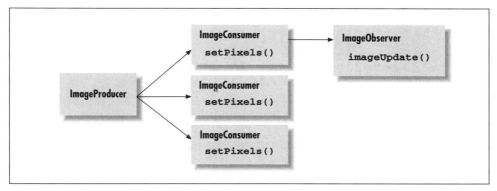

Figure 11–10: Image observers, producers, and consumers

Each consumer represents a view of the image. A given consumer might prepare the image for display on a particular medium, or it might simply serve as a filter and pass the image data to another consumer down the line.

Figure 11–10 also shows an image observer, watching the status of one of the consumers. The observer is notified as new portions of the image and new attributes are ready. Its job is to track this information and let another part of the application know its status. As I discussed earlier, the image observer is essentially a callback that is notified asynchronously as the image is built. The default Component class image observer that we used in our previous examples called repaint() for us each time a new section of the image was available, so that the screen was updated more or less continuously as the data arrived. A different kind of image observer might wait for the entire image before telling the application to display it; yet another observer might update a loading meter showing how far the image loading had progressed.

java.awt.image.ImageObserver

To be an image observer, you have to implement the single method, imageUpdate(), defined by the java.awt.image.ImageObserver interface:

```
public boolean imageUpdate(Image image, int flags, int x, int y,
                           int width, int height)
```

imageUpdate() is called by the consumer, as needed, to pass the observer information about the construction of its view of the image. Essentially, any time the image changes, the consumer tells the observer so that the observer can perform any necessary actions, like repainting. `image` holds a reference to the `Image` object the consumer is processing. `flags` is an integer whose bits specify what information about the image is now available. The values of the flags are defined as `static` identifiers in the `ImageObserver` interface, as shown in Table 11–3.

Table 11–3: ImageObserver Information Flags

Flag	Description
HEIGHT	The height of the image is ready
WIDTH	The width of the image is ready
FRAMEBITS	A frame is complete
SOMEBITS	An arbitrary number of pixels have arrived
ALLBITS	The image is complete
ABORT	The image loading has been aborted
ERROR	An error occurred during image processing; attempts to display the image will fail

The flags determine which of the other parameters, `x`, `y`, `width`, and `height`, hold valid data and what they mean. To test whether a particular flag in the `flags` integer is set, we have to resort to some binary shenanigans. The following class, `MyObserver`, implements the `ImageObserver` interface and prints its information as it's called:

```java
import java.awt.*;
import java.awt.image.*;

class MyObserver implements ImageObserver {

    public boolean imageUpdate( Image image, int flags, int x, int y,
                                int width, int height) {

        if ( (flags & HEIGHT) !=0 )
            System.out.println("Image height = " + height );

        if ( (flags & WIDTH ) !=0 )
            System.out.println("Image width = " + width );

        if ( (flags & FRAMEBITS) != 0 )
            System.out.println("Another frame finished.");

        if ( (flags & SOMEBITS) != 0 )
            System.out.println("Image section :"
                        + new Rectangle( x, y, width, height ) );

        if ( (flags & ALLBITS) != 0 ) {
            System.out.println("Image finished!");
            return false;
        }
```

```
            if ( (flags & ABORT) != 0 )  {
                System.out.println("Image load aborted...");
                return false;
            }

            return true;
        }
    }
```

The `imageUpdate()` method of `MyObserver` is called by the consumer periodically, and prints simple status messages about the construction of the image. Notice that `width` and `height` play a dual role. If `SOMEBITS` is set, they represent the size of the chunk of the image that has just been delivered. If `HEIGHT` or `WIDTH` is set, however, they represent the overall image dimensions. Just for amusement, we have used the `java.awt.Rectangle` class to help us print the bounds of rectangular region.

`imageUpdate()` returns a `boolean` value indicating whether or not it's interested in future updates. If the image is finished or aborted, `imageUpdate()` returns `false` to indicate it isn't interested in further updates. Otherwise, it returns `true`.

The following example uses `MyObserver` to print information about an image as AWT loads it:

```
import java.awt.*;

public class ObserveImage extends java.applet.Applet {
    Image img;
    public void init() {
        img = getImage( getCodeBase(), getParameter("img") );
        MyObserver mo = new MyObserver();
        img.getWidth( mo );
        img.getHeight( mo );
        prepareImage( img, mo );
    }
}
```

After requesting the `Image` object with `getImage()`, we perform three operations on it to kick-start the loading process. `getWidth()` and `getHeight()` ask for the image's width and height. If the image hasn't been loaded yet, or its size can't be determined until loading is finished, our observer will be called when the data is ready. `prepareImage()` asks that the image be readied for display on the component. It's a general mechanism for getting AWT started loading, converting, and possibly scaling the image. If the image hasn't been otherwise prepared or displayed, this happens asynchronously, and our image observer will be notified as the data is constructed.

You may be wondering where the image consumer is, since we never see a call to `imageUpdate()`. That's a good question, but for now I'd like you to take it on faith that the consumer exists. As you'll see later, image consumers are rather mysterious objects that tend to hide beneath the surface of image-processing applications. In this case, the consumer is hiding deep inside the implementation of `Applet`.

You should be able to see how we could implement all sorts of sophisticated image loading and tracking schemes. The two most obvious strategies, however, are to draw an image progressively, as it's constructed, or to wait until it's complete and draw it in its entirety. We have already seen that the `Component` class implements the first scheme. Another class, `java.awt.MediaTracker`, is a general utility that tracks the loading of a number of images or other media types for us. We'll look at it next.

java.awt.MediaTracker

`java.awt.MediaTracker` is a utility class that simplifies life if we have to wait for one or more images to be loaded before they're displayed. A `MediaTracker` monitors the preparation of an image or a group of images and lets us check on them periodically, or wait until they are completed. `MediaTracker` uses the `ImageObserver` interface internally to receive image updates.

The following applet, `LoadMe`, uses a `MediaTracker` to wait while an image is prepared. It shows a "Loading..." message while it's waiting. (If you are retrieving the image from a local disk or very fast network, this might go by quickly, so pay attention.)

```
import java.awt.*;

public class LoadMe extends java.applet.Applet implements Runnable {
    Image img;
    final int MAIN_IMAGE = 0;
    MediaTracker tracker;
    boolean show = false;
    Thread runme;
    String message = "Loading...";

    public void init() {
        img = getImage( getCodeBase(), getParameter("img") );
        tracker = new MediaTracker(this);
        tracker.addImage( img, MAIN_IMAGE );
    }
    public void start() {
        if ( !tracker.checkID( MAIN_IMAGE ) ) {
            runme = new Thread( this );
            runme.start();
        }
```

```
        }
    public void stop() {
        runme.stop();
        runme = null;
    }
    public void run() {
        repaint();
        try {
            tracker.waitForID( MAIN_IMAGE );
        }
        catch( InterruptedException e) { }

        if ( tracker.isErrorID( MAIN_IMAGE ) )
            message= "Error";
        else
            show = true;
        repaint();
    }
    public void paint( Graphics g ) {
        if ( show )
            g.drawImage( img, 0, 0, this );
        else {
            g.drawRect( 0, 0, size().width-1, size().height-1);
            g.drawString( message, 20, 20 );
        }
    }
}
```

From its init() method, LoadMe requests its image and creates a Media-Tracker to manage it. Later, after the applet is started, LoadMe fires up a thread to wait while the image is loaded. Note that we don't do this in init() because it would be rude to do anything time-consuming there; it would take up time in an AWT thread that we don't own. In this case, waiting in init() would be especially bad because paint() would never get called and our "loading" message wouldn't be displayed; the applet would just hang until the image loaded. It's often better to create a new thread for initialization and display a startup message in the interim.

When we construct a MediaTracker, we give it a reference to our component (this). After creating a MediaTracker, we assign it images to manage. Each image is associated with an integer identifier we'll use later for checking on its status. Multiple images can be associated with the same identifier, letting us manage them as a group. The value of the identifier is also used to prioritize loading when waiting on multiple sets of images; lower IDs have higher priority. In this case, we want to manage only a single image, so we created one identifier called MAIN_IMAGE and passed it as the ID for our image in the call to addImage().

In our applet's start() method, we call the MediaTracker's checkID() routine with the ID of the image to see if it's already been loaded. If it hasn't, the applet fires up a new thread to fetch it. The thread executes the `run()` method, which simply calls the `MediaTracker waitforID()` routine and blocks on the image, waiting for it to finish loading. The `show` flag tells `paint()` whether to display our status message or the actual image. We do a `repaint()` immediately upon entering `run()` to display the "Loading..." status, and again upon exiting to change the display. We test for errors during image preparation with `isErrorID()` and change the status message if we find one.

This may seem like a lot of work to go through, just to put up a status message while loading a single image. `MediaTracker` is more valuable when we are working with many images that have to be available before we can begin parts of our application. It saves us from implementing a custom `ImageObserver` for every application. In the future, `MediaTracker` should also be able to track the status of audio clips and other kinds of media (as its name suggests).

Producing Image Data

What if we want to make our own image data? To be an image producer, we have to implement the five methods defined in the `ImageProducer` interface:

- `addConsumer()`
- `startProduction()`
- `isConsumer()`
- `removeConsumer()`
- `requestTopDownLeftRightResend()`

Four methods of `ImageProducer` simply deal with the process of registering consumers. `addConsumer()` takes an `ImageConsumer` as an argument and adds it to the list of consumers. Our producer can then start sending image data to the consumer whenever it's ready. `startProduction()` is identical to `addConsumer()`, except that it asks the producer to start sending data as soon as possible. The difference might be that a given producer would send the current frame of data or initiate construction of a frame immediately, rather than waiting until its next cycle. `isConsumer()` tests whether a particular consumer is already registered, and `removeConsumer()` removes a consumer from the list. We'll see shortly that we can perform these kinds of operations easily with a `Vector`; see Chapter 7 for a complete discussion of `Vector` objects.

An `ImageProducer` also needs to know how to use the `ImageConsumer` interface of its clients. The final method of the `ImageProducer` interface, `requestTopDownLeftRightResend()`, asks that the image data be resent to the consumer, in order, from beginning to end. In general, a producer can generate pixel data and send it to the consumer in any order that it likes. The `setPix-els()` method of the `ImageConsumer` interface takes parameters telling the consumer what part of the image is being delivered on each call. A call to `requestTopDownLeftRightResend()` asks the producer to send the pixel data again, in order. A consumer might do this so that it can use a higher quality conversion algorithm that relies on receiving the pixel data in sequence. It's important to note that the producer is allowed to ignore this request; it doesn't have to be able to send the data in sequence.

Color models

Everybody wants to work with color in their application, but using color raises problems. The most important problem is simply how to represent a color. There are many different ways to encode color information: red, green, blue (RGB) values; hue, saturation, value (HSV); hue, lightness, saturation (HLS); and more. In addition, you can provide full color information for each pixel, or you can just specify an index into a color table (palette) for each pixel. The way you represent a color is called a *color model*. AWT provides tools for two broad groups of color models: *direct* and *indexed*.

As you might expect, you need to specify a color model in order to generate pixel data; the abstract class `java.awt.image.ColorModel` represents a color model. A `ColorModel` is one of the arguments to the `setPixels()` method an image producer calls to deliver pixels to a consumer. What you probably wouldn't expect is that you can use a different color model every time you call `setPix-els()`. Exactly why you'd do this is another matter. Most of the time, you'll want to work with a single color model; that model will probably be the default direct color model. But the additional flexibility is there if you need it.

By default, the core AWT components use a direct color model called ARGB. The A stands for "alpha", which is the historical name for transparency. RGB refers to the red, green, and blue color components that are combined to produce a single, composite color. In the default ARGB model, each pixel is represented by a 32-bit integer that is interpreted as four 8-bit fields; in order, the fields represent the transparency (A), red, green, and blue components of the color, as shown in Figure 11–11.

To create an instance of the default ARGB model, call the static `getRGBde-fault()` method in `ColorModel`. This method returns a `DirectColorModel` object; `DirectColorModel` is a subclass of `ColorModel`. You can also create other direct color models by calling a `DirectColorModel` constructor, but you shouldn't need to unless you have a fairly exotic application.

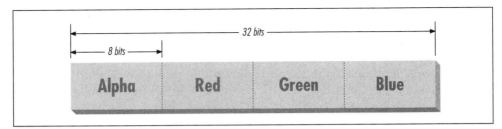

Figure 11–11: ARGB color encoding

In an indexed color model, each pixel is represented by a smaller amount of information: an index into a table of real color values. For some applications, generating data with an indexed model may be more convenient. If you have an 8-bit display or smaller, using an indexed model may be more efficient, since your hardware is internally using an indexed color model of some form.

While AWT provides `IndexedColorModel` objects, we won't cover them in this book. It's sufficient to work with the `DirectColorModel`. Even if you have an 8-bit display, the Java implementation on your platform should accommodate the hardware you have and, if necessary, dither colors to fit your display. Java also produces transparency on systems that don't natively support it by dithering colors.

Creating an image

Let's take a look at producing some image data. A picture may be worth a thousand words, but fortunately, we can generate a picture in significantly fewer than a thousand words of Java. If we're interested in producing a static image with just one frame, we can use a utility class that acts as an `ImageProducer` for us.

`java.awt.image.MemoryImageSource` is a simple utility class that implements the `ImageProducer` interface; we give it pixel data in an array and it sends that data to an image consumer. A `MemoryImageSource` can be constructed for a given color model, with various options to specify the type and positioning of its data. We'll use the simplest form, which assumes an ARGB color model.

The following applet, `ColorPan`, creates an image from an array of integers holding ARGB pixel values:

```
import java.awt.*;
import java.awt.image.MemoryImageSource;

public class ColorPan extends java.applet.Applet {
    Image img;
    int width, height;
    int [] pixData;
```

```
public void init() {
    width = size().width;
    height = size().height;
    pixData = new int [width * height];
    int i=0;

    for (int y = 0; y < height; y++) {
        int red = (y * 255) / (height - 1);
        for (int x = 0; x < width; x++) {
            int green = (x * 255) / (width - 1);

            int blue = 128;
            int alpha = 255;
            pixData[i++] = (alpha << 24) | (red << 16)
                           | (green << 8 ) | blue;
        }
    }
}

public void paint( Graphics g ) {
    if ( img == null )
        img = createImage( new MemoryImageSource(width, height,
                           pixData, 0, width));
    g.drawImage( img, 0, 0, this );
}
```

Give it a try. The size of the image is determined by the size of the applet when it starts up. What you should get is a very colorful box that pans from deep blue at the upper left-hand corner to bright yellow at the bottom right with green and red at the other extremes. (I'd show you a screen dump, but it wouldn't look good in a black-and-white book.)

We create the pixel data for our image in the init() method, and then use MemoryImageSource to create and display the image in paint(). The variable pixData is a one-dimensional array of integers that holds 32-bit ARGB pixel values. In init() we loop over every pixel in the image and assign it an ARGB value. The alpha (transparency) component is always 255, which means the image is opaque. The blue component is always 128, half its maximum intensity. The red component varies from 0 to 255 along the y axis; likewise, the green component varies from 0 to 255 along the x axis. The line below combines these components into an ARGB value:

```
pixData[i++] = (alpha << 24) | (red << 16) | (green << 8 ) | blue;
```

The bitwise left-shift operator (<<) should be familiar to C programmers. It simply shoves the bits over by the specified number of positions. The alpha value takes the top byte of the integer, followed by the red, green and blue values.

When we construct the `MemoryImageSource` as a producer for this data, we give it five parameters: the width and height of the image to construct (in pixels), the `pixData` array, an offset into that array, and the width of each scan line (in pixels). We'll start with the first element (offset 0) of `pixData`; the width of each scan line and the width of the image are the same. The array `pixData` has `width * height` elements, which means it has one element for each pixel.

We create the actual image once, in `paint()`, using the `createImage()` method that our applet inherits from `Component`. In the double-buffering and off-screen drawing examples, we used `createImage()` to give us an empty off-screen image buffer. Here we use `createImage()` to generate an image from a specified `ImageProducer`. `createImage()` creates the `Image` object and receives pixel data from the producer to construct the image. Note that there's nothing particularly special about `MemoryImageSource`; we could use any object that implements the image-producer interface inside of `createImage()`, including one we wrote ourselves. Once we have the image, we can draw it on the display with the familiar `drawImage()` method.

You can use `MemoryImageSource` to produce complex, pixel-by-pixel graphics or render images from arbitrary sources. It produces static images, though; when it reaches the end of its pixel data, its job is done. To generate a stream of image data or update pixel values, we need an more persistent image producer.

Updating Image Data

In this section we'll create an image producer that generates a stream of image frames rather than just a static image. Unfortunately, it would take too many lines of code to generate anything really interesting, so we'll stick with a simple modification of our `ColorPan` example. After all, figuring out what to display is your job; I'm primarily concerned with giving you the necessary tools. After this, you should have the needed tools to implement more interesting applications.

Image consumers

First, we have to know a little more about the image consumers we'll be feeding. An image consumer implements the seven methods that are defined in the `ImageConsumer` interface. Two of these methods are overloaded versions of the `setPixels()` method that accept the actual pixel data for a region of the image. They are identical except that one takes the pixel data as an array of integers, and the other uses an array of bytes. (An array of bytes is natural when you're using an indexed color model because each pixel is specified by an index into a color array.) A call to `setPixels()` looks something like the following:

```
setPixels(x, y, width, height, colorModel, pixels, offset, scanLength);
```

`pixels` is the one-dimensional array of bytes or integers that holds the pixel data. Often, you deliver only part of the image with each call to `setPixels()`. The `x`, `y`, `width`, and `height` values define the rectangle of the image for which pixels are being delivered. `x` and `y` specify the upper left-hand corner of the chunk you're delivering, relative to the upper left-hand corner of the image as a whole. `width` specifies the width in pixels of the chunk; `height` specifies the number of scan lines in the chunk. `offset` specifies the point in `pixels` at which the data being delivered in this call to `setPixels()` starts. Finally, `scanLength` indicates the width of the entire image, which is not necessarily the same as `width`. The `pixels` array must be large enough to accommodate `width*length+offset` elements; if it's larger, any leftover data is ignored.

We haven't said anything yet about the `colorModel` argument to `setPixels()`. In our previous example, we drew our image using the default ARGB color model for pixel values; the version of the `MemoryImageSource` constructor that we used supplied the default color model for us. In this example, we also stick with the default model, but this time we have to specify it explicitly. The remaining five methods of the `ImageConsumer` interface accept general attributes and framing information about the image:

- `setHints()`
- `setDimensions()`
- `setProperties()`
- `setColorModel()`
- `imageComplete()`

Before delivering any data to a consumer, the producer should call the consumer's `setHints()` method to pass it information about how pixels will be delivered. Hints are specified in the form of flags defined in the `ImageConsumer` interface. The flags are described in Table 11–4. The consumer uses these hints to optimize the way it builds the image; it's also free to ignore them.

Table 11–4: ImageConsumer setHints() Flags

Flag	Description
RANDOMPIXELORDER	The pixels are delivered in random order
TOPDOWNLEFTRIGHT	The pixels are delivered from top to bottom, left to right
COMPLETESCANLINES	Each call to setPixels() delivers one or more complete scan lines
SINGLEPASS	Each pixel is delivered only once
SINGLEFRAME	The pixels define a single, static image

setDimensions() is called to pass the width and height of the image when they are known.

setProperties() is used to pass a hashtable of image properties, stored by name. This method isn't particularly useful without some prior agreement between the producer and consumer about what properties are meaningful. For example, image formats such as GIF and TIFF can include additional information about the image. These image attributes could be delivered to the consumer in the hashtable.

setColorModel() is called to tell the consumer which color model will be used to process most of the pixel data. However, remember that each call to setPixels() also specifies a ColorModel for its group of pixels. The color model specified in setColorModel() is really only a hint that the consumer can use for optimization. You're not required to use this color model to deliver all (or for that matter, any) of the pixels in the image.

The producer calls the consumer's imageComplete() method when it has completely delivered the image or a frame of an image sequence. If the consumer doesn't wish to receive further frames of the image, it should unregister itself from the producer at this point. The producer passes a status flag formed from the flags shown in Table 11–5.

Table 11–5: ImageConsumer imageComplete() Flags

Flag	Description
STATICIMAGEDONE	A single static image is complete
SINGLEFRAMEDONE	One frame of an image sequence is complete
IMAGEERROR	An error occurred while generating the image

As you can see, the ImageProducer and ImageConsumer interfaces provide a very flexible mechanism for distributing image data. Now let's look at a simple producer.

A sequence of images

The following image producer, ImageSequence, is similar to the MemoryImageSource of our previous example, except that it generates a sequence of frames. As in the previous example, it reads ARGB data from an array, but ImageSequence consults the object that creates the array and gives it an opportunity to update the data between each frame.

This is a complex example, so before diving into the code, let's take a broad look at the pieces. The `ImageSequence` class is an image producer; it generates data and sends it to image consumers to be displayed. To make our design more modular, we define an interface called `FrameARGBData` that describes how our rendering code provides each frame of ARGB pixel data to our producer. To do the computation and provide the raw bits, we create a class called `ColorPanCycle` that implements `FrameARGBData`. This means that `ImageSequence` doesn't care specifically where the data comes from; if we wanted to draw different images, we could just drop in another class, provided that the new class implements `FrameARGBData`. Finally, we create an applet called `ShowSequence` that includes two image consumers to display the data.

Here's the `ImageSequence` class:

```java
import java.awt.image.*;
import java.util.*;

public class ImageSequence extends Thread implements ImageProducer {
    int width, height, delay;
    ColorModel model = ColorModel.getRGBdefault();
    FrameARGBData frameData;
    private Vector consumers = new Vector();

    public void run() {
        while ( frameData != null ) {
            frameData.nextFrame();
            sendFrame();
            try {
                sleep( delay );
            }
            catch ( InterruptedException e ) {}
        }
    }

    public ImageSequence(FrameARGBData src, int maxFPS ) {
        frameData = src;
        width = frameData.size().width;
        height = frameData.size().height;
        delay = 1000/maxFPS;
        setPriority( MIN_PRIORITY + 1 );
    }

    public synchronized void addConsumer(ImageConsumer c) {
        if ( isConsumer( c ) )
            return;

        consumers.addElement( c );
        c.setHints(ImageConsumer.TOPDOWNLEFTRIGHT |
                ImageConsumer.SINGLEPASS );
        c.setDimensions( width, height );
        c.setProperties( new Hashtable() );
```

```
            c.setColorModel( model );
        }

        public synchronized boolean isConsumer(ImageConsumer c) {
            return ( consumers.contains( c ) );
        }

        public synchronized void removeConsumer(ImageConsumer c) {
            consumers.removeElement( c );
        }

        public void startProduction(ImageConsumer ic) {
            addConsumer(ic);
        }

        public void requestTopDownLeftRightResend(ImageConsumer ic) { }

        private void sendFrame() {
            for ( Enumeration e = consumers.elements();
                  e.hasMoreElements();  ) {
                ImageConsumer c = (ImageConsumer)e.nextElement();
                c.setPixels(0, 0, width, height, model,
                         frameData.getPixels(), 0, width);
                c.imageComplete(ImageConsumer.SINGLEFRAMEDONE);
            }
        }
    }
```

The bulk of the code in ImageSequence creates the skeleton we need for implementing the ImageProducer interface. ImageSequence is actually a simple subclass of Thread whose run() method loops, generating and sending a frame of data on each iteration. The ImageSequence constructor takes two items: a FrameARGBData object that updates the array of pixel data for each frame, and an integer that specifies the maximum number of frames per second to generate. We give the thread a low priority (MIN_PRIORITY+1) so that it can't run away with all of our CPU time.

Our FrameARGBData object implements the following interface:

```
    interface FrameARGBData {
        java.awt.Dimension size();
        int [] getPixels();
        void nextFrame();
    }
```

In ImageSequence's run() method, we call nextFrame() to compute the array of pixels for each frame. After computing the pixels, we call our own send-Frame() method to deliver the data to the consumers. sendFrame() calls get-Pixels() to retrieve the updated array of pixel data from the FrameARGBData object. `sendFrame()` then sends the new data to all of the consumers by invoking each of their `setPixels()` methods and signaling the end of the frame with `imageComplete()`. Note that `sendFrame()` can handle multiple consumers; it iterates through a `Vector` of image consumers. In a more realistic implementation, we would also check for errors and notify the consumers if any occurred.

The business of managing the `Vector` of consumers is handled by `addConsumer()` and the other methods in the `ImageProducer` interface. `addConsumer()` adds an item to `consumers`. A `Vector` is a perfect tool for this task, since it's an automatically extendable array, with methods for finding out how many elements it has, whether or not a given element is already a member, and so on.

`addConsumer()` also gives the consumer hints about how the data will be delivered by calling `setHints()`. This image provider always works from top to bottom and left to right, and makes only one pass through the data. `addConsumer()` next gives the consumer an empty hashtable of image properties. Finally, it reports that most of the pixels will use the default ARGB color model (we initialized the variable `model` to `ColorModel.getRGBDefault()`). In this example, we always start sending image data on the next frame, so `startProduction()` simply calls `addConsumer()`.

We've discussed the mechanism for communications between the consumer and producer, but I haven't yet told you where the data comes from. We have a `FrameARGBData` interface that defines how to retrieve the data, but we don't yet have an object that implements the interface. The following class, `ColorPanCycle`, implements `FrameARGBData`; we'll use it to generate our pixels:

```
class ColorPanCycle implements FrameARGBData {
    int frame = 0, width, height;
    private int [] pixels;

    ColorPanCycle ( int w, int h ) {
        width = w;
        height = h;
        pixels = new int [ width * height ];
        nextFrame();
    }
    public synchronized int [] getPixels() {
        return pixels;
    }
    public synchronized void nextFrame() {
        int index = 0;
        for (int y = 0; y < height; y++) {
            for (int x = 0; x < width; x++) {
                int red = (y * 255) / (height - 1);
                int green = (x * 255) / (width - 1);
                int blue = (frame * 10) & 0xff;
```

```
                pixels[index++] =
                    (255 << 24) | (red << 16) | (green << 8) | blue;
            }
        }
        frame++;
    }
    public Dimension size() {
        return new Dimension ( width, height );
    }
}
```

ColorPanCycle is like our previous ColorPan example, except that it adjusts
each pixel's blue component each time nextFrame() is called. This should produce a color cycling effect; as time goes on, the image becomes more blue.

Now let's put the pieces together by writing an applet that displays a sequence of
changing images: ShowSequence. In fact, we'll do better than displaying one
sequence. To prove that ImageSequence really can deal with multiple consumers, ShowSequence creates two components that display different views of
the image. Once the mechanism has been set up, it's surprising how little code you
need to add additional displays.

```
import java.awt.*;
import java.awt.image.*;

public class ShowSequence extends java.applet.Applet {
    ImageSequence seq;

    public void init() {
        seq = new ImageSequence( new ColorPanCycle(100, 100), 10);
        setLayout( null );
        add( new ImageCanvas( seq, 100, 100 ) );
        add( new ImageCanvas( seq, 50, 50 ) );
    }
}

class ImageCanvas extends Canvas {
    Image img;
    ImageProducer source;
    ImageCanvas ( ImageProducer p, int w, int h ) {
        source = p;
        resize( w, h );
    }
    public void update( Graphics g ) {
        paint(g);
    }
    public void paint( Graphics g ) {
        if ( img == null )
            img = createImage( source );
        g.drawImage( img, 0, 0, size().width, size().height, this );
    }
}
```

ShowSequence constructs a new ImageSequence producer with an instance of our ColorPanCycle object as its frame source. It then creates two ImageCanvas components that create and display the two views of our animation. ImageCanvas is a subclass of Canvas; it takes an ImageProducer and a width and height in its constructor and creates and displays an appropriately scaled version of the image in its paint() method. ShowSequence places the smaller view on top of the larger one for a sort of "picture in picture" effect.

If you've followed the example to this point, you're probably wondering where in the blue blazes is the image consumer. After all, we spent a lot of time writing methods in ImageSequence for the consumer to call. If you look back at the code, you'll see that an ImageSequence object gets passed to the ImageCanvas constructor, and that this object is used as an argument to createImage(). But nobody appears to call addConsumer(). And the image producer calls setPixels() and other consumer methods; but it always digs a consumer out of its Vector of registered consumers, so we never see where these consumers come from.

In ShowSequence, the image consumer is behind the scenes, hidden deep inside the Canvas—in fact, inside the Canvas' peer. The call to createImage() tells its component (i.e., our canvas) to become an image consumer. Something deep inside the component is calling addConsumer() behind our backs and registering a mysterious consumer, and that consumer is the one the producer uses in calls to setPixels() and other methods. We haven't implemented any ImageConsumer objects in this book because, as you might imagine, most image consumers are implemented in native code, since they need to display things on the screen. There are others though; the java.awt.image.PixelGrabber class is a consumer that returns the pixel data as a byte array. You might use it to save an image. You can make your own consumer do anything you like with pixel data from a producer. But in reality, you rarely need to write an image consumer yourself. Let them stay hidden; take it on faith that they exist.

Now for the next question: How does the screen get updated? Even though we are updating the consumer with new data, the new image will not appear on the display unless the applet repaints it periodically. By now, this part of the machinery should be familiar: what we need is an image observer. Remember that all components are image observers (i.e., the class Component implements ImageObserver). The call to drawImage() specifies our ImageCanvas as its image observer. The default Component class-image-observer functionality then repaints our image whenever new pixel data arrives.

In this example, we haven't bothered to stop and start our applet properly; it continues running and wasting CPU time even when it's invisible. There are two strategies for stopping and restarting our thread. We can destroy the thread and create a new one, which would require recreating our `ImageCanvas` objects, or we could suspend and resume the active thread. As discussed in Chapter 6, neither option is particularly difficult.

Filtering Image Data

As I said above, you rarely need to write an image consumer. However, there is one kind of image consumer that's worth knowing about. In this final section on images, we'll build a simple image filter. An image filter is simply a class that performs some work on image data before passing the data to another consumer.

The `ColorSep` applet acquires an image; uses an image filter to separate the image into red, green, and blue components; and displays the three resulting images. With this applet and a few million dollars, you could build your own color separation plant.

```
import java.awt.*;
import java.awt.image.*;

public class ColorSep extends java.applet.Applet {
    Image img, redImg, greenImg, blueImg;
    public void init() {
        img = getImage( getCodeBase(), getParameter("img") );
        redImg = createImage(new FilteredImageSource(img.getSource(),
                    new ColorMaskFilter( Color.red )));
        greenImg = createImage(new FilteredImageSource(img.getSource(),
                    new ColorMaskFilter( Color.green )));
        blueImg = createImage(new FilteredImageSource(img.getSource(),
                    new ColorMaskFilter( Color.blue )));
    }
    public void paint( Graphics g ) {
        g.drawImage( redImg, 0, 0, size().width/3,
                    size().height, this );
        g.drawImage( greenImg, size().width/3, 0, size().width/3,
                    size().height, this );
        g.drawImage( blueImg, 2*size().width/3, 0, size().width/3,
                    size().height, this );
    }
}

class ColorMaskFilter extends RGBImageFilter {
    Color color;

    ColorMaskFilter( Color mask ) {
        color = mask;
        canFilterIndexColorModel = true;
    }
```

```
    public int filterRGB(int x, int y, int pixel ) {
      return
        255 << 24 |
          (((pixel & 0xff0000) >> 16) * color.getRed()/255) << 16 |
          (((pixel & 0xff00) >> 8) * color.getGreen()/255) << 8 |
          (pixel & 0xff) * color.getBlue()/255 ;
    }
  }
```

The FilteredImageSource and RGBImageFilter classes form the basis for building and using image filters. A FilteredImageSource is an image producer (like MemoryImageSource) that is constructed from an image and an ImageFilter object. It fetches pixel data from the image and feeds it through the image filter before passing the data along. Because FilteredImageSource is an image producer, we can use it in our calls to createImage().

But where's the consumer? FilteredImageSource obviously consumes image data as well as producing it. The image consumer is still mostly hidden, but is peeking out from under its rock. Our class ColorMaskFilter extends RGBImageFilter, which in turn extends ImageFilter. And ImageFilter is (finally!) an image consumer. Of course, we still don't see the calls to addConsumer(), and we don't see an implementation of setPixels(); they're hidden in the ImageFilter sources and inherited by ColorMaskFilter.

So what does ColorMaskFilter actually do? Not much. ColorMaskFilter is a simple subclass of RGBImageFilter that implements one method, filterRGB(), through which all of the pixel data are fed. Its constructor saves a mask value we use for filtering. The filterRGB() method accepts a pixel value, along with its x and y coordinates, and returns the filtered version of the pixel. In ColorMaskFilter, we simply multiply the color components by the mask color to get the proper effect. A more complex filter, however, might use the coordinates to change its behavior based on the pixel's position.

One final detail: the constructor for ColorMaskFilter sets the flag canFilterIndexColorModel. This flag is inherited from RGBImageFilter. It means our filter doesn't depend on the pixel's position. In turn, this means it can filter the colors in a color table. If we were using an indexed color model, filtering the color table would be much faster than filtering the individual pixels.

Working with Audio

So you've read all the material on drawing and image processing, and you're wondering what in the world audio has to do with images. Well, not much actually, except that true multimedia presentations often combine image techniques such as animation with sound. So we're going to spend a few minutes here talking about audio, for lack of a better place to discuss it.

As we write this, the good people at Sun are hard at work developing the API that Java applets will use for playing audio. A future release of Java will undoubtedly have support for real-time and continuous audio streams, sound management, mixing, synchronization, and filtering. Unfortunately, at the moment, we can tell you only about the basics.

`java.applet.AudioClip` defines an interface for objects that can play sound. An object that implements `AudioClip` can be told to `play()` its sound data, `stop()` playing the sound, or `loop()` continually.

An applet can call its `getAudioClip()` method to retrieve sounds over the network. This method takes an absolute or relative URL to specify where the audio file is located. The viewer may take the sound from a cache or retrieve it over the network. The following applet, `NoisyButton`, gives a simple example:

```
import java.awt.*;

public class NoisyButton extends java.applet.Applet {
    java.applet.AudioClip sound;
    public void init() {
        sound = getAudioClip(getCodeBase(), getParameter("sound"));
        add ( new Button("Play Sound") );
    }

    public boolean action(Event e, Object arg) {
        if ( sound != null )
            sound.play();
        return true;
    }
}
```

`NoisyButton` retrieves an `AudioClip` from the server; we use `getCodeBase()` to find out where the applet lives and `getParameter()` to find the name of the audio file. (The applet tag that displays `NoisyButton` must include a parameter tag for `sound`.) Unfortunately, this is about the extent of what we can do with sound right now. If you want to experiment, there are a few additional methods in the `sun.audio` classes. Stay tuned for a bigger and better API in the near future.

Glossary

abstract

The abstract keyword is used to declare abstract methods and classes. An abstract method has no implementation defined; it is declared with arguments and a return type as usual, but the body enclosed in curly braces is replaced with a semicolon. The implementation of an abstract method is provided by a subclass of the class in which it is defined. If an abstract method appears in a class, the class is also abstract.

API (Application Programming Interface)

An API consists of the functions and variables programmers are use in their applications. The Java API consists of all public and protected methods of all public classes in the java.applet, java.awt, java.awt.image, java.awt.peer, java.io, java.lang, java.net, and java.util packages.

applet

An embedded Java application that runs in the context of an applet viewer, such as a Web browser.

<applet> tag

HTML tag that specifies an applet run within a Web document.

applet viewer

An application that implements the additional structure needed to run and display Java applets. An applet viewer can be a Web browser like HotJava or Netscape Navigator, or a separate program like Sun's *appletviewer*.

application

A Java program that runs standalone; i.e., it doesn't require an applet viewer.

AWT (Abstract Windowing Toolkit)

Java's platform-independent windowing, graphics, and user-interface toolkit.

boolean

A primitive Java data type that contains a truth value. The two possible values of a `boolean` variable are `true` and `false`.

byte

A primitive Java data type that's an 8-bit two's-complement signed number (in all implementations).

callback

A behavior that is defined by one object and then later invoked by another object when a particular event occurs.

cast

A technique that explicitly converts one data type to another.

catch

The `catch` statement introduces an exception-handling block of code following a `try` statement. The `catch` keyword is followed by an exception type and argument name in parentheses, and a block of code within curly braces.

char

A primitive Java data type; a variable of type `char` holds a single 16-bit Unicode character.

class

a) An encapsulated collection of data and methods to operate on the data. A class may be instantiated to produce an object that's an instance of the class.

b) The `class` keyword is used to declare a class, thereby defining a new object type. Its syntax is similar to the `struct` keyword in C.

class loader

An object in the Java security model that is responsible for loading Java binary classes from the network into the local interpreter. A class loader keeps its classes in a separate namespace, so that loaded classes cannot interact with system classes and breach system security.

class method

A method declared `static`. Methods of this type are not passed implicit `this` references and may refer only to class variables and invoke other class methods of the current class. A class method may be invoked through the class name, rather than through an instance of the class.

class path

The directory path specifying the location of compiled Java class files on the local system.

class variable

A variable declared `static`. Variables of this type are associated with the class, rather than with a particular instance of the class. There is only one copy of a static variable, regardless of the number of instances of the class that are created.

client

The application that initiates a conversation as part of a networked client/server application. See server.

compilation unit

The source code for a Java class. A compilation unit normally contains a single class definition, and in most current development environments is just a file with a *.java* extension.

compiler

A program that translates source code into executable code.

component

Any of the GUI primitives implemented in the `java.awt` package as subclasses of `Component`. The classes `Button`, `Choice`, and `TextField` (among many others) are components.

composition

Using objects as part of another, more complex object. When you compose a new object, you create complex behavior by delegating tasks to the internal objects. Composition is different from inheritance, which defines a new object by changing or refining the behavior of an old object. See inheritance.

constructor

A method that is invoked automatically when a new instance of a class is created. Constructors are used to initialize the variables of the newly created object. The constructor method has the same name as the class.

container

One of the `java.awt` classes that "contain" GUI components. Components in a container appear within the boundaries of the container. The classes `Dialog`, `Frame`, `Panel`, and `Window` are containers.

content handler

A class that recognizes the content type of particular data, parses it, and converts it to an appropriate object.

datagram

A packet of data sent to a receiving computer without warning, error checking, or other control information.

data hiding

See encapsulation.

double

A Java primitive data type; a `double` value is a 64-bit (double-precision) floating-point number.

encapsulation

An object-oriented programming technique that makes an object's data `private` or `protected` (i.e., hidden) and allows programmers to access and manipulate that data only through method calls. Done well, encapsulation reduces bugs and promotes reusability and modularity of classes. This technique is also known as data hiding.

event

A user's action, such as a mouse click or key press.

exception

A signal that some unexpected condition has occurred in the program. In Java, exceptions are objects that are subclasses of Exception or Error (which themselves are subclasses of Throwable). Exceptions in Java are "raised" with the throw keyword and received with the catch keyword. See throw, throws, and catch.

extends

The extends keyword is used in a class declaration to specify the superclass of the class being defined. The class being defined has access to all the public and protected variables and methods of the superclass (or, if the class being defined is in the same package, it has access to all non-private variables and methods). If a class definition omits the extends clause, its superclass is taken to be java.lang.Object.

final

The final keyword is a modifier that may be applied to classes, methods, and variables. It has a similar, but not identical meaning in each case. When final is applied to a class, it means that the class may never be subclassed. java.lang.System is an example of a final class. When final is applied to a variable, the variable is a constant; i.e., it can't be modified.

finalize

finalize is not actually a Java keyword, but a reserved method name. The finalizer is called when an object is no longer being used (i.e., when there are no further references to it), but before the object's memory is actually reclaimed by the system. A finalizer should perform cleanup tasks and free system resources not handled by Java's garbage-collection system.

finally

This keyword introduces the finally block of a try/catch/finally construct. catch and finally blocks provide exception handling and routine cleanup for code in a try block. The finally block is optional, and appears after the try block, and after zero or more catch blocks. The code in a finally block is executed once, regardless of how the code in the try block executes. In normal execution, control reaches the end of the try block and proceeds to the finally block, which generally performs any necessary cleanup.

float

A Java primitive data type; a `float` value is a 32-bit (single-precision) floating-point number represented in IEEE 754 format.

garbage collection

The process of reclaiming the memory of objects no longer in use. An object is no longer in use when there are no references to it from other objects in the system and no references in any local variables on the method call stack.

GC

An abbreviation for garbage collection or garbage collector (or occasionally "graphics context").

graphics context

A drawable surface represented by the `java.awt.Graphics` class. A graphics context contains contextual information about the drawing area and provides methods for performing drawing operations in it.

GUI (graphical user interface)

A GUI is a user interface constructed from graphical push buttons, text fields, pull-down menus, dialog boxes, and other standard interface components. In Java, GUIs are implemented with the classes in the `java.awt` package.

hashcode

An arbitrary-looking identifying number used as a kind of signature for an object. A hashcode stores an object in a hashtable. See hashtable.

hashtable

An object that is like a dictionary or an associative array. A hashtable stores and retrieves elements using key values called hashcodes. See hashcode.

hostname

The name given to an individual computer attached to the Internet.

HotJava

A WWW browser written in Java that is capable of downloading and running Java applets.

ImageConsumer

An interface for receiving image data from an image source. Image consumers are usually implemented by the `awt.peer` interface, so they are largely invisible to programmers.

ImageObserver

An interface in the `java.awt.image` package that receives information about the status of an image being constructed by a particular `ImageConsumer`.

ImageProducer

An interface in the `java.awt.image` package that represents an image source (i.e., a source of pixel data).

implements

The `implements` keyword is used in class declarations to indicate that the class implements the named interface or interfaces. The `implements` clause is optional in class declarations; if it appears, it must follow the `extends` clause (if any). If an `implements` clause appears in the declaration of a non-abstract class, every method from each specified interface must be implemented by the class or by one of its superclasses.

import

The `import` statement makes Java classes available to the current class under an abbreviated name. (Java classes are always available by their fully qualified name, assuming the appropriate class file can be found relative to the CLASS-PATH environment variable and that the class file is readable. `import` doesn't make the class available; it just saves typing and makes your code more legible). Any number of `import` statements may appear in a Java program. They must appear, however, after the optional `package` statement at the top of the file, and before the first class or interface definition in the file.

inheritance

An important feature of object-oriented programming that involves defining a new object by changing or refining the behavior of an existing object. That is, an object implicitly contains all the non-`private` variables of its superclass and can invoke all the non-`private` methods of its superclass. Java supports single inheritance of classes and multiple inheritance of interfaces.

instance

An object. When a class is instantiated to produce an object, we say the object is an instance of the class.

instance method

A non-static method of a class. Such a method is passed an implicit this reference to the object that invoked it. See also class method and static.

instanceof

instanceof is a Java operator that returns true if the object on its left-hand side is an instance of the class (or implements the interface) specified on its right-hand side. instanceof returns false if the object is not an instance of the specified class or does not implement the specified interface. It also returns false if the specified object is null.

instance variable

A non-static variable of a class. Copies of such variables occur in every instance of the created class. See also class variable and static.

int

A primitive Java data type that's a 32-bit two's-complement signed number (in all implementations).

interface

The interface keyword is used to declare an interface. More generally, an interface defines a list of methods that enables a class to implement the interface itself.

interpreter

The module that decodes and executes Java bytecode.

ISO8859-1

An 8-bit character encoding standardized by the ISO. This encoding is also known as Latin-1 and contains characters from the Latin alphabet suitable for English and most languages of western Europe.

ISO10646

A 4-byte character encoding that includes all of the world's national standard character encodings. Also known as UCS. The 2-byte Unicode character set maps to the range 0x00000000 to 0x0000FFFF of ISO 10646.

Java WorkShop

Sun's Web browser-based tool written in Java for the development of Java applications.

JDK (Java Development Kit)

A package of software distributed by Sun Microsystems for Java developers. It includes the Java interpreter, Java classes, and Java development tools: compiler, debugger, disassembler, appletviewer, stub file generator, and documentation generator.

JavaScript

A language for creating dynamic Web pages developed by Netscape. From a programmer's point of view, it's unrelated to Java, although some of its capabilities are similar. Internally, there may be a relationship, but even that is unclear.

layout manager

An object that controls the arrangement of components within the display area of a container. The `java.awt` package contains a number of layout managers that provide different layout styles.

Latin-1

A nickname for ISO8859-1.

local variable

A variable that is declared inside a single method. A local variable can be seen only by code within that method.

`long`

A primitive Java data type that's a 64-bit two's-complement signed number (in all implementations).

method

The object-oriented programming term for a function or procedure.

method overloading

Providing definitions of more than one method with the same name but with different argument lists or return values. When an overloaded method is called, the compiler determines which one is intended by examining the supplied argument types.

method overriding

Defining a method that exactly matches (i.e., same name, same argument types, and same return type) a method defined in a superclass. When an overridden method is invoked, the interpreter uses "dynamic method lookup" to determine which method definition is applicable to the current object.

modifier

A keyword placed before a class, variable, or method that alters the item's accessibility, behavior, or semantics. See `abstract`, `final`, `native`, `private`, `private protected`, `protected`, `public`, `static`, and `synchronized`.

Model/View/Controller (MVC) framework

A user-interface design that originated in Smalltalk. In MVC, the data for a display item is called the "model." A "view" displays a particular representation of the model, and a "controller" provides user interaction with both. Java incorporates many MVC concepts.

NaN (not-a-number)

This is a special value of the `double` and `float` data types that represents an undefined result of a mathematical operation, such as zero divided by zero.

native

`native` is a modifier that may be applied to method declarations. It indicates that the method is implemented (elsewhere) in C, or in some other platform-dependent fashion. A `native` method should have a semicolon instead of a body. A `native` method cannot be `abstract`, but all other method modifiers may be used with `native` methods.

native method

A method that is implemented in a native language on a host platform, rather than being implemented in Java. Native methods provide access to such resources as the network, the windowing system, and the host filesystem.

new

`new` is a unary operator that creates a new object or array (or raises an `OutOfMemoryException` if there is not enough memory available).

null

null is a special value that indicates a variable doesn't refer to any object. The value null may be assigned to any class or interface variable. It cannot be cast to any integral type, and should not be considered equal to zero, as in C.

object

An instance of a class. A class models a group of things; an object models a particular member of that group.

package

The package statement specifies which package the code in the file is part of. Java code that is part of a particular package has access to all classes (public and non-public) in the package, and all non-private methods and fields in all those classes. When Java code is part of a named package, the compiled class file must be placed at the appropriate position in the CLASSPATH directory hierarchy before it can be accessed by the Java interpreter or other utilities. If the package statement is omitted from a file, the code in that file is part of an unnamed default package. This is convenient for small test programs, or during development because it means the code can be interpreted from the current directory.

<param> tag

HTML tag used within <applet> ... </applet> to specify a named parameter and string value to an applet within a Web page.

peer

The actual implementation of a GUI component on a specific platform. Peer components reside within a Toolkit object. See Toolkit.

primitive type

One of the Java data types: boolean, char, byte, short, int, long, float, double. Primitive types are manipulated, assigned, and passed to methods "by value" (i.e., the actual bytes of the data are copied). See also reference type.

private

The private keyword is a visibility modifier that can be applied to method and field variables of classes. A private field is not visible outside its class definition.

private protected

When the private and protected visibility modifiers are both applied to a variable or method in a class, they indicate the field is visible only within the class itself and within subclasses of the class. Note that subclasses can access only private protected fields within themselves or within other objects that are subclasses; they cannot access those fields within instances of the superclass.

protected

The protected keyword is a visibility modifier that can be applied to method and field variables of classes. A protected field is visible only within its class, within subclasses, or within the package of which its class is a part. Note that subclasses in different packages can access only protected fields within themselves or within other objects that are subclasses; they cannot access protected fields within instances of the superclass.

protocol handler

Software that describes and enables the use of a new protocol. A protocol handler consists of two classes: a StreamHandler and a URLConnection.

public

The public keyword is a visibility modifier that can be applied to classes and interfaces and to the method and field variables of classes and interfaces. A public class or interface is visible everywhere. A non-public class or interface is visible only within its package. A public method or variable is visible everywhere its class is visible. When none of the private, protected or public modifiers is specified, a field is visible only within the package of which its class is a part.

reference type

Any object or array. Reference types are manipulated, assigned, and passed to methods "by reference." In other words, the underlying value is not copied; only a reference to it is. See also primitive type.

root

The base of a hierarchy, such as a root class, whose descendants are subclasses. The java.lang.Object class serves as the root of the Java class hierarchy.

SecurityManager

> The Java class that defines the methods the system calls to check whether a certain operation is permitted in the current environment.

server

> The application that accepts a request for a conversation as part of a networked client/server application. See client.

shadow

> To declare a variable with the same name as a variable defined in a superclass. We say the variable "shadows" the superclass's variable. Use the `super` keyword to refer to the shadowed variable, or refer to it by casting the object to the type of the superclass.

short

> A primitive Java data type that's a 16-bit two's-complement signed number (in all implementations).

socket

> An interface that listens for connections from clients on a data port and connects the client data stream with the receiving application.

static

> The `static` keyword is a modifier applied to method and variable declarations within a class. A `static` variable is also known as a class variable as opposed to non-`static` instance variables. While each instance of a class has a full set of its own instance variables, there is only one copy of each `static` class variable, regardless of the number of instances of the class (perhaps zero) that are created. `static` variables may be accessed by class name or through an instance. Non-`static` variables can be accessed only through an instance.

stream

> A flow of data, or a channel of communication. All fundamental I/O in Java is based on streams.

String

> A class used to represent textual information. The `String` class includes many methods for operating on string objects. Java overloads the + operator for string concatenation.

subclass

A class that extends another. The subclass inherits the `public` and `protected` methods and variables of its superclass. See `extends`.

super

The keyword `super` refers to the same value as `this`: the instance of the class for which the current method (these keywords are valid only within non-`static` methods) was invoked. While the type of `this` is the type of the class in which the method appears, the type of `super` is the type of the superclass of the class in which the method appears. `super` is usually used to refer to superclass variables shadowed by variables in the current class. Using `super` in this way is equivalent to casting `this` to the type of the superclass.

superclass

A class extended by some other class. The superclass's `public` and `protected` methods and variables are available to the subclass. See `extends`.

synchronized

The `synchronized` keyword is used in two related ways in Java: as a modifier and as a statement. First, it is a modifier applied to class or instance methods. It indicates that the method modifies the internal state of the class or the internal state of an instance of the class in a way that is not thread-safe. Before running a `synchronized` class method, Java obtains a lock on the class, to ensure that no other threads can modify the class concurrently. Before running a `synchronized` instance method, Java obtains a lock on the instance that invoked the method, ensuring that no other threads can modify the object at the same time.

Java also supports a `synchronized` statement that serves to specify a "critical section" of code. The `synchronized` keyword is followed by an expression in parentheses, and a statement or block of statements. The expression must evaluate to an object or array. Java obtains a lock on the specified object or array before executing the statements.

TCP

Transmission Control Protocol. A connection-oriented, reliable protocol. One of the protocols on which the Internet is based.

this

Within an instance method or constructor of a class, this refers to "this object"—the instance currently being operated on. It is useful to refer to an instance variable of the class that has been shadowed by a local variable or method argument. It is also useful to pass the current object as an argument to static methods or methods of other classes.

There is one additional use of this: when it appears as the first statement in a constructor method, it refers to one of the other constructors of the class.

thread

A single, independent stream of execution within a program. Since Java is a "multithreaded" programming language, more than one thread may be running within the Java interpreter at a time. Threads in Java are represented and controlled through the Thread object.

throw

The throw statement signals that an exceptional condition has occurred by throwing a specified exception object. This statement stops program execution and resumes it at the nearest containing catch statement that can handle the specified exception object. Note that the throw keyword must be followed by an exception object, not an exception class.

throws

The throws keyword is used in a method declaration to list the exceptions the method can throw. Any exceptions a method can raise that are not subclasses of Error or RuntimeException must either be caught within the method or declared in the method's throws clause.

Toolkit

The property of the Java API that defines the look and feel of the user interface on a specific platform.

try

The try keyword indicates a block of code to which subsequent catch and finally clauses apply. The try statement itself performs no special action. See the entries for catch and finally for more information on the try/catch/finally construct.

UCS (universal character set)

A synonym for ISO10646.

UDP

User Datagram Protocol. A connectionless unreliable protocol. UDP describes a network data connection based on datagrams with little packet control.

Unicode

A 16-bit character encoding that includes all of the world's commonly used alphabets and ideographic character sets in a "unified" form (i.e., a form from which duplications among national standards have been removed). ASCII and Latin-1 characters may be trivially mapped to Unicode characters. Java uses Unicode for its `char` and `String` types.

UTF-8 (UCS transformation format 8-bit form)

An encoding for Unicode characters (and more generally, UCS characters) commonly used for transmission and storage. It is a multibyte format in which different characters require different numbers of bytes to be represented.

vector

A dynamic array of elements.

verifier

A theorem prover that steps through the Java byte-code before it is run and makes sure that it is well-behaved. The byte-code verifier is the first line of defense in Java's security model.

Index

Text was prepared by Erik Ray in SGML DocBook 2.4 DTD. The print version of this book was created by translating the SGML source into a set of gtroff macros using a filter developed at ORA by Norman Walsh. Steve Talbott designed and wrote the underlying macro set on the basis of the GNU troff -gs macros; Lenny Muellner adapted them to SGML and implemented the book design. The GNU groff text formatter version 1.09 was used to generate PostScript output. The heading font is Bodoni BT; the text font is New Baskerville. The illustrations that appear in the book were created in Macromedia Freehand 5.0 by Chris Reilley. This colophon was written by Clairemarie Fisher O'Leary.

About the Authors

Patrick Niemeyer (*pat@pat.net*) became involved with Oak while working at Southwestern Bell Technology Resources and experimenting with executable content in the TkWWW Web browser. He is currently a consultant in the areas of networking and distributed applications. Most recently, Pat developed components for the client/server migration at Edward Jones & Co. With the book done, Pat plans to spend the summer catching up on his life, working on his '66 Triumph Spitfire, and occasionally slipping into his alter-ego to fight crime and battle cartoonish super villainy.

Joshua Peck (*jbpeck@ooi.com*) has worked as a World Wide Web designer and consultant. He is a founder of Open Object, Inc., a company that specializes in Java consulting, training, and development. Josh holds a degree in engineering from Washington University in St. Louis.

Colophon

Our look is the result of reader comments, our own experimentation, and feedback from distribution channels. Distinctive covers complement our distinctive approach to technical topics, breathing personality and life into potentially dry subjects.

The cover of *Exploring Java* features a suitcase covered in luggage labels. Labels such as these were popular during the "Golden Age of Travel," a time that can roughly be placed between the 1880s and 1950s. The labels, which were given out by hotels, ocean-liners, railroads, and, after World War I, airlines, served two purposes. For the companies that gave them away, they were a portable and inexpensive way to advertise themselves around the world. For the travelers who affixed the labels to their luggage, they were also a form of advertisement; the colorful and exotic-looking labels told all who saw them that the person carrying that suitcase was well-traveled and adventurous and, of course, wealthy. With the introduction of the jet engine in the 1950s, traveling became less expensive and more convenient, and, therefore, more accessible to all. As being well-traveled became less a mark of distinction and as the world began to seem a smaller and smaller place, luggage labels became obsolete.

Edie Freedman designed the cover of this book, using an image from the CMCD PhotoCD Collection that she manipulated in Adobe Photoshop. The cover layout was produced with Quark XPress 3.3 using the Bodoni Black font from URW Software. The inside layout was designed by Nancy Priest.

Programming

UNIX, C and MULTI-PLATFORM

Books from O'Reilly & Associates, Inc.

Fall/Winter 1995-96

C Programming Libraries

Practical C++ Programming

By Steve Oualline
1st Edition September 1995
584 pages, ISBN 1-56592-139-9

Fast becoming the standard language of commercial software development, C++ is an update of the C programming language, adding object-oriented features that are very helpful for today's larger graphical applications.

Practical C++ Programming is a complete introduction to the C++ language for the beginning programmer, and also for C programmers transitioning to C++. Unlike most other C++ books, this book emphasizes a practical, real-world approach, including how to debug, how to make your code understandable to others, and how to understand other people's code. Topics covered include good programming style, C++ syntax (what to use and what not to use), C++ class design, debugging and optimization, and common programming mistakes. At the end of each chapter are a number of exercises you can use to make sure you've grasped the concepts. Solutions to most are provided.

Practical C++ Programming describes standard C++ features that are supported by all UNIX C++ compilers (including *gcc*), DOS/Windows and NT compilers (including Microsoft Visual C++), and Macintosh compilers.

C++: The Core Language

By Gregory Satir & Doug Brown
1st Edition October 1995
228 pages, ISBN 1-56592-116-X

A first book for C programmers transitioning to C++, an object-oriented enhancement of the C programming language. Designed to get readers up to speed quickly, this book thoroughly explains the important concepts and features and gives brief overviews of the rest of the language. Covers features common to all C++ compilers, including those on UNIX, Windows NT, Windows, DOS, and Macs.

Porting UNIX Software

By Greg Lehey
1st Edition November 1995
480 pages (est.), ISBN 1-56592-126-7

This book deals with the whole life cycle of porting, from setting up a source tree on your system to correcting platform differences and even testing the executable after it's built. It exhaustively discusses the differences between versions of UNIX and the areas where porters tend to have problems. The assumption made in this book is that you just want to get a package working on your system; you don't want to become an expert in the details of your hardware or operating system (much less an expert in the system used by the person who wrote the package!).

Programming with Pthreads

By Bradford Nichols
1st Edition February 1996 (est.)
350 pages (est.), ISBN 1-56592-115-1

The idea behind POSIX threads is to have multiple tasks running concurrently within the same program. They can share a single CPU as processes do, or take advantage of multiple CPUs when available. In either case, they provide a clean way to divide the tasks of a program while sharing data. This book features realistic examples, a look behind the scenes at the implementation and performance issues, and chapters on special topics such as DCE, real-time, and multiprocessing.

POSIX.4

By Bill Gallmeister
1st Edition January 1995
570 pages, ISBN 1-56592-074-0

A general introduction to real-time programming and real-time issues, this book covers the POSIX.4 standard and how to use it to solve "real-world" problems. If you're at all interested in real-time applications—which include just about everything from telemetry to transaction processing—this book is for you. An essential reference.

POSIX Programmer's Guide

By Donald Lewine
1st Edition April 1991
640 pages, ISBN 0-937175-73-0

Most UNIX systems today are POSIX compliant because the federal government requires it for its purchases. Given the manufacturer's documentation, however, it can be difficult to distinguish system-specific features from those features defined by POSIX. The *POSIX Programmer's Guide*, intended as an explanation of the POSIX standard and as a reference for the POSIX.1 programming library, helps you write more portable programs.

"If you are an intermediate to advanced C programmer and are interested in having your programs compile first time on anything from a Sun to a VMS system to an MSDOS system, then this book must be thoroughly recommended." *—Sun UK User*

Practical C Programming

By Steve Oualline
2nd Edition January 1993
396 pages, ISBN 1-56592-035-X

C programming is more than just getting the syntax right. Style and debugging also play a tremendous part in creating programs that run well. *Practical C Programming* teaches you not only the mechanics of programming, but also how to create programs that are easy to read, maintain, and debug. There are lots of introductory C books, but this is the Nutshell Handbook®! In this edition, programs conform to ANSI C.

Using C on the UNIX System

By Dave Curry
1st Edition January 1989
250 pages, ISBN 0-937175-23-4

This is the book for intermediate to experienced C programmers who want to become UNIX system programmers. It explains system calls and special library routines available on the UNIX system. It is impossible to write UNIX utilities of any sophistication without understanding the material in this book.

Programming with curses

By John Strang
1st Edition 1986
76 pages, ISBN 0-937175-02-1

Curses is a UNIX library of functions for controlling a terminal's display screen from a C program. This handbook helps you make use of the curses library. Describes the original Berkeley version of curses.

Understanding and Using COFF

By Gintaras R. Gircys
1st Edition November 1988
196 pages, ISBN 0-937175-31-5

COFF—Common Object File Format—is the formal definition for the structure of machine code files in the UNIX System V environment. All machine code files are COFF files. This handbook explains COFF data structure and its manipulation.

C Programming Tools

Microsoft RPC Programming Guide

By John Shirley & Ward Rosenberry, Digital Equipment Corporation
1st Edition March 1995
254 pages, ISBN 1-56592-070-8

Remote Procedure Call (RPC) is the glue that holds together MS-DOS, Windows 3.x, and Windows NT. It is a client-server technology—a way of making programs on two different systems work together like one. The advantage of RPC is that you can link two systems together using simple C calls, as in a single-system program.

Like many aspects of Microsoft programming, RPC forms a small world of its own, with conventions and terms that can be confusing. This book is an introduction to Microsoft RPC concepts combined with a step-by-step guide to programming RPC calls in C. Topics include server registration, interface definitions, arrays and pointers, context handles, and basic administration procedures. This edition covers version 2.0 of Microsoft RPC. Four complete examples are included.

Power Programming with RPC

By John Bloomer
1st Edition February 1992
522 pages, ISBN 0-937175-77-3

RPC, or remote procedure calling, is the ability to distribute the execution of functions on remote computers. Written from a programmer's perspective, this book shows what you can do with RPCs, like Sun RPC, the de facto standard on UNIX systems. It covers related programming topics for Sun and other UNIX systems and teaches through examples.

lex & yacc

By John Levine, Tony Mason & Doug Brown
2nd Edition October 1992
366 pages, ISBN 1-56592-000-7

Shows programmers how to use two UNIX utilities, lex and yacc, in program development. The second edition contains completely revised tutorial sections for novice users and reference sections for advanced users. This edition is twice the size of the first, has an expanded index, and covers Bison and Flex.

Applying RCS and SCCS

By Don Bolinger & Tan Bronson
1st Edition September 1995
528 pages, ISBN 1-56592-117-8

Applying RCS and SCCS is a thorough introduction to these two systems, viewed as tools for project management. This book takes the reader from basic source control of a single file, through working with multiple releases of a software project, to coordinating multiple developers. It also presents TCCS, a representative "front-end" that addresses problems RCS and SCCS can't handle alone, such as managing groups of files, developing for multiple platforms, and linking public and private development areas.

Programming with GNU Software

By Mike Loukides
1st Edition TBA 1996 (est.)
250 pages (est.), ISBN 1-56592-112-7

This book and CD combination is a complete package for programmers who are new to UNIX or who would like to make better use of the system. The tools come from Cygnus Support, Inc., a well-known company that provides support for free software. Contents include GNU Emacs, gcc, C and C++ libraries, gdb, RCS, GNATS, and make. The book provides an introduction to all these tools for a C programmer.

UNIX Systems Programming for SVR4

By Dave Curry
1st Edition December 1995 (est.)
600 pages (est.), ISBN 1-56592-163-1

Presents a comprehensive look at the nitty gritty details on how UNIX interacts with applications. If you're writing an application from scratch, or if you're porting an application to any System V.4 platform, you need this book. It thoroughly explains all UNIX system calls and library routines related to systems programming, working with I/O, files and directories, processing multiple input streams, file and record locking, and memory-mapped files.

Software Portability with imake

By Paul DuBois
1st Edition July 1993
390 pages, ISBN 1-56592-055-4

imake is a utility that works with *make* to enable code to be compiled and installed on different UNIX machines. *imake* makes possible the wide portability of the X Window System code and is widely considered an X tool, but it's also useful for any software project that needs to be ported to many UNIX systems.

This Nutshell Handbook®—the only book available on *imake*—is ideal for X and UNIX programmers who want their software to be portable. The book is divided into two sections. The first section is a general explanation of *imake*, X configuration files, and how to write and debug an *Imakefile*. The second section describes how to write configuration files and presents a configuration file architecture that allows development of coexisting sets of configuration files. Several sample sets of configuration files are described and are available free over the Net.

Managing Projects with make

By Andrew Oram & Steve Talbott
2nd Edition October 1991
152 pages, ISBN 0-937175-90-0

make is one of UNIX's greatest contributions to software development, and this book offers the clearest description of *make* ever written. It describes all the basic features of *make* and provides guidelines on meeting the needs of large, modern projects. Also contains a description of free products that contain major enhancements to *make*.

Checking C Programs with lint

By Ian F. Darwin
1st Edition October 1988
84 pages, ISBN 0-937175-30-7

The *lint* program is one of the best tools for finding portability problems and certain types of coding errors in C programs. This handbook introduces you to *lint*, guides you through running it on your programs, and helps you interpret *lint*'s output.

Fortran/Scientific Computing

Migrating to Fortran 90

By James F. Kerrigan
1st Edition November 1993
389 pages, ISBN 1-56592-049-X

This book is a practical guide to Fortran 90 for the current Fortran programmer. It provides a complete overview of the new features that Fortran 90 has brought to the Fortran standard, with examples and suggestions for use. Topics include array sections, modules, file handling, allocatable arrays and pointers, and numeric precision.

"This is a book that all Fortran programmers eager to take advantage of the excellent features of Fortran 90 will want to have on their desk." —*FORTRAN Journal*

High Performance Computing

By Kevin Dowd
1st Edition June 1993
398 pages, ISBN 1-56592-032-5

Even if you never touch a line of code, *High Performance Computing* will help you make sense of the newest generation of workstations. A must for anyone who needs to worry about computer performance, this book covers everything, from the basics of modern workstation architecture, to structuring benchmarks, to squeezing more performance out of critical applications. It also explains what a good compiler can do—and what you have to do yourself. The author also discusses techniques for improving memory access patterns and taking advantage of parallelism.

Another valuable section of the book discusses the benchmarking process, or how to evaluate a computer's performance. Kevin Dowd discusses several of the "standard" industry benchmarks, explaining what they measure and what they don't. He also explains how to set up your own benchmark: how to structure the code, how to measure the results, and how to interpret them.

ORACLE Performance Tuning

By Peter Corrigan & Mark Gurry
1st Edition September 1993
642 pages, ISBN 1-56592-048-1

The Oracle relational database management system is the most popular database system in use today. Oracle offers tremendous power and flexibility, but at some cost. Demands for fast response, particularly in online transaction processing systems, make performance a major issue. With more organizations downsizing and adopting client-server and distributed database approaches, performance tuning has become all the more vital. Whether you're a manager, a designer, a programmer, or an administrator, there's a lot you can do on your own to dramatically increase the performance of your existing Oracle system. Whether you are running RDBMS Version 6 or Version 7, you may find that this book can save you the cost of a new machine; at the very least, it will save you a lot of headaches.

"This book is one of the best books on Oracle that I have ever read.... [It] discloses many Oracle Tips that DBA's and Developers have locked in their brains and in their planners.... I recommend this book for any person who works with Oracle, from managers to developers. In fact, I have to keep [it] under lock and key, because of the popularity of it."
—Mike Gangler

ORACLE PL/SQL Programming

By Steven Feuerstein
1st Edition September 1995
916 pages, Includes diskette, ISBN 1-56592-142-9

PL/SQL is a procedural language that is being used more and more with Oracle, particularly in client-server applications. This book fills a huge gap in the Oracle market by providing developers with a single, comprehensive guide to building applications with PL/SQL—and building them the right way. It's packed with strategies, code architectures, tips, techniques, and fully realized code. Includes a disk containing many examples of PL/SQL programs.

DCE Security Programming

By Wei Hu
1st Edition July 1995
386 pages, ISBN 1-56592-134-8

Security is critical in network applications since an outsider can so easily gain network access and pose as a trusted user. Here lies one of the greatest strengths of the Distributed Computing Environment (DCE) from the Open Software Foundation (OSF). DCE offers the most complete, flexible, and well-integrated network security package in the industry. The only problem is learning how to program it.

This book covers DCE security requirements, how the system fits together, what is required of the programmer, and how to figure out what needs protecting in an application. It will help you plan an application and lay the groundwork for Access Control Lists (ACLs), as well as use the calls that come with the DCE security interfaces. Using a sample application, increasingly sophisticated types of security are discussed, including storage of ACLs on disk and the job of writing an ACL manager. This book focuses on version 1.0 of DCE. However, issues in version 1.1 are also discussed so you can migrate to that interface.

Guide to Writing DCE Applications

By John Shirley, Wei Hu & David Magid
2nd Edition May 1994
462 pages, ISBN 1-56592-045-7

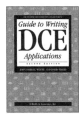

A hands-on programming guide to OSF's Distributed Computing Environment (DCE) for first-time DCE application programmers. This book is designed to help new DCE users make the transition from conventional, nondistributed applications programming to distributed DCE programming. In addition to basic RPC (remote procedure calls), this edition covers object UUIDs and basic security (authentication and authorization). Also includes practical programming examples.

"This book will be useful as a ready reference by the side of the novice DCE programmer." —*;login*

Distributing Applications Across DCE and Windows NT

By Ward Rosenberry & Jim Teague
1st Edition November 1993
302 pages, ISBN 1-56592-047-3

This book links together two exciting technologies in distributed computing by showing how to develop an application that simultaneously runs on DCE and Microsoft systems through remote procedure calls (RPC). Covers the writing of portable applications and the complete differences between RPC support in the two environments.

Understanding DCE

By Ward Rosenberry, David Kenney & Gerry Fisher
1st Edition October 1992
266 pages, ISBN 1-56592-005-8

A technical and conceptual overview of OSF's Distributed Computing Environment (DCE) for programmers, technical managers, and marketing and sales people. Unlike many O'Reilly & Associates books, *Understanding DCE* has no hands-on programming elements. Instead, the book focuses on how DCE can be used to accomplish typical programming tasks and provides explanations to help the reader understand all the parts of DCE.

Multi-Platform Code Management

By Kevin Jameson
1st Edition August 1994
354 pages, Includes two diskettes, ISBN 1-56592-059-7

For any programming team that is struggling with build and maintenance problems, this book—and its accompanying software (available for 15 platforms, including MS-DOS and various UNIX systems)—can save dozens of errors and hours of effort. A "one-stop-shopping" solution for code management proplems, this book shows you how to structure a large project and keep your files and builds under control over many releases and platforms. Includes two diskettes that provide a complete system for managing source files and builds.

Encyclopedia of Graphics File Formats

By James D. Murray & William vanRyper
1st Edition July 1994
928 pages, Includes CD-ROM
ISBN 1-56592-058-9

The computer graphics world is a veritable alphabet soup of acronyms; BMP, DXF, EPS, GIF, MPEG, PCX, PIC, RIFF, RTF, TGA, and TIFF are only a few of the many different formats in which graphics images can be stored. *The Encyclopedia of Graphics File Formats* is the definitive work on file formats—the book that will become a classic for graphics programmers and everyone else who deals with the low-level technical details of graphics files. It includes technical information on nearly 100 file formats, as well as chapters on graphics and file format basics, bitmap and vector files, metafiles, scene description, animation and multimedia formats, and file compression methods. Best of all, this book comes with a CD-ROM that collects many hard-to-find resources. We've assembled original vendor file format specification documents, along with test images and code examples, and a variety of software packages for MS-DOS, Windows, OS/2, UNIX, and the Macintosh that will let you convert, view, and manipulate graphics files and images.

Understanding Japanese Information Processing

By Ken Lunde
1st Edition September 1993
470 pages, ISBN 1-56592-043-0

Understanding Japanese Information Processing provides detailed information on all aspects of handling Japanese text on computer systems. It brings all of the relevant information together in a single book and covers everything from the origins of modern-day Japanese to the latest information on specific emerging computer encoding standards. Appendices provide additional reference material, such as a code conversion table, character set tables, mapping tables, an extensive list of software sources, a glossary, and more.

At Your Fingertips—

A COMPLETE GUIDE TO O'REILLY'S ONLINE SERVICES

O'Reilly & Associates offers extensive product and customer service information online. We invite you to come and explore our little neck-of-the-woods.

For product information and insight into new technologies, visit the O'Reilly Resource Center

Most comprehensive among our online offerings is the O'Reilly Resource Center. You'll find detailed information on all O'Reilly products, including titles, prices, tables of contents, indexes, author bios, software contents, and reviews. You can also view images of all our products. In addition, watch for informative articles that provide perspective on the technologies we write about. Interviews, excerpts, and bibliographies are also included.

After browsing online, it's easy to order, too, with GNN Direct or by sending email to **order@ora.com**. The O'Reilly Resource Center shows you how. Here's how to visit us online:

☞ *Via the World Wide Web*

If you are connected to the Internet, point your Web browser (e.g., `mosaic, netscape,` or `lynx`) to:

`http://www.ora.com/`

For the plaintext version, `telnet` to:
`www.ora.com` (login: `oraweb`)

☞ *Via Gopher*

If you have a Gopher program, our Gopher server has information in a menu format that some people prefer to the Web.

Connect your `gopher` to: `gopher.ora.com`
Or, point your Web browser to:
`gopher://gopher.ora.com/`

Or, you can `telnet` to: `gopher.ora.com`
(login: `gopher`)

A convenient way to stay informed: email mailing lists

An easy way to learn of the latest projects and products from O'Reilly & Associates is to subscribe to our mailing lists. We have email announcements and discussions on various topics, for example "ora-news," our electronic news service. Subscribers receive email as soon as the information breaks.

☞ *To join a mailing list:*

Send email to:
listproc@online.ora.com

Leave the message "subject" empty if possible.

If you know the name of the mailing list you want to subscribe to, put the following information on the first line of your message: `subscribe` "listname" "your name" `of` "your company."

For example: `subscribe ora-news`
`Kris Webber of Fine Enterprises`

If you don't know the name of the mailing list, listproc will send you a listing of all the mailing lists. Put this word on the first line of the body: `lists`

To find out more about a particular list, send a message with this word as the first line of the body: `info` "listname"

For more information and help, send this message: `help`

For specific help, email to: **listmaster@online.ora.com**

The complete O'Reilly catalog is now available via email

You can now receive a text-only version of our complete catalog via email. It contains detailed information about all our products, so it's mighty big: over 200 kbytes, or 200,000 characters.

To get the whole catalog in one message, send an empty email message to: **catalog@online.ora.com**

If your email system can't handle large messages, you can get the catalog split into smaller messages. Send email to: **catalog-split@online.ora.com**

To receive a print catalog, send your snail mail address to: **catalog@ora.com**

Check out Web Review, our new publication on the Web

Web Review is our new magazine that offers fresh insights into the Web. The editorial mission of Web Review is to answer the question: How and where do you BEST spend your time online? Each issue contains reviews that look at the most interesting and creative sites on the Web. Visit us at **http://gnn.com/wr/**

Web Review is the product of the recently formed Songline Studios, a venture between O'Reilly and America Online.

Get the files you want with FTP

We have an archive of example files from our books, the covers of our books, and much more available by anonymous FTP.

ftp to:

ftp.ora.com (login: **anonymous** – use your email address as the password.)

Or, if you have a WWW browser, point it to:

ftp://ftp.ora.com/

FTPMAIL

The ftpmail service connects to O'Reilly's FTP server and sends the results (the files you want) by email. This service is for people who can't use FTP—but who can use email.

For help and examples, send an email message to:

ftpmail@online.ora.com

(In the message body, put the single word: **help**)

Helpful information is just an email message away

Many customer services are provided via email. Here are a few of the most popular and useful:

info@online.ora.com
For a list of O'Reilly's online customer services.

info@ora.com
For general questions and information.

bookquestions@ora.com
For technical questions, or corrections, concerning book contents.

order@ora.com
To order books online and for ordering questions.

catalog@online.ora.com
To receive an online copy of our catalog.

catalog@ora.com
To receive a free copy of *ora.com*, our combination magazine and catalog. Please include your snail mail address.

international@ora.com
Comments or questions about international ordering or distribution.

xresource@ora.com
To order or inquire about *The X Resource* journal.

proposals@ora.com
To submit book proposals.

info@gnn.com
To receive information about America Online's GNN (Global Network Navigator).™

O'Reilly & Associates, Inc.

103A Morris Street, Sebastopol, CA 95472
Inquiries: **707-829-0515, 800-998-9938**
Credit card orders: **800-889-8969** (Weekdays 6 A.M.- 5 P.M. PST)
FAX: **707-829-0104**

O'Reilly & Associates—
LISTING OF TITLES

INTERNET

CGI Scripting on the World Wide Web
(Winter '95-96 est.)
Connecting to the Internet:
An O'Reilly Buyer's Guide
Getting Connected (Winter '95-96 est.)
HTML Handbook (Winter '95-96 est.)
The Mosaic Handbook for
Microsoft Windows
The Mosaic Handbook for
the Macintosh
The Mosaic Handbook for
the X Window System
Smileys
The USENET Handbook
The Whole Internet User's
Guide & Catalog
The Whole Internet for Windows 95
Web Design for Designers
(Winter '95-96 est.)
The World Wide Web Journal
(Winter '95-96 est.)

SOFTWARE

Internet In A Box ™ Version 2.0
WebSite™ 1.1

WHAT YOU NEED TO KNOW SERIES

Using Email Effectively
Marketing on the Internet
(Winter '95-96 est.)
When You Can't Find Your
System Administrator

HEALTH, CAREER & BUSINESS

Building a Successful Software Business
The Computer User's Survival Guide
Dictionary of Computer Terms
(Winter '95-96 est.)
The Future Does Not Compute
Love Your Job!
TWI Day Calendar - 1996

USING UNIX

BASICS
Learning GNU Emacs
Learning the bash Shell
Learning the Korn Shell
Learning the UNIX Operating System
Learning the vi Editor
MH & xmh: Email for Users &
Programmers
SCO UNIX in a Nutshell
UNIX in a Nutshell: System V Edition
Using and Managing UUCP
(Winter '95-96 est.)
Using csh and tcsh

ADVANCED
Exploring Expect
The Frame Handbook
Learning Perl
Making TeX Work
Programming perl
Running Linux
Running Linux Companion CD-ROM
(Winter '95-96 est.)
sed & awk
UNIX Power Tools (with CD-ROM)

SYSTEM ADMINISTRATION

Building Internet Firewalls
Computer Crime:
A Crimefighter's Handbook
Computer Security Basics
DNS and BIND
Essential System Administration
Linux Network Administrator's Guide
Managing Internet Information Services
Managing NFS and NIS
Managing UUCP and Usenet
Networking Personal Computers
with TCP/IP
Practical UNIX Security
PGP: Pretty Good Privacy
sendmail
System Performance Tuning
TCP/IP Network Administration
termcap & terminfo
Volume 8 : X Window System
Administrator's Guide
The X Companion CD for R6

PROGRAMMING

Applying RCS and SCCS
C++: The Core Language
Checking C Programs with lint
DCE Security Programming
Distributing Applications Across DCE
and Windows NT
Encyclopedia of Graphics File Formats
Guide to Writing DCE Applications
High Performance Computing
lex & yacc
Managing Projects with make
Microsoft RPC Programming Guide
Migrating to Fortran 90
Multi-Platform Code Management
ORACLE Performance Tuning
ORACLE PL/SQL Programming
Porting UNIX Software
POSIX Programmer's Guide
POSIX.4: Programming for
the Real World
Power Programming with RPC
Practical C Programming
Practical C++ Programming
Programming with curses
Programming with GNU Software
(Winter '95-96 est.)
Programming with Pthreads
(Winter '95-96 est.)
Software Portability with imake
Understanding and Using COFF
Understanding DCE
Understanding Japanese Information
Processing
UNIX Systems Programming for SVR4
(Winter '95-96 est.)
Using C on the UNIX System

BERKELEY 4.4 SOFTWARE DISTRIBUTION

4.4BSD System Manager's Manual
4.4BSD User's Reference Manual
4.4BSD User's Supplementary Docs.
4.4BSD Programmer's Reference Man.
4.4BSD Programmer's Supp. Docs.
4.4BSD-Lite CD Companion
4.4BSD-Lite CD Companion: Int. Ver.

X PROGRAMMING

THE X WINDOW SYSTEM

Volume 0: X Protocol Reference Manual
Volume 1: Xlib Programming Manual
Volume 2: Xlib Reference Manual
Volume 3: X Window System
User's Guide
Volume. 3M: X Window System
User's Guide, Motif Ed.
Volume. 4: X Toolkit Intrinsics
Programming Manual
Volume 4M: X Toolkit Intrinsics
Programming Manual, Motif Ed.
Volume 5: X Toolkit Intrinsics
Reference Manual
Volume 6A: Motif Programming Man.
Volume 6B: Motif Reference Manual
Volume 6C: Motif Tools
Volume 8 : X Window System
Administrator's Guide
PEXlib Programming Manual
PEXlib Reference Manual
PHIGS Programming Manual
PHIGS Reference Manual
Programmer's Supplement for Release 6
The X Companion CD for R6
X User Tools (with CD-ROM)
The X Window System in a Nutshell

THE X RESOURCE

A QUARTERLY WORKING JOURNAL FOR X PROGRAMMERS

The X Resource: Issues 0 through 15

TRAVEL

Travelers' Tales France
Travelers' Tales Hong Kong (12/95 est.)
Travelers' Tales India
Travelers' Tales Mexico
Travelers' Tales Spain
Travelers' Tales Thailand
Travelers' Tales: A Woman's World

O'Reilly & Associates—
INTERNATIONAL DISTRIBUTORS

Customers outside North America can now order O'Reilly & Associates books through the following distributors. They offer our international customers faster order processing, more bookstores, increased representation at tradeshows worldwide, and the high-quality, responsive service our customers have come to expect.

EUROPE, MIDDLE EAST, AND AFRICA
(except Germany, Switzerland, and Austria)

INQUIRIES

International Thomson Publishing Europe
Berkshire House
168-173 High Holborn
London WC1V 7AA, United Kingdom
Telephone: 44-71-497-1422
Fax: 44-71-497-1426
Email: itpint@itps.co.uk

ORDERS

International Thomson Publishing Services, Ltd.
Cheriton House, North Way
Andover, Hampshire SP10 5BE, United Kingdom
Telephone: 44-264-342-832 (UK orders)
Telephone: 44-264-342-806 (outside UK)
Fax: 44-264-364418 (UK orders)
Fax: 44-264-342761 (outside UK)

GERMANY, SWITZERLAND, AND AUSTRIA

International Thomson Publishing GmbH
O'Reilly-International Thomson Verlag
Königswinterer Straße 418
53227 Bonn, Germany
Telephone: 49-228-97024 0
Fax: 49-228-441342
Email: anfragen@ora.de

ASIA *(except Japan)*
INQUIRIES

International Thomson Publishing Asia
221 Henderson Road
#08-03 Henderson Industrial Park
Singapore 0315
Telephone: 65-272-6496
Fax: 65-272-6498

ORDERS

Telephone: 65-268-7867
Fax: 65-268-6727

JAPAN

O'Reilly & Associates, Inc.
103A Morris Street
Sebastopol, CA 95472 U.S.A.
Telephone: 707-829-0515
Telephone: 800-998-9938 (U.S. & Canada)
Fax: 707-829-0104
Email: order@ora.com

AUSTRALIA

WoodsLane Pty. Ltd.
7/5 Vuko Place, Warriewood NSW 2102
P.O. Box 935, Mona Vale NSW 2103
Australia
Telephone: 02-970-5111
Fax: 02-970-5002
Email: woods@tmx.mhs.oz.au

NEW ZEALAND

WoodsLane New Zealand Ltd.
21 Cooks Street (P.O. Box 575)
Wanganui, New Zealand
Telephone: 64-6-347-6543
Fax: 64-6-345-4840
Email: woods@tmx.mhs.oz.au

THE AMERICAS

O'Reilly & Associates, Inc.
103A Morris Street
Sebastopol, CA 95472 U.S.A.
Telephone: 707-829-0515
Telephone: 800-998-9938 (U.S. & Canada)
Fax: 707-829-0104
Email: order@ora.com

Here's a page we encourage readers to tear out...

O'REILLY WOULD LIKE TO HEAR FROM YOU

Please send me the following:

❏ *ora.com*

O'Reilly's magazine/catalog, containing behind-the-scenes articles and interviews on the technology we write about, and a complete listing of O'Reilly books and products.

Which book did this card come from?

_____

Where did you buy this book?
❏ Bookstore ❏ Direct from O'Reilly
❏ Bundled with hardware/software ❏ Class/seminar

Your job description: ❏ SysAdmin ❏ Programmer
❏ Other _____

Describe your operating system: _____

_____

Please print legibly

Name	Company/Organization Name

Address

City	State	Zip/Postal Code	Country

Telephone	Internet or other email address (specify network)

Nineteenth century wood engraving
of raccoons from the O'Reilly
& Associates Nutshell Handbook®
Applying RCS and SCCS.

POST CARD

O'Reilly & Associates, Inc., 103A Morris Street, Sebastopol, CA 95472-9902

BUSINESS REPLY MAIL

FIRST CLASS MAIL   PERMIT NO. 80   SEBASTOPOL, CA

Postage will be paid by addressee

O'Reilly & Associates, Inc.
103A Morris Street
Sebastopol, CA 95472-9902